D0154041

CONSENT, COERCION, AND LIMIT
The Medieval Origins of Parliamentary Democracy

The concepts of popular consent and limit, as applied to the exercise of
political authority, are fundamental features of parliamentary democracy. Both these concepts played a role in medieval political theorizing,
although the meaning and significance of political consent in this
thought has not been well understood. In a careful, scholarly survey of
the major political texts from Augustine to Ockham, Arthur Monahan
analyses the contribution of medieval thought to the development of
these two concepts and to the correlative concept of coercion.

In addition, he deals with the development of these concepts in
Roman and canon law and in the practices of the emerging states of
France and England and the Italian city-states, as well as considering
works in legal and administrative theory and constitutional documents.
In each case his interpretations are placed in the wider context of
developments in law, church, and administrative reforms. The result is
the first complete study of these three crucial terms as used in the
Middle Ages, as well as an excellent summary of work done in a
number of specialized fields over the last twenty-five years.

The book is of considerable importance not only to medieval studies
but to the history of political theory and to political theory itself. It
brings together and explains the relevance of a vast amount of material
previously known only to a few specialists, documenting Monahan's
argument that later political thought has been significantly influenced
by medieval formulations of the concepts of consent, coercion, and
limit.

Arthur P. Monahan is a member of the Department of Philosophy at
Saint Mary's University, Halifax.

McGILL-QUEEN'S STUDIES IN THE HISTORY OF IDEAS

CONSENT, COERCION, AND LIMIT
The Medieval Origins
of Parliamentary Democracy

Arthur P. Monahan

McGill-Queen's University Press
Kingston and Montreal

WITHDRAWN

HIEBERT LIBRARY
Fresno Pacific College - M.B. Seminary
Fresno, CA 93702

© McGill-Queen's University Press 1987
ISBN 0-7735-1012-5
Legal deposit first quarter 1987
Bibliothèque nationale du Québec
Printed in Canada

∞

Printed on acid-free paper

This book has been published with the help of a grant from the
Canadian Federation for the Humanities, using funds provided
by the Social Sciences and Humanities Research Council of Canada.

Canadian Cataloguing in Publication Data

Monahan, Arthur P., 1928–
Consent, coercion, and limit
(McGill-Queen's studies in the history of ideas,
ISSN 0711-0995; 10)
Bibliography: p.
Includes index.
ISBN 0-7735-1012-5
1. Representative government and representation.
2. Democracy. 3. Constitutional law. 4. Consent (Law).
5. Duress (Law). 6. Middle Ages.
I. Title. II. Series.
JC423.M65 1987   321.8   c86-094070-5

To Jean

Contents

Preface

ANY THEORY OF POLITY describing a system of government that can be called parliamentary democracy invariably stresses as an essential feature the consent of the people being governed: popular consent. This is why one modern historian of European representative political institutions has called the dictum "what touches all must be approved by all" a fundamental principle of democracy.[1]

A second feature in such a theory is reflected in the adjective "parliamentary," and has to do with the manner in which consent of the people is expressed. This is done through the medium of a representative governing body or parliament, whereby the people express consent through persons they choose to represent them in the governing body. In this way the governing body is responsible to the people insofar as those constituting the governing body's membership are elected by the people, and thus acquire their authority from the people who elect them; the representative character of the elected governing body carries the element of popular consent. The people to be governed consent to being governed by those whom they choose to represent them as members of the governing body or parliament. To put this another way: the people govern themselves *indirectly* by choosing those who will govern in their place, and by consenting to be governed by these "representatives." Consent by the people is also renewed or withdrawn through the regularity of the process of electing representatives.

The peculiar juxtaposition of end and means in the political system designated as parliamentary democracy—the end being the consent by

1. Antonio Marongiu, "Q.o.t.," p. 101. Complete bibliographical data for footnote references are in the Bibliography.

all who make up a given polity, and the means being the limited-term election of representatives by universal adult suffrage—has taken many centuries to incorporate into political institutions, and even today only a minority of the world's peoples live in societies that afford it genuine expression.

Even such a simple account of parliamentary democracy emphasizes by implication a still more fundamental underlying feature of an acceptable polity: that of limit on the exercise of political authority. Parliamentary democracy reflects the notion of limit inasmuch as authority derives from the requirement of popular consent, authority here being limited in two senses. First, the requirement of popular consent imposes a limit inasmuch as absence of such consent signals absence of authority; secondly, the mandate extending authority to the representative body is limited temporally insofar as it runs only for a specified period of time and requires further temporally limited renewal. Some forms of parliamentary democracy, notably those of the British model, include a third element of limit: the government is limited by the requirement to retain majority support of the governing body (parliament), even during the statutory time limits of an election mandate period. A government must resign whenever it fails to retain majority support in parliament on a significant issue.[2]

Another aspect of the concept of limit as it operates in any form of polity is its connection with the concept of law, but for reasons that will be obvious shortly this specific issue can best be considered separately. It is a commonplace of any theory of parliamentary democracy that political authority should act "in conformity with the law," that those who govern should do so "under the law." There are serious ambiguities in such expressions, however. Insofar as political authority, parliamentary or otherwise, is always conceded the power to make and change law, the issue of just what is meant by asserting that authority is itself limited by law is not at all clear. Such lack of clarity poses one of the most serious issues for any constitutional theory of state.

A third essential feature in any theory of polity often receives much

2. Of course, this statement is not strictly true; there is no written constitutional requirement as such that a government failing to obtain a majority in parliament must resign. There is, too, the finely balanced question of when a given issue is significant enough to warrant the need for majority house support. Such questions and their answers are the preserve of constitutional experts and prime ministers, the latter having the practical last word on divining the meaning of custom.

less explicit attention in a conventional description of parliamentary democracy. This is the element of coercion, perhaps more meaningfully expressed as sufficient power in the governing body to enforce its laws, policies, and decisions on the members of that polity. The issue of the meaning and definition of terms, always a bugbear in political theorizing, is immediately critical here. What difference, if any, is to be drawn among the terms "coercion," "power," and "authority"? The meaning of consent is obviously also critical. The issue of defining such terms is addressed directly later; and as the later material will show, the term "coercion" (*coactio*) is employed because it was the term designating the notion at issue that enjoyed the greatest currency among medieval political thinkers. Coercion indicates a traditional early Christian view of political authority given widespread currency later in the Middle Ages, especially through the authority of St. Augustine. In this view, the physical force available to the state for imposing its laws on subjects is required to overcome the sinful nature of human beings: humans need to be forced to behave as they should.

The view that ordinary people are not to be trusted to behave "properly" on their own was not an exclusively Christian attitude, of course. Plato's views on the inadequacy of the average person who, not knowing where his real best interests lie, tries to be part of a governing group of similarly ignorant common folk are well known.[3] Aristotle, too, had little faith in the working man's, especially the poor working man's, ability to govern.[4] But the Christian doctrine of Original Sin, with its assessment of the *de facto* state of human nature as somehow perverted, gave powerful support to a political theory that emphasized the need for people to be forced into behaving rightly. Unless coerced, they could not be expected so to behave.

The terms "power" and "authority," on the other hand, tend to convey a more modern attitude insofar as they appear to lack the moral connotations of the medieval term coercion. This is seen as a benefit in elaborating a political theory: morally neutral terms indicate the further value of separating a theory of government from ethical considerations, a separation usually felt nowadays to be desirable, if not essential. There is something of a historical anomaly here, however. The turn away from the Augustinian overtones of the unnatural character of political authority in the term "coercion" began with the late

3. Plato *Republic* 8.555B–64A.
4. Aristotle *Politics* 6.5.1320a30; cf. 6.4.1319b.

thirteenth-century revival of Aristotle's *Politics*, where the notion of political society is termed natural. But for Aristotle political theory also was a branch of moral philosophy.[5]

Certainly, no one can deny that any governing agency must have the power actually needed to carry out its will. For this not to be the case involves a contradiction: a government lacking the power to govern is simply not a government at all. Why, then, is this essential of polity sometimes scanted in the description of parliamentary democracy? One explanation is that acknowledgment of the need for coercion or power in a parliamentary democracy is implicit rather than explicit because of the conventional tendency towards simplification. Only one of several elements in a complex notion need be selected for emphasis; and the one feature usually given prominence in the notion of parliamentary democracy is freedom, the personal right of citizens to govern themselves, something they do by participating in government through the election process that produces their governing surrogate or representative. Further, freedom is perceived as the antithesis of coercion, resulting again in an oversimplifying tendency to construe coercion as incompatible with this form of government, although it is not. Thus, coercion is usually spoken of as having limits even when it is adverted to directly as a necessary feature of parliamentary democracy involving nothing more than the physical capacity to govern. Exercise of political authority (coercion) is legitimate only within limits; unlimited political authority is not legitimate. There are some things political authority can and may do; other things it may (should) not do, even though it can!

Expressing the notion of limit this way brings one back to the concept of law, and to the realization that another element in its meaning reflects the feature of limit. This further element relates to the question of purpose or end: what is law for if not to further the purpose of society itself, the living together of all members of a society in harmony and well-being: the common good, the good of all considered as a whole? Law properly speaking, then, should reflect the concept of limit intrinsically, its contents being limited by as well as expressive of its purpose. This is why Aristotle considered that a well-ordered society operating under the rule of law, whose contents aimed at establishing and preserving the common well-being of its citizens, reflected the element of popular consent, willingness, or acceptance to be under a

5. Aristotle *Nicomachean Ethics* 1.2.1094a19–b10.

political authority; this willingness was grounded in the fact that what "the people" willed (wanted, inclined to)—their collective well-being— was precisely what the authority, rulers, and laws aimed at as well.[6] Consent, in this sense, is to be construed as "a conscious acceptance" that need not be given expression through any direct and explicit action by the citizenry. Popular consent appears then under two aspects: (1) an active aspect according to which the people express their consent by actually doing something—voting, choosing, approving, acclaiming, concurring, and thereby providing evidence of their consent by performing a specific action; (2) a passive aspect wherein willingness, acceptance, agreement are understood to be present though not directly expressed or necessarily expressible in a specific procedure. The following account of the history of medieval political thought will show an oscillation of focus and interest between these two aspects, and only a very slow development in the direction of removing the ambiguity involved in failing to distinguish adequately between them.

The concept of limit thus emerges as fundamental in relation to the notion of coercion as well as in the analysis of consent. The concept of limit, it seems, is a more basic element in a theory of polity than either consent or coercion. The same point can be made by the briefest reflection on the notion of totalitarianism, a typical contemporary designation for the antithesis of parliamentary democracy. A conventional criticism of totalitarianism is precisely that it advances a claim to the *unlimited* exercise of coercive power: a totalitarian political power claims the authority literally and legitimately to do anything.

I would be prepared to argue on purely conceptual grounds that the kind of polity so simply and inelegantly described here as totalitarian (the term "absolutism" or "absolute" often connotes the same over-simplified meaning in ordinary contemporary usage)[7] also involves a contradiction in terms, just as does the notion of a polity having no coercive power at all. Rather than consider this view directly, however,

6. Aristotle *Politics* 4.10.1295a15. Cf. the explicit use Marsilius of Padua made of this notion.

7. But not always! Sometimes the term "absolute" is used even more loosely to mean simply the element in a polity that has the last word, the ruling entity whose decisions are not subject to limitation, rejection, or qualification from any other aspect of the political community. Thus, for example, one might refer to the conflict in the social and political history of the later Middle Ages as that between absolute rule and popular pressures: cf. Michael Wilks, "Coronation and Representation."

it may be preferable merely to inquire whether or not there is any contradiction between totalitarianism and parliamentary democracy, as the previous exercise in over-simplification might seem to imply. To put this question squarely: can one conceive of a parliamentary totalitarianism (or a totalitarian parliamentary system), that is, a parliamentary democracy wherein the elected governing body possesses the rightful legal power to do literally anything it decides?[8] An affirmative answer to this question can be established by no more complicated a procedure than soliciting replies to it from a representative sample of ordinary citizens in any modern parliamentary democracy. Many persons are prepared at least on first consideration to maintain that a parliamentary form of government has the right to enact any legislation its majority approves, so long as the parliament has been elected properly.

Nor is such an informal procedure for finding empirical evidence of a lack of contradiction between parliamentary democracy and totalitarianism the only way to establish the point at issue. There is, indeed, no contradiction between totalitarianism and the concept of parliamentary democracy as defined earlier, even allowing for the relatively loose character of the earlier definition; there is no contradiction between democracy, parliamentary or otherwise, and totalitarianism. The most basic contrast between types of polity rests on the polarity between the limited and the unlimited. What distinguishes basic forms of polity at the most fundamental conceptual level is the presence or absence of the concept of limit related to the exercise of power.[9]

There is an interesting epistemological parallel here, which would make a suitable subject for development in a different context. Ever since Aristotle's formulation of the science of logic in the mid-fourth century B.C., logicians have understood that the basic unit of human (rational) thought also must exhibit the character of limit. A definition, the basic unit in human thought whose function it is to describe

8. See the recent examination of this concept in Talmon, *Origins of Totalitarian Democracy*.

9. The nineteenth-century so-called positivist approach to law, which has been very influential in the English and American legal traditions through the writings of Austin and Holmes, offers an interesting illustration of this point. Austin held precisely that there could be no legal limit on the sovereign, that is, that the lawmaking authority by definition has power unlimited by any higher legal authority: this is the essence of his concept of sovereignty. Austin accepted nonetheless that there might be other, non-legal, forms of limit on the sovereign and that the sovereign would and could make laws limited by ethical considerations. He also accepted that limits existed for the obligation to obey "morally iniquitous laws." Cf. Hart, *Concept of Law*, pp. 203, 205.

adequately a concept or idea, must describe a concept in a limited or limiting way; it must say what it is *and* what it is not, specifying the limit of a given genus by the appropriate specific difference.[10] The Aristotelian tradition in political thought reflects this emphasis on the element of rationality, although it is not the only tradition to do so. The exercise of political authority should reflect an understanding, a reasoned or rational perception, of the purpose for governing. Such rationality clearly entails the element of limit: some governmental actions will correspond to and express the purpose for governing, others will not. It is possible to understand what the purpose of governing is, and to decide rationally what actions must be taken to achieve this purpose. Governing properly means limiting the actions of government to those that do achieve this purpose, and not performing actions that go beyond the limits of this purpose. The same mode of thinking can be found in the corresponding theory of law, according to which an essential component of law also is rationality: a proper law, entailing the obligation of obedience, must be "reasonable." Its specification for how to achieve its purpose must reflect the limits of what should and what should not be done, limits that can be understood by human reason.

There is a sense in which historical truth is distorted by designating this overall view as Aristotelian. Plato had expressed the same general theory of law and politics emphasizing the common rather than the individual good, and the necessity of understanding what to do, both individually and socially (politically), an intellectual perception itself based on clear vision: seeing things as they are.[11] It was Aristotle, however, who gave a systematic, scientific formulation to these insights.

The concept of law, then, is a fourth essential element in the development of a basic theory of polity, to be treated alongside the concepts of consent, coercion, and limit. As such it can be described loosely as the content or specification given to the concept of limit in the exercise of authority, the feature specifying and controlling coercion and directing those under authority; it directs members of a polity, both the governed and the governors, in attaining the common good, the purpose for which political authority legitimately exists.[12]

The foregoing remarks are the result of reflection on data gathered

10. Aristotle *Posterior Analytics* 2, esp. 3.

11. Plato *Republic* 7.134b; *Phaedo* 65B–66A; *Gorgias* 502A–3D.

12. I acknowledge Hart's essential caution about defining law exclusively in terms of orders issued by a coercing legislator. Such orders, however, are the paradigm case for law as it functions in political theory: see Hart, *Concept of Law*, pp. 26–41.

over a period of years in the study of medieval political thought. For some time I have been examining the meaning and extent of use among medieval political thinkers of the notion of consent, research that led naturally enough to an examination of the parallel concept of coercion. Gradually, however, I became convinced that a genuine understanding of the character of medieval thinking in the area of politics—what today can be called political science as long as the term "science" is not narrowly restricted to a purely empirical discipline that is then distinguished from political theory—required an appreciation of something other than views on consent and coercion. As subsequent pages will show, these two concepts were indeed part of the vocabulary of a very wide range of medieval political writers. Yet their presence and use are not what is most significant and most typical in the medieval contribution to the development of political theory.

The essential character and perspective of medieval political thought focuses most strikingly on the specification given to the concept of limit. This conclusion may not seem especially significant inasmuch as there is nothing exclusively medieval in the view that limit is a necessary feature of polity.[13] As already noted, both Plato and Aristotle stressed the same position centuries earlier, with Plato being clearer and more straightforward in putting the case: he contended that the proper exercise of political authority required self-control on the part of the ruler, with his activities limited to achieving and preserving the best interests and well-being of all members of society, and that the ruler was forbidden to further his own interest as such. For Plato the principal social virtue was justice, defined not as the interest of the stronger (the ruler) but as the harmony resulting from the proper ordering of all members of society, each in his appropriate place and each receiving his due in that place.[14]

Aristotle expressed substantially the same general position: good government is directed to the good of all the community, and the ruler is limited in his activities to furthering the common good; unlimited self-interest in the exercise of political power is wrong. With Plato, Aristotle designated government for the selfish interests of the ruler(s) as wrong, evil: tyrannical. The proper exercise of political authority must be limited; it must be right, virtuous in the sense of being limited by the constraints of what is "proper" for an activity whose purpose is the well-being of all rather than that of the ruler(s) alone. For Aristotle,

13. One recent study of medieval political history that also stresses the element of limit is Cam, *Law-Finders*.
14. Plato *Republic* 4.443C–E.

the best guarantee for proper limited rule is law; political authority should be exercised within the limit established by law.[15]

No novelty or uniqueness is claimed for the Middle Ages, then, by attributing to this period the general view that political authority is subject to limit, and that the specification of this limit is offered by law. Nor is there anything novel in maintaining that such a view was a fundamental feature of medieval political thinking. The specifically and peculiarly medieval connotations of this general principle, however, have not always been adequately clarified. And there has been no consistency of interpretation about whether this principle had universal application among those in the Middle Ages who claimed rights to the exercise of power. In particular, the power claimed by medieval ecclesiastical authorities in their efforts to exercise jurisdiction over temporal rulers often has been interpreted as a rejection of the principle espousing limit; limit, perhaps, for the legitimate exercise of temporal (political) authority, but no limit for the exercise of spiritual (ecclesiastical) authority.[16]

A focal point of scholarly activity reflecting this issue most clearly has been the study of medieval church / state relations, the *sacerdotium / regnum* issue that produced so much political controversy in the twelfth and thirteenth centuries and almost as much scholarly controversy in our own.[17] One result of the intensity of the more recent scholarly controversy has been the impetus given to increasingly sustained and sophisticated research into medieval source material. It is now possible to offer a much more comprehensive picture of medieval political thought, a picture in which the elements of consent and coercion, along with the fundamental notion of limit, can be located with greater confidence.

The title of this work suggests medieval origins for the contemporary theory of parliamentary democracy. The suggestion should not be construed too broadly, however, nor without sufficient qualification. Caution will be urged frequently against reading material through modern lenses. Concepts like consent and representation usually have a different, less specific, meaning for thinkers in the Middle Ages than

15. Aristotle *Politics* 3.11.1282b3.

16. A recent example of this general thesis as applied particularly to one specific late-medieval political theorist is Wilks, *Problem of Sovereignty*. Cf. Ullmann, *Medieval Papalism*; *Principles of Government*.

17. The bibliography on medieval church / state relations is enormous. For some recent lists of titles see: Tierney, "Recent Works" (reprinted in Tierney, *Church Law*); Wilks, *Problem of Sovereignty*; Ladner, "Bibliographical Survey."

in contemporary thought. They even appear as forerunners for modern political theories now seen in conflict with one another. A good illustration is the wide-ranging controversy over the meaning and implication of consent within modern democratic thinking, a controversy ranging from conservative through liberal to Marxist views, and found also within the liberal tradition. The simple meanings offered initially for consent, parliamentary democracy, and representation are not meant to ignore the contemporary lack of consensus, and even conceptual disarray, over these notions; they are only rough directional guideposts to an earlier period from which more sophisticated theories developed. Our special focus of interest is the modern doctrine of democratic representative government; nonetheless, direct democratic republicanism and forms of so-called people's democracy can also be traced to the medieval period. And certainly the more general model of limited constitutionalism, democratic or otherwise, is even typically medieval.

The organization of material here also requires some comment. An early intention to examine only writings classifiable as works of political theory has been abandoned. In its place will be found a looser but much more encompassing examination of material that also covers writings on legal and administrative theory, as well as constitutional documents and other historical data. In this way a more adequate picture should emerge about how the medieval thinker himself perceived the nature of the issues addressed here. For unless contemporary preconceptions and assumptions can be eliminated from an investigation of things medieval, leaving only the perspective of the medieval mind, however incomplete the perception of that perspective might be, there is no prospect of offering an adequate portrait of our subject.

A general Introduction presents an outline of the structure of the problem under examination, identifies the several research fields from which material can be derived, and offers a rough methodological formulation designed to provide some unity of perspective. Except for the final section, Conclusion, the remainder of the work is set out in four Parts in roughly chronological form, each dealing with a time frame that, though loose, offers a basic historical coherence. Part One presents the early medieval period, beginning with a survey of documents from the early Christian church, of which the first are the Sacred Scriptures of Christianity. It also examines the theological and political background of Christianity found in the Old Testament, the thought of the Christian Church Fathers, and the spread of Christianity through the Roman Empire through to the end of the Imperial era, continuing the historical account in cursory fashion down to the renewal of sustained Christian intellectual life in the twelfth century. An effort is made here as elsewhere to consider the relevant source material in the context of actual historical events and data.

Part Two covers roughly the twelfth century, and reflects an important division in source material that emerges at this time. Not only does the twelfth century begin to produce more significant and more sophisticated efforts at examination of the nature of political authority, of which John of Salisbury's *Policraticus* is the best example, but the development of legal studies and legal education in both civilian and ecclesiastical (canonical) forms that occurred at this time is, for our purposes, the most significant event of the period. Accordingly, attention is paid to the revival of the study of law, and in particular to the significant source material produced by both civilian and canonical legists.

Part Three continues the chronological sequence through the thirteenth century, in many ways the most fruitful as well as the most typical period of medieval life and thought. A further differentiation of material and focus is also to be noted here. Intellectual activity has become even more intense, with a corresponding general increase in the amount of documentary material; legal and administrative studies and activities also have greatly increased, so that here too material for examination has increased significantly in both quantity and quality; and, finally, historical events themselves illustrate the maturing efforts of forceful political rulers, especially the kings of England and France, to establish what today would be called nation-states. All the problems and technical difficulties, both theoretical and practical, of ruling, administering, and legislating for an increasingly more closely organized and geographically larger area came into clearer focus at this time. Both royal administration of the emerging nation-states and ecclesiastical administration of the Church by the papacy reflect these facts. Part Four extends the account through the first half of the fourteenth century.

These time frames, however, are not adhered to rigidly in the various Parts; to do so would distort the intellectual continuity of presentation. Thus, for example, no effort is made in Part One to examine data regarding ecclesiastical administration and canonical thinking down to the end of the eleventh century, data that are much better seen as background to the presentation of the twelfth-century revival of canon law in Part Two. Similarly, historical data from the twelfth century reflecting early examples of the political practice of representation are dealt with in Part Three, along with the much more substantial data on the same subject from the thirteenth century. Information concerning the organization and administration of religious orders and communities also appears in Part Three, even though some of the data relates to an earlier period.

The problem of definition of terms already alluded to is an especially vexing one in the case of "consent" (and the correlative "representation"). Intellectual history depends on much more than the discovery in earlier documents of terms having a recognizable modern currency. Some uniformity of meaning is a prerequisite of the continuity of doctrine, and the simple presence of a word in a medieval political document cannot guarantee that its user had in mind what is understood by the term today. As far as possible I have tried to let the documents speak for themselves, preferring to develop the meanings of key terms from the documents rather than imposing meanings from the outside.

The author of a work as substantial in form as this, and of a manuscript as long in preparation, inevitably has a more extensive list of acknowledgments than can be made within limits set by practicality. My indebtedness to the scholarship of others will be expressed generally, then, through the use made of it and cited in the text and footnotes. I want, however, to note a specific debt of gratitude to John R. Mac-Cormack, a colleague and friend for many years, whose shared interest in medieval intellectual and political history has made for many profitable discussions and valuable criticism of my work.

I want also to recognize several groups and individuals who assisted in more prosaic but no less necessary ways: the staffs of a number of libraries, especially the British Library, the library of Trinity College, Dublin, and that of my own university, Saint Mary's, Halifax; Florence Elliott, my departmental secretary, and Shirley Buckler and Ann Hutt of the Word Processing Centre at Saint Mary's; Valery Monahan, who typed the footnotes and bibliography in final form; Corinne Monahan, who assisted in completing the bibliography; and John St. James, who guided the manuscript so capably and amiably through the rigours of copy-editing.

I wish also to express my appreciation to the Senate Research Committee, Saint Mary's University, for providing grant monies in aid of research, the Canada Council for a Senior Leave Fellowship award, and the Social Sciences and Humanities Research Council of Canada for a subvention to assist publication.

Abbreviations

BN	Bibliothèque Nationale (Paris)
CIC	*Corpus iuris canonici*
Cod.	*Corpus iuris civilis*
Dig.	*Digesta* in *Corpus iuris civilis*
Extrav.	*Extravagantes* in *Corpus iuris canonici*
Goldast	Melchior Goldast, *Monarchia s. Romani imperii*
Gratian	*Decretum Gratiani*
Inst.	*Institutiones* in *Corpus iuris civilis*
Leg.	*Legum* in *MGH*
Mansi	Giovanni Domenico Mansi, *Sacrorum conciliorum nova, et amplissima collectio*
MGH	*Monumenta Germaniae historica*
Nov.	*Novellae* in *Corpus iuris civilis*
OND	William of Ockham, *Opus nonaginta dierum*
OpPl	William of Ockham, *Opera plurima* (Lyon: 1495)
PG	J.-P. Migne, *Patrologiae cursus completus*, series graeca
PL	J.-P. Migne, *Patrologiae cursus completus*, series latina
Sent.	A medieval commentary on the *Sentences* of Peter Lombard
Sext.	*Liber Sextus Bonifacii VIII* in *Corpus iuris canonici*
SS.	*Scriptores* in *MGH*
S.T.	Thomas Aquinas, *Summa theologiae*
X	*Decretales Gregorii IX* in *Corpus iuris canonici*

CONSENT, COERCION, AND LIMIT

Introduction

AN EFFORT TO PROVIDE a comprehensive account of the concepts of consent and coercion as employed and understood in medieval political thought is a sufficiently ambitious task as perhaps to have its goal seem foolish, if not unattainable. The quantity of available material is vast and varied;[1] and the areas of relevant and distinguishable expertise, what might be called the topology of the subject, are sufficiently diffuse to daunt even the most foolhardy. The effort can have considerable value nonetheless. It is a truism that those who ignore or forget their history are in large measure doomed to repeat it, especially in its harshest and most tragic episodes. It is equally true, of course, that more than knowledge of the past is needed in order to avoid its repetition: the productive fields of human activity are watered by more sources than the streams of knowledge.

The study of medieval history has undergone a curious if easily understandable development in the last century. When not reinforcing the Renaissance image of the Middle Ages as an era of darkness and superstition, the rationalist enlightenment of the eighteenth century had been content largely to dismiss medieval society as excessively

---

1. The judgment was made more than twenty years ago that "there are books enough to engage for years the attention of anyone curious to know how the medieval constitution of western Europe developed"; Lyon, "Medieval Constitutionalism," p. 155–83. The bibliography at the end of this work is very selective. More recent bibliographies of varying levels of comprehensiveness can be found in Marongiu, *Medieval Parliaments*; Wilkinson, *Creation of Medieval Parliaments*; Cam, "Recent Books"; *Law-Finders*; Ullmann, *Law and Politics*, contains much bibliography; Cuttino, "Medieval Parliament Reinterpreted;" Templeman, "History of Parliament"; Hoyt, "Recent Publications."

religious, theological, and superstition-ridden. Nineteenth-century romanticism, on the other hand, became fascinated with medieval literature and folklore, as well as with its architecture and painting; and considerable interest in things medieval emerged in intellectual and artistic circles in the last century.

Institutionalized Roman Catholicism provided another stimulus to a revived interest in the Middle Ages. Seeing themselves in continuity with the medieval period, and through it back to their church's origins in Roman times, many later nineteenth-century Catholic churchmen and scholars encouraged a renewal of interest in the Middle Ages. Their motive was to discover, or rediscover, a continuity of intellectual and moral doctrines and institutions that might serve as a defence against the increasingly strident rejection of Christianity as a meaningful element in human life. The Catholic revival of interest in the intellectual life of the Middle Ages was largely stimulated by efforts made within the framework of institutionalized Roman Catholicism, in European Catholic seminaries and universities first, but spreading quickly to both North and South America. Here was an essentially defensive enterprise examining the Middle Ages in a search for doctrines and formulations that would serve as a base to preserve and enlarge the ethical and religious values of the Catholic church.

Much of the impetus for the later nineteenth-century renewal of intellectual interest in things medieval thus originated in Roman Catholic circles, and had a religious *raison d'être*. Much, but not all. Nineteenth-century romanticism's interest in the Middle Ages has been noted. Further and, ironically, in a fashion that paralleled the expanding imperialism of Victorian England, English intellectual and academic circles in the last half of the nineteenth century developed a lively interest in the history and development of the institutions of British parliamentary democracy. This interest led to an examination of the medieval forms of English governance; and from this emerged the broad thesis that current British parliamentary forms reflected a political tradition whose relative superiority as a vehicle for popular democratic government was traceable back at least to the thirteenth century. The monumental historical scholarship of Bishop William Stubbs presented this thesis in its most authoritative and properly nuanced form,[2] a thesis that, probably inevitably, was given a more

2. Stubbs, *Constitutional History of England*, especially vol. 2. An excellent summary of the Stubbs thesis concerning the origins of the British parliamentary system and of later reaction to it, can be found in the 1955 lecture of Edwards, *Historians and Medieval English Parliament*.

simplified expression by less perceptive and more fervent followers of the great Anglican historian.

The Stubbs thesis has been the stimulus in both the English-speaking world and western Europe for massive research into the origins of parliamentary and representative systems of government, a notable manifestation of which was the founding in 1936 of the International Commission for the Study of Assemblies of Estates-General (later renamed the International Commission for the History of Representative and Parliamentary Institutions); and the end of this spate of research activity seems not yet in sight. Medieval historians engaged in this enterprise tended initially to focus their interest on the data concerned with the events of political history, and on political forms and institutions. The medieval and earlier periods were assiduously combed for evidence of aboriginal and nascent forms of parliamentary institutions and for illustrations of types of political representation.[3] In what is by now an almost bewildering array of material and interpretation resulting from a hundred years of historical research and controversy, a number of generally distinguishable positions have emerged in roughly chronological sequence. The original thesis that the British parliamentary system in its unique and superior form was traceable directly back to the late thirteenth-century parliament of Edward I (1295), with certain fundamental elements in place even earlier (for example, the Magna Carta, 1215) produced negative reactions of two kinds. The first was a revisionist interpretation of English medieval history, according to which the political realities of the thirteenth century simply did not reflect what was advanced by the original positive and enthusiastic thesis;[4] the second, a product of the

3. A distinguished series of studies, monographs, and collections of papers has come from the International Commission for the History of Representative and Parliamentary Institutions. Originally conceived in 1933, it was established formally in 1936 as the International Commission for the History of Assemblies of State, a subcommittee of the International Committee of Historical Sciences, and changed its name to the ICHRPI in 1950. To date it has published more than sixty volumes. Antonio Marongiu has produced a large number of articles: see the list printed in "Theory of Democracy and Consent," in Cheyette, ed., *Lordship and Community*, pp. 404–21. There are other extensive references here. Many notable contributions have been made by Gaines Post in a series of articles written in the 1940s and 1950s, most of which are reprinted in *Studies in Medieval Legal Thought*, and by Yves Congar, "Quod omnes tangit." See also Gaudemet, "Unanimité et majorité"; and for a careful examination of the connection between public representation and royal taxation in medieval England, see Harriss, *King, Parliament, and Public Finance*.

4. Richardson and Sayles, "Origins of Parliament."

effort to examine medieval political institutions across western Europe on a comparative basis, advanced the view that comparable and roughly contemporary data from other parts of western Europe showed similar kinds of political evolution to that evident in England.[5]

As greater insight into the character of medieval political institutions developed it became clear, and generally although not universally accepted, that there is a genuine sense in which the origins of the modern parliamentary system can be traced back to the Middle Ages, and that some continuity can be found in substance as well as form.[6] Research then began to focus on the issue of where these "popular" elements themselves originated. An operative feature behind one form of reply to this question of origins seems to have involved an assumption concerning the Middle Ages in general, namely, that a popular or democratic attitude would not have developed in the medieval European mind as such. Medieval European thought and institutions, it was accepted, were formed largely by the Christian church, an institution whose attitudes, especially in the Middle Ages, were antithetical to democratic or popular forms of expression, and indeed whose institutional character as typified by the thirteenth-century papacy was a kind of paradigm of absolutism. The source of any medieval manifestation of popular or democratic views on political organization and institutions, then, could be expected to have derived from other than Christian sources, sources such as the Celtic and Germanic tribes of pre-Christian Europe, or to have been imported somehow from Greek democratic thinking. One specific form of this attitude, a form incidentally that accounts significantly for earlier lack of interest in medieval legal history, held that Roman jurisprudence in both civilian and canonical forms was absolutist in content and tone, and that constitutional concepts emerged in spite of medieval forms of Roman law; the fertile ground of English common law, which retained original Teutonic notions of liberty and was uninfluenced by Roman law, was thought to be the soil in which the origins of modern constitutionalism developed.

Medieval scholars with a liberal bent operating in the Catholic tradition, on the other hand, were inclined often to interest themselves largely in matters of theology, philosophy, and political theory, rather

5. Cf. various writings of Marongiu, cited in n. 3 above.
6. For a recent well-balanced account of medieval constitutional history see Wilkinson, *Creation of Medieval Parliaments*.

than with the history of political forms and institutions. Political theory and not political institutions attracted their attention, particularly inasmuch as the institutional Church of the Middle Ages seemed a particularly hard case for anyone looking to discover attitudes and institutions congenial to liberal democratic values.

The steady and sustained activities of research into medieval thought of recent decades have produced a much more realistic, if less dramatic, picture of the continuum of human political activity and thought through the medieval period. Medieval life and thinking perceived in the round, to the extent that this is yet possible with the limited evidence even now available to the most assiduous scholar, can be seen as both more and less in phase with twentieth-century attitudes than much of earlier research was prepared or even able to acknowledge. Much more in the way of data is now available; and the patient, painstaking and careful presentation of it by contemporary scholars working in depth on a host of individual and even apparently isolated research topics has made it possible to show threads of continuity and development that link the Middle Ages much more precisely both to what went before and to more recent, modern attitudes.[7]

The tools of historical interpretation, however, require appropriate application. This is especially true regarding items of much earlier vintage and available only in a language whose elements of important meaning developed in a context significantly different from our own. It is now clear as well that the interpretation of medieval political thinking involves the further need for some kind of sustained interdisciplinary approach. A noticeable feature, precisely, of recent medieval research activity in the area of medieval politics is that progress has been made in several areas of research by scholars who, while expert in a specific field, have found it possible to extend their investigations into other areas as well. A contemporary magisterial

7. The area of research having undergone the most extensive development in the post–World War Two era is canon law. Tierney has provided elegant support for the thesis of continuity between medieval and modern political thought: *Religion, Law and Growth.* The work as a whole is a statement in more summary form of the same general position found here. A more striking emphasis on the continuity between medieval and later political thought and legal development, alleging a revolutionary character in the development of the institutional Church and Church law from the Gregorian movement of the later eleventh century, is in Berman, *Law and Revolution.* Both these works came to my notice after the present manuscript was in draft form. See also Skinner, *Foundations of Modern Political Thought,* 1:3–22, 49–68; 2:113–84.

practitioner in medieval political research recently accepted, in advance, criticism for his failure to incorporate material from a list compiled by himself of some twenty-five areas of specialization, with the justification that a fully comprehensive approach would require a multi-volume effort, and that even then the effort would not be complete: "Completeness cannot be aimed at in this subject."[8] The present work attempts to correlate only a small list of elements, for none of which anything more than minimum competence may be claimed. The attempt, however, reflects a judgment that only by bringing together the best in contemporary medieval scholarship from a variety of areas is it possible to gain the overview needed to make comprehensible this important and exceedingly interesting chapter in the history of western political thought.

Contemporary scholarship dealing with the medieval notions of consent and coercion falls roughly into three categories: history of medieval political institutions, history of medieval political theory, and history of medieval law, the last having emerged into importance and prominence only comparatively recently. Research in all these areas quite properly has linked consent with the notion of "representation." A central feature, understandably, has been an appreciation of the meaning of the term "consent" itself. Further, and again quite understandably, there has frequently been a tendency to construe the meaning of consent according to its usage in modern political theorizing: namely, as agreement among representative members of an institutionalized assembly, council, or parliament to decisions and actions of that assembly.[9] Consistent with such an interpretation, evidence of the element of consent then has been taken as evidence for the presence of the limiting feature of political authority so cherished by modern advocates of parliamentary democracy—popular consent; that is, the exercise of legitimate political authority is seen as limited by the requirement that those exercising authority must have approval from the (majority of the representatives in parliament of the) people.

In fact, medieval political history and its documentation are amply supplied with references to assemblies, parliaments, and councils to which representatives were summoned and came, such representatives being possessed of all the authority (*plena potestas*) necessary to

8. Ullmann, *Law and Politics*, p. 13, n. 1.

9. As noted earlier, of course, the modern theory of representative democracy is not the only intellectual construction employing the notion of popular consent; nor are representative democrats agreed on its meaning.

represent and give consent.[10] Such evidence then has been interpreted to show medieval examples, more or less inchoate perhaps, of parliamentary institutions where the political authority (of the monarchy, for example) was conditioned and limited in some way by the power resting in the hands of the representative members of the convened assembly. In order for the government to function, for the king to rule, according to this interpretation, representatives of some sort had to provide their consent. The representatives, then, limited and controlled the exercise of political authority by the monarch by giving or withholding consent.

A more strict interpretation of the terminology in the sources for the history of medieval political assemblies, however, led other scholars to reject so sanguine a view of medieval political institutions in terms of finding the cradle of modern democracy.[11] An alternative view of the medieval notion of consent has been advanced according to which the consent offered in the typical medieval assembly was, in fact, something *required* of the attending representatives.[12] The act of consenting was involuntary on the part of the representatives, and necessarily conformable to the royal authority as unlimited and, in the last analysis, absolute—having no constraints whatever. Accordingly, the emerging monarchies of the thirteenth century could be seen as forerunners of the modern absolute or totalitarian state.[13]

Investigation into the doctrinal sources of medieval political theory also has uncovered evidence of the element of consent among thirteenth-century political theorists such as Thomas Aquinas and John of Paris, for example. Here, too, as with many interpretations given to medieval institutions, there has been a tendency to construe a medieval theory of consent according to modern usage of the term, wherein agreement (consent) is seen as a necessary condition for the

10. See the important Post article, "*Plena potestas*."

11. Maitland is often credited with having taught this lesson forcibly: see Cam, "Evolution of the English Franchise," especially p. 427; cf. Schuyler, "Historical Spirit Incarnate."

12. Post, "A Roman Legal Theory of Consent"; see also Post, "*Plena potestas*" and "A Romano-Canonical Maxim."

13. Reconciliation of these conflicting views of the medieval meaning of consent requires the distinction between passive (= compulsory in this context) and active meanings of the concept. Realization of the theoretical necessity to move from the former to the latter entails an adequate theory of the individual. As will be seen, William of Ockham is the only political thinker among those whose views are examined to show any doctrinal sensitivity to this crucial point.

legitimate exercise of authority. Neither has the historian of medieval
political theory had any difficulty finding evidence of the concept of
limit as an essential condition for the exercise of political authority.
Thus it has been relatively easy, probably to the point of the connection
often being made unconsciously, to connect the concepts of consent
and limit in the way they are connected in modern political theory. The
consequent interpretation of the general thrust of medieval political
theory, then, shows it as insisting on the limited character of legitimate
political authority, and as inimical to any theory of absolutism or
totalitarianism.

A countervailing interpretation also has been postulated, however,
emphasizing the apparently inconsistent attitude shown by medieval
Christian theorists in their emphasis on the absolute primacy of the
authority of the Church as a second "power."[14] A reading of many
medieval theoreticians on the authority of the Church as the dominant,
spiritual, society has led to the contention that their claims here were
for a full-blown absolutism for ecclesiastical authority over any and
every political or temporal power. The particular focus for this version
of medieval political theory may be found in the enormous body
of research and publication dealing with the so-called church/state
problem in the Middle Ages.[15] And again, as in the case of controversy
among historians of medieval institutions, those who affected a careful
and strict interpretation of the terminology in the sources treating of
the *sacerdotium/regnum* controversies, principally as regards the relevant ecclesiastical documents, have tended to advance the more critical
view that the medieval Church laid claim to a form of absolute authority
or sovereignty.

Recent decades have seen a wide-ranging development of interest in
the study of medieval law, both civil and canon, a development in some
sense stimulated by precisely the issues already mentioned, and having
to do also with curiosity about the nature and operation of medieval

14. A trenchant expression of the thesis that it was the medieval canonists who
articulated the theory of papal political omnipotence can be found in Ullmann, *Medieval
Papalism*. But cf. Tierney, "Some Recent Works;" and "Continuity of Papal Political
Theory;" Gaudemet, "Collections canoniques." Tierney's generalized conclusions concerning the contributions of medieval canonists to the development of western
constitutionalist theory are in *Religion, Law and Growth*; cf. Berman, *Law and Revolution*,
esp. pp. 199–254.

15. Bibliographies on this subject can be found in many recent publications: Tierney,
Crisis of Church and State; "Continuity of Papal Political Theory"; Wilks, *Problem of
Sovereignty*; Watt, *Theory of Papal Monarchy*.

political and administrative institutions. It is now quite clear, so much so that one may raise the question of why anyone should ever have doubted the fact, that the political and administrative institutions developed in the nation-states emerging from feudalism in the thirteenth and fourteenth centuries employed and incorporated principles and procedures found in and adapted from Roman law. Modern research into the history of medieval law has provided many correctives and solutions for the apparently conflicting and ambiguous interpretations previously asserted in the history of medieval political theory and institutions;[16] and even though much remains to be examined among medieval legal sources, it is now possible to offer a reasonably comprehensive and comprehensible interpretation of the medieval theory of polity, and at least mitigate the more extreme and contradictory interpretations of earlier research in this field.

A much more comprehensive and intrinsically more plausible picture is now emerging of the general thirteenth-century notions of state and human society, and of the relationship of the highly organized institutions of the Christian church with the developing national political entities of France and England, as well as with the increasingly anachronistic entity of the Holy Roman Empire; of the character and institutions of the emerging nation-states; of the inappropriateness of trying to analyse and interpret ideas and political forms from the medieval era with tools of meaning and definition developed in later centuries; and, finally, of the gratuitously offensive and unnecessary assumption, formulable in any era but peculiarly attractive to our own, that earlier thinkers somehow functioned in an inconsistent, incoherent, and even contradictory manner. Thirteenth-century western Europe was not the Europe of the late twentieth century. But this fact does not make our medieval European predecessors fools; at least it does not make them any more susceptible to folly than ourselves. History is a continuum, and the seeds of one era's flowering are to be found in preceding times; an accurate account of history will acknowledge these facts. Accuracy and adequacy in the perception of earlier times, however, require careful elimination of later assumptions and prejudices. Historical investigation must accept

16. In particular see the extensive and refined research in the various writings of Tierney, Post, Stickler, and Watt as well, of course, as the pioneer work on canonical sources by Kuttner. Cf. also Berman, *Law and Revolution* and Skinner, *Foundations of Modern Political Thought*.

what it finds, even though the finding of anything at all presupposes that somehow one knows what to look for.

To understand medieval political thought one must begin with the most fundamental and most obvious feature of that period in western European history: its people were Christian. Medieval Europeans saw themselves as followers of Jesus Christ, committed to living as their Divine Master had instructed them, and as the leaders and institutions of the Christian church directed. The importance of this fact cannot be overestimated. It means, first of all, that every example of medieval political thinking will be an example of "Christian" political thinking, that every text of medieval political theory can be expected to reflect the influence of Christianity and be an expression of a "Christian attitude" towards its subject. The point at issue here, however, is not as simple as it might seem. Many efforts have been made, and at least an equal number of more or less derisory criticisms levelled, at describing a Christian attitude to various subjects and intellectual disciplines.[17] Hence, extremes in such an enterprise must be avoided.

To attribute too much to the attachment of the term Christian to a concept or theory is to fall victim to a peculiarly mischievous form of category mistake, as well as to fly in the face of empirical evidence to the contrary, evidence usually massive in quantity once an effort is made to discover and sift it thoroughly. There is no such thing as "Christian political theory" if such a term is taken to mean a single uniformly formulated doctrine that all Christian political writers articulate and to which they give assent. The notion of there being a single univocally formulated and universally expressed position subscribed to by all Christians on any subject is a myth; there are virtually as many specific formulations of any intellectual discipline by Christians as there are Christian formulators working in that discipline.

It is equally a mistake, however, to deny out of hand any connection between Christianity and a given intellectual discipline or tradition. This extreme can appear in either of two forms, distinguishable on the basis of whether or not the proponent considers it possible for an intelligent human being to make a personal commitment to Christianity. Many thinkers of the last several centuries have maintained directly, even bluntly, that the doctrines of the Christian religion are

17. A standard context for an examination of the compatability of Christianity with any form of rational discourse has been an examination of whether there can be such a discipline as Christian philosophy; see Gilson, *Spirit of Mediaeval Philosophy*; cf. Gilson, *Philosopher and Theology*; Maritain, *Essay on Christian Philosophy*.

not compatible with rational thought and, consequently, that no reasonable person can formulate an adequate intellectual position on any subject that will accommodate a personal acceptance of Christianity: a person simply cannot be a believing Christian and, simultaneously, a seriously rational thinker in any area of human thought.[18] Accordingly, there can be no such thing as a validly Christian approach to any intellectual discipline, no such thing as a Christian political science, for example. The two halves of the compound concept are incompatible; the concept itself contains a contradiction.

The second form of this extreme appears among thinkers who take a positive view towards the Christian religion. Again there is a denial of any such thing as a Christian approach to a given subject; not, however, because Christianity is seen as incompatible with rational thought, but simply because in some mysterious way a religious belief such as Christianity is considered not to interfere with the integrity of human intellectual activity.[19] This point of view asserts, for example, that there is no such thing as Christian political science; there is only political science, whose students and practitioners share a common commitment to the essentials of a particular intellectual discipline, the abstract integrity of which is impervious to distortion from a religious source.

The facts of the matter are other than what is suggested by either of these extremes. Notions such as a "Christian philosophy," "Christian political science," and so on are meaningful, and it is not difficult to appreciate their meaning provided that the definitions offered are not drawn so narrowly as to preclude them having any meaning at all. The term "Christian political science" can be held not to be self-contradictory provided only that the effort to give it meaning proceeds in a commonsensical manner. A definition developed in this fashion is necessarily loose and largely descriptive, containing the inevitable elements of ambiguity with which ordinary speech is fraught; but it can be both significant and useful. A Christian political science or, better, a Christian *approach* to political science is simply that approach, along with its results, that a believing Christian could be expected to take towards this intellectual discipline. Difficulties still can be found in such a formulation, of course, not the least of which has to do with defining what is meant by "political science," but these can be left aside. It should

18. Gilson, *Spirit of Mediaeval Philosophy*, p. 3 and p. 427, n. 5.

19. C. Cierp, in Kleutgen, *La philosophie scolastique*, 1:ix, cited in Gilson, *Spirit*, p. 427, n. 4.

be noted, moreover, that this definition includes an element of content in the term "approach," content deriving from the Christian religion.

This element of content is noted in the definition; its substance, however, is susceptible in some way to examination in terms of empirical evidence. Simply put: a Christian approach to political theorizing can be expected to contain and reflect views accepted by the Christian who is formulating it, and these views themselves can be identified as elements of Christian doctrine that have a connection with the area of politics. The evidence concerning the relevant elements of Christianity, as well as our understanding of them, requires a historical judgment. Consequently, these elements also must be disentangled from their history, a task not as difficult to achieve, however, as this description might indicate.

The documents themselves are, first and foremost, the authoritative texts of the Christian religion, texts accepted by Christians as the direct expression of truths revealed by God: the Sacred Scriptures, which include both the Old and the New Testaments. As well there are the other authoritative writings of the institutional Christian church, texts and documents given approval by the Church either as products of individual Christian writers whose works have been accepted by the institutional Church or as products emanating directly and formally from the institutional Church itself.

In addition to matters of literary text and context there are the important factors of historical and sociological character related to the community into which the religious writings of Christianity were received. The founder of Christianity, Jesus Christ, presented himself as a "saviour" to a specific religious community that was also a specific racial and historical entity: the Israelites. The earlier of the two most authoritative documents among the Christian sacred writings is also a history of the Israelites as "the Chosen People." Details of the history of the tribes of Israel, including details of their social and political organization, are thus part and parcel of the revealed writings of Christianity, and enjoy some form of authority among Christians from this fact. This is not to say that the cloak of authority thrown over the general contents of the Old Testament is an adequate basis for prescribing the facts of Jewish political and social history as the paradigmatic structure for a Christian political society. However, one should expect some connection.

On the negative side it must be recognized that the Christian community in the first centuries of its existence was a purely religious community, with neither the characteristics nor the aspirations for functioning as a political society. Its members were themselves members individually of a political society formally holding different religious views, and within which for the most part Christians were an insignificant and powerless element. The early Christians living as either citizens or slaves within the Roman Empire during the first three centuries of the Christian era did not see themselves in any position to implement political theory, whether or not they might have wished to apply ideas and precedents detailed in the Old Testament.

More to the point for our purposes, there was little incentive among early Christians to formulate anything at all in the way of political theory, even among early Christian intellectuals, of whom the numbers were not large. Formulation of political theory, even more particularly than is the case with many other forms of intellectual activity, is for the most part a subsidiary, subordinate, and secondary activity, following on and responding to actual social and political realities and perceived opportunities. These facts account largely for the absence of any really serious or sustained effort by early Christian writers to produce anything approximating a treatise on politics.

There are other reasons for this lacuna, not the least of which is a fundamental feature of Christianity itself, namely, that it is an "other-worldly" religion, directed in its focus of interest to a world other than the one presently inhabited by humans. The explicit words of its founder assert: "My kingdom is not of this world."[20] Accordingly, the early Christians were not primarily concerned with the details of social and political organizations in this world, except as these details impacted on their other-worldly religious interests. Nonetheless, the writings of Christianity do contain elements having both direct and indirect connections with the order of polity, which one can expect to find in any effort by a Christian to formulate a theory of polity. These elements in the Christian Scriptures are fundamental texts in the formation of Christian attitudes towards the world of politics; attention is directed to them in the first portion of Part One.

20. John 18.36.

The Early Medieval Period

1. CHRISTIAN SCRIPTURAL SOURCES

IN ADDITION TO what might be called the particular ambiance of other-worldliness reflected generally in Christian doctrine and derivative directly from the Christian Scriptures, there are individual biblical texts that exhibit a definite attitude towards political matters, if not some form of political thought itself. These texts can be expected to exert an important influence on the thinking of any Christian, for whom their contents in some sense have the authority of divine revelation. The Scriptures possessed an authority that simply could not be gainsaid by a Christian; their contents were accepted as truth, guaranteed by God Himself. Thereby, they enjoyed status as the highest authority, and were to be studied assiduously. What is at issue, then, is the simple but crucial fact that medieval Christian thinkers were influenced by the Christian Scriptures, as they understood them. Neither the truth of these texts themselves, nor the accuracy of the interpretation given them, is thereby at stake, however. The medieval Christian perception of their truth and the medieval interpretation given them are the critical issues; and both of these are historical phenomena.

Of greatest importance were statements made directly by, or directly attributed to, Jesus himself. The sources of these were the writings of the New Testament, particularly the Gospels of Matthew, Mark, Luke, and John, authors considered to have been divinely inspired as well as having known Jesus at first hand. The rest of the New Testament canon had equal authority as divinely inspired, as did the contents of the Old Testament. A major qualification applied to the earlier Testament, however; it described a religious dispensation that had been superseded by the religion established directly by God through Jesus Christ. The religion of the New Testament, accordingly, took precedence over that of the Old; primacy of truth and authority was conceded to the texts of the New Testament wherever they varied from or failed to reflect the contents of the Old. Elaborate and sophisticated methods of exegesis were developed in the course of time for dealing with the Christian Scriptures, by which relative weightings and means of assessment and interpretation could be applied to the sacred texts; but the details of such exegetical methodology need not be provided here.[1]

Of course, the Christian Scriptures were not composed in any of their several parts for the purpose of outlining a theory of government; but this fact should not be taken in too simplistic a fashion. For as we shall see shortly, the Old Testament does offer an account of the government of God's Chosen People, the Israelites. As well, the obscurity still surrounding the issue of precisely how the early Christians saw themselves in continuity with the original Chosen People makes it very difficult to appreciate the political thinking of the early Christians. In the event, too, the earliest Christians lived under the political sovereignty of the Roman Empire, whether as citizens or something else, and they perceived their social, economic, and political circumstances as affording little prospect for their own independent polity, even had they aspired to such. Just what the early Christians understood by the New Testament description of them as members of the "kingdom of God," a term not found in the Old Testament or in other Jewish literary sources, is also interesting, but it is a side issue and need not distract from our principal concern.[2] Nor should subsequent political thinking among either the early Christian or contemporary Jewish societies that almost certainly reflected the influence of political realities on the circumstances of the two groups. How medieval Christians perceived the polity and political thought of early Christians is our concern, rather than how the early Christians themselves saw these things. And it was really much later when Christian writers undertook a systematic winnowing of Scriptural texts in the search for data and directives for organizing both temporal and

1. The earliest explicit efforts to apply an exegetical methodology to the Christian Scriptures were made by Origen, although he did not attempt himself to lay down a set of explicit rules for the exegesis of Scripture: Origen, Homilia 12, in Numeros, *Origenes Werke*, 7:2, p. 93. Cf. Smalley, *Study of the Bible*.

2. See Grant, "Idea of Kingdom of God."

spiritual societies, with results that in some instances were truly amazing.[3]

A number of Scriptural texts, however, have always been accepted as having unmistakable and important connections with a theory of polity; and they were so recognized from the beginning of Christianity. One New Testament statement explicitly attributed to Christ bears directly on the political. Queried about whether or not to pay taxes to Imperial Rome, the occupying power under which the Jews were currently living, Christ is reported as having replied: "Render to Caesar the things that are Caesar's, and to God the things that are God's."[4] The particular significance of the issue of "tribute to Caesar" can be seen from the fact that there are two other references to it in other Gospel accounts: the question of how to respond to the obligation of paying taxes to Caesar appears also in Mark 12:13–17, while Christ is accused of having forbidden the payment of tribute to Caesar in Luke 23:2.

The single statement in Matthew, however, is by far the most important text of the three, and must be seen to constitute the cornerstone of any Christian doctrine of politics. Given the Christian's attitude towards the New Testament, it is only to be expected that a Christian theory of polity will accept the admonition to "render to Caesar what is Caesar's." The statement is largely hortatory, of course, but not entirely so; its context shows this clearly. Nor was it ever so interpreted. It raises inevitably the further question of what, precisely, is Caesar's; but this question itself accepts that something belongs to the temporal and political.

Christians are here instructed to act in appropriate ways towards two,

3. In his edition of Aegidius of Rome's *De ecclesiastica potestate* Scholz lists more than two hundred Scriptural texts employed by medieval advocates of papal power: Aegidius of Rome, *De ecclesiastica potestate*, pp. 214–15; see also John of Paris, *On Royal and Papal Power*, p. 166. The pervasiveness of biblical ideas and terminology in medieval formulations of principles of government is shown by Ullmann: "Bible and Principles of Government." Cf. Foreville, "Recours aux sources scripturaires." Ullmann also shows here how the Latin Vulgate Bible used Latin terms reflecting concepts from Roman law that were not necessarily identical in meaning then with either those of the Greek Septuagint or the more distant conceptual framework of the Hebrew formulation of Jewish thinking found in the Old Testament. The Vulgate text transmitted Roman legal language and ideas to the medieval Christian West, and did so in a manner both religiously authoritative and largely unnoticed. Ullmann contended further that no single source was more influential than the Bible on political and legal thinking in the Middle Ages, and expressed amazement at the gap in medieval research on this score. Unfortunately, the gap remains largely unclosed.

4. Matt, 22.21.

and two distinct, authorities, the (human) authority of Caesar and the (divine) authority of God. A necessary and immediate inference from such an instruction is that Christians are to accept two different and distinguishable spheres of governance, the temporal and the spiritual, each of which is legitimate. Denial of legitimacy to temporal political authority, then, is not consistent with the Christian religion. Consequently no professing Christian, especially one occupying a position of prominence or importance in the Christian church, should be expected to deny the legitimacy of temporal authority as such. Nor does one find any instance of such direct denial of political legitimacy by a Christian thinker.[5]

Thus, it should be surprising to find historians failing to acknowledge this fact. Yet how often has the history of medieval western Europe been presented in terms of instances where Christian leaders, especially popes, have denied the legitimate exercise of temporal authority by kings and emperors, claiming for ecclesiastics some form of absolute authority over temporal affairs?[6] To deny that one or other of the medieval popes or any of their theologian or canonist supporters ever claimed that temporal rulers lacked *all* legitimacy is, of course, not to deny that medieval Christian churchmen made claims of superior jurisdiction over temporal rulers, or that some medieval churchmen in certain circumstances claimed actual temporal jurisdiction over temporal rulers. Still less is it to question that some medieval ecclesiastics denied to temporal authority a form of jurisdiction generally acknowledged today to be a perfectly legitimate exercise of secular political power. Nor is it to deny that the claims of at least some medieval churchmen exceeded the limits of propriety in an acceptable political theory. Medieval Christian thinkers and churchmen had many arresting things to say about the relationship between church and state, and about the relative superiority of spiritual over temporal authority. This

5. One of the most extreme formulations of the theory of papal supremacy, by Aegidius of Rome, still provides explicit acceptance of the legitimacy of temporal authority: see Part 3, 3D, below.

6. There is an almost irremovable ambiguity in the term "absolute." Another view of this ambiguity, from the opposite side and involving language normally seen as contradictory to the above, is seen in Post's designation of Philip the Fair as a "constitutional" monarch, on the grounds that he based his major decisions on the expert legal opinions of members of his royal council: "Vincentius Hispanus," p. 179, especially note 73; cf. Strayer, "Philip the Fair." Treharne also speaks of "the essential conditions of royal absolutism in thirteenth-century England," these conditions being the implied limitations on royal authority: "Constitutional Problem," p. 56.

is particularly true in the case of advocates for the *plena potestas* of the papacy—papal supremacy—where some formal statements assert very broad claims. Nonetheless, the most fundamental Christian text on politics accepts the legitimacy of the lay exercise of temporal power as such, and no medieval Christian could be expected to repudiate this position.

Other biblical texts should be mentioned also in order to see the full range of elements likely to be found in a Christian formulation of political theory. A general, but absolutely compelling, feature of the contents of both Old and New Testaments is the admonition that rulers are constrained to obey God, to be obedient to the laws of God. A corresponding feature is the enjoining of Christians to obey human rulers insofar as these rulers enjoy their authority as given them by God. Citations from both Old and New Testaments to substantiate these two points are many, and the issue is sufficiently well known not to require references to them all. Old Testament sources are the more numerous, but both St. Peter and St. Paul are also explicit on the point. Christians are advised by Paul to be obedient to their masters, political and otherwise, inasmuch as the source of all authority is God Himself. To be obedient and subordinate to one's master is in some way to be obedient and subordinate to God Himself: "Let every soul be in subjection to the higher powers" (Romans 13:1). "Render to all their due: tribute to whom tribute is due; custom to whom custom; fear to whom fear; honor to whom honor" (Romans 13:7). On the point of all authority deriving from God: "He who resists the power withstands the ordinance of God" (Romans 13:2 and 5; cf. Titus 3:1 and 2; 1 Timothy 2:2). These texts from Paul are quoted by other Christian writers from the second century onwards, along with the Matthew text concerning tribute to Caesar; the latter is cited by St. Justin Martyr in his *First Apology* 17.[7] St. Peter also instructed Christians to be subject to their masters, even to the extent of accepting injustice: "For if one who suffers unjustly bear his trouble for conscience sake, this is grace" (1 Peter 2:18).[8]

Christians, then, not only accepted the legitimacy and integrity of temporal political authority; they accepted that those who exercised such authority did so on behalf of God Himself, from Whom political

7. Justin Martyr *First Apology* 17; cited in Carlyle and Carlyle, *Mediaeval Political Theory*, 1:129.
8. Cf. Matt. 3.4–6; Luke 13.14–16.

authority somehow derived. They also accepted that they had a moral and religious obligation to obey temporal authority, and that it was directed to the common good.[9] Another clear feature of both Old and New Testament texts on temporal political authority was that such authority was exercised for the purpose of fulfilling a divine plan.[10] This had two aspects: (1) temporal authority as such was subordinate to God's (spiritual) authority; (2) Christians had an obligation to God (to the order of the spiritual) that transcended their obligations to temporal authority.

Finally, one should mention the New Testament text given copious consideration and interpretation among medieval theologians and jurists, Luke 22:38: "Here are two swords; to which He [Christ] replied: 'That is enough.'" Clearly lacking explicit reference to any order of polity as well as any clear directive about how Christians were to behave, this text became fundamental for papal monarchists intent on showing that both spiritual and temporal authority fell somehow under papal jurisdiction: there were two swords in the possession of the Church. The use, and abuse, of this text by thirteenth- and early-fourteenth-century advocates of papal power illustrates well the ingenuity that could be employed by the medieval mind to advance a particular theory virtually independently of any intrinsic meaning in the sacred text to warrant such an interpretation.[11]

2. THE POLITY OF THE ISRAELITES

In addition to reflecting these attitudes and admonitions regarding a theory of polity, the Christian Scriptures also offered the Old Testament account of the political history and system of God's Chosen People. One can read here the advice given the Israelites by their God Who enjoined on them obedience to Himself. For the most part Christians have understood that the "kingdom of Christ" was not of this world; and when this notion was taken in conjunction with other statements in the Gospels and Epistles referring to Christianity as a "new" law or dispensation, it was construed as a warning not to try to create a heaven on earth, as well as not to renew the kind of society their Jewish predecessors had described in the Old Testament. There have

9. Ibid.
10. 1 Peter; cf. texts cited in n. 8 above.
11. Cf. Aegidius of Rome *De ecclesiastica potestate* 1.7–9; 2.13–15.

been exceptions to this general interpretation, however;[12] and even where the generalization holds, a Christian's political theorizing, especially that of a medieval Christian, can be expected to be influenced by knowledge of the history and political system of the Chosen People, the Jews. The details of this history and polity, therefore, are important background material for early and medieval Christian political thought. A qualification: no advocacy is being made for the historical accuracy of a would-be literal Old Testament description of the Jewish polity, nor for the accuracy of the medieval understanding of this account. Even less is there any actual or implied validation of the political theory embedded in this account. Only very recently have scholars employed the sophisticated tools of modern textual exegesis and linguistics in combination with new data from archaeology and anthropology to provide a fuller and more coherent picture of early Jewish history. A much earlier, simplistic reading of the Old Testament, however, was what influenced medieval political thinkers from Augustine to Ockham and beyond concerning the origins of the Israelite temporal polity as a monarchy.[13]

A fundamental feature of the Israelite polity was that it was monarchical throughout much of its existence, and monarchical in a very specific way. The relevant Old Testament sources reveal that early Jewish society did not make a clearcut distinction between the roles of spiritual and temporal leadership and authority. While they understood the distinction between spiritual or religious activity, such as offering sacrifices to the Lord, and political or temporal activity, such as defending the tribe against physical aggression and waging war, they made no rigid distinction between persons who were to perform these different functions and exercise the authority requisite for them. Leaders in the early period of Jewish history exercised both offices concurrently. According to the traditional account of Hebrew history their earliest rulers were judges and prophets, with the priestly caste claiming and exercising separate prerogatives only as time went on.

Beginning with the Book of Genesis, the Old Testament offers an

---

12. Cohn, *Pursuit of the Millenium*. Cf. Beskow, *Rex Gloriae*.

13. For a standard contemporary account of the Jewish monarchy see Bright, *History of Israel*, pp. 184–339; and a briefer account of the history of the Israelites: Albright, *Biblical Period*. The basic Old Testament account of the Jewish monarchy is found in Deuteronomy 17 and 1 Samuel. What follows in the text summarizes that account and contains only essential reference citations within the text itself. I have not examined the literature on the Essene cult or the Dead Sea scrolls.

account of the creation of the world along with a description, largely genealogical for the earliest period, of how human society in the persons of the Israelites began with the original couple and spread across part of the territory now called the Middle East. The author of Genesis, commonly accepted to have been Moses, himself the divinely appointed leader of the Chosen People who had freed them from captivity in Egypt, traced his own lineage through the genealogy back to Adam. The genealogical account also presents the history of the Jewish monarchy.

The first specific mention of a king for the Jewish people is of Melchisedech, "the king of Salem and priest of the most high God" (Genesis 14:18). However, earlier references were made to there being kings of other tribes than the Israelites.[14] Moses also was the combined spiritual and temporal leader of his people, as is clear from the lengthy account given of his life in Exodus and Deuteronomy. He was chosen directly by God to lead the Israelites; and throughout his life he enjoyed a direct, if irregular, relationship with the Lord, from Whom he received the set of laws by which the Chosen People were to be governed. The Jews at this period clearly were being ruled politically by their highest spiritual leader. Equally clearly, each of the twelve tribes making up the Chosen People had its own temporal leader or prince; and the male members of the tribe of Levi, from the family of Aaron, were specially designated to perform the religious duties of offering sacrifice and acting as judges in matters of law. These latter persons did not share directly in the inheritance rights of the Jewish law, but enjoyed a special status through which they lived from the fruits or offerings made "to the Lord as the priests' due from the people" (Deuteronomy 17:1–8).

At a certain point in their history, God informed His people that "I will set a king over thee as all nations have . . . him whom the Lord shall choose" (Deuteronomy 17:14–15), a promise that was fulfilled when the prophet Samuel was told by God to anoint Saul. Saul thus became

14. The properly medieval context for inquiry concerning early examples of temporal rulers was the examination of the question whether kingship preceded priesthood, an issue having to do with the priority of the two spheres. Medieval knowledge of early communities other than the Israelites was very limited, naturally; and modern research provides for judgments not open to earlier periods. One source of medieval information on early non-Israelite societies, saying nothing for the moment about the accuracy of data from the source, was Augustine *De civitate Dei* 16.17. Cf. Hugh of St. Victor *De sacramentis* 2.2.7; John of Paris *De potestate regia et papali* 4.

formally the first king of the Israelites, in the sense that he became the first purely temporal or political leader of the Chosen People who was not concurrently chief priest and spiritual leader as well. A separation of powers by persons occurred at this point. The relevant Scriptural text contains interesting details concerning the procedure by which Saul came into office, as well as a somewhat ambiguous reference to the reason for the event. The Jewish people as a whole seemingly had asked the elderly Samuel to "make us a king . . . give us a king to govern us" (1 Samuel 8:5–6), because his own sons were failing to provide appropriate judicial services. Samuel interpreted this request as a rejection by the Jews of his own role as prophet; but when he took up the matter with the Lord, he was told that the Jews were rejecting God Himself rather than His prophet, Samuel, and that he was to describe to the Jewish people the specific and unpleasant consequences that the imposition of a king's "rights" on them would entail. Samuel did so, adding his own comment that the Chosen People would soon "cry out" against such a regimen. The Israelites ignored their prophet's advice, however, and repeated the request for a king "so that we will be like all nations, and our king shall govern us and go out before us, and fight our battles for us" (1 Samuel 8:20). When Samuel reported back again to the Lord, he was instructed to "hearken to their voice, and make them a king" (1 Samuel 8:22), God apparently being prepared to accede to His People's request even though He thought it was a mistake and was unhappy about it.

The prophetic account of the establishment of a monarchy among the Israelites, then, shows a reluctant God consenting to a popular demand, and a clear warning of the dangers involved in the demand itself. There is also the mournful inference that, in requesting an earthly king, the Chosen People were somehow rejecting their divine, invisible ruler. The later account of the Jewish monarchy by the Old Testament historians repeatedly emphasizes this mistake, the disloyalty to the Lord it involved, and the suffering experienced by the Jews as a result.

The Lord then identified Saul to Samuel as the person chosen by God to be "prince over my people Israel" (1 Samuel 9:16), and Samuel anointed Saul, saying: "Has not the Lord anointed you to be prince over Israel?" (1 Samuel 10:1). Samuel called together all the people of Israel, arranging them by tribes and by families within tribes; and employed a lottery system for the selection first of a tribe, then of a family within that tribe, then of an individual within that family to be

identified as the person who should be king. The lot fell ultimately to
Saul, whom Samuel already knew to be God's choice; and Samuel then
identified Saul to the people, Saul himself appearing to the Jews as
"taller by a head than any of them" (1 Samuel 10:23). The people for
their part then "all cried and said God save the king" (1 Samuel 10:24).
Finally, Saul instructed the people concerning the law of the kingdom,
and left a book containing the law in the presence of the Lord (1
Samuel 10:25). An earlier text wherein God had promised to establish
a king for the Israelites is more explicit on the requirements for this last
activity: "After he [the king] is raised to the throne of his kingdom, he
shall copy out to himself the Deuteronomy of this law in a volume,
taking the copy of the priests of the Levitical tribe, and he shall have it
with him, and shall read it all the days of his life, that he may learn to
fear the Lord his God, and keep his words and ceremonies, that are
commanded in the Law" (Deuteronomy 17:18–19). The same text
speaks of the king's sons reigning "after him" (Deuteronomy 17:20);
but this did not actually occur in the case of Saul. Having become
displeased with Saul's unworthy behaviour, the Lord chose someone
else directly while Saul was still alive.

The factual details in the Old Testament account of the establishing
of the Jewish monarchy in separation from the role of the priesthood
are worth enumerating in review: (1) The action itself of establishing
the monarchy was taken at the request of the Jewish people. (2) God's
view of a temporal monarchy separate from the spiritual leadership of
the Chosen People was negative, although He acceded to it. (3) God
Himself chose the recipient of monarchical authority directly, the
choice being made known first to God's minister-priest. (4) The person
chosen by God to be king (Saul) was anointed by God's minister-priest
before he was identified to the people; the actual procedure for
identification of the person to be king involved an established system of
casting lots. (5) The person identified by this procedure was recognized
by the people as "superior"—in the case of Saul he was seen to be
physically taller and stronger; later, however, when God became
unhappy with Saul's tenure and chose David to succeed Saul, the Lord
asserted that He "does not judge according to the look of man . . . but
according to the heart" (1 Samuel 16:7); God's minister, it seems,
proclaimed that the person selected to be king had been chosen by
God, and that he was unlike all the other people. (6) All the people then
acknowledged the chosen one as king: yet not literally all, for one
group refused to do so at the time, offering their allegiance only after

Saul had proven himself successful in battle. (7) The law of God was then explained to the people by God's minister-priest, who reiterated that this law was the framework for the exercise of the monarch's authority. This represents a repetition of an earlier procedure wherein the chosen leader of the Jews, as both priest and king, was also instructed by God to rule by following and correctly interpreting God's law.

A striking example of the way the Jewish monarchy was identified as the model for a proper temporal polity is the very late medieval text, *Vindiciae contra tyrannos*, a sixteenth-century pseudonymous work of French provenance called one of the two most important political writings opposed to absolute monarchy in the two centuries preceding Locke's *Second Treatise on Government*.[15] Not only does the *Vindiciae* text specifically invoke the Jewish monarchy as model, it also invokes the principle of popular consent and the view that political authority devolves on a ruler through the people's agreement; and it finds evidence for both these elements in the Israelite model, emphasizing the typically medieval reference to the Jewish monarchy as divinely established and thereby "proper." The author's formula is that God "chooses" the king, while the people "establish" him in office.[16]

15. Oakley, "Road from Constance"; also "Figgis, Constance"; Laski, ed., *Natural Law*, pp. 118–20. The *Vindiciae* text was available in England as early as 1589, and went through three English editions before the end of the seventeenth century.

16. "The people of Israel demanded a king. God gave and appointed the law of royal government contained in the seventeenth chapter, verse fourteen of Deuteronomy. . . . You see here, that the election of the king is attributed to God, the establishment to the people: now when the practice of this law came in use, see in what manner they proceeded.

"The elders of Israel, who presented [sic] the whole body of the people . . . came to meet Samuel . . . they demanded a king of Samuel, who asking counsel of the Lord, he made known that He had chosen Saul for the governor of His people. Then Samuel anointed Saul, and performed all those rights which belong to the election of a king required by the people. Now this might, perhaps, have seemed sufficient, if Samuel had presented to the people the king who was chosen by God, and had admonished them all to become good and obedient subjects. Notwithstanding, to the end that the king might know that he was established by the people, Samuel appointed the estates to meet at Mizpah, where being assembled as if the business were but then to begin, as if the election of Saul were then only to be treated of, the lot is cast and falls on the tribe of Benjamin, after on the family of Marti, and lastly on Saul, born of the family, who was the same whom God had chosen. Then by the consent of all the people Saul was declared King. Finally, that Saul nor any other might attribute the aforesaid business to chance or lot after that Saul had made some proof of his valour in raising the siege of the Ammonites in Jobish Gilead, some of the people pressing the business, he was again confirmed king in a full assembly at Gilgal. Ye see that he whom God had chosen, and the lot had

Other Old Testament texts also reflect the element of popular consent to temporal authority in a suitably enigmatic way: for example, "All the people made him their prince" (Judges 11:11). Finally, it should be noted again, the Old Testament account of the Jewish monarchy consistently represents the efforts of the Israelites to function "like other nations" under a separate temporal ruler as a mistake. The Jews seem to have preferred their own peculiar form of political order, a theocracy wherein God alone was king and His chosen priests both ministered and administered God's reign, this reign being a worldly one, but not exercised directly by any earthly or merely temporal monarch.[17]

3. EARLY CHRISTIAN SOURCES

Medieval Christian views and doctrines on the nature of polity were established on a foundation perceived as the fundamental truths and directives of Christian revelation found in the New and Old Testaments, particularly those Scriptural texts to which reference already has been made. These texts, as has been seen, accepted the legitimacy of temporal authority: "Where there is no ruler the people will fall" (Proverbs 11:14), and enjoined obedience to the ruler as a religious obligation. Other documents also figured in the background to which the medieval mind was inclined because of its bent towards the acceptance of authority. They were the writings of earlier Christian thinkers, such as they were known. It is essential, then, to have a sense as well of what these other source materials were; for they show directly, first of all, what were major sources for medieval political

---

separated from all the rest, is established king by the suffrages of the people" (see n. 15, above). At the time I prepared my summary of the Old Testament account of the origins of the Jewish momarchy, I had not seen the *Vindiciae* text.

17. Grant, "Idea," p. 439. This account of the origins of the Jewish monarchy from the perspective of the medieval Christian believer obviously ignores many difficulties and apparently irreconcilable elements in the sequence of the Old Testament text. A fully coherent account, taking into consideration later interpolations and problems of textual sequence has become possible only fairly recently as a result of brilliant contemporary efforts at textual exegesis and reconciliation with archeological, anthropological, and linguistic data: cf. Bright, *History of Israel*. Specific reference to the Old Testament account of the origins of the Jewish monarchy are in John of Salisbury, Thomas Aquinas, Aegidius of Rome, John of Paris, Marsilius of Padua, as well as the canonists: see Part 3 below. For information on the legal use of Scriptural texts see Foreville, "Recours aux sources scripturaires."

thinking and, secondly, they present some of the raw material with which later Christian thinkers worked in the formulation of their own views.

For the most part, early Christian writers were no more interested in developing a political theory as such than were the writers of the Old and the New Testaments, although, as with the fundamental texts of Christianity, some of the products of early Christian writing reflect elements for a theory of politics at least indirectly. For example, in defending their fellow Christians against various forms of Roman persecution, Christian apologists of the second and third centuries emphasized certain notions clearly reflecting an attitude towards the areas of politics and temporal authority. First, they insisted that Christians recognized the legitimacy of temporal authority in general: Justin Martyr quoted the Matthew text: "Render under Caesar the things that are Caesar's";[18] while Irenaeus spoke of a temporal government as established by God, citing Proverbs: "By me kings reign and princes administer justice."[19] Secondly, the Apologists made much of the rights of Christians to practice obedience to a higher religious authority. Theophilus of Antioch, in the second century, insisted that Christians were obliged to obey their civil ruler, but not obliged to adore the Roman emperor;[20] Tertullian expressed the same opinion.[21] Somewhat later, the more intellectually sophisticated Christian thinker, Origen, actually raised the question why Christians should be asked to obey civil authority inasmuch as this power comes from God, when civil authority actually persecutes them. His reply was to the effect that power can be misused without being lost; then Origen went on to locate the reason for man's position of servitude to authority in the order of sin.[22] Irenaeus,[23] and later Ambrosiaster writing in the mid-fourth century (366–82), interpreted a basic Pauline text on a Christian's obligations towards obedience (Romans 13:1) as meaning that the prince is "a ruler over sins" (*minister poenarum*).[24] St. John Chrysostom

18. Justin Martyr *First Apology* 17.

19. Irenaeus *Adversus haereses* 5.4; cited in Carlyle and Carlyle, *Mediaeval Political Theory*, 1:129.

20. Theophilus of Antioch *Ad Autolyeum* 3.14; (*PG* 2:41A), cited in Daniel, "Omnis potestas," p. 45.

21. Tertullian *Ad Scapulam* 2.7 (Corpus Christianorum, Tertulliani opera, 2:1128), cited in Daniel, "Omnis potestas," p. 45.

22. Origen, cited in Daniel, ibid.

23. See n. 17 above.

24. Ambrosiaster *Commentarium in epistolarum ad Romanos* 13.1 (*PL* 17:162D), cited in Daniel, "Omnis potestas," p. 49.

also identified sin as the reason for humans being obliged to submit to civil authority, though making as well the point that the Divine Will and Wisdom have established that governments exist.[25]

4. ST. AUGUSTINE

The most important early Christian writer whose views influenced later medieval theories on the nature of polity, however, was St. Augustine, whose impact here as well as in many other areas of medieval thought was decisive for almost a millenium. And this is true even though the great African Church Father nowhere formulated anything like an *ex professo* treatise on politics. Individual statements and somewhat larger texts having some connection with political thought can be found in a variety of writings in the large Augustinian corpus, but Augustine nowhere offered any specific presentation of a theory of polity. The *City of God* has been interpreted at times as if it were such a document, but it is not. The operating distinction between "heavenly" and "earthly" cities in its basic structure has been pressed to provide an Augustinian formulation of the nature and relationship between the spheres of the spiritual and the temporal, but such an interpretation casts this sometimes ponderous literary masterpiece in a false perspective.[26] Its author did not directly address the *sacerdotium / regnum* issue. Augustine, however, did offer some basic themes that connect with a theory of polity. With all Christians he held that the ultimate purpose of human life in this world is an eternal life after death: true human happiness is to be found in an unending life beyond this world.[27] Further, Augustine accepts and applauds the view that a happy person's life in the world will be social, while acknowledging that terrestrial life is often miserable; he also notes that the saints in heaven enjoy a social life.[28]

Augustine maintained with St. Paul and other early Christians that submission to political authority, as to any form of authority, is submission to God Himself.[29] Political obedience, thus, is a religious

25. John Chrysostom *Sermo IV in Genesim* 203 (*PG* 54:596–97), cited in Daniel, "Omnis potestas," p. 51.

26. See Gilson's review and assessment of various interpretations of the "two cities" image in his foreword to *Augustine, City of God*, Fathers of the Church series. The original French version appears in *Métamorphoses*, chap. 1 and 2.

27. Augustine *De civitate Dei* 19.4.

28. Augustine *De civitate Dei* 19.5; see also *De bono conjugale* 1.1; *De civitate Dei* 19.12; *Quaestiones propriae ex epistolis ad Romanos* 7.

29. Augustine probably was influenced here by Origen; see Daniel, "Omnis potestas," p. 51.

obligation. For him political authority was instituted by God as a remedy for sin, seemingly denying that human government is a natural or essential feature of human society. He maintained that in the state of nature, by which he means the state enjoyed by Adam and Eve in the Garden of Eden before their commission of the Original Sin, human beings had no need of a social organization employing force or coercion. The primitive state of the first (two) humans being one of full rationality and freedom, there was no need for physical force to be employed to guarantee proper behaviour; government of one human by another was not part of this "natural" state of mankind. God willed that rational creatures should have dominion over irrational creatures, but not over one another.[30]

Because his argument on this point is somewhat tortured in expression and was so influential in later medieval political theorizing, it bears reformulation. Augustine contended that by nature no human is a slave, either to another human or to sin. Yet slavery as a social institution is seen to be legitimate in current positive law, while this same law enjoins general preservation of the law of nature. Therefore the legitimation of slavery, the forceful subordination of one human to another, is evidence of a violation of the original law of nature for which slavery must be a punishment. Had no violation of the law of nature occurred, the punishment of slavery would not have been necessary. Coercion, then, even so severe a form of coercion as slavery, is a form of punishment and is a good for a wrongdoer.[31] Had there been no initiating sin or wrongdoing, the corrective punishment of physical coercion would not be needed; and in this sense it can be termed unnatural. Augustine here uses the term "coercion" (*coactio*) to designate the power of the state; and he does so elsewhere as well.[32] Basically, Augustine accepted slavery as a legitimate social institution; the fact that Roman law enshrined it in legislation is one of the premises from which his doctrine of coercion as punishment, and the state as somehow unnatural, flows.

Augustine, however, never discussed the issue of the origin of the state either directly or in detail. The text in which his views on the origin of political authority are most directly expressed centres on an

30. Augustine *De civitate Dei* 19.15.

31. Augustine *De civitate Dei* 19.16.

32. Augustine *De Genesi ad litteram* 9.9, cited in Carlyle and Carlyle, *Mediaeval Political Theory*, 1.167.

exhortation to those in authority in society, especially the *paterfamilias*, to act from a sense of service.[33] The general impression given in this and other texts, however, is that he does not distinguish political from other forms of authority, and that his paradigm case for the exercise of authority is that of master over slave. Like slavery, which he accepts as legitimate if not natural, the institutions of government, coercion, and punishment are brought into human society by sin. They are God's just punishment for human sin, the providential dispensation for dealing with the disorder and strife that are the consequence of sin. For Augustine, the essence of political authority is its coercive character; without coercion the state is not a state. Political authority and its coercive power and aparatus are what transforms a society into a state. For him society has its origins in the order of nature, but the state is a dispensation rooted in sin. Clearly for Augustine, human nature is social, not solitary, and in their original natural state (prior to the commission of the Original Sin) all humans are equal and subject only to God and not to one another, though there is some natural gradation of one human to another even in the original state: for example, of wife to husband and child to parent. But such gradation does not extend to that of ruler over ruled.[34] Exercise of political authority, then, is legitimate but not natural; the natural as so defined did not fully survive the sin of Adam and Eve. Thus, there were only two real examples of humans living in the original state of nature, and these two for only a portion of their lives.[35]

33. Augustine *De civitate Dei* 19.14–15. Markus, "Two Conceptions." Post makes a case for softening the denial by Augustine that political authority and the state are "natural": *Studies*, pp. 500–502; see also Chroust, "Fundamental Ideas," pp. 17–18.

34. Markus, "Two Conceptions," p. 77.

35. A later medieval text on the issue of whether the exercise of authority by one human over another is natural extends the Augustinian doctrine in a conscious effort to bridge the gap between the original Augustinian terminology and the Aristotelian conception of political society as natural. St. Bonaventure speaks of there being three ways in which a human can be said to exercise authority (*potestas dominandi*): (1) the power to use something in his possession: it functions in every state of human nature, including that of original innocence; (2) the power of domination, as commonly understood, encompasses one human's power to command another human being who is capable of understanding and obeying; this power obtains both in the state of original integrity and innocence before the Fall and in the state of fallen nature: examples are the authority a husband has over a wife, and a parent over a child; (3) the power of domination, properly speaking (*proprie*) is identifiable with coercive power, It is operative only in the state of fallen human nature, wherein the authority some humans have over others is in some sense a preternatural punishment for sin (*quodammodo praeternaturaliter in punitionem*

Augustine's emphasis on the legitimacy of political authority and of coercion as an instrument of public policy directly parallel his view concerning the subject's obligation to obedience. Both the legitimacy of temporal power and the obligation to obey it are integral elements of the divinely ordained and instituted order encompassing the universe and mankind's place in it after the Fall. Further, Augustine urges the view that human legislation is necessary to prevent, or at least inhibit, the worst excesses of human wickedness, since the dispositions of human nature that reflect the natural moral law are not sufficient in themselves, after the damage caused by the Original Sin, to guarantee against wrong behaviour. Human laws, however, do not inhibit or command every feature of human activity, only its most fundamental features.[36] Human nature is in itself, so to speak, social; but its state is damaged as a result of the Original Sin, such that humans are organized into legally and politically organized societies possessed of the element of coercion to provide the structures and correctives that ordinary people need to promote their well-being. Human nature and the natural moral law it embodies somehow need actual temporal legislation as an instrument that enables human beings actually to realize themselves in history.[37]

Augustine did speak at one point about a political subject not being obliged to obey laws that are "against the society of the city of God";[38] that is, the subject is not required to perform a sinful act even if enjoined to do so by some actual law. But what Augustine seems to have had in mind here was the Christian's right to reject a positive law in direct violation of God's law, best exemplified by state legislation that bears directly on the subject's obligation to perform specific forms of

---

peccati): Bonaventure, 2 *Sent.* 44.2.1 *ad* 4; 44.2.2, cited in Markus, "Two Conceptions," p. 83. Bonaventure here is giving ultimate expression to the Augustinian concept of the non-natural character of political authority; fully aware himself of the alternative Aristotelian formulation. Bonaventure's contemporary Thomas Aquinas was to make the Augustinian formula redundant. Another mid-thirteenth-century repetition of the Augustinian position can be seen in Richard of Middleton, 2 *Sent.* 44.1.2, also cited in Markus, "Two Conceptions," p. 83, n. 7a; cf. the views of William of Ockham below.

36. See references in Chroust, "Philosophy of Law of St. Thomas Aquinas," pp. 4–5, nn. 18–20.

37. See the many references to Augustinian texts in Chroust, "Fundamental Ideas," pp. 73–74, nn. 83, 84.

38. Augustine *Confessions* 3.8. Post cites this reference from its use in Gratian's *Decretum* as *Conf.* 2, and offers a mistaken reference: see D.8 c.2. Post cites c.3 in *Studies*, p. 501, n. 15.

idolatrous (non-Christian) religious worship. Certainly, he never engaged in any effort to develop a theory of limitation of political authority.[39] His excursus on justice as an essential element in a true state functioned essentially only as a debating point in denying that Christianity caused the fall of Rome, rather than an element in a theory of limited government.[40]

Nevertheless, these efforts at defining a state in terms of justice were to find echoes in later medieval political writings, as was his repetition of the basic Ciceronian conception of justice, the Stoic formula of "giving everyone his due" that itself originated in Plato's *Republic*. The channel for communication of this conception of justice to the later Middle Ages was Cicero himself, via his *De inventione*,[41] a shorter version of Cicero's formulation in Isidore's *Etymologies*,[42] and the *Elementarium* of Papias,[43] as well as echoes of Cicero in Augustine and Ambrose. The Isidorean text was the most influential, the *Etymologies* being one of the most important textbook authorities in the Middle Ages, cited again and again by most medieval theologians and scholars.

39. Anton-Hermann Chroust maintains that, according to Augustine, "we should reject or ignore [sic] all those human, temporal or positive laws which do not flow directly from the *lex aeterna*, that is, from the eternal fountainhead of all justice and lawfulness"; Chroust, "Fundamental Ideas," p. 74. However, he gives no reference for this view, which I find too explicit and merely logically consistent with Augustine's doctrine of eternal law. In my judgment Augustine is not so consistent when it comes to squaring the emphasis he clearly places on the right of a ruler, even a tyrant, to coerce with the view that positive law must reflect eternal law. In a later article Chroust offers references from Augustine to support the view that the edicts of a secular lawgiver must conform fully to the dictates of the *lex naturalis moralis* and the *lex aeterna* in order properly to be law, but again the issue of whether or not something less than a proper positive law carries coercive legitimacy is not addressed directly: Chroust, "Philosophy of Law of St. Thomas Aquinas," pp. 4–5, especially nn. 16, 17. Chroust acknowledges that Augustine conceded, with regret, that not all human laws reflect or encourage only the dictates of the *lex aeterna* and *lex naturalis*: Chroust, "Fundamental Ideas," p. 74.

40. Augustine offers a second definition of state in *De civitate Dei* 19.24, and uses it throughout the work: see nn. 63–69 below.

41. "Habitus animi communi civilitate conservata, suam virique tribuens dignitatem": Cicero *De inventione* 2.61.

42. Isidore *Etymologiae* 15.2.1: I cite references from the Oxford edition: *Isidori hispalensis episcopi etymologiarum sive originum libri XX*, 2 vols. (Oxford: Clarendon Press, 1910).

43. The *Elementarium doctrinae rudimentum* of Papias the Lombard, written about the middle of the eleventh century, served for many centuries as an encyclopedic reference manual for scores of later medieval writers. More than ninety manuscript copies are extant and it was printed first in 1476.

Later medieval legal writings take the same notion from Ulpian's legal formulation found in the *Corpus Iuris Civilis*.[44] Another, "forgotten," definition of justice coined by St. Martin of Braga (d. 579), and mistakenly attributed by Paucapalea in the twelfth century to Gregory the Great, offered a more natural-sounding formulation: "an unspoken covenant of nature devised for the aid of many."[45] Isidore of Seville provided a somewhat more satisfying statement on this issue: He agreed that subjects are to obey their rulers, but was explicit in insisting that justice is an essential element in the state, and that the king must practice justice: "If not, thou shalt not be king."[46] This and many other Isidorean views, especially those concerning the nature and purpose of law, found their way directly into later medieval legal and political theory by way of the *Decretum* of Gratian.[47]

The view that humans are naturally social, while government of humans by other humans through the use of coercion is the result of moral failure, had roots in Greek as well as Christian sources. Stoic ethical theory maintained that all humans are equal in their natural state, and capable therein of living in harmony with one another rationally without the need for social structures that subordinate individuals to one another by physical force. Seneca, too, imagined a primitive state of innocence wherein humans were free from all external compulsion and government, and property and slavery were unknown. Some classical Roman writers also ascribed the development of institutions of the "law of nations" (*ius gentium*) to the realities of war and human avarice.[48]

This view was strongly reinforced by Christians, who similarly accepted the notion of basic equality among humans, and were able to "locate" the originally harmonious and rational condition of human nature in the Garden of Eden prior to the commission of the Original Sin by Adam and Eve. A chief effect of the first sin was to disorder human nature and fracture the harmony between human reason and the emotions (the medieval term "passions" to designate the emotions strikes the right chord in conveying the Christian doctrine on Original Sin). Consequently, external forms of control over human behaviour

44. Ulpian, cited in *Dig.* 1.1.1.2.

45. Martin of Braga, "Formula honestae vitae," in *Martini episcopi Bracarensis opera omnia* 246; cf. *PL* 72:27.

46. Isidore *Etymologiae* 9.3.5.

47. See Part 2, 4, below.

48. Seneca *Epistola 90*; cf. Ovid *Metamorphoses* 1, ll. 90–162, esp. 135–36; Lucan *Letter I*; cf. other references in Cohn, *Pursuit of the Millenium*, pp. 187–91, 357–58.

are needed to compensate for the loss of control by reason over the emotions. According to this view, political authority and the coercion integral to its operation are legitimate as permitted, and even instituted, by God in order that rulers might maintain law, order, and justice, elements now beyond the ordinary abilities of sinful humans to practice in respect of one another.

Gregory the Great reflected the same view in the sixth century,[49] probably following Augustine directly. He went even further, however, maintaining that a good ruler may be taken as a sign of his subject people being good, while an evil ruler is evidence that his subjects are themselves evil.[50] Gregory thus pressed very far the view that in all his actions, evil as well as virtuous, the ruler is a representative of God Himself and an instrument of Divine Providence. Augustine was not so extreme in his own expressions; hence, the more consistent Gregorian view on the obligation to submit to political authority should not be attributed to Augustine.[51] Speaking in the tradition of the Greek Fathers, St. John Chrysostom also emphasized the obligation of obedience to temporal political authority; but he implied, though he did not develop, a distinction between obedience to the office and obedience to the person holding the office.[52] Lactantius maintained that social duties derive from the dignity of the Son of God, rather than from any form of social necessity;[53] while St. Ambrose held that the function of the state was in conformity with the Divine Will, and that its purpose was justice and kindness.[54] Isidore of Seville, whose definition of law in his *Etymologies* was reproduced in Gratian's *Decretum*, asserted that the purpose of laws was to curb human wickedness and protect innocence.[55]

The view that human government is the result of sin and that the

49. Gregory *Libri moralium in Job* 21.15; cited in Carlyle and Carlyle, *Mediaeval Political Theory*, 1:127.

50. Gregory *Libri moralium in Job* 25.16; cf. *Regulae pastorales* 3.4 and *Libri moralium in Job* 25.24.

51. Arquillière, *L'Augustinisme politique*, p. 155. Carlyle offers three reasons for the more radical Gregorian position: a deliberate effort to repudiate the anarchical tendencies existing in the early Church; the position held by the Roman emperor after Constantine's edict making Christianity the state religion of Rome; finally, influence from the Old Testament conception of the King of Israel: Carlyle and Carlyle, *Mediaeval Political Theory*, 1:157–58.

52. John Chrysostom, cited in McIlwain, *Growth of Political Thought*, pp. 152–53.

53. Lactantius *Instituta divina* 6.10.

54. Ambrose *De officiis* 1.22–129; cited by Post, *Studies*, p. 500.

55. Isidore of Seville *Etymologiae* 5.10; and 5, *passim*; cf. Gratian D.4 C.1.

legitimacy of coercive power rests on the legitimacy of divine punishment for sin provides the standard medieval account for temporal rule until the appearance of Aristotle's *Politics* in the mid-thirteenth century. Only then do we find currency given to the view that political society is natural as the means of fulfilling the naturally imperfect character of the individual human, who can neither survive physically nor fully develop personally alone. The so-called Stoic-Christian-Augustinian doctrine, whose most influential exponent was Augustine himself, then gave way among later medieval thinkers to the more rigorous formulations of Aristotelianism, a fact that has led some interpreters of the Middle Ages to juxtapose the earlier and later medieval theories concerning the character of temporal rule in terms of the distinction between the view that human government is conventional (the earlier view) and the notion that it is natural.[56]

The introduction of Aristotle's *Politics* did produce something of a revolution in political thinking in western Europe after its translation into Latin about 1260; but it is a serious oversimplification to draw too firm a contrast between earlier and later medieval views on the character of temporal rule in terms of what is "natural." From earliest times Christian writers accepted temporal rule as legitimate and normal; and however much their account of it was construed in terms of sin and punishment, none of them referred to it as "conventional" any more than they denied its necessity. Further, no articulation of the Christian theology of Original Sin held that its consequences involved a change in the "nature" of human beings. The orthodox Christian doctrine of original sin consistently maintained that while human nature was wounded, perverted, or somehow rendered inharmonious by the sin of Adam and Eve, it was not substantially changed into a different nature. After the Fall, Adam and Eve were not characterized as unnatural or conventional, whatever these terms might mean; they were viewed as possessing the same human nature that was theirs before their transgression, albeit distorted, wounded, perverted. Their sinful condition after the Fall was seen as a debilitated one rather than

---

56. See Post, *Studies*, pp. 494–513; Markus, "Two Conceptions." p. 337A. The distinction between "natural" and "conventional" originates in social contract theory (especially as formulated by Rousseau in the *Contrat social*), according to which humans form political society by contractual consent: society and its authority come into being by "convention," conventional agreement. The distinction here between the state of nature (the "natural") and the state of society (the "conventional") is thus clear. Equally clear, however, is its inapplicability to medieval thought that did not exhibit the social contract frame of reference.

as changed substantially, as displaying features needing correctives to compensate for the debilitation and to restore so far as possible the balance and order among the elements that constituted it.

A political theory expressing this theological doctrine directly perceives political authority as unnecessary in circumstances or conditions where human nature functions perfectly and consistently with the proper ordering of its elements—conditions that are contrary to present circumstances and that only obtained for the natural state of Adam and Eve in the Garden of Eden. Coercive political authority is certainly necessary in the present conditions of "sinful" human nature, however, where all humans suffer from the harmful effects of the Original Sin. Early Christians, including Augustine, accepted the realities of human government and organization as perfectly legitimate, necessary, and useful. The advantages of living in some form of organized society are virtually self-evident, and so they seemed to both early and later medieval Christian thinkers, whether or not they were familiar with the first chapters of Aristotle's *Politics*. Lack of acquaintance with the Stagirite's views on the nature of polity, as well as lack of express interest in the subject as such, however, probably contributed greatly to the failure by Augustine and those who followed his views to formulate an adequate and comprehensive theory of polity.

Augustine accepted, and even argued for, the legitimacy of political organization. He notes that God (the heavenly city) makes use of the "peace" that is the aim of temporal society for His own purposes, and seeks the merging of human wills that is useful in achieving mortal human peace.[57] He even describes human society in this world in terms of peace, defining a state (or city) as "a multitude of reasonable beings voluntarily associated in the furtherance of common interests."[58] Significantly, he again speaks clearly in terms that accept the normal character of political society and government, and identifies what came to be a standard reference point in later medieval political theory, the point just noted that the purpose of political organization and government is peace. Augustine notes specifically that earthly peace is conducive to the attainment of heavenly, eternal peace, and states that this is why St. Paul advised Christians to be obedient to temporal masters; he also asks the Church to pray for kings and other high persons, citing 1 Timothy 2:2.[59]

57. Augustine *De civitate Dei* 19.17.
58. Augustine *De civitate Dei* 19.24; cf. *Epistola 138* 2; *Epistola 155* 3.
59. Augustine *De civitate Dei* 19.26.

Augustine's conception of "city" and the basis for his distinction between its heavenly and earthly forms is theological rather than philosophical, however, and involves the Christian doctrine of predestination.[60] As noted earlier, accordingly, there is no direct correspondence between his two cities and the distinction between spiritual and temporal spheres of authority. The theological basis for Augustine's two cities is itself "spiritual," so that neither of them has a direct correspondence with the order of the temporal. The city of God is constituted of those "citizens" chosen by God (via predestination) to fulfill themselves with Him eternally in heaven: some have achieved this goal already; others living at present in the world in all the various forms of temporal jurisdiction will achieve it at their death; while still others yet unborn are destined even later to become citizens of the heavenly kingdom. The earthly city, however, is the kingdom of Satan: its citizenry are those humans predestined to Hell from all eternity, some already dead and others at present alive or as yet unborn, but all having no specific connection with any particular temporal polity. Here, fundamentally, is the explanation for insisting that Augustine's *City of God* cannot be considered a treatise on political theory, or even as containing directly the basic elements for this form of work. As noted before, its author was not concerned primarily with issues of political theory, even though his *magnum opus* contains elements for one and set something of a style for later medieval repetition of Augustinian views that did impact on politics.

Another element in Augustine's doctrine that became deeply woven into the political thought of the later medieval period, and had far-reaching consequences thereby, was his effort to define the state. Augustine took his cue here from a reading of Cicero's *De re publica*,[61] and with Cicero he maintained the traditional position that the purpose

60. A careful explanation of Augustine's doctrine relating the concept of Christian predestination to his definitions of the two cities is found in Gilson's foreword to the English translation of *City of God*, in Fathers of the Church series, 8, pp. lv–lxxxi. Gilby offers a telling comment on the restrictive character of the "two cities" concept as a basis for political theory, a restriction to which Augustine himself was much too astute to fall victim; Gilby also notes the later medieval introduction of a third city, in a text relating to the Lateran Council of 1179; cf. Congar, "Maître Rufin," cited in Gilby, *Political Thought of Thomas Aquinas*, p. xxvi, n. 1.

61. Cicero's definition, as quoted by Augustine in *De civitate Dei*, 19.21, was *Populum esse definivit coetum multitudinis, juris consensu et utilitatis communione sociatum*. The Ciceronian definition must be from a portion of the dialogue that is lost. But see Cicero *De re publica* 2.42. Cf. Carlyle and Carlyle, *Mediaeval Political Theory*, 1:4–8.

for which political society functioned was the common good.[62] However-
er, his formulation was dictated from the beginning by the overall
intention behind the composition of the *City of God*. This was to offer a
sustained and unassailable rejection of the thesis that the Christian
church was responsible in any way for the decadence and weakness that
had led to the decline of the Roman Empire. Augustine's counterclaim
is that the Empire had been responsible for its own enfeebled
condition, that its political, social, and moral degeneracy was the result
of the false and pernicious attitudes on which it had been based.[63]
Warming to this subject Augustine asserts that, in the final analysis, one
had to deny that the Roman Empire was even entitled to call itself a
state.[64] To achieve this self-serving conclusion he employs Cicero's
definition of a state, according to which justice is a necessary feature of
a sound political community,[65] and offers the following argument to
show that the Empire failed to meet the Ciceronian criterion: Justice
not based on Christian law as well as on the law of nature is incomplete;
hence a state not founded on Christian law is an incomplete embodiment of its necessary feature of justice. Like all earlier and even all
contemporary political organizations, Rome was not based on Christian law, and hence was not a true state.[66] Gregory the Great took this
Augustinian view a further logical step several centuries later, when he
made the inference that the obligation of securing divine justice upon
earth rested ultimately on no one but the pope as Christ's vicar in this
world.[67] From this formulation it was only a short step to the later claim
by Innocent IV that the pope is the *iudex ordinarius* of all humans,[68] a
fundamental claim giving rise to much of the thirteenth-century
struggle between church and state.[69]

There is a reference in the Ciceronian definition of the state to

62. Augustine *De civitate Dei* 19.21; cf. 2.21, John of Salibury reiterated the same
point, of course, as did Thomas Aquinas and all other medieval political theorists, those
of the latter part of the thirteenth century and later being able to reinforce this principle
even more strongly by reference to Aristotle's *Politics*. Cf. Eschmann, "Thomistic
Glossary"; Lewis, "Organic Tendencies."

63. Augustine *De civitate Dei* 2.22.

64. Ibid., 19.21.

65. See n. 60 above.

66. Augustine *De civitate Dei* 19.21.

67. McIlwain, *Growth of Political Thought*, p. 160.

68. Ibid.

69. Augustine's final position on the definition of state simply rejects the original
definition as too narrow: *De civitate Dei* 19.24.

"consent" by the people to the law that gives structure to the political community as it aims at the essential purpose of achieving justice;[70] and Augustine reiterates this reference to consent in his own position.[71] But the original Ciceronian text is itself oblique and lapidary, obviously not containing anything of the modern notion of consent as designating a procedure for validating political authority. Augustine was even less concerned with any such feature, and his handling of the Ciceronian definition was perceived to be less than adequate by later Christian writers. Isidore of Seville saw fit to reorganize Augustine's wording for the definitions of both state and law, thereby producing a better co-ordination between Ciceronian and Christian views.[72] These Isidorean definitions enjoyed great currency in the technical writings of the later medieval period, having been preferred by Gratian.[73] Isidore, not Augustine, set the form of the definitions for these important concepts in medieval political theory, a form that explicitly took juridical and sociological elements into account,[74] elements Augustine himself acknowledged as significant, but reference to which did not appear specifically in his definitional statements.

Augustine had second thoughts about the use he had made of the Ciceronian definition of state as necessarily involving the virtue of justice. He returned to this issue much later in the *City of God*, and acknowledged the narrowness with which he had applied Cicero's formulation. He then amended his position, not to say rejected it completely; he proferred a second definition of temporal society according to which its essential feature was nothing more than common agreement among its members with regard to the purpose of their coming together.[75] The new definition enabled Augustine to accept virtually any grouping of humans under any common purpose as a state (or city), thereby justifying his own designation of all the humans predestined to hell because committed commonly to the cause of the Evil One as "citizens" of a state. The latitude to the new

70. See n. 61 above. Cf. Cicero *De re publica* 1.25; 3.5. Cicero expressed a theory of government based on consent: *De re publica* 3.13.23 and *De officiis* 1.17.53. See Gough, *Social Contract*, p. 19 and nn. 3 and 4.

71. Augustine *De civitate Dei* 19.21 and 24.

72. Isidore *Etymologiae* 9.4.5; 5.3.4.

73. Gratian, D.4 c.1 and c.2; D.1 c.1–12; D.2 c.2.

74. A typical illustration is found in Thomas Aquinas's treatise on law, where he asks specifically whether or not the Isidorean definition of positive law is appropriate: *S.T.* 1–2.95.3.

75. Augustine *De civitate Dei* 19.24. Cf. *Letters* 138.2.10, 155.3.9

Augustinian meaning for state is sufficiently broad to include all actually existing states, as well as past and future historical polities, even those whose rulers are tyrants who decline to limit their power to the rules of God's law. By using so broad and loose a definition Augustine offers further evidence here that he was not seriously interested in developing a political theory as such. It also indicates that the later extension of doctrine by Gregory the Great just noted, while perhaps logically consistent with certain Augustinian remarks, extended their meaning beyond the point to which Augustine himself was prepared to go. Augustine, then, presents two conflicting definitions of the state, one identifying justice as its essential feature, the other citing only a shared common purpose. And while his preference favoured the latter, he does not reconcile it with the first, thereby failing to provide either an adequate concept of justice or a satisfactory view concerning its place in a polity.

While thus offering an incomplete and only indirect theory of polity, Augustine does accept the concept of there being a good for the state, political society, as a whole. Again he follows Cicero in expressing the general Roman view that individual interests are subordinate to those of the polity itself.[76] Ulpian's famous formulation on the point held that public law dealt with the very status of the Roman state, and with the public authorities and sacred matters necessary for the public welfare: "Public law pertains to the Roman state as such ... Some things are for public use and others for private use. Public law has to do with matters sacred, priestly, and magisterial."[77]

Augustine clearly subscribed to the same view, that the supremacy of justice had as its goal and purpose the attainment of order and peace that gave expression to the *ratio societatis*. St. Ambrose expressed the same view somewhat later: the *ratio societatis*, justice, is to be associated with the public law pertaining to the duties of magistrates in administering the public community for the welfare of all.[78] And it was this Augustinian-Ambrosian theory of justice as the normal *ratio societatis*, combined with the principles from Roman law concerning the power

---

76. Cicero *De oratore*, 1.46.201. However, Cicero could be cynical also regarding civil authority appealing to the general interest: see *De officiis* 3.11; cf. Post, *Studies*, pp. 254–55.

77. "Publicum ius est quod ad statum rei Romanae spectat ... sunt enim quaedam publice utilia, quaedam privatem, publicum ius in sacris, in sacerdotibus, in magistratibus consistet": *Dig.* 1.1.1.2.

78. Ambrose *De officiis* 1.28 (*PL* 16.61).

of the prince and its relation to the common or public utility, that encouraged John of Salisbury to write his small treatise on "reason of state."[79]

5. SUMMARY

The early period of Christian thought and history of politics may be reviewed at this point in terms of our interest in the concepts of consent, coercion, and limit, keeping in mind the restricted nature of the documentary and doctrinal background known to those whose views are under consideration. Thus, for example, it must be remembered that Aristotle's *Politics*, though written in the mid-fourth century B.C., was unknown directly either to later Roman writers or to Christians of the early Christian period; this essential document in the history of western political thought came into general circulation in western European intellectual circles only in the mid-thirteenth century.[80] Plato, too, was known only imperfectly. Roman moralists and political writers such as Cicero and Seneca were generally aware of the doctrines of "Platonism," as were Christian authors such as Justin Martyr and Augustine. But their knowledge was quite imperfect, and did not extend to direct access to the major Platonic writings in ethics and political theory: the *Republic* and the *Laws* do not seem to have been known directly to either the Roman or the early Christian intellectual tradition.[81]

What can be learned of the Christian attitude towards politics from the writings of early Christianity shows no express concern at all with the issue of consent as a feature of either the theory or the practise of political authority. The biblical account of how the Jewish people received their first king, Saul, does refer to his having been acclaimed by all the people, and to the employment of a lottery process by which the candidate for monarchical office was identified to the people. Yet the context in which these elements occur shows that the lottery process was not a means for making the position of political leadership genuinely open to a group of possible candidates; it was simply the proce-

79. Post uses the expression "small treatise on reason of state" to characterize a portion of John of Salisbury's *Policraticus*: Post, *Studies*, p. 259; cf. esp. nn. 32–34. See other references to medieval use of the concept "reason of state" in Post, *Studies*, pp. 257–58.

80. See Muckle, "Greek Works, Part I" and "Continuation."

81. Ibid. Cf. van Steenberghen, *Aristotle in the West*.

dure used by human agency, but presumably controlled by the divinity, through which God made known the person He had chosen for this role. Clearly God chose Saul to be king of the Jews, and the Israelites recognized clearly and accepted that the choice lay with God and not themselves. Their consent was a form of agreement by way of acceptance of an action already taken by their God. Against such a background the element of popular acclaim cannot be construed as anything more than post factum and pro forma acknowledgment of a decision already made. There is no trace here of the notion that the people to be governed have any direct jurisdiction or right of prior determination in the choice of ruler. Consent in this latter sense was not part of the Jewish vocabulary of governance.

The element of coercion, however, was present in the Jewish system of politics, though its articulation is not frequently explicit. God's chosen ruler for the Israelites was viewed as an instrument of God's law and of His vengeance; it was the ruler's responsibility to uphold and enforce the divine law on the Chosen People, and this he did through his kingly office. Unquestionably, the king possessed the power needed to accomplish this task. The only qualification or reservation placed on this power had to do with the king's willingness to enforce God's law on His people, rather than with any ability or right to do so.

The feature of limit is also clearly to be found in the Old Testament account of the exercise of monarchical rule, at least by implication. The king's authority extended to the interpretation and enforcement of God's law, and only to that limit. A ruler who transgressed the limits of the law laid down by God for His Chosen People did wrong and exceeded his divine mandate. When this occurred, such a ruler could be deprived of his political authority, but apparently only by God Himself. This actually happened in the case of Saul, the first Jewish king, who was said to have been deprived of his royal office during his own lifetime by God. The mechanics of how this was done are obscure, however, and there seems to have been no formal act of deposition nor any immediate consequences of the act of divine revocation of authority: God informed Samuel that Saul was no longer king, but the Jewish people as a whole apparently were not informed of the deposition, and Saul continued in office until his death. Only then did the second divinely appointed monarch, David, actually succeed to office, even though his selection by God had taken place earlier. It must be noted, however, that no completely certain and accurate account of either the theory or the practice of the Jewish monarchy can be derived from the Old Testament. Such an account was simply not of direct or serious interest to the writers of the Jewish Scripture.

Another illustration of the same point, which involves an issue that emerged in later medieval theories of government, is the absence of any reference to the possibility of deposing an evil or tyrannical ruler. While it is clear that a Jewish ruler was limited in the legitimate exercise of authority to enforcing laws provided by God, there seems to have been no parallel expression of the limits of the obligation to obey the king. Nor was there any expression given to the possibility of it being legitimate for any member(s) of the community to challenge or depose an unjust ruler. Like the selection of the king, this matter seems to have been left directly to God; the Jewish people were to have faith that their Lord would provide all things needful, and would deal with His people properly, giving them a king as and when they required one, and removing him as and when this might be necessary. The disposition of events was "left to heaven"; and the actual course of events was explicable post factum according to this principle.[82]

Neither does the concept of consent appear explicitly in any of the formally expressed political views of early Christian thinkers, at least not in what they say concerning the exercise of temporal political authority—not even in respect of what can be called pro forma consent by way of the popular acclamation of temporal rulers. This should not be surprising. The earliest Christians who were Jews were, and recognized themselves to be, members of a conquered people; accordingly, they could not be expected to advance any claims for rights in the choice of their political masters. As well, even Christians like St. Paul who were Roman citizens did not operate in a context

82. It may be argued that some ambiguity exists in the Old Testament text regarding the original selection of the first Israelite monarch by lot, and that this process could have been perceived by the people as genuinely open to all, "democratic" in the way that choice of magistrates by lot in democratic Greek city-states was. I interpret the texts differently, however; for it seems clear that, at least for the authors of the Scripture here, the description of events is being offered from the "inside," by persons knowing what actually happened; and according to this view the choice of ruler was not genuinely open when the casting of lots occurred. Rather, the outcome already had been determined by God. The only ambiguity, then, has to do with whether the people saw the lottery as nothing more than an identification process or as genuinely determining the choice. It does not seem that the notion "anyone will do (to serve as king)" was an operative principle. John of Paris made precisely this remark in commenting on how the Israelites came by their first king: "God did not commit to them the right of choice ... rather He reserved it to Himself": *De potestate regali* 19 *ad* 35.

where they saw as relevant the notion of exercising actual and deliberate consent regarding the rulers of the Roman empire. What was relevant was the obligation to obey; and naturally enough this was where the early Christians placed their emphasis in expressing views on the nature of polity.

There is no question, then, about acknowledging and accepting the reality and legitimacy of the coercive power of the state in exacting obedience from its members. The early Christians, as we have seen, were enjoined to obedience, on moral and religious grounds. But within limits. The temporal ruler was to be obeyed as long as his orders did not impose on Christians actions forbidden by the divine authority to which they owed a higher allegiance and superior obligation, the authority of God and His laws. There was never any doubt from earliest times that the obligation Christians accepted towards any actual political authority, however stringently this obligation might be expressed by their own religious leaders (many of whom explicitly insisted that it extended to obedience towards evil rulers and tyrants), did not extend to the requirement of acting against the higher authority of their God. The authority of an earthly ruler was limited to "what was Caesar's"; what was God's (law) was not Caesar's. That simple distinction at least was clear, though its specifications were not spelled out; and many early Christians accepted the distinction at the cost of their own lives through religious martyrdom.

Not too much should be made, however, of there being necessarily a conscious awareness among early Christians of the abstract political concept of limit. The early Christian martyrs were not engaged in the formulation of political theory. The strength of their religious commitment, rather, gave practical expression to the principle that there are limits beyond which political authority may not legitimately enforce its authority, as is the case whenever a citizen decides not to obey a law. Of course, a person refusing to obey may intend simply to disobey rather than question the law's legitimacy. The issue, however, is that anyone disobeying a law on the grounds that a law is not legitimate invokes the principle of limit, whether or not the allegation of illegitimacy is correct.

The Augustinian view of polity offers another instance of Christian thought where the element of consent attracts no specific interest at all, while the concepts of coercion and limit function generally in ways identical to those already seen in earlier Christian writers. Augustine did not enquire about what role, if any, the people as a whole are to play in the establishment or exercise of political authority; its reality seems to have been accepted by him as a given. Christians, and by extension presumably all persons, are obliged to obey existing political authority, even in circumstances where this authority may be evil or tyrannical: political authority derives from God Himself, and its coercive application as well as its reality are justifiable in terms of using such physical force as is required to direct the sinful human condition into proper behaviour. Again, a limit is implied on the legitimate exercise of political authority, a limit restricting temporal authority to an arena that does not conflict with the laws of God. But Augustine offers no encouragement, nor even much solace, to those who find themselves in a situation where political authority acts beyond its legitimate limits.[83] The temporal role for a Christian is simply to suffer evil and tyranny where it occurs, recognizing that the imposition of human authority is a consequence of sin and represents suitable punishment from God for human transgressions. Augustine does speak in one place about popular acclamation for political authority; but the reference is a passing one and the concept he had in mind seems more ritualistic than anything else.[84]

6. CONSENT IN EARLY CHURCH PRACTICES

One aspect of early Christian life in which the element of popular consent does seem to have functioned in practice was in the selection in Apostolic times of leaders in the various Christian communities. Though the evidence is scanty and provides no theoretical basis for the practice described, it seems that in the first Christian communities persons were selected for the responsibilities of conducting religious services and affairs by a process involving the total community. Several texts of the Acts of the Apostles speak of the Christian community as a whole being involved in a type of decision making: Acts 1:23–26, 6:5, 11:2, 15:4, and 22; and several kinds of activity are mentioned. 1 Cor. 49:3 also mentions that Clement of Rome approved this Apostolic

83. Carlyle was sceptical about how influential was Augustine's view that implied a lack of any practical limit on the exercise of political authority, but I think his interpretation here is a bit too reverent: Carlyle and Carlyle, *Mediaeval Political Theory*, 1:169.

84. Augustine defines a society ultimately in terms of the people being "voluntarily associated:" *De civitate Dei* 19.24; but nowhere does he attempt to describe how this voluntariness is to be given expression.

practice when he spoke of the Apostles and other important early Christian leaders as having placed persons in authoritative positions "with the approval of the whole Church."[85]

Hippolytus reflected the same attitude in the period after Clement;[86] and the era from the second through the fourth centuries shows several instances of individual church communities refusing to be administered by a bishop other than the person accepted by them. In a text that has had a long and impressive history, Pope Celestine I promulgated the rule at the beginning of the fifth century that "no one should be a bishop unless accepted (*invitus*),"[87] a directive that was adopted by a Church council in Orleans in 549, and by the Council of Paris of 557.[88] There is similar evidence from the early Christian centuries of some lay participation in Church councils and other organs of general Church governance, although the details are sketchy concerning what actual role the laity played, and no evidence exists for any theory justifying such activities.[89] Considerable caution must be used, then, in construing these data as bearing implications for political theory, even a theory of ecclesiastical polity.

What was likely being reflected in the New Testament sources that mention community (popular) participation in the selection of spiritual leaders, as well as in the similar examples from the early Christian centuries, is informality in the procedure for choosing a leader rather than a conscious determination to use a specific mechanism guaranteeing an explicit and essential role to the people of the community as a whole. Marsilius of Padua, whose views on the requirement of popular consent have earned him the reputation in some quarters of being a late-medieval forerunner of democratic theory, was positively cynical in his interpretation of instances of popular rule in the early Christian community. He speculated that the early Christian churches may have been so bereft of qualified persons either to select a proper minister or

---

85. A recent but brief summary of the element of communal consensus in the Apostolic Church is Schnachenburg, "Community Co-operation in New Testament." See also in the same journal an article on the election of bishops in the early Church: Legrand, "Theology and Election of Bishops."

86. Hippolytus, cited in Congar, "Quod omnes tangit," p. 225. This article is one of the most important studies of the Roman legal dictum *quod omnes tangit* (*q o t*): see Part 3, 1A below.

87. "Nullus invitis detur episcopus. Cleri, plebis et ordinis consensus ac desiderium requiratur": Celestine I *Epistolae* 4.5, cited in Gratian, D.61 c.13 and D.63 c.26.

88. Cited in Congar, "Quod omnes tangit," p. 226.

89. Ibid.

actually to fill the leadership role that it was necessary to broaden the base for selection as widely as possible in order to get maximum advantage from sound judgment wherever it might be found.[90] Whatever the explanation for these early examples of popular involvement in decision making in early Christian communities, and whatever form they might have taken, knowledge of the instances themselves was not lost. And their significance for later centuries was considerable.

7. THE EARLY MEDIEVAL CHRISTIAN COMMUNITY

Sixth-century views and practices concerning the function of the Christian community as a whole in the appointment of a bishop consciously reflected the practices of Apostolic times as they were understood. Selection of bishops in the early medieval period, at least in parts of Italy, also involved an element of popular choice or consent. As with the procedure of earlier times, what seems to have been present here was an informality that probably precluded serious formal deliberation; it is even more probable that no particular interest was taken in the development of a theory of ecclesiastical polity. The element of popular participation in episcopal election, nonetheless, was not only sanctioned, it was directly encouraged.

The fifth-century letter of Celestine I already mentioned had stipulated that no bishop ought to be given to those unwilling to receive him. Later, Pope Leo I wrote to Rusticus, Bishop of Narbonne, that "no one ought to be considered a bishop unless he had been elected by the clergy, accepted by the people, and consecrated by his co-provincials with the co-operation of the metropolitan."[91] These two texts warrant careful consideration, if for no other reason than that they became important elements in later medieval formulation of the canonical procedure for appointing bishops.

Celestine's single remark clearly does not stipulate a specific consenting function for the laity of a diocese; nor is there any suggestion that the general "willingness to receive" must be expressed in any

90. Marsilius of Padua *Defensor pacis* 1.3.4; 2.17.7.

91. Leo I *Epistolae* 167, cited in Gratian, D.62 c.1. The *Decretum* text shows a slightly different wording from the original, which reads: "nulla ratio sinit ut inter episcopos habeatur qui nec a clericis sunt electi; nec a plebibus sunt expetiti, nec a provincialibus episcopis cum metropolitani iudicia consecrato. Cf. Benson, *Bishop-Elect*, pp. 23–34; Chodorow, *Christian Political Theory*, pp. 199–205.

formal way or necessarily prior to the bishop being placed in office. It is not even clear that "those who must be willing to receive their bishop" include the laity as distinct from the clergy, although it is certainly plausible to assume that this is so. The letter of Leo I to Rusticus is more explicit, but again it is far from comprehensive regarding either theory or procedure. The clergy of the diocese as a whole are to be involved in the selection of their bishop, but the procedure of involvement is not spelled out. The diocesan laity as a whole are also to be involved, though how this is to be done is even less clearly explained. Presumably, the selection is actively performed by the clergy, and is conducted before the candidate for episcopal office is named; and he is actually chosen by the clergy as a whole ("elected by the clergy"). The people's activity of "accepting" presumably also occurs before the successful candidate assumes office; but the distinction between "electing" and "accepting" indicates a difference in function between clergy and laity, and as well seems to provide a less well-defined role for the lay people. The wording of these two texts does not make it possible to derive any more information on the issue.[92]

Documents of any kind devoted specifically to the nature of politics and society are rare in the period from the fifth to the eleventh century, a reflection of the fact that literature of any kind was rare in this politically unstable and frequently chaotic period in western Europe; it reflects as well the fact that the theory of politics itself was not a subject of great concern. The few elements produced were almost all of the "mirror for princes" (*speculum principum*) genre, handbooks of largely moral advice to rulers about how to conduct themselves in office. This type of document illustrates an almost complete absence of genuine theorizing about the nature of government, as well as a common and virtually unqualified acceptance of political rulers as necessary and legitimate features of human society. Beyond this the "mirrors" did little more than "reflect" the character and qualities a ruler should possess, rather than the structure and elements appropriate for a political society. They stressed the moral qualities a ruler must exhibit, the virtues he ought to possess or acquire, and the corresponding vices to be avoided or eliminated. No intellectual tradition existed in the Dark Ages that devoted attention to the nature and forms of political society. As mentioned earlier, the fundamental political writings of

---

92. See the later use made of this text, and of the Leonine text as well, by Gratian, nn. 87, 91 above.

Plato and Aristotle were unknown directly, and their existnce had not yet left any significant trace on Christian thought. More importantly, however, the emperor Constantine's decision in the fourth century to make Christianity the state religion of the Roman Empire had resulted, though not immediately, in a virtual identification between Christian church and state, or at least in a confusion of the spiritual and temporal spheres.[93]

The formality of the distinction remained nonetheless, with continuing recognition of the Gospel admonition to distinguish between God and Caesar. In fact, one of the most widely cited documents in the later medieval church / state controversy had its origins at this time: the late fifth-century letter of Pope Gelasius to Anastasius, outlining a doctrine of the two spheres.[94] However, it became more and more difficult to distinguish the two spheres in practice. Christianity spread institutionally throughout the geographical confines of the Empire in some sense because of its official status, and did so in a way that saw its own administrative framework usually paralleling the old Imperial political structure. When the Empire as a political reality ultimately collapsed in western Europe the administrative structure of the Church remained, and often was expected to serve needed political as well as ecclesiastical purposes; and in fact it frequently did so. Furthermore, collapse of the Empire had meant collapse as well of the cultural, intellectual, and educational forms and institutions in virtually the whole of western Europe except Ireland. Little remained as a basis on which to rest serious intellectual activity of any kind.

The "mirror for princes" type of political treatise had its origins in the sixth century with Gregory the Great, and took its form from its prototype, Gregory's *Pastoral Care*.[95] This work, in turn, was patterned after the *De officiis* of Cicero,[96] and was a handbook for the moral guidance of clerics in the exercise of their duties. Such was the basic material that was transmuted into later directives for the exercise of temporal political authority, a further illustration of the intellectual

93. See *Histoire de l'église*, ed. Fliche and Martin, 3.

94. Gelasius *Ad Anastasium*; English translation, in part, in Tierney, *Crisis of Church and State*, pp. 8–9.

95. Gregory the Great, *The Pastoral Care*, ed. Ingvar Carlson (Stockholm, Almquist & Wiksell, 1975). There were two earlier Christian texts similar to Gregory's *Liber regulae pastoralis*: the *Second Oration* of Gregory Nazianzanus, with which Gregory was familiar, and the *De sacerdotis* of St. John Chrysostom.

96. Cicero *De officiis*, trans. Walter Miller (Cambridge: Harvard University Press, 1961).

simplicities of the period. Leadership functions in both church and state were perceived alike in one-dimensional terms: success in the exercise of authority, whether ecclesiastical or temporal, required that the ruler be possessed of and exercise the appropriate moral virtues. The attitude embodied in these political treatises did little more than display the contrast between the responsibilities of leadership and those of obedience in any political context.[97] The function of a ruler was simply to rule, for which certain moral qualities of character were necessary; the function of others was to obey. The qualities necessary in a ruler, as in a subject, were moral, internal. If he possessed these, his behaviour in office would be right and good, by definition, so to speak; similarly, the corresponding actions of his subjects would be proper inasmuch as they reflected the requisite virtues of obedience. Such a view does not even raise the question of the need or utility for any corporate constitutional power to limit or regulate the ruler from "outside." No emphasis is placed on political structures or forms of political expression, no interest expressed in setting down conditions under which authority is to be recognized and exercised.[98]

However, one signal exception can be seen to this generalization: the exercise of authority must be limited by law, power must always be used under the law. This feature is always found in the *speculum* texts either explicitly or implicitly; and it survived them by being transmitted through them, and was expanded on in later centuries when intellectual life and expression concerning a theory of polity became suitably sophisticated once again.[99]

8. THE POLITY OF THE PRE-CHRISTIAN TRIBES

Reference has been made already to the connection between barbarian tribal societies and the search for the origins of modern European

97. This genre of literary effort had a lengthy history in the Middle Ages; its most popular example was the enormously successful late-thirteenth-century exemplar, the *De regimine principum* of Aegidius of Rome.

98. Whatever the poverty of data in the literary tradition, formal coronation and consecration procedures existed in various western European Kingdoms: among the Britons in the sixth century, the Visigoths in the seventh, and the Anglo-Saxons and Franks in the eighth. See Kern, *Kingship and Law*, pp. 34–50.

99. The feature of limitation by law is the single concept emphasized by Professor Cam in her ultimate assessment of the value of the British parliamentary system of democracy, whose genuine origins she found in the thirteenth century: the conception of popular rights, the rights of the people, protected by limitations on the authority of the monarch: Cam, *Law-Finders*.

democracy. Of particular interest is the tradition among Germanic, Anglo Saxon, and Celtic tribes of choosing a leader or king. Particular impetus towards examining the data of tribal and folk ways among the "barbarians" of pre-Christian Europe developed from the perception that the medieval Christian churchman's attitude towards the exercise of authority tended to see it as essentially God-given, originating in the divine. Such a perception among many early modern constitutional historians of western Europe led them to look to the "barbarian" societies for the source of an alternative attitude. This impetus has been encouraged and accentuated in more recent times through the widespread circulation and influence of an interpretation of medieval political theory and history advanced some years ago by Walter Ullmann.[100] According to this interpretation, medieval political theory was dominated and controlled by two largely antithetical views concerning the nature of authority: a "hierarchical or downward" view, according to which authority resides ultimately in the divinity and flows downward from God to the humans to whom God dispenses it; and a "popular or upward" view, wherein authority is considered to reside in the people as a communal entity, and to rise from the people to those whom they designate to exercise it.

Like most intellectual tools devised to control and interpret a vast and varying array of data, the Ullmann thesis reflected a serious oversimplification, attributing at least by implication too little to the Christian contribution to medieval political thinking in respect of the notion of popular consent, and too much in this respect to pre-Christian tribal attitudes and values. There does seem to have been a

100. Ullmann has made regular and extensive use of the ascending and descending thesis in interpreting medieval political theories and practices since the late 1950s; see especially his *Principles of Government*, 3rd, ed., pp. 19–26, and p. 20, n. 1; cf. Wilks, *Problem of Sovereignty*, pp. 15–63. Cf. the review of Ullmann, *Principles of Government* by Kantorowicz: *Speculum* 39 (1964): 344–51. The most interesting application of the Ullmann thesis for our purpose is in his article "Bible and Principles of Government": see n. 3 above. Unquestionably the biblical sources were very influential on medieval political thinking, and unquestionably they did reflect the descending theme. What needs to be acknowledged is that these same sources also reflect, though much less forcibly, elements of the ascending theme. It is, therefore, an error to locate these latter elements only in non-Christian and non-Roman sources. Gaudemet repeats the basic contention that the Germanic tribes reflected a popular element in their political structure, at least in the sense that they practised a form of popular consent that was expressed in a physical rather than an abstract form (= actual individuals actually doing something). However, he speaks of "Germanic traditions strengthening the canonical principle of unanimity: Gaudemet, "Unanimité et majorité", p. 155.

feature of popular involvement in the selection of leaders among the early Germanic and Celtic tribes, as far as it is possible to gain a coherent perspective on this subject from available evidence.[101] At least in theory it seems that the chief men or nobles of the tribe were expected in some way to consent to the elevation of their principal leader. But available data do not make it possible, and there are grounds for scepticism about whether it will ever be possible, to formulate a fully defensible theory concerning the origins of Germanic kingship as early as the first century, B.C.

Earlier modern judgments on the nature of kingship among the Germanic tribes rested largely on evidence from Roman sources, principally the *Germania* of Tacitus;[102] but this is now recognized to be an unsafe guide, at least for the period after which Tacitus wrote. And more recent scholarship also has produced some scepticism concerning Tacitus's distinction between the Germanic and Celtic tribes, a distinction he based on geographical rather than ethnographic considerations.[103] It can be assumed that Germanic tribal kings existed at the time of Tacitus—the *Germania* dates from ca. A.D. 98. But even as late as the fourth and fifth centuries kingship was not an essential part of Germanic society; some Germanic tribes possessed kings by this time, some not.[104] Further, in a way somehow akin to the Christian notion of the ruler as the anointed of God, and certainly in a manner sufficiently akin to serve as ground for rejecting too straightforward a contrast between the Christian and the pre-Christian tribal traditions on this point, the Celtic and Germanic tribes of early medieval western Europe viewed their leaders as an embodiment or personification of the tribal divinity, reflecting a mystical, religious contact with the diety who controlled the tribal destiny. So viewed, the tribal leader possessed certain quasi-divine qualities; and this was why he was acceptable and accepted as a leader.[105] Consequently, his designation and acceptance as leader by the community as a whole was not an exercise in popular sovereignty in a modern sense, any more than was the rule of a

101. Substantial contributions to the study of the early tribes of western Europe can be found in Binckley, *Celtic and Anglo-Saxon Kingship*; Chaney, *Cult of Kingship*; Ejerfeldt, "Myths of the State"; Wood, *Law and Society*; Wallace-Hadrill, *Early Germanic Kingship*; *Long-haired Kings*; and Wood, "Kings, Kingdoms and Consent."
102. Tacitus *Germania*, in *Dialogues, Agricola, Germania*.
103. Wallace-Hadrill, *Early Germanic Kingship*, pp. 2, 4, n. 11.
104. Wallace-Hadrill, *Early Germanic Kingship*, p. 8.
105. Chaney, *Cult of Kingship*, pp. 16–17.

medieval European king who was solemnly assumed or declared by political theorists of the time to be exercising authority with the people's consent. Rather, it was probably little more than a kind of popular acclamation for a special individual perceived as divinely favoured and chosen, something comparable to the Jewish people's acclaim for the divinely chosen monarch, and the Christian community's assent by acclamation to the choice of bishop for a diocese.

Moreover, whatever variation may have existed in practice among the different prehistoric forms of tribal kingship in western Europe, variations that lasted into the period of recorded history, hereditary kingship had become common, if not virtually universal, by the early period of the post-Roman Imperial era. Accordingly, the view that the exercise of political authority among European tribal societies at this time was elective in any meaningful sense cannot stand. It seems that the central feature controlling the practice of royal succession among the Germanic tribes by this time was "blood" or royal kinship, rather than the claims of any particular family member. Strict hereditary succession, therefore, did not always occur. Even in the most stable royal families, no heir was certain to succeed; even though most did, some did not. And when all the heirs survived and the kingship was divided among them, a practice that continued into Merovingian times, the division did not have to be territorial.[106] Most of the early Germanic codes of law[107] implied that inheritance by all male heirs was the norm, although most of these "kingdoms" did not apply their own inheritance laws to inheritance of the kingdom itself.[108] The Visigothic kingdom of the seventh century was not hereditary, for example, while the Frankish kingdom was.[109] Even the case of the non-hereditary character of the Visigothic kingdom requires careful examination, however. While it has ben held up as an example of the notion of elective monarchy, the practice of succession based on heredity appeared very early in Visigothic history, and few seventh-century Visigothic rulers came to exercise royal power solely as the result of a strictly elective process. It is more accurate to speak of an occupative throne, inasmuch as association, designation, and simple usurpation all

---

106. Wood, *Law and Society*, p. 23.

107. A useful collection of data on early medieval codes of law is Joseph Balon, *Ius medii aevi*, 3 vols.

108. Wood, "Kings, Kingdoms," p. 26.

109. Ibid.

were significant factors as well in determining who came to power at a given time.[110]

The fact that there seems to have been at least some form of electoral or acclamatory function provided to the people, or perhaps only to the nobles or warriors, in the Germanic notion of kingship shows that it is correct to speak of some kind of upward movement in respect of sources of authority; and it is clear that the Germanic terms for king derive from kin, people, and tribe.[111] There is also evidence of the concept of limiting the royal authority in features of Germanic law such as the right of resistance, the possibility of deposition, and the participation of all free men in judicial and criminal procedures through the notions of self-help and blood feud.[112] But as has been seen, the concept of limit is not uniquely Germanic or barbarian; as applied to the exercise of authority it can be found in Christian political thought from its beginnings, as well as in Greek political theory and Roman law. And the specific notions of deposition and equal participation in governance in some manner by all members of the society were known and practised in some forms of medieval monasticism as early as the sixth century.[113]

There are examples of the explicit use of consent with respect to lawmaking in the early medieval period, probably reflecting interesting fusions of Germanic and Christian concepts, these latter likely derived themselves from Roman law. The Laws of the Burgundians, fifth century, were said to have been drawn up by the common will of all,[114] and the Fourth Council of Toledo (633) seems to show evidence of a rudimentary contract between ruler and people, entailing consent.[115] Some rudimentary form of legislative assembly existed in the Carolingian era, a reflection perhaps of the sort of popular legislative assembly found in the Scandinavian countries of the same period. According to the chronicler of the *Annals of Lorsch* for 802, changes in the law were to be produced by the action of the *populus christianus*: what was meant apparently was not a genuinely popular assembly, but a convocation of those having a place at "chapter"—the aristocracy,

110. Wood, *Law and Society*, p. 24.
111. Ejerfeldt, "Myth of the State," p. 163.
112. Ibid.
113. See *infra*, Part 3, 2B.
114. Gough, *Social Contract*, p. 25, citing *MGH*, *Leges*, Nat. Germ. 2.1.14, p. 34 et n. 2.
115. Gough, *Social Contract*, p. 25, citing Mansi, *Concilia*, 10.638.75 at n. 1.

provided they were Christians.[116] Changing the law was a specific responsibility of this assembly, and those called to such a meeting were summoned for this particular purpose. Such changes were the work of the assembly as a whole, and were to be introduced as new legislation by the judgment of all (*Capitula legi salicae addita . . . ab omnibus iudicatum est*: cap. 1, n. 142; *iudicatum est ab omnibus ut, si Francus homo*: cap. *De functionibus publicis,* c. 5; *legis salicae per omnium consensum addenda esse.*[117] At this time the royal *fideles* constituted the assembly of "free men," so this is probably the group charged with legislative responsibility.[118] Whatever variations from this principle may have occurred then and later, this early ninth-century example of required consensus among the nobles seems to have been the norm.[119] Another probable example of the same principle at work was the stipulation in the Edict of Pista of 25 June 864 that "law is to be made with the consent of the people (*consensu populi*) and formulation by the king."[120] Alcuin (d. 804) also used the expression *vox populi, vox dei*; but it is likely that the medieval usage of this formula intended not so much to indicate the wisdom and value of the opinions of the many, as the more prosaic notion that such an expression of popular will is practically irresistible. And again it seems that *populus* here designates the nobility rather than the people as a whole.[121]

---

116. Balon, *Ius medii aevi,* 2:206.

117. Ibid., 2:480–81, n. 1408.

118. Ibid.

119. Ibid. *Q o t = quod omnes tangit,* the incipit for a Roman legal principle according to which "what touches everyone should have everyone's consent": see Part 3, 1A.

120. "Quoniam lex consensus populi et constitutione regis fit," *MGH, Leg.* 2.2.273. Carlyle notes that this formula "only sum[s] up the general principles and practices of the time": Carlyle, *Political Liberty,* p. 17; cf. his earlier comments to the same effect in the context of conclusions about the general conditions of lawmaking and royal authority in the ninth century: Carlyle and Carlyle, *Mediaeval Political Theory,* 1:235–39, esp. p. 238.

121. Gallacher, "Vox populi."

PART TWO

The Twelfth Century

1. JOHN OF SALISBURY: THE POLICRATICUS

IN THE TWELFTH CENTURY one has moved into a much more differenti-
ated set of socio-political conditions than those of the earlier medieval
period. Larger-scale political stability occurred more frequently and
on a broader geographical scene as efforts got under way towards the
centralizing of political authority that was to produce the modern
nations of Europe, especially England and France. The conquering
Normans had held England since the third quarter of the eleventh
century, and were extending royal control across much of the central
island. The Capetian dynasty had established itself about the same time
in the roughly geographical northern centre of what was to become
France, and had begun a somewhat similar process of extending their
authority outward from the Parisian capital.

The Christian church had experienced the stimulating purgative of
the Gregorian reform in the latter half of the same century, and had
emerged generally purified in respect of its religious and moral ideals
and behaviour, as well as with a greatly increased sense of its autonomy
from political affairs and control, and of confidence in its own
institutions and administrative structures. Development of these
structures was to provide the medieval church with the ability and the
will to appear as a formidable foe for temporal rulers and lords then
struggling to exert greater authority over enlarging geographical
areas. The first, and truly universal administrative and power-wielding
entity to emerge on this scene was the Church. Concomitantly came the
temptation to vanity, and the mischievous sense of superiority that
beclouded many a churchman's perception of his responsibilities and

functions: the abstract principle that the spiritual is superior to the temporal is readily susceptible to practical abuses.

The spiritual life of the medieval church was being revivified all this while, in the renewal of the old norms for morality and religious worship, and in the re-emergence of the monastic movement that was so integral an aspect of the Gregorian reform. Hundreds of religious communities of both men and women sprang up across the face of western Europe, variant forms of the earlier Benedictine mode of religious community and more austere forms as well. From them came many of the resources, human and other, for Church renewal, and for the inspiration that led to a re-examination of Christian life and thought in the centres of learning that developed in the thirteenth century into the great universities of Europe. The same widespread development of religious and clerical activity also produced the personnel to staff both the purely spiritual and the administrative structures of the medieval church.

The renewal of intellectual activity in the twelfth century, and the increasingly necessary focus on the political and administrative activities of both ecclesiastical and secular developments, produced a revival of interest in the theory of politics. An outstanding product of this activity was the *Policraticus* of John of Salisbury, written in the style of a "mirror of princes" with which earlier centuries were familiar, but significantly superior to all previous examples.[1] A twelfth-century England churchman, humanist, and man of letters, Salisbury was one of the most educated persons of his generation, and had connections both ecclesiastical and secular extending from Rome through Paris to Canterbury and including popes, kings, and saints. Subtitled "the frivolities of courtiers and the footsteps of philosophers," John's

---

1. The standard modern edition of the *Policraticus* is *Ioannis Saresberiensis episcopi carnotensis policratici*, ed. Clemens C. I. Webb, 2 vols. (London: 1909; reprinted Frankfurt a. Main: Minerva, 1965). Its most relevant political parts are translated into English in *The Statesman's Book of John of Salisbury*, trans. John Dickinson (New York: Russell and Russell, 1963). Much interesting autobiographical data having to do with John's formal education can be found in *The Metalogicon of John of Salisbury: A Twelfth Century Defense of the Verbal and Logical Arts of the Trivium*, trans. Daniel D. McGarry (Berkeley: University of California Press, 1962). A recent analysis of Salisbury's political theory is in Berman, *Law and Revolution*, pp. 276–88, where John is called the "founder of western political science." Berman rightly locates John in the context of new legal, ecclesiastical, and political currents, but overestimates the unity of his thought in its effort to synthesize a wide variety of elements from disparate intellectual sources. Berman also errs at one point in presenting Salisbury's doctrine: see n. 32 below.

Policraticus was written in 1259 and dedicated to a personal friend, Thomas Becket, then chancellor to England's King Henry II, before he became archbishop of Canterbury and fell later as a martyr in one of the more famous episodes of the church / state conflict in medieval England. The work itself has been referred to as the only important political treatise written before the re-emergence of Aristotle's *Politics* in western England,[2] and as the earliest and one of the most influential of medieval writings on politics.[3]

It is a presentation of dos and don'ts for the Christian ruler, thus exemplifying directly the category of treatise that outlines the specifics of personal moral perfection required of a ruler. Yet it is a vastly more sophisticated example than earlier models. Its contents reflect its author's erudition, with John using the traditional literary form to present both religious and secular classical material in the expression of his views. The work provides thereby a unique insight into the range and character of the intellectual life of the period.[4]

There is no need for a full account of the contents of the *Policraticus*, but a brief survey will show John's basic theory of polity. According to Salisbury, a ruler's function is to act as "head"[5] of the body politic (though he does not actually use this latter term); Christian priests are its "soul."[6] In exercising authority, moreover, the ruler has an obligation to obey the law; he must not act either arbitrarily or exclusively in his own interests. Actions that are either arbitrary or exclusively self-interested on the part of the ruler are contrary to the very function of rule; they are tyrannical.[7] The archetype of political authority for the author of the *Policraticus* is the prince, a single all-powerful ruler[8] who, nevertheless, does well to receive advice from a group of wise men whom he should gather around himself.[9] John simply accepts that a polity should have but one head, neither arguing for this mode of

2. Dickinson, *Statesman's Book*, p. xvii.

3. Dickinson, *Statesman's Book*, p. vii. On the influence of the *Policraticus* for later medieval and Renaissance jurists, see Ullmann, "Influence of John of Salisbury." John also was familiar with the contemporary developments in canon law: see n. 39 below.

4. For the classical and earlier Christian sources reflected in the *Policraticus* see Liebeschutz, *Medieval Humanism*.

5. John of Salisbury *Policraticus* 5.6.548D. Page references to the *Policraticus* here (548D) and elsewhere are to the Webb edition.

6. John of Salisbury *Policraticus* 2.5.539B.

7. Ibid., 4.1.513B.

8. Ibid., 4.1.514A.

9. Ibid,. 4.6.522C; 524D. Cf. n. 31 below.

governance nor directly considering alternative forms. The later medieval practice of explicitly considering oligarchy and democracy as possible alternative forms of government appears only after the mid-thirteenth-century emergence of Aristotle's *Politics*.

The prince or ruler holds authority directly from God; his exercise of it, like the power itself, is somehow religious and sacral, reflecting the special character of the person possessing it.[10] John cites St. Paul: "The power which the prince has is therefore from God: who therefore resists, resists the ordinance of God" (Romans 13:2).[11] The purpose or object in exercising princely power is the good of everyone in society, the good of the people as a whole, whose representative the ruler is.[12] In pursuing the common goals of all, the ruler must exercise power in accordance with the requirements of the common good,[13] requirements established in and reflected by the law.[14] Thus, the ruler is constrained by law, limited to exercising power in accordance with the law; and he is himself subject to the law even as ruler. The limits of the law circumscribe the legitimacy of the ruler's power.

In holding that the ruler must function under the law, John bases his position on the Christian Scriptures, citing texts from both the Old and New Testaments, and appealing directly to Old Testament directives given to the kings of Israel.[15] Other instances have been seen of Scriptural texts being used to maintain that the exercise of authority must always conform to the law, the primary ones being the Old Testament insistence that the rulers of the Israelites had no other function than to direct the Chosen People in accordance with the law given them directly by God.[16] And Salisbury cites precisely these Old

10. See Liebeschutz, *Medieval Humanism*, p. 46. For the notion of the sacral character of kingship see Kantorowicz, *King's Two Bodies*.

11. John of Salisbury *Policraticus* 4.1.514A.

12. Ibid., 5.2.539B. cf. 4.2.515B. The concept of the ruler as "representative" of the people appears frequently in medieval political writing, and the concept's meaning requires careful interpretation.

13. See the lengthy list of obligations of the ruler towards the public usually expressed in terms of morally virtuous acts to be performed: *Statesman's Book*, p. li. See also the citation from the earlier (fifth century?) work, *De duodecim abusionibus saeculi* 9, reproduced by Dickinson at p. liii, and p. liv, n. 162.

14. John of Salisbury *Policraticus* 4.2.514C–D. John speaks of the law here in terms strongly reminiscent of the Roman legal concept of law as a gift of God: *Dig.* 1.3.2; cf. Post, *Studies*, p. 259, nn. 32 and 34.

15. John of Salisbury *Policraticus* 4.4.518C–9B.

16. See Part 1, 2–3, above. An earlier and clear expression of the principle that the temporal ruler is bound to obey the laws of his own jurisdiction in the same way clerics are bound by the canons of ecclesistical law is in the ninth-century work of Hincmar of

Testament directives. Earlier Christian apologetic writers had repeated the same principle, and had extended its application by stipulating that for the case of Christians living under "pagan" (that is, non-Christian) political regimes, non-Christian rulers also were entitled to exercise jurisdiction only within the limits of the law (of the Christian God).[17] According to this view Christians, and by implication all other subjects of political authority (even the political authority of non-Christian rulers), could not legitimately be required to act contrary to the law (of the Christian God). The notion that a ruler should obey his own laws was stated clearly by Isidore of Seville, who connected the law with the concept of justice; Gratian cited Isidore on this point.[18] The later treatises on kingship consisting largely of admonitions to follow justice and mercy, to seek wisdom, and fear God, and which contrasted king and tyrant in a highly standardized way—the "mirror for princes" literature—follow Isidore's general position.

John of Salisbury reiterates the principle. But the force with which he does so, and the central location he gives it in his text, are evidence of something not seen before in Christian political writing. Learned as well as intellectually astute, John saw a need in his own day for placing particular emphasis on the view that a ruler must conform to the law. He was familiar with an important new phenomenon on the intellectual scene in the mid-twelfth century, the renewed awareness of and interest in the contents of Roman civil law;[19] and he was familiar with a maxim of that code that held that the king is above the law.[20] The

---

Rheims *De ordine palatii* (*MGH*, *Leg.* 2.2). Hincmar cites Augustine on the point in *De vera religione*; for other relevant texts from Hincmar, and their references, see Carlyle and Carlyle, *History of Mediaeval Political Theory*, 1:231–34 and notes. Hincmar also quotes Gregory the Great and Ambrose, showing the continuity and sources for the view.

17. See Part 1, 3–4, above.

18. Isidore *Etymologiae* 9.3; see also 3.47; 49; 52. Gratian quotes Isidore *Etymologiae* 9.52 at D.9 c.2.

19. See section 3 below.

20. The well-known Ulpian text, *princeps legibus solutus est*: *Dig.* 1.3.31; cf. Post, *Studies*, p. 259. But see also Ulpian's view that the ruler will love and cultivate justice: "digna vox," C.1.14.4; cf. Kantorowicz, *King's Two Bodies*, pp. 95, 104, and n. 51; Post, *Studies*, pp. 259, 302, and note the texts Post has collected showing how canonists used the concept of the ruler's "worthy speech" to express the general will of the state and its people as applicable to the pope: p. 302, n. 132. Another dictum from Ulpian used to imply an absolute quality in authority was "quod principi placuit habet legis vigorem": D.1.4.1; see references in Post, "Vincentius Hispanus," 165–66, and nn. 27, 28. Post rejects this interpretation for both dicta: "quod principii placuit" and "princeps solutus" in the same article, pp. 159–84, *passim*.

vigour with which John made his own case reflects his knowledge of this Roman legal dictum; and John would have none of it. He devotes considerable space to a rejection of this notion, citing Matthew 7:2: "By what judgment ye judge, ye shall yourselves be judged."[21] He goes further, and offers an interpretation of the Roman maxim: it should not be taken to mean that a prince can act legitimately outside the law, but only that a ruler has no human political power higher than himself to which he owes obedience. John is speaking of what today would be called the sovereignty of the ruler of any state. He did not intend to preclude the notion of a hierarchy of forms of temporal authority, but simply to insist that whoever exercised authority over any temporal sphere had no superior in respect of the exercise of political authority in that sphere. Consequently, the obedience he gives when he binds himself to the law is an obedience freely given.[22] The steps John takes here show unmistakably that he is arguing directly against an alternative view. He contends that a human political ruler is the supreme human authority in his own sphere: while making no explicit reference to Roman law when he rejects the maxim that a king is above the law, John makes it clear that he was familiar with this Roman legal dictum.

Familiar with it he certainly was, as he was with Roman law in general. John also was prepared to cite Roman legal authorities when it suited him. The principle that the ruler should be subject to the law in fact was not a peculiarly Christian view, but a maxim of Greek political theory at least as far back as Plato[23] and Aristotle;[24] it also can be found in Roman political and legal thought. John of Salisbury was aware of its Roman origins, though not directly of the Greek precedents; and he quotes directly from the Justinian Code the admonition to a prince concerning his need to acknowledge himself bound by the law.[25] John

21. John of Salisbury *Policraticus* 4.7.527A–C.

22. Ibid., 4.2 and 4.4, *passim*.

23. Plato, *Republic* 2.359A; 6.484A–485B. Plato does not express the maxim in so many words; but his distinction between tyrant and true ruler rests on the principle that the latter knows the politically good and makes laws that express it, to which all are enjoined in obedience.

24. Aristotle *Politics* 3.16.1287a18. Cf. John of Salisbury *Policraticus* 4.1.513B and 4.2.514D–5A, where he cites Demosthenes as well as the Roman jurist Papinian on the same point. This reference to Demosthenes shows John's familiarity with the civil code: see *Dig.* 1.3.2. Tierney notes a similar reference to Demosthenes in Accursius, *Gloss* and *Cod.* 7.33.12, "Divina": Tierney, "Prince is not Bound," p. 3.

25. John of Salisbury *Policraticus* 4.1.514B; cf. *Cod.* 1.14.4. See also *Policraticus* 4.6.522C.

also employs the Roman civil code for his own definition of the term "law," parallelling language from Justinian's *Digest* and citing Chrysippus.[26]

John enters one qualification on his insistence that the ruler is bound by law, a move that reflects a refreshing improvement over earlier and more simplistic medieval handling of general formulae containing sophisticated concepts. He distinguishes between two types of law, flexible and inflexible; and the distinction enables him to admit that a ruler can dispense in certain circumstances from the former, although never from the latter. A ruler can mitigate or dispense from the verbal strictness of a flexible law, says John, "provided that the purpose of the law is preserved in its integrity by the compensation made to propriety or public utility."[27] This view, however, does not make clear the precise character of the distinction between flexible and inflexible laws. As well, John seems to draw very narrowly the limits of the ruler's discretion, even in the case of flexible laws.

Salisbury also distinguished between law and equity, and held that the ruler is bound ultimately by the latter rather than the former. Addressing the dictum that the prince is bound by the law and working with it as a maxim in Roman law, John maintains that the ruler should conform to equity rather than to the letter of the law. His technique is the same here as that seen earlier in his interpretation of the superficially or literally contradicting formula that the king is above the law: he simply rejects the literal meaning and offers a more reasoned and sophisticated interpretation. According to John, a ruler should practise equity rather than merely providing a literal interpretation or application of the law, "not through fear of the law but out of love for justice."[28]

Ambiguities remain in this formulation because of Salisbury's failure

26. Ibid., 4.2.514c–d; the text cites *Dig.* 1.3.1 and 2 at 515a. Webb cites the definition of law as from Azo, but without specific reference, while Dickinson notes that Fitting has found it in an ancient introduction to the *Institutes*: *Statesman's Book*, p. 6, n. 1. Interestingly, perhaps, Azo's *Summa institutionum* was also the terminological source for the definition of law used by Marsilius of Padua: Lewis, "Positivism of Marsiglio of Padua," pp. 545–48, 552–55; cf. Wilks, "Coronation and Representation," p. 255. Webb identified literally dozens of citations made by John to the *Corpus iuris civile*: Webb, *Policratici*, 2:482b–83b.

27. John of Salisbury *Policraticus* 4.7.527c. John's distinction between flexible and inflexible law reflects a point made by Ivo of Chartres concerning the difference between variable and invariable law.

28. Ibid., 4.2.515a.

to spell out exactly what he means by distinguishing equity and justice from the law. This failure parallels the earlier one concerning the distinction between flexible and inflexible forms of law. Apparently, John appreciated that the specific contents of a given piece of legislation, "the law" in a given form of expression, did not comprehend the essence of justice as a whole, and might even fail altogether to embody this essence. (John's derisory remarks in another context about the fatuity of the debate among his contemporaries over the philosophical problem of "universals" ring a little hollow here.)[29] Yet it is the essence of justice in itself that is the fundamental element engaging the correlative features of authority for the law-giver and obedience for the subject. John appreciated that it was justice, not merely a legal form of words, that constituted the reality and foundation of law; but he provided no specific criterion for detecting its presence or absence in a given case.

All in all, John's position affords very little flexiblity to a ruler in his response to law. The reason for this, quite simply, is that the metaphysical and cosmological frame of reference within which he operated, as well as the consequent theological formulations he employed, were both rigid and inadequate. For this reason also the ambiguities or difficulties in his position would not have been as obvious to John as they seem to a modern reader. To Salisbury, for example, there would not have been any ambiguity or apparent contradiction in his view that the prince is both above the law and yet bound by it; for he would never have associated the concept of an acceptable arbitrariness or personal value-judgment with the former principle. For John authoritative decision making and action cannot be arbitrary, by definition. John would never have accepted the view that illegal measures, that is, measures actually contrary to the law in the highest sense of the term law, could be justified in any circumstances, not even for the common good. To Salisbury this would be a contradiction in terms. At the same time there is some suggestion that John would have been prepared to concede sufficient initiative to the supreme authority in a state to act to protect and defend the necessities and essential interests of the commonweal, even in circumstances where his authority might be seen normally to be circumscribed by existing legislation. There are further ambiguities here that John fails to eliminate, but that he might well have acknowledged had he

29. John of Salisbury *Metalogicon* 2.17–20.

perceived them. Salisbury certainly never denied to a ruler the right to determine (legislate) matters for the sake of the common good; nor did he deny a king the right to dispense from a given law, or the power to pardon.

The issue of consent appears in the *Policraticus* when John considers how a ruler comes into office. One can see in this consideration a feature not addressed directly in any previous Christian text dealing with the nature of polity; and the fact that John raises it indicates that the question was recognized by him as having current interest. His handling of it, however, shows only a slight advance in sophistication of theory. Salisbury's doctrine on accession to temporal authority reflects directly his conception of kingship as sacral in character because emanating from a divine source, and no interpretation of it can be construed as particularly congenial to democratic thought. He actually employs the terms "election" (*electio*)[30] and "to elect" (*eligere*),[31] but the context shows that he is speaking of the ruler as chosen (elected) by God. The fact of the ruler being designated by God is what constitutes the real foundation of his authority. John had read carefully the Old Testament description of how God provided the first king for the Jewish people, and he repeats the fundamental element described in this procedure: selection of the king by God.

He also lists details of an election process, however, showing an awareness of the complexities of political theorizing on the specific issue of procedure. Salisbury's views concerning how a temporal authority comes into office are clear and quite comprehensive as he presents them in the early portion of *Policraticus* 5, 6, and they are based squarely and explicitly on texts from Samuel and Numbers. John notes three distinct elements in the proper method of choosing and installing a ruler: (1) "the secret ministry of God's providence," that is, a direct action of some kind by God Himself; (2) some "action by God's priests"; (3) concurrence in placing the ruler in authority by "the votes

---

30. *Policraticus* 5.6.548D.

31. Ibid., 5.6.549A; 549C. John also invokes the concept of consent when he asserts that a king whose affairs are to prosper rightly should take the counsel of men of letters: *Policraticus* 4.6. But this text seems to envisage that the ruler might be illiterate; and further there is no clear requirement that the ruler must accept any such advice, or that royal decisions in contradiction of such advice would lack authority. John would certainly have agreed that a ruler should accept the advice of his council without, however, raising the specific question of whether or not legitimate exercise of royal authority explicitly required agreement from the king's councillors.

of all the people" (*totius populi vota concurrent*).³² Further, John distinguishes this procedure from two other methods that, arguably, were being urged or at least displayed in current practice: hereditary succession and succession through relationship. He also states flatly that the proper procedure does not include the element of popular acclamation: *Sic autem plane nulla est populi acclamatio.*³³ Finally, Salisbury's denial of popular acclamation as an essential element in royal election is specifically connected to the ritual of coronation, to which he makes direct reference.³⁴ His point seems to be that acclamation by the people was not an integral part of the biblical account of how Moses handled the installation of Josuah as leader of the Jewish community and that, accordingly, it need not be a feature of the coronation ceremony for a king.

John here is making two points of interest to our concern: (1) the authority of the Old Testament account of accession to political office as involving consent of the people shows such consent to be adequately expressed by the people's mere presence when certain actions are performed by priests; (2) the role of the community as a whole is thus passive. Accordingly, acclamation by the people, in the sense of some active role or some act to be performed by the people, is not an essential part of the coronation procedure. Concurrence of the whole people, then, is an essential condition for the legitimate designation of political authority only in the sense that the formalities of the act are to be carried out in public, "in the presence of the people"; what the "votes of the whole people" really express is only a form of public acknowledgment of the person already selected by God through some earlier

---

32. Ibid., 5.6.548D–9A. The Dickinson translation is in error on this point; it lists the three elements in the electoral procedure as apparently three different ways of selecting a ruler: "sometimes 1) ... sometimes 2) ... and again 3)": *Statesman's Book*, p. 83. John makes another reference to the choice of Saul as the first Jewish king at *Policraticus* 8.18, 785C. Probably following the Dickinson translation of the *Policaticus*, Berman makes the same error: *Law and Revolution*, p. 285. Berman refers to Salisbury's use of two Old Testament examples where temporal succession was at issue: the identification of Moses as leader of the Israelites, and Moses' decision regarding the paternal inheritance for the daughters of Salphaat. But, curiously, he makes no mention of Salisbury's paradigm case for accession to temporal authority, God's selection of Saul as the first Jewish monarch. John's analysis of this case identifies the three essential elements in accession to political authority, all of them falling under the fundamental principle that the ruler is chosen by God.

33. John of Salisbury *Policraticus* 5.6.549B.

34. Ibid.

action, acknowledgment by physical presence in a public ritual. John's direct reference to the non-essential character of popular acclamation in respect of the coronation ceremony may well reflect a willingness to limit the people's role in royal accession in a way similar to that seen in Gratian's contemporary and parallel views concerning the limited role of the people in the election of bishops. What John had in mind was a form of juridical or ritualistic concurrence for a person already selected by another means, the essential element of which was divine designation, and not a method for establishing the identity of a ruler by popular choice.

John was willing in practice to accept hereditary succession as the actual mechanism for identifying the individual selected for the exercise of political authority; heredity seemed to him to provide generally adequate presumptive evidence for the essential ingredient of divine selection. But what counted ultimately was the moral probity of the ruler, something the male heir could be presumed to possess.[35] In this connection John was prepared also to accept the element of popular consent, but only as confirmatory in a purely ritualistic way of the legitimacy of hereditary succession: the role of the people's consent is once more merely concurring in its function, and does not entail actual selection. Salisbury thus continued to employ the apparently traditional Christian notion of ritualistic popular approval, and grounded this notion in the accepted authority of relevant Old Testament texts. And though explicit evidence is lacking on this point, there is good reason to speculate that John also would have conceded some role to the people in consenting to the provision of ecclesiastical rulers, inasmuch as this notion was current at his time and was expressed in ways with which John would have been fully familiar. But here, too, the notion of popular consent expressed an element of pro forma concurrence, nothing more substantial.[36]

John also was prepared to indulge a ruler in the legitimate exercise of authority even when he failed to display the full range of required virtues; and he advised obedience to an evil king: "as long as his vices are not absolutely ruinous [he is to be shown] obedience in every way."[37]

35. *Policraticus* 6.6.549C; 4.11, *passim*. The same view can be found in Augustine *De civitate Dei* 5.24. But see Liebeschutz, Medieval Humanism, pp. 47–48. John also quoted Scripture to support the view that hereditary succession of authority was proper: *Policraticus* 5.6.549C; 4.11.533B: cf. Num. 27:1–6; Ps. 89:29.

36. John makes frequent reference to Gratian's *Decretum*: see *Policraticus* 2:486B–7A.

37. John of Salisbury *Policraticus* 8.20.793B; cf. 8.18, *passim*.

This text makes clear, however, that limits exist for the obligation of subjects to submit to political authority, showing another instance in which Salisbury was prepared to expand his inquiry into the nature of polity and try to come to grips with one of its significant issues. John spells out the limits of obedience to authority in excessively abstract and moralistic language; yet he does not shirk the logical consistency of drawing the ultimate inference from his earlier insistence on the feature of limit. He is prepared to justify tyrannicide, though his justification is couched in ill-defined and very general terms. Just as the legitimacy of a ruler's authority was limited or circumscribed by the law that gave expression to the purpose for which he exercised authority and to which he was obliged to subordinate and regulate his own behaviour, so was the obligation of obedience on the part of those subject to authority limited to acceptance only of such authority as was not ultimately destructive of its very purpose.[38] The limits of this obligation to obey might be very broad, but limits there were.

A doctrine of tyrannicide is regularly and properly attributed to John of Salisbury, but his formulation on this point is neither very straightforward nor very precise. His acceptance of the legitimacy of assassinating a tyrannical ruler probably was grounded in Cicero's explicit countenancing of such an act,[39] even though John makes no reference to Cicero and develops his own justification largely on the basis of an appeal to Old Testament instances where the killing of a tyrant seemingly was approved. He makes a number of explicit statements favouring tyrannicide: "By the authority of the Scriptures it is a lawful and glorious act to slay public tyrants";[40] "it is just for public tyrants to be killed";[41] "to kill a tyrant is not merely lawful, but right and just;"[42] but his development of the doctrine is less forthright and

38. Ibid., 6.25.626B.
39. Cicero *De officiis* 3.6.32; cf. *Policraticus* 3.15.512C.
40. John of Salisbury *Policraticus* 8.20.793B.
41. Ibid., 8.20.795A.
42. Ibid., 3.15.512D. Further less specific references to tyrannicide are at 8.17: "The tyrant ... is generally to be killed" (8.17.778A). A recent article explains the confused character of John's views on tyrannicide by suggesting that the *Policraticus* text operates at both a theoretical and a practical level: Rouse and Rouse, "John of Salisbury." This thesis is not entirely satisfactory. That John might have feared tyrannical behaviour from Henry II of England is certainly plausible; but I prefer to think that confusion or inconsistency in John's views here reflects failure to work through the implications of his own thought, rather than an explicit effort to warn Henry indirectly about how God might act through an assassin to punish the king's tyranny.

satisfactory. Having listed several examples from history that seem to show that tyrannicide is justified, John mentions a number of qualifications to its apparent legitimacy: "None should undertake the death of a tyrant who is bound to him by oath or by the obligation of fealty";[43] poisoning seems not to be a legitimate method for dispatching a tyrannical ruler, on the grounds that John knew of no law that permitted it;[44] and finally: "Removal of tyrants from our midst ... should be done without loss of religion and honor."[45] No further specification is provided, however, concerning how the requirement to maintain religion and honour might be met.

John has little or nothing to offer his reader concerning either political forms or policies, much less the specific legislation through which the ruler should give expression to his purpose of promoting the common good. The function of the ruler, he says, is to strike terror into his subjects. Thereby, seemingly, the prince will awe and coerce them into "being good," doing what they should do, obeying the law.[46] John is clearly more than willing to attribute coercive power to the ruler.[47] It is an essential requirement in any ruler; and John even defines the antithesis of the good ruler, a tyrant, in terms of "force misused."[48] Interestingly, too, especially in light of the subsequent use of this terminology, John employs the word "sword" to designate the coercive power of political authority.[49] The language and mode of speech of his contemporary Bernard of Clairvaux appear in the *Policraticus* when John speaks of the power of the state as a sword, received from the Church, which has two swords in her own right.[50] Salisbury knew Bernard's views on the subject as well as the terms of their formulation, just as he knew the great Cistercian personally.

Like many earlier and later medieval texts on political issues, the *Policraticus* moves on a purely abstract plane, frequently to the

43. John of Salisbury *Policraticus* 8.20.796c.
44. Ibid.
45. Ibid.
46. John of Salisbury *Policraticus* 4.1.514A–B.
47. Ibid., 4.1.513c–4B. Even tyrants have a right to the exercise of coercive power: Ibid., 8.18.786A.
48. Ibid., 8.18.786A.
49. Ibid., 4.3 *passim*.
50. A recent article shows that, while John and Bernard of Clairvaux employ the "two swords" formula, Salisbury's position distorts that of Bernard and gives it the more radically papalist interpretation that became common in the later thirteenth century: Kennan, "*De consideratione*."

irritation of a modern reader hoping to discover some tincture of connection with the real world, some indication that its author perceived the practical significance of at least some of his more striking theoretical postures. Salisbury's *Policraticus* is a constant disappointment in this respect, although in other writings he was quite capable of offering perceptive and penetrating personal comments on the realities of his day.[51] A final comment might be made connecting John of Salisbury with his own time: an interesting comparison can be drawn between John's approach to a theory of temporal polity in the *Policraticus* and the theory of ecclesiastical polity presented in the great contemporary canonical legal work, the *Decretum* of Gratian, with which Salisbury must have been familiar and whose views would have had great interest for him.[52]

2. OTHER TWELFTH-CENTURY SOURCES

A. *The Norman Anonymous*

As its title indicates, the *Norman Anonymous* is an early twelfth-century document of northern European provenance written by an unknown author.[53] Basically a political treatise of polemic intent, it incorporates an extreme expression of the superiority of kingship over the Church, on the grounds that the king is *rex sacerdos* in the Melchisedechian model, and thereby exercises a sacral power. Its author speaks of the king as reflecting the divine nature of Christ, whereas the priest reflects human nature. And while reference is made in the text to "election,"[54] its meaning is "predestination"; and the author speaks of a subject's obligation to obey his king as a foretaste of heavenly liberty. Naturally enough, the work argues against the dictum of Celestine I, by then generally accepted, regarding episcopal election, that a bishop should

51. See John of Salisbury's chatty account of his own student life in *Metalogicon* 2.17–20. John understood well the implications of his views for the England of his day, of course, even though he made no reference to the contemporary scene.

52. See n. 36 above.

53. G. H. Williams, ed., *The Norman Anonymous of 1100 A.D.*, Harvard Theological Studies 18 (Cambridge: Harvard University Press, 1951). See Berman's account of the *Norman Anonymous*, which contrasts it with Salisbury's *Policraticus* and terms it "the last important pre-Western (that is, premodern) treatise on government": Berman, *Law and Revolution*, pp. 276–77.

54. *Norman Anonymous*, p. 198.

not be given to those unwilling to receive him (*nullus invitis detur episcopus*).[55]

B. St. Bernard of Clairvaux

Two other twelfth-century Christian writers also should be mentioned in connection with the political thinking of the period, although neither of them was a political thinker in any direct sense. Both commented on such issues indirectly, however, and did so in documents that acquired considerable authority and significance in later medieval times. St. Bernard of Clairvaux (1091–1153), the great twelfth-century Cistercian mystic and theologian, was a man of many facets and one of the dominant figures of his era. Inveterate Church reformer and scourge of heretics both inside and outside the Christian church, preacher of the Second Crusade against the Moslem infidels, he was a close friend, confidant, and correspondent to many persons in high places, ecclesiastical and temporal.[56] He composed a treatise offering advice to a fellow Cistercian, close acquaintance, and former student who succeeded to the throne of Peter as Pope Eugene III in 1145, a work that soon came into general circulation under the title *De consideratione*.[57] Its author offers some striking comments on the character and substance of papal authority that not only caught the attention of their recipient, but came quickly into widespread use and acceptance. Bernard's intention was to proffer sound if traditional advice to the Roman pontiff concerning matters for which the papacy had supreme responsibility. The language he employed, however, stressed in the first instance the universal, all-encompassing feature of papal authority in such a way that the distinction he went on to make between the spiritual and the temporal could be blurred easily. Bernard's actual distinction between the two spheres of authority proceeded with a reference to two "swords," the spiritual sword and the temporal sword; and the basic

55. Celestine I *Epistolae* 4.5, cited in Gratian, D.61 c.13 and D.63 c.26.

56. So much research has been done in recent decades on Bernard that a new and comprehensive biography taking all the latest scholarship in account is needed. The standard brief biography in English is Watkin Williams, *Saint Bernard of Clairvaux*. An earlier, much more substantial effort is E. Vacandard, *Vie de St. Bernard*, 2 vols.

57. Bernard of Clairvaux, *De consideratione ad Eugenium papam*, ed. Jean Leclercq and Henri Rochais, Sancti Bernardi opera, vol. 3 (Rome: Editiones Cistercienses, 1963). An English translation has appeared: *Five Books on Consideration: Advice to a Pope*, trans. John D. Anderson and Elizabeth T. Kennan (Kalamazoo: Cistercian Publications, 1975).

intent behind this language was to distinguish between two forms of "coercive" action available to the Church, that is, to spiritual authority, in the pursuit of its own legitimate spiritual purposes.[58]

Bernard held that both the spiritual and the temporal swords were legitimate possessions of the Church for use in furthering its spiritual purposes; but he advised the pope against using the material sword, that is, coercive physical power, even for legitimate spiritual purposes: the material sword, while legitimately in the pope's possession and thus available to him for use, should not be used by him or any other cleric. The use of physical coercion, even for spiritual ends, should not be practised by clerics at all, but should be left to lay authority. Otherwise, clerics who should interest themselves exclusively in matters of the spiritual order and direct their authority exclusively to spiritual affairs, might become contaminated by contact with material things. The Bernadine advice, however clearly it was formulated—and considerable evidence exists to show that its formulation was sufficiently clear to its contemporary readers to be understood in terms of the interpretation just offered—came later to be used in support of much broader claims for papal authority than Bernard originally intended.[59] The Cistercian mystic did not have in mind the use to which his remarks were put later in extending claims for papal authority over temporal affairs in a manner that would be seen today as an illegitimate intrusion of ecclesiastical authority into the sphere of temporal politics; yet the lapidary character of his text made such an interpretation very easy.

To be fair to Bernard as well as to twelfth-century interpretations of what he might have meant by his doctrine of the two swords, a number of points can be made: (1) The Bernardine text itself did not assert, nor was it the author's intention to assert, that the Church *should* itself employ physical coercion for any purpose whatever. What it precisely

58. A sustained effort to unravel the original Bernardine "two swords" doctrine from the use the image was put to by later medieval papalists is in the work of Stickler, "De ecclesia potestate"; "De potestate gladii materialis"; "Il 'gladius' nel Registro di Gregorio VII"; "Il 'gladius' negli atti del concilii e del R.R. Pontefici"; "Il potero coattivo materiale: Der Schwerterbegriff bei Huguccio." The Kennan article has a good review of recent scholarship and a bibliography on this and other aspects of Bernard's views on the relationship of church and state, and offers a balanced judgment on the advisability of reading a full-blown theory of papal monarchy into the *De consideratione*; Kennan, "*De consideratione*," pp. 101–15 and n. 112.

59. See, for example, the interpretation of the two-swords image in Aegidius of Rome *De ecclesiastica potestate* 1.7.8 and 9.3.9.

denied was that the spiritual authority should use coercion for attaining legitimate spiritual aims, even though it had the right to do so. (2) Inasmuch as Bernard conceded to the spiritual authority a right to use physical coercion in the promotion of spiritual ends, even though the Church should not do so, it is conceivable that he might also have conceded to the spiritual authority a comparable right to the use of physical coercion in furtherance of the Church's temporal purposes (assuming that for him the Church could be said to have temporal as well as spiritual purposes). In fact, however, he was completely silent on this point, so that it is not possible to state exactly what his views on it were. (3) Bernard was equally silent concerning what form any physical coercion applied by temporal authorities on behalf of the spiritual aims of the Church might take.

Bernard's two-swords terminology found an immediate echo in the mid-twelfth-century, as noted earlier. John of Salisbury's *Policraticus* repeated the Bernardine formula in the Cistercian's own terminology, but expressed the doctrine in such a way as to offer a seemingly clear statement of total ecclesiastical sovereignty: "The prince is the servant of the priest, and exercises that portion of the sacred duties which are unworthy of sacerdotal hands."[60] While John's statement can still be construed to mean that Salisbury was speaking only of the use of physical coercion in the pursuit of the Church's spiritual goals, it is comparatively easy to appreciate that the words could have been construed quite differently, to mean that John was asserting that the whole of the prince's temporal authority was under the spiritual power to which it belonged by right.[61] It was in this latter sense just noted that the formula and phraseology of the two swords came into regular and frequent use for centuries later as a foundation stone in various pro-papalist theories of church / state relations. Yet Bernard never intended to produce a comprehensive doctrine on the relationship between spiritual and temporal authorities; even less had he in mind to develop a theory of temporal polity.

60. John of Salisbury *Policraticus* 4.3.516A.
61. This was, of course, the standard interpretation of the later papal monarchists such as Aegidius of Rome: see n. 58 above; cf. Kennan, "*De consideratione*," pp. 76–84. Ullmann, who construed John and Bernard as both holding extreme hierocratic views on papal sovereignty over temporal authority, did not note the differences in their use of the swords image: Kennan, "De consideratione," pp. 81, 104, n. 127. Cf. Ullmann, *Growth of Papal Government*, pp. 426–37, esp. p. 427.

C. Hugh of St. Victor

Hugh of St. Victor was another prominent twelfth-century theologian whose writings were extremely influential in the later medieval period. His work *On the Sacraments*[62] also contains a scrap or two of comment concerning the authority of the Church, texts that tend to reappear in subsequent medieval political writings.[63] But like Bernard, Hugh was not primarily interested in political theory, whether of church or state; and for the most part he simply repeated Bernard's two-swords doctrine, thereby incidentally making the treatise *On the Sacraments* an important vehicle for the transmission of the Bernardine theory. It is difficult, then, as it was with Bernard, to extract anything resembling either a full or fully coherent doctrine of polity from Hugh's text, nor even a fully articulated doctrine of church / state relations. Hugh, however, did offer a slightly broader intellectual perspective on the point of the superiority of the spiritual over the temporal.

3. THE RENEWAL OF THE STUDY OF LAW

While it is essential to examine twelfth-century political treatises such as the *Policraticus*, unquestionably the major developments in political theory and the notions of consent and coercion in this period are to be found in the law, in the theory and practices associated with the courts and with legal administration, both civil and ecclesiastical. A fundamental feature here paralleled the renewed intellectual, administrative, and political activities of both church and state and was an integral part of them: the twelfth century saw a remarkable revival of the formal study of law.

Throughout even the most chaotic periods following the collapse of the Roman Empire in the West, there had been some retention of the knowledge and practice of the system of Roman civil law, some awareness of this great monument to the Roman genius for political

---

62. Hugh of St. Victor, *On the Sacraments of the Christian Faith*, trans. Roy J. Deferrari (Cambridge, Mass.: Mediaeval Academy of America, 1951). This translation is based on what Deferrari called a critical text of the *De Sacramentis* prepared by Brother Charles Henry; this Latin text has yet to be published. An earlier Latin text is found in *PL* 176.

63. Aegidius of Rome made extensive use of the *De sacramentis* of Hugh of St. Victor, as well as of Bernard of Clairvaux: *De ecclesiastica potestate* 1.4, 1.5, 2.2, 2.4, 2.6, 2.7, 2.10, 3.11.

organization and administration.[64] Its persistence in Gaul from the fifth through to the tenth centuries was rather more significant than has been thought by earlier historians, although it is found there not so much in the retention of the classical rules of Roman law as in the post-classical Roman legal practices of the period preceding the Germanic invasions. In some instances formal traces of Roman law persisted, but usually without any real understanding of the formulae, so that their juridical value had been lost. The Carolingian renaissance of the late eighth and early ninth centuries saw some conscious effort at renewal of the law, both civil and ecclesiastical; and some references to actual Roman legal precedents began to reappear. In practice, however, the situation was the reverse; the fusion of Frankish and Germanic populations produced a mixture of social and economic elements, and custom began to assume greater importance in the developing context of feudalism, for which Roman law had never been designed. The Roman legal system, however, retained its prestige and technical value among the clerics of the Christian church, where it continued to exercise a fascination for scholars rather than practitioners. In addition, moreover, the old Roman law in its last formulations had provided a privileged position for the Church; and for this reason, as well as for the attraction of its intellectual and formal rigour, clerics were disposed to retain an interest in it. Thus it began its long history as a *droit savant* which, in the words of a contemporary legal historian, "though made in another era and for another society, [it] remained as a model, guide and sometimes an inspiration."[65]

The real locus for the Roman legal system itself, of course, had moved to the East after the collapse of Rome in the fifth century; and the most impressive of all Imperial Roman efforts to systematize the law had been made in Byzantium: the early sixth-century codification ordered by Justinian, which has been given his name.[66] By this time it was too late for any general application of the code in western Europe, the political structure of which had largely disintegrated into more or less geographically isolated and politically insignificant enclaves. Only

64. A brief, useful treatment of the prevalence of Roman law in the early Middle Ages is Gaudemet, "Survivances romaines"; see also Gaudemet, *Formation de droit séculier*; "Doctrine des sources"; and a reprint collection of his articles, *Formation du droit canonique médiéval*, which contains the first article noted above as Text II.

65. Gaudemet, "Survivances romaines," pp. 205–6.

66. The standard modern edition is *Corpus Iuris Civilis* (*Dig.*, *Cod.*, *Inst.*, *Nov.*), ed. T. Mommsen et al., 3 vols.; new printing Berlin, 1954, of the 12th ed., 1911.

the gradual return of something approximating general political stability in the twelfth century made possible any significant and widespread revival of the rule of Roman law. A conscious part of this revival involved the perception of the greatness of the Roman legal system, and of the need for its renewed study. The Gregorian reform movement in the Church provided the stimulus to bring this perception to full focus in the twelfth century.

The actual revival of the study of Roman civil law began in northern Italy, where lawyers and students of law gathered in Bologna from the second quarter of the century.[67] By the end of the century, the knowledge of Roman law, and its influence was widespread in continental western Europe. A parallel development took place with respect to the law of the Church, canon law. And it is no longer possible to deny or even doubt that the same happened in England as well. Some slight Roman influence had been evident even in Anglo-Saxon England, and this had been modestly increased as a result of the Norman Conquest.[68] But the study of Roman law in England began with Vacarius at Oxford, about the middle of the twelfth century, very shortly after Bologna had developed in northern Italy as the major centre for the study of both civil and canon law.[69] Vacarius was born about 1120, and studied both Roman and canon law at Bologna under the "Four Doctors," themselves the immediate pupils of the founder of the great Bolognese school of glossators, Irnerius. Vacarius became a *magister* of law, and was brought to England about 1143 by Archbishop Theobald of Canterbury to assist in the administration of that see; he was transferred to York in the 1150s.[70]

There is evidence that a centre for the study of Roman law existed at Oxford before the end of the twelfth century; and by the early decades of the thirteenth century law had become a separate faculty, along with arts and theology, here as well as in most of the newly established

67. A brief accessible treatment of the medieval revival of the study of Roman law is in Ullmann, *Law and Politics*, pp. 81–116, with bibliographical data at p. 84, n. 2. See also Kuttner, *Harmony from Dissonance*; Gilmore, *Argument from Roman Law*; and *Ius Romanum medii aevi*. Medieval interest in Roman law began with the rediscovery about 1070 of Justinian's *Digesta*, the central element of ancient Roman jurisprudence: Kuttner, ibid., p. 6. Cf. Berman, *Law and Revoution*, pp. 85–164.

68. Post, "A roman-canonical Maxim." Post provides bibliographical data on the early influence of the two laws in England: *Studies*, pp. 184–88, nn. 69–91, and p. 315, n. 12.

69. Post, *Studies*, p. 185.

70. See Steen, "Vacarius and the Civil Law."

universities. (Frederick II established a school of law at Palermo that was intended to be a new Bologna.)[71] As regards later and more specifically political applications and influence of Roman law in England, it is known that French legists were in England during the reign of Edward II,[72] that the great canonist Hostiensis advised Henry III occasionally, and that the younger Accursius was in England for a short time with Edward I.[73] Connections between Bolognese legal scholarship and English legists were continued into the thirteenth century by Thomas of Marlborough, who had close connections with canonists at Bologna, as well as by William of Drogheda later in the century.[74]

The dissemination in England of both Roman and canon law was assisted greatly by clerics who brought their knowledge as well as manuscripts in both laws with them from the continent to churches such as Exeter's. The great English civil legist Bracton was connected with Exeter, although he likely learned his Roman law at Oxford, where both the *corpus iuris civilis* (the Roman civil law code) and Roman canonical treatises were under formal study by the middle of the thirteenth century.[75] The students were clerics, many of whom subsequently took employment in both civil and ecclesiastical administrations, and in noble households and sheriffs' offices, as well as in the king's chancery and at various levels of ecclesiastical administration, performed the tasks of writing letters, drafting legal documents, and keeping court proceedings. Influences from the renewal of legal studies and activity that began in the mid-twelfth century thus spread in much the same way and for much the same reasons as influences from the study of Aristotelian philosophy were to spread throughout Europe in thirteenth-century European universities: the subject matter in itself was of such compelling interest, and was perceived to be so clearly valuable and superior to any other currently available material, that its attraction was overwhelming.

The parallel twelfth-century developments in Roman and canon law occurred naturally and frequently in the same places, Bologna and Oxford being good examples. Because less well known than the history

71. Congar, "Quod omnes tangit," p. 232.

72. Post, *Studies*, p. 315; cf. n. 67 above. See also Richardson, "English Coronation Oath," p. 69, n. 124; Haskins, "Francis Accursius."

73. Post, *Studies*, p. 315, n. 10.

74. Post, *Studies*, p. 185; cf. n. 76.

75. Ibid.

of European civil law, a brief account should, perhaps, be offered of the origins and development of the law of the Christian Church.[76] Institutionalized Christianity always possessed some form of co-ordinated and authorized rule of faith and practices, the Sacred Scriptures being the most obvious and fundamental example. Canon (or Church) law may be said to have had its formal beginnings in 325, however, with the Council of Nicaea, this first ecumenical council bringing together the heads of the most important churches in Christendom for the explicit purpose of "making law" for the whole Church. There had been earlier councils, but Nicaea represented the first "universal" gathering of Christian churches to make decisions that immediately and subsequently were to be accepted as binding throughout the entire Church.

Another feature of the ecumenical council of Nicaea was its deliberate policy of collecting and presenting council decisions in a series of rules or "canons" organized in a systematic fashion under specific categories.[77] The same procedure was followed by subsequent authoritative conciliar gatherings, so that a series of ecclesiastical decisions came into existence, rules or canons promulgated by a variety of authoritative Church gatherings. These canons from various Church councils, then, could be formed into a more or less comprehensive collection to serve as the basic content of Church law, and to become the object of examination, analysis, and interpretation. Collections of canons produced by tacking the canons of one council on to those of other councils became the standard form for compiling law-books in the Church. This procedure resulted in a collection of material marked by diversity and even chaos in its contents, however, insofar as the different sources from which ecclesiastical decisions emanated were varied and even potentially at cross purposes. The conciliar decision-making gatherings themselves ranged from the relatively infrequent ecumenical councils to a wide variety of regional, provincial, and even local diocesan gatherings; and they took place in

76. A good, brief account in English of the history of Christian ecclesiastical (canon) law is Mortimer, *Western Canon Law*; see also van Hove, *Prolegomena ad Codicem Juris Canonici*; Stickler, *Historia juris canonici latini*. Cf. Ullmann, *Law and Politics*, pp. 119–60; Gilby, *Political Thought of Thomas Aquinas*, pp. 23–54.

77. Decisions of the Council of Nicaea can be found in Mansi, *Sacrorum conciliorum nova et amplissima collectio* (Florence: 1759–1798; reprint and continuation; Paris and Leipzig: 1901–1927), 1.

widely different geographical locations and under widely varying cultural, social, political, economic, and other conditions.

From time to time attempts were made to produce order from this diversity, but it was not until the twelfth century that these efforts met with generally acknowledged success. About the year 500, a Scythian monk named Dionysius Exiguus produced a reasonably systematic but modest collection of canons. His collection contained an itemized list of decisions from eight councils of the Greek church, of which Exiguus had made a careful Latin translation, as well as canons from several councils of the Latin church.[78] Exiguus also produced a second edition of his first collection, containing a larger number of canons from the Latin church councils, and added later a collection of some thirty-nine judgments (decretals) of various popes, the bulk of them from Innocent I. These two books, the second edition of Exiguus' first compilation and the later collection of papal decretals, came to be known as the *Dionysiana*,[79] and were very influential in the early history of canon law. They were, however, by no means the only canonical collections made in this particular period.

The era from the sixth to the eighth centuries saw an almost complete breakdown in any form of centralized Church administration and authority, with the result that conciliar and other decision-making activity usually took place only at a local, or at best regional, level. And with there being little possibility for universal administration, there was virtually everywhere an ignoring of the general rules of canon law. The Carolingian reforms of the late eighth and early ninth centuries brought a partial effort to remedy this state of affairs; but what followed was a further period of confusion and diversity, during which canonists felt free to interpret sources as they pleased and in accordance with local customs and temporary needs. A fresh effort to reform and systematize Church law was made in the eleventh century, a good example of which was the *Decretum* of Burchard, prince-bishop of Worms, in the first decade of the century.[80] Burchard continued to

78. The first collection of canons by Dionysius Exiguus has a modern edition by A. Strewe (Berlin: 1931). Useful articles on the various early collections of canons can be found in the *Dictionnaire de droit canonique*.

79. This collection, along with some minor additions, circulated in the Frankish kingdom at Charlemagne's direction, and was known as the *Dionysio-Hadriana*: edited in *PL* 67:39–134; see Stickler, *Historia iuris canonici*, pp. 106–15.

80. Burchard of Worms *Decretum* (*PL* 140:537–1090). For bibliographical data see: Fransen, "Suite de Recherches," p. 514 and nn. 1 and 2.

employ a very informal approach towards his source material, however, not hesitating to ignore the fact that particular laws had a civilian rather than a Church origin, for example, or even simply ascribing them arbitrarily to a pope, Church council, or Church father, especially St. Augustine. He also frequently altered, adapted, and edited texts in order to achieve a preferred interpretation.

Another eleventh-century canonical collection of very great importance for the history of canon law was the *Decretum* of Ivo of Chartres, compiled about 1094.[81] Probably its most important contribution to the development of canon law was Ivo's preface, where he offered a method for interpreting and harmonizing disparate items. Confronting the extremely formidable problems of how to handle canons of varying provenance, Ivo commented on how to unravel contradictions and arrive at a decision concerning several conflicting rules. Among other things he advised a distinction between variable and invariable laws: application of the distinction was shown to resolve many an apparent contradiction insofar as the contradiction could be resolved by dispensing in a particular case from a general but variable law. Both contradictory rules thus can be accepted as sound; but the one is general and the other particular. Something of this distinction appeared in the views of John of Salisbury seen earlier concerning flexible and inflexible laws;[82] and it is more than likely that Salisbury derived his position from familiarity with the legal theory of his day, to which Ivo would have made a great contribution, and whose general

81. Ivo of Chartres *Decretum* (*PL* 161:47*ff.*). An English translation of part of the Prologue is found in *Scholastic Miscellany*, pp. 238–42.

82. The method of trying to reconcile conflicting opinions and texts was not exclusive to students of the law in this period, although it was peculiarly necessary in the legal field. It appears formally also in theology with Abelard's *Sic et non*, generally considered to have been the prototype of the so-called scholasticism, the standard medieval methodology in theology and philosophy. Carlyle has a useful, if dated, summary of Ivo's method of classifying authorities in Church law, following Augustine, with appropriate citations to Ivo's works: Carlyle and Carlyle, *Mediaeval Political Theory*, 2:162–63; see also his remarks on Burchard of Worms, p. 161. Cf. Kuttner, *Harmony from Dissonance*, pp. 4–6. It is also worth noting that the Ivo prologue containing his advice on interpretation and reconciliation of disparate texts circulated widely in the twelfth century as a separate treatise, entitled *De consonantia canonum*. Early in this century Paul Fournier identified Urban II as promoter of the distinction between general and particular (inflexible and flexible) canons: "Tournant de l'histoire de droit." But see a later Kuttner article that identifies Ivo, rather than Urban II, as author of a text in the *Collectio Britannia* on which Fournier based his thesis: "Urban II and the Doctrine of Interpretation."

method of textual reconciliation would have been commonplace by the middle of the twelfth century.[83]

4. THE DECRETUM OF GRATIAN

The first and most important legist to consider directly in an examination of medieval canon law's contributions to the notions of consent, coercion, and limit is Gratian, not only because he stands at the beginning of what might be called a fully professional approach to his material, but because his success in establishing canon law on a firm and systematic basis set the whole frame of reference in which this discipline operated for centuries to come. Aptly titled "a concordance of discordant canons," the *Decretum* of Gratian was written about 1140.[84] It was the first really successful effort at a systematic compilation of Church law, and became the foundation of medieval and all subsequent canon law, remaining one of the fundamental collections of ecclesiastical jurisprudence, and attracting a host of commentaries, analyses, and glosses from the beginning of its existence.

Only comparatively recently, however, has Gratian's monumental work been subjected to the careful scholarly investigation needed to provide a comprehensive picture of its meaning and historical significance outside the limits of Church law; and only in the past decade has a coherent and satisfying statement emerged concerning what its author was about. Gratian, moreover, was himself a teacher as well as a student of Church law, and he trained the first generation of canon-law specialists who developed the school of canon law at Bologna in the 1140s and 1150s, shortly after the *Decretum* had become the standard text in this new discipline. Among the early decretists (commentators

---

83. John may have known Ivo's *Decretum* directly, and that of Burchard of Worms as well. He cites Cyprian *Epistola* 1.10 at *Policraticus* 1.8.406c, found in Ivo *Decretum* 2.31, and in Burchard *Decretum* 5.21. The same citation also appears in Gratian *De consecratione* D.2 c.95; but if, as is now generally accepted, the *De consecratione* is not an authentic part of the original Gratian text, then either John would have had to have seen the Cyprian text elsewhere, or the interpolation was made soon after Gratian completed his collection about 1240.

84. An excellent recent monograph on Gratian's work is Chodorow, *Christian Political Theory*. Chodorow examines the dating of the *Decretum*, pp. 7–12 and in Appendix I. Even though its information is sketchy and largely negative, the standard biography of Gratian is still Kuttner, "Father of Canon Law." Cf. Noonan, "Gratian Slept Here." The Noonan article deals at length and sceptically with much hearsay data about the Master, and the critical apparatus shows the most recent references on the subject.

on Gratian's *Decretum*) was Roland Bandinelli; he became Pope
Alexander III in 1159, and was the first of the great lawyer popes of the
Middle Ages.

The text of the *Decretum* is a massive document of some fourteen
hundred folio-size pages in modern edition.[85] Recent research has
made it clear from comparisons between the standard printed text and
its early manuscript tradition that significant additions of individually
interpolated items and even of whole sections (for example, the
treatises on consecration and penance) have found their way anony-
mously into the original work.[86] Similar investigations have produced a
much more satisfactory interpretation of Gratian's purpose in compiling the *Decretum*, with its author emerging as something more than a
disinterested legal scholar having no stake in, or being uninfluenced
by, the political world of his day. He now can be seen as consciously
involved in efforts to the twelfth-century Church in Italy towards
pressing its claims for ascendancy over the temporal powers of the day,
and as a canonist whose *magnum opus* aimed at nothing less than
establishing a basis for a Church-dominated society.[87] Gratian's success
in this regard makes his *Decretum* one of the most significant works of
political theory of the mid-twelfth century; it contains an ideal of
Church government that, in the later language of Richard Hooker, can
be called a genuine theory of ecclesiastical polity.

In containing a theory of polity, then, the *Decretum* deserves
attention, even though its views are only indirectly applicable to the
order of the secular.[88] The legal texts Gratian collected and organized,
as well as his own comments on them, were intended to present a

85. The *Decretum* is volume 1 in the modern edition of *Corpus iuris canonici*, ed. A.
Friedberg (Leipzig: 1879; reprinted Graz, 1959).

86. The work of Professor Jacqueline Rambaud has been crucial in this connection:
Rambaud, "Plan et méthode"; 'Corpus juris civilis'"; "Divers types d'abrégés"; "Décret
de Gratian et droit romain"; "Etude des manuscrits;" "Paleae dans le Décret de Gratien."
Madame Rambaud was responsible for the list of *paleae* published in *Histoire du droit et des
institutions de l'église en occident*, 7, L'âge classique, pp. 52–129. Other scholars who have
contributed to the clarification of the Gratian text are Vetulani, Kuttner, and Gaudemet.
Cf. Vetulani, "Etudes sur la division en distinctions"; "Suite d'études I"; "Suite d'études
II"; "Nouvelles vues sur le décret de Gratien"; Kuttner, "New Studies in Roman Law";
"Additional Notes"; Gaudemet, "Romische Rect in Gratians Dekret."

87. Chodorow, *Christian Political Theory*, pp. 63–64, 97.

88. See similar remarks concerning later canonical writings connected with the
conciliar movement that rightly urge caution in using essentially canonical or theological
material to construct medieval political thought in Black, *Monarchy and Community*.

picture of an organized and appropriate administration for a Church society, a society perceived as a community whose purposes were spiritual rather than temporal, heavenly rather than earthly. But such a spiritual society inevitably must have a relationship with the political or temporal society in which it finds itself; accordingly, the specifications of this relationship, or at least some of them, are likely to be addressed in developing a theory of a Church society. The focus for such specifications will be the function of the ecclesiastical polity, of course, and the details of the view presented will reflect this focus. Thus, the nature and character of temporal polity are not treated directly, with the consequence that direct questions concerning the integrity and limits of the temporal polity are likely to go unanswered because they are not directly asked.

Gratian was not interested primarily in the nature of political society, in political theory as we understand that term, a point equally important when it comes to assessing the political thought of other medieval canonists and theologians. Nor was he interested directly in the problem of the relationship between church and state, although his *Decretum* contains much material touching on this issue, material later carefully weighed and sifted by medieval canonists and Church leaders, and by more than a few modern scholars as well for whom this problem has been of concern. But Gratian did not deal directly with the *sacerdotium / regnum* problem; he was interested exclusively in aspects of an ecclesiastical constitution, and offered no explicit guidelines for any resolution of the problem of specifying the precise boundaries between church and state. The opposing theories on church / state relations that emerged in the century and a half following the appearance of the *Decretum*, then, may each have had proponents who claimed Gratian in support of their views; and the authority of the Gratian text was offered as justification for views that its author himself had not expressed. Items on this question that Gratian himself never cited were also interpolated into the Master's text: the *capitula* in Distinction 96 dealing with the Donation of Constantine, for example, are accretions to Gratian's original text.[89] This whole Distinction and its twelfth- and thirteenth-century glosses and commentaries became extremely important material for later interpretation of the relation-

---

89. Chodorow, *Christian Political Theory*, p. 56 and p. 54, n. 53. For more references regarding the view that Gratian was concerned exclusively with the nature of the ecclesiastical constitution, see Chodorow, "Magister Gratian."

ship between the two powers of church and state. For his own part, however, Gratian actually concerned himself only with the question of what rights a secular power had in dealing with ecclesiastical property and involving itself with ecclesiastical affairs; the larger issue of theory concerning the interaction of the spheres of the spiritual and temporal lay outside his purview.

The contents of the *Decretum*, nonetheless, are of great interest for our purposes. They represent a massive, though necessarily still selective, effort to compile texts from Church sources dealing with the life, structure, and organization of the Christian church; papal and episcopal pronouncements, statements, letters, declarations and legal decisions composed by Church authorities of various kinds, and authoritative texts and *dicta* of one sort or another from the Apostolic period of the Church down to Gratian's own day, accompanied by brief but usually incisive comments from Gratian himself by way of explanation, interpretation, and assessment. Gratian's *Concordance of Discordant Canons* is obviously quite a different type of document from, and written in quite a different context than, John of Salisbury's *Policraticus*, which contains an *ex professo* statement on the nature of temporal polity. But Gratian's work does contain material in which the notions of consent, coercion, and limit are handled, even though the context always has to do directly with ecclesiastical rather than temporal issues of governance. Such use as will be made of Gratian's treatment of these notions must always keep this fact in mind.

As befits a treatise dealing with the law, Gratian begins the *Decretum* by explaining the meaning of this term; and it has been observed often that the whole introductory part of the work is simply an expanded commentary on the section of law in the *Etymologies* of Isidore of Seville.[90] Though clearly famliar with the contemporary twelfth-century state of knowledge of Roman law, Gratian chose to define law by using ecclesiastical rather than secular sources. He quotes Isidore to the effect that law "should be according to nature and according to custom, and suitable to the place and time of the *patria*, necessary and useful, as well as honest, just, possible, manifest and for the common

90. Chodorow considers the treatise on the nature of law more than the beginning of Gratian's work; rather, it represents the beginning of a systematic effort of legal theorizing aimed at providing "adequate protection for the community against the caprices of its governors. ... It constituted the theoretical foundation for the reform program of the party with which the work was associated." Chodorow, *Christian Political Theory*, p. 98. See Gaudemet, "Doctrine des sources."

utility of all the citizens."[91] Gratian offers a second, earlier citation of Isidore, when he asserts that "a ruler makes law with the counsel and consent of the people,"[92] an Isidorean text repeated by Thomas Aquinas along with Gratian's definition of law.[93] He also cites Isidore to the effect that the purpose of law is to curb wickedness and protect innocence,[94] reflecting the view common among medieval lawyers and theologians that laws should not attempt to cover more than the major human vices to which the majority of people are so prone that they cannot be expected to abstain without the constraints and coercion of the law.[95]

Gratian then acknowledges the legitimacy of variables in the law relating to differences in environment, language, customs, and institutions, a notion that subsequently became a standard feature in the formal definition of law formulated by both canonists and civilians.[96] This notion, of course, can be found in the earlier Augustinian tradition as well as in Augustine himself,[97] from whom Isidore likely took it; so Gratian was breaking no new ground here. It was repeated and given greater emphasis by late-thirteenth-century political thinkers such as Thomas Aquinas[98] and John of Paris,[99] both of them strongly influenced by Aristotelian as well as early Christian and Roman formulations. The same notion, obviously reflecting the same Augustinian-Isidorean authorities, appeared in Alexander of Hales, St. Bonaventure, and Matthew of Aquasparta.[100] As regards the Isidorean definition, which makes reference to law as being made with "the counsel and consent of the people," Gratian merely cited it without comment of his own;[101] accordingly, there is no way of knowing precisely what the Master understood by this formula-type expression. The fact that he did cite the Isidorean text, however,

---

91. Isidore *Etymologiae* 5.2 (= 5.21).1143b11, cited at Gratian, D.4 c.2.

92. *Gratian*, D.2, c.1.

93. Thomas Aquinas, *S.T.* 1–2.90.3 *sed contra*; 1–2.95.3. Aquinas cites Gratian in the first of these texts.

94. *Gratian*, D.4, c.1; Cf. Isidore *Etymologiae* 5.20.

95. The section defining law, like the whole of the *Decretum*, immediately became a standard text and the object of ceaseless repetition and interpretation.

96. *Gratian*, D.4 post c.1.

97. Augustine *De civitate Dei* 19.18.

98. Thomas Aquinas, *S.T.* 1–2.95.3; 97.4.

99. John of Paris *De potestate regia et papali* 3.

100. Chroust, "Philosophy of Law of St. Thomas Aquinas," pp. 13–19.

101. *Gratian*, D.2 c.1.

guaranteed that the notion of popular counsel and consent would receive the kind of widespread and authoritative reference that inclusion in the *Decretum* provided.

The only formal and *ex professo* treatment of the notion of consent that Gratian offers in the *Decretum* occurs within the framework of his discussion for procedures to select a bishop.[102] Reference has been made earlier to texts and practices dealing with episcopal election in the early Church, and to the involvement of the entire Christian community in the appointment of ministers and spiritual leaders.[103] Reference back to the ancient sources and practices had been revived in the eleventh century as part of the Gregorian reform efforts to wrest episcopal and other forms of ecclesiastical administration back from the control of lay rulers. In the fifth century, the practice had been for each ecclesiastical province (a grouping that included a number of bishoprics or dioceses) to exercise primary responsibility for the election of its episcopal members; but the exercise of preference by the bishops of a province was not always decisive, and other persons frequently had to be consulted. The participation of the diocesan clergy and laity, as well as the consent of the metropolitan, came to be regular features in the process; and these elements, considered inseparable insofar as each was essential, were sanctioned and publicized by the papal authority of the day. As already noted earlier, Celestine I (422–32) directed that "a bishop should not be given to those unwilling [to receive him]," and stipulated that the consent and wishes of the clergy, people, and nobility were required.[104] Pope Leo I (450–64) had restated this guiding principle in more explicit terms: "He who governs all should be elected by all";[105] and "No one shall be designated a bishop who has not been chosen by the clergy, accepted by the people and consecrated by the bishops of the province with the approval of the metropolitan."[106]

---

102. A recent fine examination of medieval procedures for choosing a bishop is Benson, *Bishop-Elect*; cf. Gaudemet, "Participation de communauté." This article has a useful bibliography at p. 308, n. 1. Cf. Gryson, "Elections ecclésiastiques."

103. Part 1, 6–7.

104. Celestine *Epistolae* 4.5 (*PL* 50:434).

105. Leo *Epistolae* 10.4 (*PL* 54:628); cf. *Epistolae* 10.6, 13.3, 14.5, 167.1.

106. "Nulla ratio sinit ut inter episcopus habeantur qui nec a clericis sunt electi nec a plebibus sunt expetiti, nec a provincialibus episcopis cum metropolitani iudicio consecrati": Leo *Epistolae* 167 (*PL* 54:1203); cited in *Gratian*, D.62 c.1. St. Cyprian also expressed the view to his clergy that his style of exercising episcopal office involved "doing nothing without your advice [*consilio*] and without agreement of the people [*consensu*

Different roles are assigned formally by Leo to the clergy, people, fellow provincial bishops, and metropolitan; and it is noteworthy that his term for people was *plebs*, designative of the common people rather than of any noble or privileged section of the community as a whole. The Leonine text is strongly reminiscent of a remark by Pliny the Younger that "the emperor of all the people should be chosen by all the people" (*imperator omnibus eligi debet ex omnibus*),[107] and shows just how persistent this theme was in both Roman and Christian notions of polity, and in both temporal and ecclesiastical formulations by Christian thinkers. Elsewhere, Leo also made clear his willingness to accept the necessity of an episcopal election having the approval of the imperial power.[108]

Almost certainly following the text of Leo in a conscious manner, medieval writers, canonists, and theologians normally distinguished between *populus* and *plebs*. Sometimes the term *populus* meant all the people, the *plebs* as well as the nobility; but generally it was assumed that the *populus* was constituted of the "greater men," the greater and better part (of the whole people): *maior pars*; *sanior pars*; *maior et sanior pars*.[109] A thirteenth-century decretist described the distinction between *populus* and *plebs* as follows: "The difference between *populus* and *plebs* is the same as that between animal and man, genus and species, for the nobles, and the nobles taken as a group, constitute the *populus*. The *plebs* do not find senators and consular men among them . . . that is, the *universus populus* are those better born in respect of three elements: nobility, dignity, antiquity."[110] Full implications of the distinction between *populus* (the nobles) and *plebs* (the masses of the lower classes) are expressed graphically in the early fourteenth century by Marsilius of Padua.[111]

The most famous and most often cited early historical instance of

plebis]": Cyprian *Epistolae* 14.1.2 and 4; cited in Congar, "Quod omnes tangit," p. 226 and n. 59. Cf. Part 1, n. 91.

107. "Imperator omnibus eligi debet ex omnibus": Pliny the Younger *Panegyricus* 7.6; cited in Benson, *Bishop-Elect*, p. 25, n. 8.

108. Benson, *Bishop-Elect*, p. 26, n. 22, citing Hinschius, *Kirchenrecht*, 2:513–15.

109. For the meanings of these various terms see Part 3, 2A, below.

110. *Summa*. "Antiquitate et tempore" on *Decretum* (Vat. MS. Palat. lat., fol. 37) D.2. c.1; cf. *Inst*. 1.2.3.4, cited in Post, *Studies*, p. 374, n. 16. The author's point would have been clearer had he written *plebs et populus*, rather than the other way about; for clearly the *plebs* (all the people considered as a whole) is a genus of which the *populus* (the nobles) is a species.

111. See Part 4, 1B, below.

episcopal appointment involving the people directly was Ambrose's appointment to the see of Milan in the late fourth century.[112] Here it seems that the election by the clergy in a formal procedure, if indeed there were any such procedure, "coincided" with an expression of genuinely popular support and acclaim, a paradigm case as it were of what was regularly seen and referred to among medieval canonists and theologians as the ideal coming together of the essential clerical and lay elements in an episcopal election to yield full or complete consensus. Later this was called election by quasi-inspiration,[113] and was recognized as the most perfect form of agreement for a Christian community, unanimity by consensus.[114]

The original doctrine of canonical election had become largely ignored and forgotten during later centuries, when the secular powers were accustomed to choosing persons to fill the episcopal offices in their territory. It was disregarded virtually completely in the early Frankish period, when the king exercised an almost unrestricted right to appoint bishops. But from the mid-ninth century a noticeable difference can be seen in practices in the west Frankish region. Here, probably because of greater maturity and intellectual advances, efforts can be seen to revive the ancient principles. The procedure of episcopal election by clergy and people was used for vacancies at Rheims (845), Rennes (866), Chalons (868), Tours (869), and Laon (876), which were filled in "the canonical manner."[115] The collection of canon law accepted by Charlemagne for use in his kingdom, the *Hadriana* (787),[116] contained a set of canons on the election and consecration of bishops, one of which stipulated that a bishop was to be elected by all the bishops of his province, and consecrated by at least three of them, with the metropolitan confirming.[117] Another eighth-century canonical collection, the *Hispana*,[118] reproduced the canons of Antioch, canon

112. The Ambrosian popular election became the standard reference point and precedent for such a procedure in medieval canonical and theological writings.

113. This was one of the three formally designated and acceptable modes of ecclesiastical election approved by the Fourth Lateran Council in 1215 (canon 24); see Moulin, "*Sanior et maior pars*," p. 296. The other two forms were the compromise (*compromissum*) and ballot (*scrutinium*).

114. Moulin, "*Sanior et maior pars*," pp. 369–71, 491–93.

115. *MGH, Epistolae*, 6:81, p. 73, II.16–17; cited in Ullmann, "Election of Bishops," p. 81, and n. 3.

116. See n. 78 above.

117. See article on the *Hadriana* in *Dictionnaire de droit canonique*, 5:1083–84.

118. See the article on the *Hispana* in *Dictionnaire de droit canonique*, 5:1159–62.

16 of which also describes episcopal election, while canon 22 of the section, titled *Statuta ecclesiae antiqua*, asserts that "a bishop is not to be ordained without consulting his clergy and without the approval of the laity."[119]

The undoubted leader in urging canonical reforms and the revival of ancient practices in the ninth century was Hincmar of Rheims,[120] who consistently held that the proper elements for elevating a bishop were the clergy and people of his diocese. Hincmar knew the law and practice of the Church, and urged his views on canonical election at the Council of Valence in 855. The council, however, approved a kind of compromise position, preserving the right of clergy and people to elect their bishop, contingent on permission to do so being granted by the king (the *congé d'élire*): the approved method indicated that the king was to be approached with the request that he permit a canonical election by clergy and people. The permission obtained, consultation was then to begin among the clergy and people, in order that a suitable person might be chosen "with the consent of the whole clergy and people."[121] It seems that the essential element in the election was that of consent by clergy and people: the royal permission, Hincmar always insisted, was merely formal. Later tenth-century practices, which saw aristocratic control replace the earlier royal control, thus were seen by contemporary religious authorities as deviations from the canonical norm even though they were accepted.[122] By the eleventh century bishoprics again were being treated for the most part by emperors and other powerful rulers as private churches. Remnants of the old practices could still be found, however: the canonical form was followed by Cardinal Humbert;[123] and it was invoked by Pope Nicolas

119. Gratian cites a canon from the Fourth Council of Toledo (633) asserting that "he whom the clergy and people of his own city have not elected, and whom neither the authority of the metropolitan nor the assent of the provincial bishops has chosen—he shall not be bishop": *Gratian*, D.51 c.5. Cf. Benson, *Bishop-Elect*, p. 27.

120. Hincmar, archbishop of Rheims, was a person of remarkable intellectual abilities and accomplishments who wrote extensively on public government with a level of sophistication not matched again until much later. The standard work on Hincmar is still Schrors, *Hinkmar von Reims*; cf. Ullmann, *Law and Politics*, pp. 241–42, and brief bibliographical note at p. 241, n. 2; Ullmann, "Election of Bishops," p. 83; Carlyle and Carlyle, *Mediaeval Political Theory*, 1:230–34 and later, *passim*.

121. Mansi, *Sacrorum conciliorum amplissima collectio*, vol. 15, col. 7, chap. 7; cited in Ullmann, "Election of Bishops," p. 85.

122. Ullmann, "Election of Bishops," pp. 84–85.

123. Humbert *Adversus simoniacos* 5.5 (*MGH, Libelli* 51:108 and 3:6), cited in Benson, *Bishop-Elect*, p. 32.

II in a papal election decree employing the precise distinction found in the earlier Leo text, which Nicholas quotes directly.[124]

A major ingredient in the religious reform movement of the twelfth century had to do not only with the necessity to eliminate the moral imperfections that had insinuated themselves into both the lives and administrative practices of the members of the Christian church; as well there was a perception of the need to have realized literally as far as possible the ideals expressed in the Gospels for the conduct of human life in the Christian community. Some information concerning this ideal and how the first Christians went about embodying it was to be found in the Gospels and other early Christian sources; and on the issue of appointing bishops a careful search of late-Roman church directives and practices had turned up the texts of Celestine and Leo already noted, as well as much other parallel data from earlier canonical collections.

The reformers perceived their major task in reviving appropriate methods for the appointment of bishops to be the elimination of direct and conclusive involvement by lay authorities; and for this reason they moved towards the exclusion of all direct lay participation. The ideal for canonical election freshly advocated was a procedure involving "clergy and people", with the implication at least that what was needed was the consent of all concerned: canons of the cathedral chapter, cathedral and monastery clergy, nobility, ministers, and the ordinary lay community. Gregory VII himself stressed that episcopal election should be by both *clerici et populus*, but he did not specify clearly how these two elements were actually to participate, and did not distinguish between their respective roles.[125] The reform group as a whole tended to concede the right of the emperor (or other appropriate lay ruler) to exercise some form of consent in canonical election, but to minimize it by incorporating it with the consent of the people (*plebs*).[126] A later development weakened lay involvement in episcopal elections even further, and even diminished the value of clerical participation.

---

124. *MGH, Const.*, 1:540.382.8; cited in Benson, *Bishop-Elect*, p. 42 and n. 83. Cf. Leo I *Epistola* 10.4.6.167 (*PL* 54:632, 634, 1203).

125. Benson, *Bishop-Elect*, p. 33. See Chodorow, *Christian Political Theory*, pp. 201–4; Sägmuller, *Bishopswahl bei Gratian*.

126. Benson, *Bishop-Elect*, p. 40. Cf. the earlier distinction between *plebs* and *populus*. To combine the role of lay ruler with that of the common people as a whole is to reduce it in a striking fashion, and I'm not certain that would have been fully and explicitly intended by all commentators.

Distinguishing between office and jurisdiction produced the doctrine that only electoral confirmation conferred authority on a bishop: insistence by canonists and popes that electoral confirmation (of an episcopal candidate) was the crucial act tended to diminish the significance of any election process (regardless of what parties might participate in the election). The election was thus transformed into something through which a prelate might be chosen, but which transferred no power to him; the electors were deprived of any efficient power, for if the person elected acquired no rights through his election, the election itself was not essential except perhaps pro forma.[127] Even in these circumstances, however, formal election was not quite absolutely nothing; its very retention even as a formality offered some evidence of an actual role for electors in the process.

Gratian devoted three Distinctions of the *Decretum* almost entirely to an analysis of the issue of episcopal election, Distinctions 61–63, as well as portions of text in other locations.[128] The position he took was that seen earlier in Leo I, although Gratian spelled out more clearly the respective roles of clergy and laity in the election procedure. The author of the *Decretum* certainly was aware of both the early Celestine and Leonine texts. He cites the Celestine text twice, at Distinction 61, c. 13 and Distinction 61, c. 26; the Leo I text at Distinction 62, c. 1. Curiously, however, he does not do so in a completely straightforward way; he quotes neither text in his *ex professo* treatment of episcopal election, although one might have expected him to do so. He mentions the Celestine text only in connection with the problem of diocesan clergy having preference in episcopal elections over those outside the diocese, and he does not use it in a way that invokes its contents as a general principle. Nor does he quote the portion of it stating that "all should be involved" when citing it with reference to the election of a bishop. Neither did he cite the Leonine text in this connection, at Distinction 63, c. 26 and 27. It has been suggested that Gratian was determined not to employ for canonical purposes dicta known to be derived from Roman law; hence his careful editorial work with these two texts that showed traces of the Roman maxim *quod omnes tangit*, a formula Gratian was prepared to accept, but not apparently to acknowledge as Roman in origin.[129] Whatever Gratian's reservations in

127. Benson, *Bishop-Elect*, pp. 45–55, 90–115.
128. Distinctions 60–63, esp. D.63 c.7 and c.8; cf. D.23 cc.1–3; D.51 c.5.
129. Chodorow, *Christian Political Theory*, pp. 205–20.

this connection, later canonists, expecially canonist-popes, had no compunction about identifying the Roman origins of the maxims they cited in support of their decisions.

Gratian asserted that it was his intention to defend the thesis that "laymen must not involve themselves in any way in [episcopal] election";[130] and he provides the details of his position in his comments at D.63, *post* c. 25: "Laymen should not be excluded from the election ... [however, they are] not to perform the election, but rather to give consent to it. For election belongs to the priests and the duty of the faithful people is to consent humbly [by way of popular acclamation of the newly elected episcopal candidate].[131]" Elsewhere in the same Distinction he stated: "It is clear to everyone that election belongs only to clerics."[132]

The Magister's main point is a distinction between the right to elect, which belongs to the clergy of a diocese, and the right to consent, which is basically only a right to acclaim and belongs to the people (among whom the lay ruler is included). Gratian did not invent the distinction, which rests ultimately on the ambiguity in the term "to elect" (*eligere*), which can both designate the juridical action of selecting one person from many, and also be used more loosely to express acceptance or approval. Leo I had reflected this fifth-century double usage of the term when he employed it to describe the rights of both clergy and laity alike in episcopal election.[133] However, Leo could and did distinguish between the "electoral" functions of the clergy (*eligere*) and of the laity (*expetere*); and Leo's distinction was followed in the later texts of episcopal election that transmitted the early form, those of Cardinal Humbert and Nicolas II mentioned earlier. Leo's statement had come into regular citation among the canonical collections of the late eleventh century, and was fully known by Gratian: "*Electio clericorum est, consensus plebis.*"[134]

For Gratian the dominant role in canonical election must rest with the clergy, but the people, including the prince, need not be excluded

130. *Gratian*, D.63 c.1.

131. *Gratian*, D.63 post c.25.

132. *Gratian*, D.63 post c.34. Cheney notes an injunction from Deut. 22:10 used to demarcate and limit the rights of the laity generally in the medieval church—"Thou shalt not plow with an ox and an ass together"—noting its presence in *Gratian*, C.16 q.7 c.22 and in *Decretals*, 3.13.22: Cheney, *Becket to Langton*, p. 156.

133. Leo *Epistolae* 10.4 and 6 (*PL* 54:632 and 634); *Epistolae* 167 (*PL* 54:1203).

134. *Gratian*, D.62 dict. ante c.1.

completely; they were to express their consent or approval by way of acclamation. And apparently this could be done either at the time of the election itself or at the time of episcopal enthronement. He seems to have been anxious to preserve some role for the people in episcopal election, but it was not to be a dominant one even though it may have been essential; Gratian is not explicit concerning the point of whether a candidate for a bishopric duly chosen (elected) by his clergy could assume office in the face of a refusal to accept him by the laity. Presumably such a candidate could not do so, following the Celestine formula that, to be a bishop, one must be accepted (*invitus*). What is clear, however, is that the role he assigns to the clergy is both dominant and essential, although even here Gratian's concern is not so single-minded as to have him clarify exactly how the clerical election was to be performed or precisely which clerics are to be assigned which roles. He simply expands on Leo I: "In the Church of God, a ruler is rightly established when the people acclaim the one whom the clergy will have elected by a common vote."[135]

A particular feature of Gratian's treatment of episcopal election offers an opportunity for further analysis of his overall constitutional theory, inasmuch as that term is applicable to his views on the character of ecclesiastical polity. As insisted on earlier, Gratian presented no theory of temporal polity, as that was never his intention. However, his overall views do offer a constitutional theory of the Church; and it is possible to extrapolate from here to the temporal plane. Indeed, this is the best that can be done. Unfortunately, the feature to which we now turn shows a negative, rather than a positive, aspect of Gratian's constitutional theory. An extension of the Magister's doctrine of canonical election was his concern for the quality of Church leaders produced by the procedure; and such concern and its expression form an essential part of any constitutional theory and theory of law. Gratian apparently saw the need to protect the ecclesiastical community somehow against the possibility of misuse of authority by a prelate who found himself in office as a result of even the proper functioning of the election procedure. As it might be put in terms of the concepts that are

135. *Gratian*, D.63 dict. post c.25; cf. D.62. dict. ante c.1. Wilks offers a good example of the traditional roles provided for clergy and laity in a text from Placidus of Nonantula *De honore ecclesiae* 37: "Sed magis communi electione clericorum et consensu populorum, maiorum scilicet et minorum, inter quos videlicet tam reges quam principes numerantur": (*MGH, Libelli*, 2:585), cited in Wilks, "Coronation and Representation." p. 270.

the subject of this study, he perceived the need to give some kind of expression in law to the theoretical concept of limit in the exercise of authority. The legal theory presented in the *Decretum*, however, fails signally to provide adequate procedural protection for the community against possible caprice and abuse by its rulers.

It has been contended that medieval legal theory in general did not admit of law being made, but simply of being perceived or discovered, a point of view that led some historians to a revision of the early history of English parliaments according to which these gatherings were essentially judicial and not legislative bodies.[136] A careful examination of Gratian's views in the *Decretum* shows that such a narrow view of the function of authority in terms of laws must be rejected; the Magister saw clearly that authority—ecclesiastical authority, of course, in the specific terms of his interests—possessed power extending to the activity of lawmaking as well as law-discovering; and he was concerned to establish a relationship between this power as exercised by given human office-holders and the contents of acceptable laws as such.

Aware of the Roman legal maxim that the ruler is above the law, Gratian was not prepared to construe the formula literally when discussing the position of the pope in relation to the established laws of the Church, any more than was John of Salisbury in discussing temporal rulers.[137] Gratian contended that the legislative power of an ecclesiastical ruler was restricted inasmuch as he himself was required to obey the law under ordinary circumstances.[138] But in a position that gives the lie to the thesis that medieval legal theorists did not admit that the power to legislate rested in the hands of those in authority, Gratian accepts that properly constituted Church authority can make law, and that in so doing can properly go beyond the "normal" requirement that even the ruler must be under the law.[139] As Salisbury did in respect of a temporal ruler, Gratian applied to the pope the famous legal maxim that the prince is above the law as well as the dictum that he is bound by

---

136. Chodorow provides bibliographical data on this point in *Christian Political Theory*, p. 133, n. 1.

137. *Gratian*, D.45 dict. post c.13; cf. Chodorow, *Christian Political Theory*, pp. 133–35.

138. *Gratian*, C.25 q.2 dict. post. c.16; cf. Chodorow, *Christian Political Theory*, pp. 142–47.

139. *Decretum*, c.25 q.1 dict. post c.16; cf. C.25 q.2 dict. post c.21; C.22 q.4 dict. post C.23; C.22 q.4 dict. post c.23; C.25 q.2 dict. post c.21: this last text, as Chodorow points out, is similar to Bernard of Clairvaux, *De consideratione* 3.4.14; Chodorow, *Christian Political Theory*, p. 146, n. 25.

the law,[140] and in so doing displayed a serious lacuna in his constitutional theory. On the one hand, he argued for a restriction of legislative power in the supreme ecclesiastical ruler by requiring him to obey the laws; on the other hand, he acknowledged an exception to this rule by conceding to the pope the right to go beyond the law when legitimately engaged in the specific task of lawmaking. Gratian thus introduced into his governmental theory the essential tension between a ruler's sovereign power to make law and the principle that he is bound by the law, a tension found in any theoretical formulation that is not absolutist in the crudest possible way. But the author of the *Decretum* failed to provide any specific method for expressing and resolving this tension in a meaningful fashion, any test for determining if and when the lawmaking activity of the legislator moved from the legitimate role of lawmaker, which continued somehow to reflect the limits of the ruler's function, to that of arbitrary tyrant, or any way of redressing effectively a situation where the lawmaker becomes a tyrant.

The best Gratian seems to have managed in this connection was to advise that a pope (or other "prince") should act out of consideration for the equity of reason when granting a privilege against the general provisions of a law,[141] the kind of general formulation to appear shortly also in the *Policraticus* of John of Salisbury and to be reflected as well in the views of another contemporary, Bernard of Clairvaux.[142] The pope should exercise his power to legislate and judge in accordance with the precepts of God. But if he failed to do so (as also apparently would be

140. Chodorow, *Christian Political Theory*, p. 147. Gratian also taught simple inalienability for the pope, repeating a formulation of papal immunity from judicial action created by the early sixth-century forger of *Constitutum Sylvestri*. The text purported to be a decree from a Roman synod of 324, presided over by Pope Sylvester and the emperor Constantine. Perceived as the juristic expression of an important principle it enjoyed considerable currency, appearing in the *Pseudo-Isidoriana*, as canon 20 in *Collectio 74 titulorum*, as well as in the collections of Ivo of Chartres and Gratian: Moynihan, *Papal Immunity*, pp. 22–23. In a curious way this long-lived and influential text provides negative evidence for the prevalence of the notion of popular consent in ecclesiastical affairs: it stipulates that no one—emperor, king, cleric or the people—can judge the pope: "Nemo enim ab augusto neque ab omni clero neque a regibus neque a populo iudex [= papa] judicabitur": Gratian, C.9 q.3 c.13. The whole issue of the medieval view on the inalienability of papal authority has received careful study in Moynihan, *Papal Immunity*; cf. Oakley, *Council over Pope*; de Vooght, *Pouvoirs du concile*.

141. *Gratian*, C.25 q.1 dict. post c.16.

142. Bernard of Clairvaux *Epistolae* 131, cited in Chodorow, *Christian Political Theory*, p. 146, n. 25; *Sancti Bernardi Opera*, 7; English translation in Bernard, *Letters*, trans. Bruno Scott James.

the case for the exercise by duly elected and consecrated bishops of their authority in ways that had them acting "wrongly"), those subject to his authority were still obliged to obey. In his views and wording Gratian continued the patristic tradition on this point, balancing the concept of authority (*potestas*) possessed by an ecclesiastical ruler with that of charity (*caritas*), the latter being a kind of procedural *deus ex machina* to keep the exercise of authority within the bounds of reason and equity, or at least to mitigate the harsh effects of any failure to do so.

Gratian's doctrine is defective at this point; he leaves the reader of the *Causa* with the impression that the pope ultimately must be considered superior to the community over which he is set, and that in practical terms he is loosed from its laws. The only qualification mentioned is that members of the Church should not be asked to perform an evil action. Ultimately, the only hedge Gratian seemed to see as a guarantee against bad (ecclesiastical) governance was to ensure that good men were promoted to office. It was not until later in the twelfth and thirteenth centuries that canon lawyers began to develop a theory for controlling rulers that expressed the element of reserving some authority to the community, thus enabling it to exercise power against its governors if and when the necessity for so doing arose. Gratian's doctrine on episcopal election may have contained the seeds of this element in constitutional theory insofar as it assigns a kind of acclamatory role to the community over which authority is to be recognized as operating in the Church, a role to be exercised as part of the election procedure, and an elective function to the clergy as well. But Gratian's overall position is inadequate because incomplete; he offers no mechanism for either the community as a whole or for the clergy to employ in dealing with abuse of authority. John of Salisbury's doctrine of tyrannicide is similarly inadequate in its formulation and specification with respect to the exercise of temporal authority, but it does advance the issue somewhat.

PART THREE

The Thirteenth Century

1. THE DEVELOPMENT OF LEGAL CONCEPTS

A. Quod omnes tangit: *What Touches All*

GRATIAN'S *Decretum* is only the first example we have seen of the literary products illustrating the growing sophistication in both forms of the law that began to develop in the twelfth century. This development continued apace throughout the next century as well, and had a major influence on the emergence of specific forms of juridical and political structures, especially in England, France, and the city-states of northern Italy.

New political and legal issues and problems emerged as the increasing complexities of both church and state, and of the relations between the two, reflected the centralizing activities of both ecclesiastical and lay leaders of the time. A number of considerations must be kept in mind here: (1) For their part, the canonists continued to present and speak for the interests of the ecclesiastical constituency; their remarks were intended to apply to that constituency, had relevance directly only in the ecclesiastical sphere, and for the most part were only indirectly relevant to political society. (2) The professional interests of the canonical and civilian legists and of the personages they supported begin now, clearly and extensively, to diverge; the differing interpretations and theories advanced in the two legal jurisdictions illustrate this fact. (3) At the same time, however, some standardization developed in both ecclesiastical and political jurisdictions regarding procedural aspects of administration and litigation. What might be called public law developed in both church and state; legal experts and theorists became more important in both civil and canonical legal spheres, and some uniformity of concepts and procedures resulted from the interaction of professionals and their theories in both spheres.

It is important for this reason to extend the examination of medieval sources for political theory to cover the development of both legal theory and practice concerning the notion of consent. As noted earlier, the term "consent" appeared in Gratian in a reference to the need for consent by the whole people to valid laws, and Gratian himself derived it from Roman law and the texts of certain Christian writers. The period of close study and sophistication in development of basic legal notions and formulae that began in the twelfth century, however, saw a more specific question being asked in this connection: what precisely and jurisdictionally was meant by the notion of consent by the people? And as soon appeared, there is a cluster of legal terms and elements involved here, the meaning and application of which are closely connected. The issue of who, in the sense of how many persons, there are whose consent is required, is always relevant, and begins to be recognized as such. So is the matter of how persons whose consent is needed should act to express consent: do they, must they, act as individuals directly on the issue at hand; or is there some way another person can act for them singly or together? The notion of representation appears here as crucial on a number of accounts: (1) Can one person be represented by another? (2) If so, how does the representative acquire his status? (3) What powers must the representative have (be given) in order to represent? (4) What are the consequences for the person represented of the actions of his representative? Examination of the medieval meaning and use of the concepts of consent, coercion, and limit requires further inquiry into these issues in medieval legal thought.

Perhaps the single element with the longest history of use in legal practice of direct concern is the principle that "what touches all must be approved by all" (*quod omnes tangit ab omnibus tractari et approbari debet*), henceforth referred to simply as *q o t*.[1] The maxim appears in Gratian[2]

1. Fundamental research on this principle can be found in Post, "A Romano-Canonical Maxim" and "A Roman Legal Theory of Consent" and Congar, "Quod omnes tangit"; see also Post, "Roman Law and Early Representation," "Plena potestas"; Marongiu, *Medieval Parliaments*, and "Q.o.t., principe fondamental"; cf. Cheyette, *Lordship and Community.*

2. *Gratian*, D.63 post c.25.

and was known by him as a dictum of Roman law, although he seems not to have quoted it directly from Roman legal sources nor to have acknowledged its Roman provenance. Interest in *q o t* had begun to develop in canonical circles as a consequence of the eleventh-century reform activities in connection with efforts to wrest episcopal election from the control of lay rulers. Bernard of Clairvaux offers an excellent illustration of the principle, as well as of his own recognition of its importance as a legal maxim, when he wrote in the mid-twelfth century to the clergy of Sens, and cited an "ancient rule" that everyone affected by an episcopal election should participate in that election.[3] The maxim itself brings together all the elements in the cluster of concepts mentioned earlier: consent, representation, and the representatives' mandate.

Q o t has long been known to have had considerable currency in the thirteenth century, where it was a familiar maxim in both civilian and canonical jurisprudence and texts. Its presence in the royal writ by which Edward I directed the calling of parliament in 1295 was taken by the great nineteenth-century English historian Bishop Stubbs as conclusive evidence that this gathering marked the beginning of the English parliamentary system.[4] Stubbs credited Edward with having raised *q o t* to the status of a constitutional principle, and thereby to have acknowledged a limitation on the royal prerogative. With the attention of medieval political historians thus drawn to it, the maxim *q o t* became a focus for much careful examination of medieval political documents and other texts; and its appearance and use have now been noted in a wide variety of sources and contexts, so much so that the uniqueness perceived by Stubbs in the Edwardian parliamentary call of 1295 must be severely qualified. It was employed by cathedral chapters to assert

3. "Omnibus scribendum fuit de eo quod spectat ad omnes": Bernard of Clairvaux *Epistolae* 236; English translation in Bernard, *Letters*. Cf. *Epistolae* 36.

4. Stubbs, *Constitutional History of England*, 3 vols. Helen Cam offered a recent summary of the Stubbs position: "To him [Stubbs], as to any nineteenth century Englishman, parliament stood for democracy, and its representative element was its essential feature. He sees the Anglo-Saxon Witan as the assembly of the people; the Anglo-Saxon *duris Regis* as inheriting its traditions and feudalism slowly broadening down to admit the representative element, deliberately incorporated by that 'buccaneering old Gladstone,' Simon de Montfort. Edward I, replacing the feudal by the national principle, arrived at the right formula in 1295; his son in the Statute of York defined the place of the Commons in the constitution; his grandson accepted their control over taxation. Such is Stubbs' picture." Cam, "Stubbs Seventy Years After," p. 195; cf. Edwards, *Historians and Medieval English Parliament*.

their rights to attend provincial councils, and was so confirmed by Honorius III in 1225–27;[5] Matthew Paris used it about 1240 as the basis for asserting the rights of archdeacons to be consulted before the higher prelates of England could grant a subsidy to the king;[6] it appeared as a *regula iuris* in the *Liber Sextus* issued by Boniface VIII as a compendium of canon law;[7] and it was the basis for his antagonist Philip IV's summons to the French estates general of 1302,[8] as it had been earlier for Frederick II's call to the cities of Tuscany in 1231 to send *nuntii* with full powers, and later the same year for his request to the commune of Genoa to send representatives to a meeting in Ravenna: Frederick is the first secular ruler known to have applied *q o t* by summoning proctors with mandates.[9] Even earlier, in 1200, Innocent III had summoned proctors to his *curia* from six cities of the March of Ancona; and he called a form of assembly again in 1207.[10] After mid-century this procedure was continued in both the Kingdom of Sicily and the Papal States, and became common also in Spain, England, and France.[11]

The principle of *q o t* itself can be found in the Justinian Code of 531, where it is invoked as a maxim of private law in respect of joint interests in a single issue: "What touches all similarly is to be approved by all" (*ut quod omnes similiter tangit, ab omnibus comprobetur*).[12]

---

5. *X* 3.10.10, cited in Post, *Studies*, p. 325, n. 253.

6. Matthew Paris *Chronica major* 4.57, cited in Post, *Studies*, p. 325, n. 254.

7. See n. 58, below.

8. Post, *Studies*, pp. 149, 165, and 166, n. 4. The references in nn. 5–8 are cited also in Post, "A Roman Legal Theory," p. 66, an article that is the best summary statement of Post's general thesis on the medieval legal meaning of consent. It is not reproduced in Post, *Studies*.

9. For the Tuscany meeting see *MGH, Leg.* 4.2.151–4; for the Ravenna meeting see *MGH, Leg.* 4.2.155; Huillard-Bréholles, *Historica diplomatica*, 4:266; and the *Annales* of Bartholomaeus Scriba in *MGH, SS.* 18.177–79. On representation in Frederick's southern kingdom see Calisse, *Storia del parlemento in Sicilia*, Appendix, 43 and 46; Marongui, *Istituto parlementare*, pp. 123–27; cited in Post, *Studies*, p. 89, n. 113.

10. Theiner, *Codex diplomaticus dominii temporalis Sanctae Sedis*, 1:42–43, cited in Post, *Studies*, p. 86, esp. nn. 102, 103.

11. Post, *Studies*, pp. 89–90.

12. The terminology in the formula varies in both Roman Law and medieval canonist and civilian repetition and interpretation. Sometimes *comprobetur* in the original Justinian text becomes *vocandi sunt*; sometimes *approbetur*; sometimes *consentietur*; sometimes the *similiter* becomes *equaliter*: see Post, *Studies*, pp. 168–80. Other Roman precedents that came to be associated with *q o t* are found in *Dig.* 10.2.27, 10.2.48, 11.1.1, and 39.3.9.1; *Cod.* 5.51.5; and especially Paulus's statement in *Dig.* 42.1.47. See

The issue for an understanding of the history of medieval political thought in respect of *q o t*, then, is not so much to discover its incidence of use, as to discern what its users understood the principle to mean. On its face the directive in a political document that "a matter affecting all should be considered and approved by all" appears as ready evidence of the constitutional principle that the people as a whole must be consulted and must approve legislation on any issue that affects them all. But was this its meaning in the medieval period? Certainly the notion of consent was a fundamental element in feudal society; the whole theoretical and legal fabric of feudalism rested on the concept of voluntary agreement between persons in respect of mutual services to be rendered. However, there was no feature of representation in the basic feudal relationship. The magnates and monarch of England who signed the Magna Carta in 1215, for example, consented to its terms,[13] but in doing so they did not represent anyone or anything: they agreed in and for themselves. Consultation was also an essential element in monarchical and other forms of ruling practice in the Middle Ages, being an integral feature of both feudal and ecclesiastical law, as well as reflecting an element embedded in centuries of custom.[14]

As formulated in one specific text in the Roman civil code, *q o t* laid down the rule that when several individuals had joint and indivisible rights or interests in a given matter, their joint administration could be ended only with the consent of all the individuals concerned.[15] The principle of *q o t* was in general use in Roman law, however, and had specific applications that varied somewhat from the one just noted. Another section in the Justinian Code stipulated that consent of all those having an interest must be obtained: for example, all those to whom joint water rights are due from the operation of an aqueduct must consent to any issue involving the aqueduct.[16] The code also held

---

McIlwain, *Constitutionalism, Ancient and Modern*, pp. 48 *ff.*; cf. Post, *Studies*, pp. 170–71. Post cites and quotes six texts on *q o t* from Roman sources: *Cod.* 5.59.5.2, *Dig.* 39.3.8, *Cod.* 11.59.7.2, *Dig.* 42.1.47, *Dig.* 11.2.1, and *Dig.* 11.2.2 (Post, *Studies*, p. 221), and cites a number of others: *Dig.* 39.3.9.1, *Dig.* 21.1.13.5, *Dig.* 40.9 30.4, *Dig.* 42.1.36.39, *Dig.* 50.1.19 and 160.1, *Dig.* 11.2.1, and *Dig.* 11.2.2. (Post, *Studies*, pp. 169–75).

13. See William S. McKechnie, *Magna Carta*.

14. An interesting illustration from early-thirteenth-century England is the much-disputed speech attributed to Archbishop Hubert of Canterbury on the occasion of the "election" of King John: see *Statesman's Book*, pp. xlviii–xlix, quoting Matthew Paris, *Chronica major*, Rolls series, 57.2:454 and 455.

15. *Cod.* 5.59.5.2.

16. Ulpian, *Dig.* 39.38; cited in Post, *Studies*, p. 169, n. 10.

that a judgment falls equally on all the plaintiffs or defendants having a joint interest as parties to a given case.[17]

What the Roman legal maxim *q o t* asserted generally was that the rights and interests of all the individuals combined in a joint matter or "thing" must always be taken into account in a manner consistent with their interests in the joint matter. This did not always mean that individual voluntary consent from each of the individually concerned parties was necessary for the joint matter to be disposed of. Sometimes this specific form of consent was necessary, but sometimes it was not; the precise character of the relationship the individuals had to the joint matter determined what was required of each of them in terms of consent. "What touches all must be approved by all," then, did not always mean in Roman law that no action could take place on a matter of joint or common interest without the specific individual consent of all parties concerned. What it meant, rather, at least in terms of what might be called its common-denominator meaning across a broad spectrum of use, was that all persons jointly concerned in a matter had to be given a hearing and offered an opportunity for defence of such rights and interests in that matter as they possessed. As a minimum it guaranteed access to the courts for anyone having an interest or right (*ius*) in a given matter, as well as the right to be heard.

The revived interest in and study of Roman law in the twelfth century had led to the rediscovery of this maxim; and the imagination and ingenuity of the new breed of medieval legists put it to use in a wide variety of civil and canonical legal issues. The formula *q o t* was known to Gratian in its Roman origins, as already mentioned; he made reference to it several times, although not specifically with respect to the role of the people in expressing consent. For his own reasons Gratian seems to have suppressed any reference to the maxim coming from Roman legal sources, just as he was inclined to do whenever he used other elements from Roman law. And when he did employ *q o t* it was not in connection with his advocacy of the role of the people in expressing consent (in the matter of episcopal election). Gratian's use of the maxim was with reference to issues of joint clerical concern, administrative and jurisdictional.

The prevalence of citation of *q o t* by many canonists and legists subsequent to the appearance of Gratian's *Decretum* has long been

17. Ulpian, *Dig.* 3.3.31.1, 3.5.30.7; *Cod.* 3.40: Wenger, *Institutes of Roman Law*, p. 89; cf. Yves Congar, "Quod omnes tangit," p. 211, nn. 3 and 4.

known, as has the prevalence of its use in ecclesiastical court procedures as early as the middle of the twelfth century. No particular significance has usually been attached to these data, however, some historians having been inclined to ignore the evidence or dismiss it as involving little more than a rhetorical flourish.[18] The frequency and form of its use in this period, nonetheless, require more careful consideration.

When adjudicating an issue involving the appointment of a rural dean, Pope Innocent III used *q o t* directly; he held that deans should be appointed with the joint consent of bishop and archdeacon, inasmuch as a dean's responsibilities and authority relate to both these offices.[19] The same pontiff also quoted *q o t* explicitly elsewhere, noting that it had the authority of a Roman imperial judgment. He observed, in a letter to the Latin patriarch of Constantinople in 1206, that the very nature of law, itself a postulate of justice, stipulated that nothing should be decided to the prejudice of anyone who had been neither summoned nor convicted nor absent by his own fault.[20] Innocent had been trained in the law at Bologna, and illustrates here a commn tendency among twelfth-century canonists to use Roman law almost as an auxiliary to canon law, referring normally to the authoritative character of the laws of Justinian.

A gloss of the period 1210–14 on one of Innocent's decretals, relating to a case involving the archbishop of York and the rector of a hospital, refers directly to two locations in the Justinian Code where *q o t* is expressed, although the text of Innocent did not quote the maxim directly.[21] Johannes Teutonicus in a gloss written about 1217 on another Innocent III decretal also invoked the maxim directly.[22] St. Bernard of Clairvaux shows that the maxim was known and in use in ecclesiastical affairs in the mid-twelfth century when he wrote about

---

18. Pasquet, *Origins of House of Commons*, pp, 25, 173 *ff.*; Petit-Dutaillis and Lefebre, *Studies and Notes*, p. 345; White, *Making of English Constitution*; Pollard, *Evolution of Parliament*, p. 59; Jolliffe, *Constitutional History of England*, pp. 349 *ff.*; Riess, *History of English Electoral Law*, p. 2 and n. 4; Adams, *Constitutional History of England*, p. 186. Post offers a survey assessment of other earlier interpretations of *q o t*: *Studies*, pp. 166–67.

19. X 1.23.7, cited by Post, *Studies*, p. 171, n. 26. Cf. Gratian, C.7 q.10 c.1.

20. X 1. q.33, c.8; cf. Gratian, C.8.10.1.33; cited in Post, *Studies*, p. 171, n. 25.

21. The gloss quotes the maxim as "omnes enim vocari debent quos casa tangit," and cites *Cod.*5.59.5.2 and *Dig.* 39.3.8. The gloss itself is on X 2.28.48, and is found in the *Apparatus* to Compilatio 3.2.19 (De appellat.) c.6, ad 5, cited in Post, *Studies*, p. 172, and n. 27.

22. "Omnes illi quos res tangit vocandi sunt," supported by Teutonicus with a reference to Paulus, *Dig.* 42.1.27, cited by Post, *Studies*, p. 172 and n. 28.

1143–44, apropos of a controversy surrounding the appointment of William Fitzherbert as archbishop of York, that "everyone involved in an issue should have been consulted" (*omnibus scribendum fuit de eo quod spectat ad omnes*).[23] Innocent IV, undoubtedly the most distinguished of the medieval canonist-popes, commented on a decretal of Alexander III that "agreement by all who are touched by the matter is necessary in the consideration of the matter as well as in its voluntary disposition."[24]

Representative samples from both canonist and civilian sources of the twelfth and thirteenth centuries exist in ample numbers to show the currency of *q o t* and the developing tendency to apply it in a variety of ways. Legists and canonists at this time brought the Justinian maxim into use over all kinds of several-, joint-, and common-rights issues, and applied it imaginatively to different issues: the rights were individual rights, with individual consent indispensable if any change were to be made, when the matter pertained to all severally, as when several persons had an easement, or when two or more prelates or administrators had administrative rights in common, or when several individuals or corporations (or individuals and corporations jointly) had rights to patronage or presentation.[25] A formal legal maxim containing the element of consent underwent gradual development and application. The civilians and canonists formulated as a general maxim that every kind of legal right (*ius*) was accompanied by the right of consent. An early thirteenth-century decretist asserted that "the consent of all is required whose right (*ius*) may be taken away," meaning that consent is required of all who have any power or authority in respect of the matter involved.[26] The great English canonist and civilian jurist at Oxford, William of Drogheda, referred about 1239 to the *Digest* texts on servitude to support his view that if a proctor is appointed in the presence of a judge, the judge's consent as well as that of the litigants was necessary.[27]

But what was the nature of this "consent" that was required? It seems that while consent was required from all who had rights in an issue, the

23. Bernard of Clairvaux, Epistolae 236, in *S. Bernardi Opera*, 8.

24. Innocent IV in *Apparatus on X*, 1.36, cited by both Post and Congar. For other instances of medieval usage of *q o t* see Post, *Studies*, pp. 171–80; Congar, "Quod omnes tangit," pp. 189–96.

25. Post, *Studies*, p. 175.

26. Post, "A Roman Legal Theory," p. 69.

27. Post cites a number of instances where William employs *q o t* and quotes its Roman sources in *Studies*, pp. 192–96.

nature of the consent required might be different as the relevant rights in an issue might differ. There could be different rights in respect of different parties to the same issue. Consent, then, need not be equally shared, even though it might be commonly shared. The significance of consent in this legal context seems to have been procedural at base.

The legal activity that began with respect to matters involving common and several rights and the consent appropriate to them occurred both on continental Europe and in England during the latter half of the twelfth and the early thirteenth centuries. But it also had begun by the end of the twelfth century to extend into the sphere of corporate and community rights as reflected, for example, in the growth of English common-law procedure. It was long the practice in England for every hundred, vill, and borough to send representatives to the county court, and apparently a vote of taxes sometimes was made there. The oldest unit to be represented in English administrative practice was the vill, in 1110; the shire and the hundred were accorded representation in 1166, and the cathedral chapter in 1226. Hence, this concession of the right of representation in England precedes the actual adoption of the *q o t* formula.[28] In addition, there was the purely procedural sense in which four knights of the shire represented the county court when they carried its record of cases to the king's court. This latter practice was not corporate representation as such, but merely part of the administrative machinery of late-twelfth-century English government. But shortly the system acquired new significance, and the notion of these knights actually embodying the element of representation of the rights of the knights of the shire as a community, and as such conveying it to the king's court, began to emerge.[29] Thus, the meaning of consent in respect of community or political rights is inextricably bound up in this period with the history and character of civil and canon law.

Of course, there is a sense in which the principle of consent in association with rights is a natural and relatively ubiquitous feature of any society, discernable in primitive as well as in sophisticated forms of social organization. The phenomenon of affording the right of consent in some fashion to the community as a whole existed in early Christian communities regarding the choice of leader, as we have seen;[30] it has been observed, too, in Jewish history and in early Celtic and Germanic

28. Cam, *Law-Finders*, pp. 168–69.
29. Post, *Studies*, p. 200; cf. Plucknett, *History of Common Law*, p. 140.
30. See Part 1, 6.

tribal societies. It can be found in a more specified form in early Frankish private law, where the consent of all of several occupiers of a piece of land was needed for a new settler to be admitted;[31] and also in an informal but trenchant fashion in the demands of the revolting Norman peasantry in 997.[32] Law and custom in the feudal period of western Europe also protected many types of joint and common rights. Development of the Christian concepts of community and of the Church as some type of a unity in which all its members shared a "mystical body," in St. Paul's phrase, also must have contributed strongly to the concern for how the Church's members might express themselves and participate freely in its reality.

Many factors, then, lie behind the medieval impulse to give expression to the element of consent as an essential feature of organized society; and it would be a mistake to single out only one to explain the particular meaning and form the element took in this particular era. Nonetheless, the particular legal developments that did occur in the twelfth and early thirteenth centuries provided a form through which the notion of consent could be given meaning, and greatly stimulated efforts both to give it expression and to specify its meaning. Such activity occurred in both ecclesiastical and temporal spheres, in both of which centralizing political and administrative pressures were very apparent. Cross-fertilization of legal and administrative concepts and procedures was common, and much more widespread than many earlier medieval historians have been prepared to recognize and acknowledge.

The Roman legal maxim *q o t* had been in use in the medieval Church in the twelfth century in respect of canonical appointments to church office and as a general legal principle. Its value in developing and reinstituting proper procedures for the canonical election of bishops has already been mentioned.[33] It can be seen, too, as a principle at work in the group activity of the Church as a whole, where the issue was the rights of the individual and protection of personal liberty: decisions by a group (collegial or corporate person) only applied to the individual members of the group in respect of their personal goods and obligations to the extent that such decisions had been approved by each

31. Kuebner, "Settlement and Colonization," p. 34, with reference to the Salic law, *Titulus de migrantibus*, p. 45. Cf. Post, *Studies*, p. 181 and n. 56.

32. William of Jumièges, *Gesta Normanorum ducum*, pp. 73, *ff.*, cited in Richardson, "Origins of Parliament," p. 176, n. 2.

33. Part 2, 4.

and every one of them.[34] A useful distinction was soon formulated between what touches all as individuals (*ut singuli*) and what touches all as members of a group (*ut collegiati*). In cases of the former the consent of each individual was required in respect of what touched his individual rights. In cases of the latter only the consent of the collegial whole was required, although each individual member of the whole must be able to exercise his rights of membership in the whole: for example, by being summoned to the corporate consideration of the matter and by being able to participate through voting in the group decision, which might then carry by majority vote with the dissenting voters bound by the majority group decision.

The maxim *q o t* can also be seen in the conciliar activities of the thirteenth-century Church, and historians have been right to see it and its importance in the letter *Vineam domini* of 19 April 1213, by which Innocent III invited participants to the Fourth Lateran Council,[35] and wherein he asserted that he wished to convoke an ecumenical council according to the practices of the early Fathers to discuss serious matters concerning the common interest of all the faithful. Precedents for this manner of convocation can be found in the twelfth century, of which the calling of the Third Lateran Council by Alexander III in 1179 is only one example.[36] It was at the latter, as well, that the Church formulated the position that clerics could not be subject to taxation by any temporal authority unless they consented to be so taxed (*quod omnes tangit ab omnibus approbari debet*, with a clerical twist!).[37]

Significantly, the maxim was seen to be applicable to monetary exactions on the clergy from ecclesiastical powers as well. Innocent III was the first medieval pope to conceive the idea of following temporal rulers in the tendency to impose taxes on the clergy; he considered a general levy for papal curial needs, but never implemented his plan. In fact, the medieval papacy was never markedly successful in levying taxes on its own clergy; and one of the bulwarks regularly mounted by the clergy in defence of their financial autonomy *vis-à-vis* the papacy was the invocation of *q o t*. Not even the papacy had the power to levy taxes by unilateral decision. Such an action touched all (and all individually, in some sense); therefore, approval by all was required, that is, free consent by those being taxed. Pope Honorius III attempted

---

34. Congar, "Quod omnes tangit," p. 215.
35. Ibid., p. 215, and n. 22. Cf. Foreville, Représentation et taxation du clergé."
36. Congar, "Quod omnes tangit," p. 216, and n. 25.
37. Ibid., pp. 217–18, and n. 29.

to levy a general tax on the clergy through the bull, *Super muros Jerusalem*, of 28 January 1225; but when his legate presented the papal directive to the synod of Bourges on 30 November of that year, he was met with a formal reply from the assembled French clergy that "they were astonished not to have been consulted on this matter which is of special interest to us, and about which agreement by one individual or another would count for nothing since the matter touches every-one..."[38] A papal legate sought a levy of 1 per cent of clerical revenues on behalf of the papacy at a French church council held in Paris on 8 November 1263; the bishops in council refused the papal demand, and then proceeded to grant a much lesser amount. They asserted that "the prelates concerned agreed voluntarily [to make a grant of money] and not from any requirement to accept the subvention specified for the Holy Land in the lord pope's letter, not out of any coercion, but freely."[39] A similar example of English clerical recalcitrance based on *q o t* can be seen in the Council of Westminster, 13 January 1226.[40]

Q o t had obvious value in connection with opposition among potential taxpayers, and was used for their own purposes by both clerical and lay taxpayers as a defence against calls on their purse. It was also highly useful as a procedural maxim in ecclesiastical jurisdic-tional and administrative issues, and had been so used from at least the middle of the twelfth century. By the thirteenth century it was beginning to assume the character of a general principle. What did its users understand it to mean?

The maxim *q o t* was used from the time of Innocent III in two different senses, to address two distinguishable issues in the area of legal theory and practice. On the one hand, and consistent with its original formulation in Roman civil law, it embodied a principle of legal procedure, guaranteeing in effect that at a minimum every

---

38. Ibid., p. 218, and n. 32.

39. Cited in Gaudemet, "Aspects de législation conciliare." Post cites a similar incident concerning the French clergy's objection to a papal demand for taxes to support a war in 1264; in this case, however, the objection failed: Post, *Studies*, p. 147, n. 181; cf. Congar, "Quod omnes tangit," p. 215; Foreville, "Représentation et taxation."

40. Congar, "Quod omnes tangit," p. 219, citing Matthew Paris at n. 35. See also the English clergy's objection to papal assessment without invoking *q o t*, at London, 1245: *Councils and Synods*, p. 391. A good summary of the meaning of consent involved in English royal efforts to develop a system of public taxation in the twelfth and thirteenth centuries is Harriss, *King, Parliament*, pp. 3–159; a bibliography on the origins of medieval public taxation is at p. 3, n. 1. Cf. Foreville, "Représentation et taxation," for an early French example of the clerical tax issue.

individual affected by a matter under litigation had a right to be summoned to and heard in any court exercising jurisdiction over the matter at issue. On the other hand, it was seen to reflect at least something of the character of a general principle advocating consultation and consent in some formal way from all those whose interests were an issue in a public or community matter.

The examples of the maxim already mentioned fall largely but not exclusively into the first category of procedural meaning and interpretation. Some of the actual instances of its use that have been cited are sufficiently ambiguous in meaning to make it difficult to place them exclusively in either of these two categories of meaning. The element of procedure is seemingly always present, but the more general meaning may be present in some of the documents as well, although less clearly so. In fact, the ambiguity of meaning may well be present in the documents and in the historical circumstances themselves, with differing parties to the issue assuming different interpretations of $q \, o \, t$. In instances where there is a conflict of interests the parties in conflict often tend to construe things differently and to their own advantage.

It is sometimes very difficult to know precisely what $q \, o \, t$ meant in a given medieval context. Its formulations and applications in the thirteenth century have been analysed very carefully by Gaines Post, who summarized the legal activity surrounding the maxim with the conclusion that the thirteenth-century lawyers borrowed and fused together three notions that freed the classical meaning of $q \, o \, t$ from its narrow application to consent in the procedural aspects of the private law of joint rights, and made it applicable to the government of communities. The three principles were: (1) the right of the majority in a corporation or other community to determine an issue even in the presence of a dissenting minority; (2) continuance of the classical procedural principle that made consent by all who had interests an intrinsic feature of due process; (3) subordination of consent, both of individuals and of the majority as well, to the idea of corporate, community, or common good—the public welfare, of which it was acknowledged that the ruler was the sole protector and judge.[41]

So interpreted, at least in terms of the legal theory it conveyed in the thirteenth century, $q \, o \, t$ was something less than a constitutional

41. Post, "A Roman Legal Theory," pp. 71–73. The distinction between the king as a person and the Crown, found in both Glanville and Bracton, certainly qualified the view that the ruler was the sole judge of the common good, at least in England.

principle providing limitation on the royal authority by requiring actual popular consent through representatives of the people to royal decisions. According to theory, at any rate, what constrained or limited the king's activities was the traditional limitation of his being bound by the law; it was the law that required him to summon all those in his kingdom who had an interest in the issues of state or who would be affected by royal actions in respect of these issues.

The ruler had long been required by private feudal law to consult and obtain the consent of his barons to measures that affected their interests; there was nothing new on this front in the thirteenth-century theory of $q o t$, except perhaps the improved specifications for how this consent was to be asked for and expressed. The theory of summoning and the consenting, then, did not reflect a developing notion of the political sovereignty of the people; it reflected a specific instance of the king being bound by the law. And it seems that a further legal concept was being fitted alongside this traditional element of the king having to obtain consent for all extraordinary measures he wished to undertake and that "touched all"; namely, that the king as embodiment of the common good, as regent of the polity standing in the place of the whole community, had a peculiar and unique responsibility for the state of the kingdom as a whole.[42] Roman law had held that any important matter touching the state of the realm touched the king and was his business, and that the public business of the ruler in his public office was sometimes the business of the people as a whole (*populus*).[43] In this position his judgment was unique and not to be gainsaid; the king was superior in authority here both by law and by tradition.

Accordingly, the consent of those he was obliged to call to his parliaments had to be construed in the light of the king's ultimate authority over matters of state; it might mean merely that the king was required to call "all who were touched"; it might even mean that those who were called had an obligation to appear; it might mean further that, having been called, those who were called had the right to state what their interests in the matter were, and perhaps the right to object to the king's proposals; but the theory did not encompass the right of those called to deny the king his requests. Feudal law afforded the barons the right to deny any request going beyond the limits of their

42. See Post, "Ratio publicae utilitatis;" *Studies*, pp. 310–414. The latter section of *Studies* offers a detailed examination of the concept of the royal prerogative considered as superior to other interests because related to the common good, society as a whole.
43. *Cod.* 6.51.1.

feudal contract; and presumably this ground could be claimed by the king's subjects in insisting that their consent was required. But the theory here envisaged a role for the ruler involving more than that of superior party in a personal contract: the notion of the ruler as protector and judge of the common good was a thrust towards the non-feudal concept of sovereignty.

The theory may well have run this way; the case for so interpreting the legal history of western Europe in the thirteenth century is both intriguing and plausible. But political realities seldom move only on fuel from theoretical sources. Practical realities such as the interests and determination of the personalities concerned, as well as the actual circumstances themselves, are factors often at least as significant.

B. Representation

There is another important theoretical question as well, which bears on the meaning of consent as an element of popular sovereignty. Those called to a parliament or estates general in a public and "political" application of the maxim $q\,o\,t$ in some sense can be recognized as "representatives." But of what are they representative; precisely what does the notion "to represent" mean here? Another exigesis on medieval terminology and its meaning is called for.[44]

The notion of representation is closely associated with the element of popular consent in many forms of democratic polity. This is particularly true in respect of modern democratic representative theory, where it is accepted as virtually self-evident that a direct form of democracy, where every individual citizen has the right and the opportunity to participate in legislative decision making, is simply not feasible in the large constituencies that are a normal feature of today's states. A certain nostalgia may still reside in some democratic imaginations for the recreation of a dimly remembered and often distorted impression of the meetings of all the citizens in the agora of a Greek city-state, each speaking his mind and each casting a vote on the issues under discussion. But however attractive to the memory and imagination, such scenes are recognized as things that can never be in the present: the people in a modern polity are simply too numerous, and hence the notion of getting them all together for discussion and decision making is unrealistic.

---

44. Documentation on the medieval conception of representation is also voluminous, although frequently the same bibliographical data refer also to the $q\,o\,t$ dictum: see n. 1 above.

Mechanisms for the working of many modern democratic forms of polity, accordingly, come equipped with some method by which the people are "represented" in the activities of legislating and governmental decision making. Only some, relatively few, citizens actually engage in the practice of government; the exercise of governmental authority, nonetheless, is held to be democratic because all the people still express themselves indirectly; they elect those who govern. The people consent to being governed by a relatively small group of lawmakers who represent the people as a whole. Citizens of a democracy, so the theory goes, are governed by the persons they choose to represent them; they consent to being ruled by persons they themselves choose as their representatives. So closely are the notions of consent and representation woven together in a modern theory of democratic polity that it is often difficult to disentangle one from the other. But if consent and representation are nowadays closely connected and understood in terms of one another, this has not always been the case throughout the history of the development of political systems. For this reason, just as it was necessary to examine the notion of consent in its medieval meaning and use, the same must be done for the concept of representation and for the issue of the correlation between the two.

Not surprisingly, the use and meaning of the notion of representation exhibits a similar history to that of consent. Its meaning, and more specifically its meaning and use in connection with the sort of notion that comes almost automatically to the mind of a modern student of political theory, developed only slowly during the medieval period. The rather precise and technical meaning almost unconsciously connoted by the modern term was not present in the earliest instances of its use among medieval writers, simply because the notion of one person standing in place of another for the performance of public acts was not a commonplace one. Again it was the development and expansion of the study and practice of law in the twelfth century that was responsible for the development of the concept of representation; and again it was the canon lawyers rather than their civilian counterparts who led the way.

As we have seen, the Church underwent considerable administrative expansion and centralization throughout the twelfth century; and, accordingly, it was within the Church that there was an increasing need for the development of procedures to ensure uniformity and equity across distance. As the medieval Church reactivated its perception of the value of an organized and centralized ecclesiastical society in the

aftermath of the Gregorian reform movement, and as the consequences of this revitalizing activity spread throughout western Europe
in terms of church expansion, there was a need for the Church as a
religious community to develop a means of expressing itself as a whole,
as well as the need to develop practical methods for the administration
of this burgeoning and increasingly complex social institution. The
serious beginnings of sustained efforts to exercise political control over
large geographical areas, especially noticeable in England in the
twelfth century, also stimulated the development of instruments and
institutions for the exercise of a centralized public administration.

Feudal and Germanic law had made it difficult for any but principal
parties, administrators of communities, and feudal lords to function in
court; and when they did so they seem to have acted directly for
themselves, that is, they offered consent (or otherwise) directly and on
their own behalf as the persons involved. The revival of Roman and
canon law acted as both cause and effect to the growing sophistication
in secular and ecclesiastical administrations, and produced a development of concepts and procedures that superseded the limited character of feudal law. These new concepts eventually made possible the
articulation of a new theory of polity.

Roman law also contained maxims that gave specification to vaguely
retained notions of political authority residing in the community as a
whole and passing to the ruler through some kind of consent. Thus,
the notion that somehow power rested on a collective base, never wholly
lost through the early medieval period because of various stimuli
available from both Christian community traditions and Germanic
sources, received support from formal legal authorities of standing,
and became an object of interest to both canonists and civilians. Not
that the Roman sources offered an unmixed and uniform set of
maxims for the education and edification of medieval students of law.
Alongside the dictum that political authority derives from the people
ultimately and the principle of *quod omnes tangit*, for example, one can
also find the *lex regia*, interpreted to mean that the people had
permanently ceded all power to the ruler.[45] It was to be some time
before these various and apparently conflicting *dicta* on the nature of
temporal political authority and the place of popular consent in it were
reconciled in a formulation expressing a modern representative theory
of democratic polity.

45. *Dig.* 1.4.1.

In addition to *q o t*, two other Roman-derived concepts came gradually into play in the realm of medieval private law, with implications and
advantages that were then extended widely in both ecclesiastical and
temporal jurisdictions. They were the concept of corporation as a
collective or corporate entity (*universitas*)[46] that itself could be considered a person, and the concept of proctor or procurator (*procurator*) as
an individual able to embody, represent, function in place of another
(first, another individual but very soon a corporate person as well).[47]
When these two notions came fully into play, and the meaning of
representation was given a base in the individual rights of all members
of a political society, the theory of modern parliamentary democracy
with its employment of elected representatives possessed of legislative
authority became fully coherent.

The concept of corporation or *universitas* developed slowly in the
late twelfth century, the term itself being used to designate something
other than the person of feudal and Germanic law who had been identified simply as a real individual. A corporation was a fictive person, a
group of individual persons having a common interest; the corporate
person or corporation was then conceived of as the seat of the rights
and interest of the community as a whole. The concept of proctor was
simply that of one person functioning on behalf of another; and as one
might expect it came into use first in terms of one real person acting on
behalf of another real person. Only with the development of the notion
of corporation as a person could the concept of proctor be applied to
corporate person; and only then could the notion of a corporate entity
being "represented" by a single individual begin to acquire meaning.

Until about the middle of the twelfth century there is little evidence
in legal literature to indicate the use of the notion of proctors, and what
evidence there is shows an application of the concept in terms of the
representation of individual persons only. Gratian apparently was
familiar with the function of proctor only as an agent for real
individuals and individual churches, not for corporations. But very
shortly thereafter examples begin to appear among the canonical
jurists of reference to proctors as legal representatives of corporations.[48] It was through the activity of the decretists working in the
second half of the twelfth century that this procedure concerning

46. See Post's research on the development of corporate identity at the University of
Paris: "Parisian Masters Corporation."
47. See Post, *Studies*, pp. 61–162.
48. Ibid., pp. 56, 63.

corporations and representation, the origins of which the canonists had found in Roman legal principles, was given widespread application in ecclesiastical courts. More important than the theoretical formulations involving these notions, however, was the extensive application to which they were put. The mid-century activities of Pope Eugene III (1145–53), contemporary of Gratian, Bernard of Clairvaux, and John of Salisbury, and himself thoroughly trained in both Roman and canon law, encouraged the dissemination of Roman legal principles of this sort. By the end of the twelfth century another papal expert in the two laws, Innocent III (1198–1216), was making widespread use of ecclesiastical corporations and proctors in canonical practice; and canonists of the period became very active in applying and expanding the notions of corporation and proctor to a wide variety of ecclesiastical litigation and administration.[49]

The last third of the twelfth century also saw the appearance of references to corporations and their representatives become much more common in both laws. Civilian as well as canonical jurists began to adapt the Roman procedure to both secular and ecclesiastical courts, although practical acceptance of the new notions and the more sophisticated procedures seems to have been slow. The practice of corporate representation was almost non-existent before 1150; and it was not in common use except in the Church until the last quarter of the century, even in Italy.[50] But after the first decade of the thirteenth century, the system of corporate representation by agents given full powers grew steadily. Innocent III played an important, if not original and decisive, role in adapting the new method of representing communities in ecclesiastical and secular assemblies. The Italian communes in this way became familiar with a breadth of legal experience, formulae, and procedures developed by legists and canonists that enabled them to give constitutional expression to their developing political forms; and other temporal jurisdictions began to show evidence of similar benefits throughout the thirteenth century.[51]

Development of a system of proctorial representation for corporate communities lay behind the thirteenth-century examples of the calling of great assemblies in both ecclesiastical and temporal jurisdictions. But what did "representation" signify in these circumstances? The concept of representation needs also to be understood in its medieval

49. Ibid., pp. 66–67.
50. Ibid., p. 68.
51. Ibid., p. 88.

context, for it is another of the essential elements in a modern theory of parliamentary democracy. This means that it must carefully be connected with, but at the same time distinguished from, the two notions of corporation and proctor. For there is a sense in which the procurator can be said to "represent," to be the representative of the corporate entity whose authority he bears; and indeed the term "represent" (*repraesentare*) is used in medieval documents precisely to designate this function. But the traditional medieval theory of corporation did not yet contain the notion of representation associated with the modern theory of democracy, although the beginnings of the development of that notion can be found in this era. The idea of representation arose almost insensibly at first in the religious community, where the notion of bringing together in some way the whole Church can be seen to underlie the actual late-twelfth and thirteenth-century efforts of various popes to hold general Church councils. It has been maintained that, without even using the term explicitly, Pope Clement V gave a precise meaning to representation for the first time when he invited certain bishops to come together for the purpose of sending common delegates to the Council of Vienna in 1311, a gathering consciously intended to be and accepted as being a representation of the universal Church.[52] What was striking about this event from the point of view of our interest in the theory of consent was the clear awareness of the gathering as embodying the notion of a collective unity, a social community, and of it having been brought together for the defence and advancement of the common interests of the Christian community as a whole.

Twelfth-century jurists had begun to be aware of the notion of corporation and of its value in dealing with the increasing complexities of administration and jurisdiction in both temporal and ecclesiastical polities. At the same time, the more theoretical aspects of the problem of what representation was present in those exercising authority were coming under consideration, however indirectly. The functioning communes of the Italian city-states, for example, gave focus to some of the canonist views. Applying the principles as they understood them of how the ruler represents his subjects, they described elected magistrates in a commune as acting in the place of the commune itself (the *universitas*), and of all the members of the *universitas*. In the words of one historian of the period they thus began "arriving at the formula-

---

52. Lagarde, "Idée de représentation."

tion of the idea of representation before the term itself came into use."[53]

The *Glossa ordinaria* speaks of "decurial leaders who act for the community as a whole and are deputies for the whole state" (*decuriones qui praesunt universitatis et deputata loco totius civitatis*).[54] Pillius speaks of those "who having been elected by all have power conferred on them by all" (*cum omnibus sint electi ab omnibus est eis concesse potestas*).[55] Hugolinus deduced the modern concept of representation from this idea of election: "the whole or the greater part, or those elected by the greater part of the community, act accordingly as the community as a whole would act" (*quod universalis vel maior pars, vel illi qui a maiore parte universitati electe sunt, faciunt perinde est ac si tota universitas faceret*).[56] And Roffredus asserted that "what was done by order of the consuls of a camp was seen to have been done by order of all of the citizens,"[57] a maxim recalled explicitly by Boniface VIII in the *Regulae iuris*, 68 and 72.[58] What is apparent here is the realization of the value of giving procedural specification to a theoretical concept. Perhaps the clearest medieval (and later) expression of this value appears in the assertion, which is both theoretical (via definition) and procedurally conclusive, that the weightier part (*sanior pars*) of any group *is* the majority (*maior pars*). Acceptance of this definition identifies the procedure (method) whereby the community expresses its will.

Thirteenth-century canonists working at applying such principles to the Church made them more precise, while at the same time, however, moving specifically away from the element of communal delegation of authority to the ruler. They were less interested in how the community power which lay behind the authority exercising it came voluntarily into its possessor's hands from the different members of the community, than in the explicit but simple notion that he held it from the community. The issue of how the ecclesiastical authority, pope, bishop, or abbot, came by his authority was of sustained interest among canonists and theologians at this time largely only through the "back door," so to speak. The issue of how a ruler acquired his authority

---

53. Ibid., p. 432.
54. *Glossa ordinaria* 1.160, cited by Lagarde, "Idée de représentation," p. 432, n. 2.
55. The Pillius text is also cited by Lagarde, ibid.
56. Hugolinus, cited by Lagarde, ibid.
57. Roffredus *Quaestiones sabbathiae* 27, cited by Lagarde, ibid.
58. Boniface VIII *Regulae iuris* 68 and 72, cited by Lagarde, ibid.

came into focus from the perspective of how it might be taken from him in circumstances where he abused it. Though not doing so entirely adequately (some of the monastic constitutions being an exception), ecclesiastical and canonical writers did address the problem of how a malevolent or perverse spiritual authority, even a pope, might be removed from office. And here the theoretical notion that his authority devolved on him in some way from the community over whom he exercised it could be put to use.

Late-thirteenth-century civilian jurists who addressed the same general issue of how an authority represented or acted for his community were more successful in beginning to delineate the notion of how power transferred from people to "representative," though still without a clear modern specification for the term, and without employing it. In mid-century Roffredus (d. 1250) spoke of the magistrate as "representing the image of the whole state" (*totius civitatis imaginem repraesent*).[59] Later, taking advantage of groundwork laid by the canonists in respect of the development of the concept of personification of collective life, and less deterred by the idea of treating the concept of the people in terms that dissociated it from the individuals who constituted it, jurists came to associate the idea of representation naturally with the fiction of a collective personality (public corporation). Albert of Gandino inquired specifically whether a community could plead in a criminal court through a proctor. His first response was in the negative, on the grounds that every private person must appear himself and that, inasmuch as the *universitas* is embodied in the single person who stands for the whole community, that person represents the power of the [corporation's] one person, and hence the ruler himself must appear. But he goes on to say that, in a second sense, it must be admitted that the syndic precisely represents the fictive personality of the whole community (*repraesentat vicem universitatis*); and if the syndic is thus representative, his being present can be taken as if the *universitas* were present in person.[60] Here is a text clearly designating a political authority as representing (in the modern sense of that term) the community over which he has authority. The term was so employed from the end of the thirteenth century, by jurists first;

59. Lagarde, "Idée de représentation," p. 433, and n. 49.
60. Albert of Gandino *Tractatus de maleficiis*, reproduced at the end of *Tractatus de maleficiis*, ed. Venice, 1584; cited by Lagarde, "Idée de représentation," p. 433, n. 59.

and beginning with Bartolus of Sassoferrato[61] it became common currency.[62]

The term "representation" did not receive any very precise political of juridical meaning, however, during the century in which it began to receive concrete expression. The term "to represent" was itself ancient, appearing in classical glossaries in connection with the concept of justice, and in classical literature in the sense of "to reproduce"; it appears once in Tertullian with the modern connotation.[63] A typical thirteenth century theological meaning for the term can be seen in Thomas Aquinas's use of it in the *Summa theologiae*, where it connotes the etymological sense of image or allegory.[64] It appears frequently with this meaning in a political context also; a temporal or ecclesiastical authority, prince, king, ruler, pope, bishop et al., is said to "represent" (in the sense of being an image or a symbol of) the community over which he exercises authority. In this meaning there is a fusion of the classical meaning of jurisdiction with the Christian element of allegory.[65] The term underwent a somewhat different transformation in meaning among both the civilian and canonical jurists of the Middle Ages; and it was their efforts that finally produced the modern meaning for the term. By the beginning of the fourteenth century, they were beginning to use "represent" to express the personification of a collective life and to determine the rights of the instrument or individual charged with its interests. The juridical reality being represented, however, was not the same for all.

There are two distinct elements in this evolved notion of representation: that of personification of a collective life, and the designation of the instrument representative of the collective life. The second of these may seem the more important, because it is precisely this feature that occurs first to the modern mind when the concept of representation is involved, and because historical reflection leads rather easily to the realization that the technique for designating a representative instrument or entity and for bringing it into being was likely to have been

61. There is a biography and account of Bartolus's doctrines produced early in this century: Woolf, *Bartolus of Sassoferrato.*

62. Lagarde, "Idée de représentation," p. 434 and n. 2.

63. Tertullian *De jejuniis* 13, cited in Lagarde, "Idée de représentation," p. 434 and n. 2.

64. Thomas Aquinas *S.T.* 1–2. 95.3.

65. Cf. Kantorowicz, *King's Two Bodies*, esp. pp. 273–313.

developed over time as the need for it was perceived. Yet the element of personification of a collective entity is equally important; and it is the more crucial of the two when trying to locate the medieval origins of democratic constitutional theory. For while it is possible to find many instances of the notion of representation in medieval political texts, the meaning normally conveyed is that of symbolic representation or personification of an entity that is a whole, conceived of as an abstraction, rather than a collective whole constituted of individual parts. Thus, for example, when John of Salisbury and even later Thomas Aquinas spoke of a political ruler as "representing" the people,[66] what they had in mind was that the ruler in some allegorical, symbolic way embodied or personified the whole community. Not as an individual, of course, but in virtue of holding office the ruler "was" the community as a whole. He stood for the community as their regent, the one who exercised power "for them," the power of the universal whole.

This notion can be seen in fully explicit form in Aquinas, when he uses the term "represent" and the notion of the ruler as "he who has the power of the whole" (*vis universitatis*) in the same text.[67] In this sense the community is not so much a collective whole of individual members each with individual rights as a part of the whole, as it is an abstraction or, better, an image of a whole. Ultimately, this is why the question of how the people were to express their consent to having the personification of the commonweal exercise authority held so little interest for many medieval political writers and legists. The ruler was seen, primarily, not to represent the individual citizens' social interests and personal rights, but to represent the community as a disembodied whole. Only when society as a collective whole came to be viewed as a collective whole of individuals, each with individual interests and rights, did the notion of representing the community begin to reflect the feature of representation associated with a democratic form of polity. The historical question, then, of when the first forms of parliamentary democracy can be seen in western Europe can only be answered in terms of a representative gathering or institution that reflects this meaning of representation.

To summarize and advance this discussion at one and the same time:

66. For John of Salisbury *Policraticus* 5.6.548D, 549A and C: Part 2, 1 above; for Thomas Aquinas, see n. 67 and Part 3, 3A.

67. Thomas Aquinas *S.T.* 1–2.95.3; cf. John of Salisbury *Policraticus* 4.6.523A; 5.2.540B; 4.3.516D. Aquinas repeats almost verbatim a formulation of Bulgarus from the Justinian Code, *Dig.* 50.167–76, cited in Lagarde, "Idée de représentation," p. 432, n. 1.

the notion of a collective whole of individuals developed in the practice of the Church and among the canonists of the thirteenth century, but this concept received "theoretical" consideration among civilian jurists only later. The perception, then, of political society as a collective whole whose individual members had individual rights and interests to be "represented" by political authorities came later among civilian jurists and theorists of temporal polity than among canonists, whose interests, however, were directed to a theory of spiritual or ecclesiastical, rather than temporal polity. At the same time, any retention of the older Germanic and feudal notions of law and personal rights and interests delayed the perception of personal rights and interests in public law insofar as these older conceptions focused virtually exclusively on private law. Even while the perception was developing of the practical advantages in formulating a mechanism for the expression of legal interests and rights at a distance—delegation of authority, representation as involving the designation of an organ or person to embody these interests and rights, which became the essential feature of the second element in the modern juridical concept of representation—the actual developments themselves were seen for some time to apply to matters of private law and to be applicable to issues to be treated as if they were matters of private law. Accordingly, even where the evolving concept of representation was applied to circumstances and issues we accept as public, and even in circumstances that might be seen as public (for instance, parliaments and estates general or their equivalents, of which scattered examples can be found throughout the thirteenth century), these events and the documents and contemporary terminology associated with them do not yet illustrate clearly the sense of representation and required popular consent associated with modern democratic institutions.

C. The Concept of Full Powers (Plena potestas)

Another concept of considerable interest and importance in the study of medieval political thought and practice, and one intimately bound up with the notions of corporations and representation by proctors, is that of "full powers" (*plena potestas*).[68] Representatives of corporate

---

68. Basic literature on *plena potestas* is plentiful: see Post, "*Plena potestas*"; Benson, "*Plenitudo potestatis*"; Edwards, "*Plena Potestas*"; Clarke, *Medieval Representation*; Cheyette, *Lordship and Community*.

persons were required to have full powers to consult and consent; hence an understanding of what was meant by this requirement for consultation and consent entails an understanding of the meaning of *plena potestas.* Again the concept had an origin in Roman law; and again its adaptation and extension among medieval legal procedures came about through the revived interest in Roman law among canonist and civilian jurists of the twelfth and thirteenth centuries.[69]

The notion that someone is truly a representative or delegate of someone else only to the extent that he has "full powers" to act for the person he represents is commonplace in modern legal and political theory, even though its reality in the latter sphere is often hazy at both ends of the representational spectrum. The electorate sometimes expresses dissatisfaction with its elected representative for taking a position with which they do not agree and thereby failing to "represent" them properly; similarly, elected representatives frequently nowadays do their best by using modern polling techniques to discern the views they are supposed to represent, and lay themselves open to the accusation that they are simply following rather than leading their constituents.

The concept of full powers can be found often in medieval legal and political thought, where its presence and use, like that of the notion of consent, sometimes has been taken to presage the existence of some form of representative parliamentary government. It appears, for example, in the mandates carried by knights and burgesses to the earliest English parliaments, and by delegates of cities and towns to Spanish *cortes* and French *états-généraux*; and for this reason it has been interpreted as implying an almost political or sovereign consent limiting royal authority in such gatherings.[70] An appreciation of its original meaning in Roman law and of its medieval applications by legists in both laws, however, yields a more modest interpretation of the evidence for its medieval currency being a significant sign of a modern theory of popular sovereignty. The emperor Alexander Severus described the requirements and limits of the authority needed by a proctor in order to represent his principal adequately in court; the legislation appears in the Justinian Code at 2.12.10. There is evidence that this legal principle was known and commented on in Italy perhaps

---

69. Post, *Studies*, p. 93 and n. 9.

70. This interpretation can be seen in Clarke, *Medieval Representation*, p. 291 and pp. 200–98.

as early as the ninth century,[71] although no explicit reference to *plena potestas* in respect of representation in secular or civil jurisdiction has been found even as late as the end of the twelfth century. There is good reason to suspect that the concept was in use in civil administration by this time, however, because it is referred to in the 1180s in a canonical treatise on legal procedure.[72]

The concept appeared much earlier and in a different context in sixth-century papal correspondence: summoning his vicar, Anastasius of Thessalonica, Pope Leo I stipulated that his request for the vicar to appear before him rested on the pope's concern for him, and not on the full papal authority to summon (*in partem sollicitudinis, non in plenitudinem potestatis*).[73] The term "full powers" appears again in a decretal of Gregory IV to the bishops of Gaul, Europe, Germany, and all provinces dated at Colmar, 8 July 833;[74] and this document was the basis for a spurious interpolation by the Pseudo-Isidore to a genuine decretal of Vigilius.[75] These three classic statements of *plena potestas* applied to the papacy, two authentic and one a forgery, were rediscovered in the eleventh century; and the canonists of the later part of this century and subsequently employed them in both canonical and political treatises: Gratian reproduced all three in the *Decretum*.[76] As early as the period 1182–85 a canonical book of procedures (*ordo iudiciarius*) asserted that a proctor should receive full powers;[77] and in 1200 Innocent III was summoning proctors from Italian city-states to come to the papal curia with full powers.[78] The notion is found also in Rogericus[79] and Azo,[80] as well as in Accursius, one of the most authoritative of thirteenth-century legists.[81] The fourteenth century

71. Post, *Studies*, p. 93 and n. 9.

72. *Ordo iudiciarius Bambergensis* (ca. 1182–85), cited by Post, *Studies*, p. 93, n. 10.

73. Leo I, Epistolae 14.1 (*PL* 54:671), cited in Benson, "*Plenitudo potestatis.*" p. 198, n. 12.

74. *MGH, Epistolae*, V, 72–81, no. 14, cited in Benson "*Plenitudo potestatis*," p. 200, n. 24.

75. *Decretales Pseudo-Isidoriana*, ed. P,. Hinchius, p. 712, cited in Benson "*Plenitudo potestatis*," p. 202, n. 32.

76. Benson "*Plenitudo potestatis*," p. 203.

77. See n. 72 above.

78. Post, *Studies*, p. 97 and pp. 108–9, citing Theiner, *Codex diplomaticus temporalis sanctae sedis*, 1, nos. XLII and XLIII.

79. Rogericus *Summa codicis* 2.8, *De procurationibus*, ed. Palmieri, *Scripta anecdota glossatorum*, 1:27 f., cited by Post, *Studies*, p. 93, n. 11.

80. Azo, Lectura to *Cod.* 2.12.10, cited by Post, *Studies*, p. 93, n. 11.

81. Buckland, *Textbook of Roman Law*, p. 525.

shows similar widespread instances of its use by both canonical and secular legal authorities: by the civilian jurists Bartolus of Sassoferrato, Baldus Ubaldus, and Francesco Tigrini, among others.[82]

An important feature of the medieval legists' treatment of the original Roman private-law concept of full powers was their fusion of it with other Justinian sources referring to the *procurator Caesaris*,[83] a field of law where discretionary power is involved. They extended the concept in this way to apply to the element of "general mandate," that is, authority given to an agent or representative allowing him general or free discretion in actions he was authorized to take on his lord's behalf, being authorized thus in effect to commit his lord without specific prior authorization or the need to check back for such authorization.

Examples of the maturity of the procedure applying the concept of full powers developed by theorists and authorities in both secular and canon law can be found throughout the thirteenth century,[84] with the same concept and its formulas for mandate serving not only for representation in courts and ordinary business transactions, but also to express the powers both of ambassadors appointed by princes and cities to negotiate truces, treatises, and other contractual agreements, and of royal procurators and papal legates as administrators.[85] Application of the concept of full powers to the temporal political sphere began first in Italy, and spread to the Holy Roman Empire.[86] It can be seen also in the England of Prince John, when in 1215 he sent procurators to Pope Innocent III with a mandate wherein the English chancery clearly expressed Roman formulas.[87] An interesting example of the general practice of representation of corporate groups is found in the 1252 articles of confederation between Dublin and Drogheda, wherein the two Irish towns agreed on common counsel among representatives of the towns.[88] A confederation embracing Dublin, Drogheda, Cork, Limerick, and Waterford provided in 1285 for two or three citizens of each town to meet triennially at Kilkenny on the

82. Post, *Studies*, p. 94 and nn. 15, 16, 17.

83. Ibid., p. 95.

84. Post lists a number of examples. Ibid,. pp. 95–102.

85. Ibid., p. 103.

86. Ibid., p. 106.

87. Ibid., p. 107.

88. Gilbert, *Historical and Municipal Documents of Ireland*, p. 131, cited in Richardson, "Origins of Parliament," p. 176.

morrow of Trinity.[89] It seems that by the middle of the thirteenth century the Roman formulas concerning consent and full powers were in use for almost every kind of agency and representation.[90]

As already noted, however, consent was given in terms of mandate *before* the negotiation began. If the affair was between equals (for example, two or more kings) or between autonomous communes and princes, the agents were ambassadors. But if it was between ruler and subjects or subject communities, the agents of the latter were proctors, who represented their constituents before a superior authority. Consent, then, whether the negotiation was judicial, legislative, administrative, or merely consultative, could be quite different in quality from the consent of equals to a contract or treaty, even though the procedure may have been strikingly similar and the element of full powers was always a prerequisite. Accordingly, instances of representatives with delegated powers coming to various medieval public assemblies and parliaments with full powers of consultation and consent must be treated cautiously as evidence of what might be called popular sovereignty.

Delegates of Lombard communes attended the Diet of Roncaglia in 1158, though with what specific powers is not clear.[91] Pope Innocent III summoned *procuratores* from six Italian cities to his curia in 1200, instructing that they must arrive with *plena potestas*;[92] their function was to submit to the pope's demands, not to be given the option of refusing obedience and thereby limit papal authority. Frederick II was the first secular ruler known to have summoned proctors with full powers, in 1231;[93] and after the middle of the thirteenth century the procedure of proctorial representation continued in the Kingdom of Sicily and in the Papal States. It also became normal in Spain, England, and France.[94] By 1268, Roman formulas of *plena potestas* as an essential element of the proctorial mandate were adapted in respect of the summoning of knights of the shire to English parliaments;[95] and soon the kings of both England and France, following precedents established by the lawyers and cathedral chapters in provincial ecclesiastical councils in

89. Gilbert, ibid., cited in Richardson, ibid., p. 176.
90. Post, *Studies*, p. 107.
91. Ibid., pp. 108, 381, 88.
92. Ibid., p. 109 and n. 82; cf. pp. 85–88.
93. Ibid., p. 89; cf. pp. 85–88, 381.
94. Ibid., p. 110.
95. Ibid., p. 90.

both countries, began expressly to employ the Roman maxim of *q o t* in court procedure. As so employed it involved full powers as an integral element in the rationale for the representation of individual and corporate interests before the king and his court and council in assembly.[96] After the middle of the thirteenth century the use of consent involving full powers was frequent, even common, in both civil and canonical jurisdictions. By 1300 it was normal to use it in sending representatives to assemblies of both temporal and ecclesiastical character, whether provincial ecclesiastical councils, chapters of religious, general ecclesiastical councils, or high courts and councils of princes: in this latter connection, for example, to the English parliament by 1268 or possibly earlier (1254, 1265); to the *cortes* of Aragon by 1307 and probably much earlier; to the French Estates General of 1302 and thereafter.[97]

But what did consent from representatives mandated to medieval assemblies with *plena potestas* actually mean? In ordinary judicial procedure, the original locus for the actions of agents possessed of full powers, it signified as a minimum full acceptance of or consent to, the court's decision of the case in question. Did it mean the same thing in a royal assembly or in ecclesiastical councils of various sorts? The cautious conclusion of Gaines Post is that "the procedure by which representatives were summoned and by which they brought powers from corporate communities, defended the 'liberties' of their constituencies, and accepted the will of the king and council was quite analogous to that of litigation in courts ordinary. But the assembly was no ordinary court; the king was the highest judge and administrator in the land; he presided over the assembly in the fullness of his prerogative ... more important, representatives were not summoned to the assembly as litigant parties ... [but] primarily to consent to an extraordinary demand by the king for a subsidy."[98]

96. Ibid.
97. Ibid., p. 110. Charles H. Taylor produced a series of articles on French assemblies of the early fourteenth century to show that this was a period of experimentation in the calling of the *états-généraux*, and that no definite methods then existed for the calling of such assemblies: "Assemblies of French Towns"; "Some New Texts of the Assembly of 1302"; "An Assembly of French Towns in March, 1318"; "Composition of Baronical Assemblies in France, 1315–1320"; "French Assemblies and Subsidy in 1321"; see also Brown, "Assemblies of French Towns"; "Subsidy and Reform in 1321"; "Taxation and Morality"; "Royal Salvation."
98. Ibid. Cf. Harriss, *King, Parliament*, pp. 1–74.

D. *The Royal Prerogative*

One needs, then, to take into account the notion of royal prerogative as well as the details of legal procedure. And here apparently a new factor emerges that might be said to have operated at cross purposes to the development, deliberate or accidental, of the mechanisms of popular sovereignty. For at the same time as there was some awakening to the possibilities of limiting royal authority in terms of emphasis on the mechanisms for requiring the ruler to seek and obtain consent, there was also an emerging emphasis on the notion that the king, as responsible in his office for the public welfare, had the right to require his subjects to agree with his judgments concerning what these responsibilities entailed. The point here might be expressed roughly as follows: insofar as the king through his office was responsible for the welfare of the whole realm, he could be assumed to "know" what was to be done on its behalf and had the right to demand that its interests be protected and advanced in ways consistent with the perceived realities of his public responsibility. His subjects, for their part, had an obligation to conform to this right as it rested in turn on the monarch's obligation to protect the public domain. Thus, while consent was something that, by traditional feudal law as well as by the maxims of classical Roman law then so much admired, the ruler was required to seek from his "people," the notion of consent began to receive yet another twist.

Accordingly, when the king of England, for example, needed an extraordinary subsidy, feudal law demanded that he obtain the consent of all whose rights and liberties were affected, and this consent was voluntary: the contractual character of the agreement between King John and his barons enshrined in chapters 12 and 14 of the Magna Carta is an illustration.[99] But virtually concurrently with this historical event, and under the influence particularly of Roman law again, the legal experts of popes and kings were beginning to assert a new doctrine: namely, that in an emergency or special case of necessity such as a just defence against an invader, which touched both king and

---

99. See Stubbs, *Select Charters*, pp. 296–306, esp. pp. 298–99. For an English translation with running commentary see Swindler, *Magna Carta*, pp. 244–351, esp. pp. 270–78. Treharne interprets the Great Charter as affording to the "Common council of the realm" the power to grant or refuse a voluntary aid to the king, and the power by majority vote to bind a dissident minority to pay a granted tax: "Constitutional Problem," p. 63.

kingdom, the *status regis et regni*,[100] the rights and welfare of the people, the king possessed a superior right to ask for aid and to have it granted to him as a matter of right. Much of this theory also was derived from Roman law;[101] and it reflected a dawning conception of the notion that the public good, state sovereignty of a nascent type, could be appealed to to overcome and transcend private and feudal rights. The same point of view can be found consistently in medieval political treatises, where the emphasis was on the direct connection between political authority and the common good. The sole justification for the exercise of political authority was the pursuit of the common good; it was only for this that the ruler functioned, and it was his responsibility to further the common good, while his subjects had the obligation to obey his commands in respect of this furtherance.[102] The new legal developments, then, reinforced a formulation from traditional theories of polity, which themselves had found new theoretical support in the late thirteenth century from Aristotle's *Politics*.[103]

In such circumstances, it is more than plausible that the element of consent in royal assemblies turned out to be much like its counterpart involving agents with *plena potestas* in ordinary courts. *Plena potestas*, then, seems to have been similar in an assembly to what it was in a court; in theory it involved an expression of consent, given before the action began, to the court decision and decision of the royal council. Theoretically, the case of necessity was, as it were, tried in the assembly; and the representatives were, in a sense, attorneys protecting the rights and interests of the communities against the royal claim of public utility, while at the same time binding the communities by their consent to the decision.[104] Consent even to taxation was therefore consultative and judicial, rather than voluntary and democratic. Only when parliament ceased to be a council and a court, in effect, and when the

---

100. Again, it is Post to whom we are indebted for the basic research on this concept: see *Studies*, pp. 241–414; cf. pp. 91–162 also for reprint of his article on *Plena potestas* and consent in medieval assemblies. Harris's work on medieval royal taxation in England reinforces this interpretation: Harris, *King, Parliament*, pp. 21–47; but see Mitchell, *Taxation in Medieval England*, p. 150.

101. Ulpian *Dig.* 1.4.2, 1.3.8, 1.3.40, and 10.16.10; *Inst.* 1.1.4; cited by Post, *Studies*, p. 114, n. 97. But note his point that the same concept of public good, common good, was available to medieval thinkers also from Aristotle and Cicero.

102. Emphasis on the common good as the aim of political rule is general, indeed universal, among medieval political writers.

103. Aristotle *Politics* 1.1.

104. Post, *Studies*, p. 116.

king was deprived of the practical right to refuse a properly presented, popularly supported petition could *plena potestas* in England or elsewhere signify genuine popular sovereignty.[105]

So much for the legal and political theory. There were other, practical considerations, however. Some possibilities deriving from the private-law origins of the notion of proctorial representation could be appealed to in efforts to circumscribe and constrain the exercise of royal authority. The features of providing only a limited mandate or of being required to refer back to their delegating corporation, the need for sufficient instruction to be given to the proctor, and so on: these could be used as at least a kind of procedural barrier against royal demands; and there were examples of this sort of delaying tactic actually being used in both temporal and ecclesiastical jurisdictions.[106] It was precisely to forestall such efforts that the central authority came to insist that proctors and representatives must carry *plena potestas* into courts and assemblies. These efforts themselves also are to be seen, for the most part, before there was a general understanding and acceptance of the view that the royal authority enjoyed a superior status relating to public or common utility and necessity; that is, before the efforts of the royal authority became largely successful in establishing the view that the royal prerogative could deny a position of equality to those persons it brought to its courts and assemblies for the necessities of state. Even where legal elements of limitation were appealed to, their acceptance as valid required the approval of the court or assembly in which the matter was being considered. Accordingly, even when accepted, they did not reflect an unqualified right of popular sovereignty in the modern sense.

Political events themselves in the thirteenth century were also giving impetus to the gradual focusing of attention on the issue of the relationship between a ruler and his people. The centralizing activities of the English and French monarchs, in particular, inevitably brought them into contact and frequently into conflict with their own people, especially those who exercised any authority of their own. It has long been understood that the basic political arrangements of feudal times were personal, that is, that individuals bound themselves to one another on a personal basis; accordingly, mutual obligations of

---

105. Ibid., p. 117.

106. See Post's careful consideration of the legal notions of "sufficient instructions," "reference back," and limited mandate in *Studies*, pp. 127–60.

protection and obedience, for example, were grounded in personal contracts or agreements between the parties concerned. Such arrangements are not the stuff of which a modern theory of state[107] is constructed, even though these feudal arrangements may have encompassed considerable territory and displayed few "protectors" and many "obeyers."

What we understand today as a nation or, more frequently, nation-state (although a nation does not have to be any particular geographical size), is a political association wherein the relationship between governor and governed is precisely *not* based on personal relationship or contract, but on something at once more abstract and more substantial, having to do with common features and interests and an acceptance of the power relationships between governor and governed based on these considerations. Of course there is nothing new about the formulation of this concept of the state: it is the classical as well as the modern meaning for the term, and as such was known in the Middle Ages as well. But what was lacking in the early medieval period was actual experience of its reality. Political society in western Europe in those centuries had become so fragmented that the notion of there being anything other than a personal arrangement with a local protector had become dim, while the corresponding notion of extending protection on anything other than a personal basis also lacked expression.

A significant consequence of this fact, expressed in comparably oversimplified terms, was that when an ambitious medieval European political ruler began to extend the areas of his jurisdiction he was inclined to see this expansion in purely personal terms, just as those over whom he was seeking to extend his control also saw the issue in personal terms. It was their personal interests or rights that were being assaulted, often in the literal sense of these terms, and what they sought to defend and protect were personal, rather than what we might call social or political, values. To continue the gross oversimplification: the struggles—and there were many, some violent, others not—between

107. The origins of the modern state is another much controverted issue whose *status questionis* and examination was addressed by Post in "Ratio publicae utilitatis," which reviews the state of the question (*Studies*, pp. 241–47. See also Post, "Public Law, the State, and Nationalism," published as "Two Notes on Nationalism in the Middle Ages," *Traditio* 9 (1953): 281–320, and revised for 1963 publication as titled above in Post, *Studies*, pp. 434–93; and "Naturalness of Society and the State," in Post, *Studies*, pp. 494–561. Cf. Tierney, *Religion, Law*; Strayer, *Medieval Origins of the Modern State*.

the politically centralizing activities of the medieval nation builders and their own people, especially the feudal nobility of those nascent states over whom political authority in the first instance had to be exercised, were perceived by the protagonists themselves, at least in the beginning, as a struggle for personal rights and interests. What the nobles of England were doing when they gathered at Runnymede in 1215 to exact the Magna Carta from King John, was protecting something perceived by them as personal rights and privileges established by contract, rather than essential features of a political society. Only gradually did such a perception change; and with the change in perception came the development of the modern state and the modern theory of the state, in which the elements of sovereignty and interests of state rather than personal contract are so fundamental.

There is a sense in which the thirteenth-century developments in this area actually show a kind of dual and opposing set of directions, and this on two levels. On the level of theory, much of it worked out by justifying in theoretical terms the claims being made by one side or the other in an actual conflict of interest, both the people (for which read, largely, the noble class) and the ruler (by way of his advisers, usually) found material at hand on which to ground their respective interests. Faced with royal requests or efforts at imposition of authority, often by way of taxation, the "people" could claim that their consent was required, and that all who were touched by these potential exactions had to be consulted and to approve. Both their feudal rights and the more dimly perceived notions of political authority resting in the people, notions now coming to the attention of students of both canonical and civil law, could be and were appealed to in this respect.

For his part the king, who was also a beneficiary of the results of the great new studies in the law, might claim on the one hand that he was "above the law," that the people had ceded all their authority to him even though they might have possessed it originally (*lex regia*); or, even more subtly and with greater prospect of theoretical if not practical agreement, that he was the people as its symbol or regent; and that he had the responsibility to further the common interests of the people as a whole, that his interests precisely were *not* merely personal, and that as such his decisions required agreement and were not negotiable: they did not require the consent of the people, or if they did, the form of consent to which his obligations extended were only those of consulting, and that this was precisely why he went to the trouble of inviting persons to come to his parliament and court possessed of the *plena potestas* necessary to consent!

The second level of opposition between the contending parties, of course, was practice. And again the two sides can be seen to be able to turn practices and practical realities to their respective advantages. The king found it useful to invoke the newly recognized forms of consent, representation, and *plena potestas*; an energetic, intelligent, and properly advised monarch could be expected to employ such mechanisms and procedures to his advantage, and through them advance his, that is, the national, interest over the personal interests of the leaders of the society he was attempting to govern. The convened representatives of this society, on the other hand, if perceptive and strong-minded enough, might for their part force the actuality of events beyond the limitations of the ruler's notion that they were obliged to agree with him, and extract from him privileges, concessions, rights that little by little could lead to a form of governance in which the people as a whole might ultimately come to enjoy such rights.

In the meantime, however, a kind of inversion between theory and practice was taking place: the practice of the nobles in terms of their own interests involved an attempt to limit the prerogatives of the king and to oppose the theoretical position according to which political society as a whole, in whose interests political authority is to be exercised, was embodied in the king. In attempting to protect their own interests and, thereby, placing themselves in opposition to the king, the nobles actually advanced not only the theory but the practice of a political society in which functioning authority actually does pursue the common good, and is limited in its exercise of authority by mechanisms designed to protect the common good from tyrannical acts and to guarantee the personal rights and interests of all those subject to authority.

However formulated, or indeed without being formulated at all, the notion of collective sovereignty was in the air from early in the thirteenth century: first in ecclesiastical circles, but spreading quickly to temporal political ones as well. The attitudes and activities of Frederick II as the first secular ruler to summon proctors with mandates reflect the temporal scene clearly. One indication of the growing sense of the Church as a collective whole was the expression given it by the fact of laity being invited to general Church councils, as well as the relatively large number of such gatherings throughout the century. Here was a concrete, rather than theoretical, expression of the view that an ecumenical council should be more than a gathering of bishops as the post-Constantinian ones had been; such a council should be "a faithful image of the whole Christian community."[108] There was, of course, no question of the lay delegates being involved directly in theological or canonical matters: in his bull of 13 April 1213 convoking the Fourth Lateran Council Innocent III informed the invited secular princes that they were only to be heard on certain issues that concerned them; and Gregory X in 1274 also invited the secular princes "inasmuch as certain issues are to be dealt with which pertained to them."[109]

One of the features of fourteenth-century political activities was the example of repeated efforts by the lords and representatives to parliament to limit royal authority by requiring clarification and specification of what was involved in a royal appeal to a case of public utility and necessity. Such efforts took the form of requiring specifics for any claim by royal authority that its demands rested on some exclusive and superior judgment requiring consent.[110] Political efforts of this sort were more successful in England than anywhere else in western Europe in the late medieval period, but they were not completely successful even there until later.[111] A reflection of such thinking is to be found also in the late thirteenth century in the political theory of Godfrey of Fontaines.[112]

2. THE HISTORICAL SCENE

A. Electoral Practices: Majority Rule

It has been said often enough that the controlling element in medieval life and thought was the Christian church. This is why so much attention has been paid thus far in our inquiry into medieval views on consent and coercion, and to the doctrines dealing with, and attitudes towards, these concepts among the basic documents of Christianity and in the works of Christian writers. It has also been said that political

108. Lagarde, "Idée de représentation," p. 426. However, as late as the end of the thirteenth century, in the case of William Durandus, and into the fourteenth century with John of Paris and Augustinus Triumphus, a general Church council was conceived of an essentially a convocation of bishops: Lagarde, "Idée de représentation," p. 426, n. 3; on John of Paris and the function of a general council in deposing a pope, see Part 3, 3E.

109. Lagarde, "Idée de représentation," p. 426, n. 2.

110. Post, *Studies*, pp. 146–47 and n. 181.

111. Post's qualified judgments on England are in *Studies*, pp. 154–62, esp. pp. 161–62.

112. See Part 3, 3C below.

thinking is a secondary, subordinate form of intellectual activity, conditioned by, as much as it conditions, the kinds of activity it purports to prescribe—that events shape theory at least as much as the other way around.

For this reason it is important to examine the practices employed in the medieval political context that involve the presence or absence of what we understand today by the term "consent," the practices that provide for involvement of members of a community in the basic political activity of the group. As noted already, the notion of majority was developing around the meaning of corporate person as giving legal status to individuals considered as a group. The majority came to be seen as able to decide for the corporation, and thus bind any dissenting minority to the decision made. The development of this notion of majority rule came only slowly, however, both in theory and in practice.

One of the basic decisions in any polity is the selection of a leader, the activity of determining who, as well as how, someone is placed in a position of authority in the group. Interestingly, the Church itself provides the most significant data from the medieval period on this point.[113] The Christian church was the most important community or society with which the individual medieval person was concerned; its significance for the medieval Christian far outweighed that of the particular political society in which he happened to find himself. A reasonably detailed picture has been drawn of the views of early and early medieval Christian writers concerning consent as a conceptual element in the theory of politics; a brief parallel investigation is now in order concerning the actual practices of the Church in regard to this notion. How did the medieval Christian church in fact go about the business of appointing its leaders? More specifically, what procedures, what techniques or mechanisms were actually employed to designate those persons who were to exercise ecclesiastical authority? As elsewhere, in the area of polity actions speak as loudly as words. The actual techniques employed to place persons in positions of authority attest at least as much as any theory to the attitudes people hold concerning this matter; for in the last analysis it is electoral techniques or procedure

113. See the important research of Moulin, "Science politique"; "Gouvernement des communautés religieuses"; "Origines religieuses"; "Sources des libertés"; "Sanior et maior pars." The last article has a bibliography. Cf. Gaudemet, "Unanimité et majorité"; Gryson, "Elections ecclésiastiques au IIIe siècle."

that condition the character of both the selection process itself and the regime of which it is an element.

How, then, did the Church designate its community leaders? Looked at even cursorily, the Christian church provides a fascinating case study in this respect. From the beginnings of its institutional existence its very claims to divine origins and superior status *vis-à-vis* temporal political regimes made it essential, or at least highly prudent and practical, for the Church to provide the very model in appropriate forms and procedures for its collective actions, the validity and integrity of which should be unchallengeable. For this reason the Church was obliged very quickly to practice methods for selecting its leaders that were seen to be of the highest order of propriety, appropriateness, and regularity. From the early centuries of its existence it thus developed electoral and deliberative techniques of a complexity and minuteness of detail not employed in the temporal order until centuries later; techniques, moreover, that could be looked to as models by medieval political theorists and practitioners of temporal politics precisely because they were known and were known to be practised in the most significant social organization of the Middle Ages. The Church's influence in this respect can be seen even in more modern electoral practices, although only in an attenuated way. Certain forms and procedures derived from ecclesiastical concepts and models have been introduced on such a broad basis and over so long a period of time that they simply have become part of the generally accepted way of handling these matters.

In fact, the electoral practices developed in the Christian church during the medieval period were the forerunners of much of modern western parliamentary practice. The techniques of election by majority—absolute, relative, and qualified—as well as most of the electoral techniques currently in use in civil politics, had their origins in the Church institutions and religious orders of the Middle Ages, rather than in the practices developed in earlier Roman times, which long since had fallen into disuse or been abandoned.[114] This is not to say that all or even some of these techniques were practised either widely or regularly in the medieval Church; rather only that the formulation of the techniques can be seen to have occurred in the medieval period, and that at least some examples of use can be identified.

114. Moulin, "Sanior et maior pars," p. 24, n. 1. For an examination of Roman legal practices see Gaudemet, "Unanimité et majorité, pp. 150–54; cf. Grossi, "Unanimitas"; Petrani, "Genèse de la majorité qualifiée."

The concept of *maior pars*, literally the greater part—not always identifiable with the numerically larger part, as will be seen—was a concept in Roman law, where consent of the majority, in this case presumably a numerical notion, was accepted as consent by all the members of a corporation.[115] The classical Roman context for this notion, however, was that of private law. Again it was the activity of medieval legists and canonists that began the extension of this concept to other areas and contexts; and the terminology *maior et sanior pars* began to appear as the designation of that portion of any group that could be identified as committing the group as a whole. As already seen, legists and canonists frequently referred to passages on consent and *q o t* in both the *Digest* and *Codex* of the Justinian collection; and when a case was seen to touch a corporation as a whole, the lawyer applied the theory of *maior pars* to corporate consent. What was approved by the *maior pars*, sometimes specified as a two-thirds majority of members present in a general assembly, bound the community as a whole. Majority approval meant, moreover, that the dissenting minority had no further legal rights in the matter.[116] The procurator for a *universitas*, for example, was to be chosen as representative of the corporation by the whole *universitas* or by the *maior et sanior pars* of at least two-thirds of its members in assembly.[117] The thirteenth-century English legist Bracton applied the corporate fiction to the kingdom as a whole in the case of business touching the king and kingdom; he maintained that the *maior pars* (not further defined) of magnates and prelates represented the community of the realm.[118]

The earliest election form acceptable and in use in the Christian church for the selection of popes, bishops, and abbots had been selection by unanimity: *electio concours; electio concorditer et unanimiter facta, communi voto eligere*;[119] and even before this procedure was reduced to a formula and to formal ecclesiastical approval it was probably the technique practised among the early Christian communities. Certainly in its formula expression as described and legalized in medieval canonical literature it was what medieval Christians understood to have been early Christian practice. Election by unanimous

115. *Dig.* 50.1.19 and 160.1; cf. Post, *Studies*, pp 175–76.
116. Post, *Studies*, p. 212, n. 180.
117. Ibid., p. 42 and n. 90.
118. Ibid., pp. 198–99 and n. 123.
119. Moulin, "*Sanior et maior pars*," p. 370.

consent, by consensus, seems to have been the normal method for designating Church leaders during the first ten centuries of the Christian church, and it has been contended that the tenth century knew no other form of election.[120]

The impetus and attraction for this electoral procedure were virtually overwhelming from the beginning of Christian community activity, although the details of such procedure are largely unknown. How, for example, did one express a negative view or abstain; was it even possible to do either? The *Rule of St. Augustine* specified that the community should live in perfect harmony and that "there should be one soul and one heart in God among you."[121] Moreover, a division of opinion in the community was always considered an object of scandal. Nevertheless, Pope Leo I indicated that differences of view were not in themselves reprehensible, nor were they evidence of a state of mind inimical to true religion.[122] But for centuries the position of a minority view on a matter of significance to the Christian community, especially in respect of the designation of leaders, seems to have been tenuous indeed; and the practice was probably common of suppressing quickly any discordant elements by having the losing minority move to accept and agree with the majority and thus restore unanimity. Similar disinclinations towards continuing expression of opinions ajar from those holding sway were reflected in temporal political affairs as well; there were serious penal provisions in some of the codes of Germanic law for members of a minority position who persisted in their eccentric views: exile, for example, or a fine.[123] It is questionable, however, whether such civil legal provisions had any influence on the continuing emphasis in Christian communities on voluntary unanimity.

The tendency to unanimous consent can also be seen in the Italian city-state communes of the later Middle Ages, as well as the practice of minorities moving very quickly to join their votes to the majority and produce unanimity.[124] The notion of a unanimous election held such an attraction for the canonist Hostiensis as late as the thirteenth century that he maintained that such an election was valid even if it lacked the canonical necessities of form.[125] The first papal election in

---

120. Ibid., p. 371.
121. Ibid., p. 371, and nn. 12, 13.
122. Ibid., p. 371. Moulin notes that the Leonine text in *PL* omits reference to this incident, suggesting it might have been interpolated: n. 13.
123. Ibid., p. 372, n. 16; p. 373, n. 22.
124. Ibid., p. 373, n. 22.
125. Hostiensis, *Summa aurea*, cited in Moulin, "*Sanior et maior pars*," p. 373 and n. 23.

nearly five centuries that did not involve unanimity among the electors occurred as late as 1130, when Innocent II was named pope without receiving general agreement from the electors.[126] The election was contested, however, and required the intervention of Bernard of Clairvaux. Bernard declared in favor of Innocent, but not in a fashion that specifically upheld the majority principle; he found for the person elected on the grounds of his being the "more worthy candidate."[127] As late as 1447, one finds Pope Eugene IV advising his cardinals in respect of papal election to elect "an ordinary man by way of unanimity rather than a very remarkable personnage by a simple majority."[128]

Despite the general prevalence of election by unanimity or consensus in the early and early medieval Church, however, there were instances where election by simple majority occurred. The election of St. Cornelius to the papacy in 251 was by majority; some decisions of the Council of Nicaea in 325 were by majority, as were others at the Council of Antioch (341), the ecumenical Council of Chalcedon (451), the general Council of Africa in 418, and the Roman Council of 499.[129] A decree formulated by St. Symmachus and approved at this latter Roman council affirmed the validity of elections made by simple majority, and did so specifically in opposition to a decree of the Emperor Honorius that had required papal elections to be by way of unanimity.[130] Pope Vigilius was elected by simple majority in 538;[131] Gregory of Tours mentioned a bishop as having been so elected in the mid-sixth century (by the majority of his clergy);[132] and there is an interesting case of episcopal election in the reign of Clotaire II (584–629) wherein the king put forward a minority candidate, Sulpicius, only to be informed that this would be a violation of an ecclesiastical edict of 614, according to which episcopal nominations required at least a majority vote of clergy and faithful; the king, it was submitted, had only the right to insist on the election being run again so that Sulpicius could be designated by a majority.[133]

A new and vexing element concerning the election procedure for

---

126. Moulin, "*Sanior et maior pars*," p. 374; cf. n. 27.
127. Ibid., p. 383; cf. n. 69.
128. Ibid., pp. 374–75; cf. nn. 29, 30.
129. For these examples of election by majority see Ibid., p. 375.
130. Ibid., p. 376.
131. Ibid.
132. Ibid.
133. Ibid.

ecclesiastical authorities was introduced by St. Benedict in formulating the rules of his Order in the sixth century. Benedict was concerned to cover circumstances where one of his monastic communities might not express unanimity in choosing an abbot. He stipulated that a person could be chosen without the unanimous consent of the community, provided that the individual chosen was "the wisest," having regard to the personal qualities of "worthiness of life and wisdom of doctrine."[134] Clearly, Benedict envisaged the acceptability of election by only a part of the electorate, and by a part that might be less than a majority, even much less than a majority; the worthiness of one candidate could override the strength of electoral support for any other candidate. In this fashion Benedict introduced the notion that an electing group could have a "better part" (*senior pars*), that is, a part of its total complement, regardless of the size of the part, whose individual members were better judges of a candidate or issue than even the major part might be, and who thus were entitled to have their decision accepted. This Benedictine notion seems to have been introduced explicitly into canon law by Gregory VII, and the concept of *senior pars* remained there until the 1917 revisions of the canonical Code.[135] It had been in actual use in monastic communities and other ecclesiastical jurisdictions ever since Benedict formulated it; and there are numerous medieval instances of elections of ecclesiastical officials being contested by minority groups who claimed that their candidate was superior to the person elected.

The just-mentioned case of Pope Innocent II in 1130 was a peculiarly graphic and characteristic example, the resolution of which by Bernard of Clairvaux highlighted a particular area of ambiguity surrounding the concept of *senior pars*. In fact Innocent had been elected pope as a majority candidate, but the election was contested when supporters of a minority candidate insisted that their man was "the better"; that is, according to the terminology and technical concepts invoked, that as a voting portion of the college of cardinals they were the *senior pars* of the electorate as a whole. Bernard found for Innocent on the grounds of him being the better candidate; and in this way he identified the majority portion of the electorate as *senior*. A

134. Ibid., pp. 376–78. The critical edition of Benedict's Rule is *Sancti Benedicti regula monasteriorum*, ed. Dom Cuthbert Butler (Fribourg: Herder, 1935). Moulin notes that the term *eligere* appears nine times in the Benedictine Rule with the meaning of "choose," "prefer," "name," but never with the technical meaning "elect": n. 45.

135. Moulin, "*Sanior et maior pars*," p. 380.

good number of contemporary canonists and historians are inclined to hold that in most, if not in all, cases of medieval practice there was a practical identification between the notions of *majority part* and *better part* of an electoral group; and this is probably true. Nonetheless, a conceptual difference exists between these two notions, and the Gregorian formula introducing the procedure directly into canon law in 1179 through the relevant canon of the Third Lateran Council expressed the distinction: *"sanior et [sic] maior pars."*[136] The Fourth Lateran Council (1215) repeats the distinction between majority vote and better vote at least to the extent of clearly differentiating the system of the *sanior pars* from other forms of election procedure.[137]

The focus of the electoral technique appropriate for papal elections was also specified more precisely by the Lateran Council of 1179; the principle of two-thirds majority of present members was introduced.[138] The effort here clearly was to eliminate the dissension and scandal that were the normal consequences of contested papal elections, there having been two such elections in recent times: 1130 and 1158. The text on papal election repeated the reference to the concept *sanior pars*, but its novelty rested in the presumption that a two-thirds majority *ipso facto* constituted the *sanior pars* of the electorate. The two-thirds-majority principle for papal election has not been modified since, but only later was the specific identification between this principle and the notion of *sanior pars* made explicit in canonical legislation.[139] The technique of calling for a two-thirds majority spread to other than papal elections in the late twelfth and thirteenth centuries. It is known to have been used in an episcopal election in 1199;[140] a canonical text of 1212 stipulated that the election of a suitable episcopal candidate by a two-thirds vote is valid, and the same went for a coadjutor.[141] The Council of Lyon (1274) extended the principle to chapter elections;[142] and soon the common teaching of canon law affirmed that two-thirds

136. Ibid., pp. 384–85.
137. Ibid., p. 385.
138. Ibid., pp. 385–86.
139. Ibid., p. 388.
140. Ibid., pp. 389–90. Apparently, the election was disallowed; however, the successful candidate was less than thirty years of age.
141. X 1.6.40; cited in Moulin, "*Sanior et maior pars*," p. 390 and n. 105.
142. Moulin, "*Sanior et maior pars*," p. 390 and n. 107. Salmon notes that the Carthusians determined in 1256 that adoption by a majority of votes was sufficient for a decision to have the force of law, and seems to imply that what is at issue here is a simple majority: Salmon, *Abbot*, p. 92, n. 27.

of those assembled should be present in order for elections and chapter actions to be valid.

It must not be assumed in all this talk of a two-thirds majority in an electorate, however, that the manner in which this majority was expressed was necessarily by way of formal polling or voting among the electorate. This was only one of three ways formally noted and approved by the Fourth Lateran Council in 1215 (canon 24): the other two were unanimity by quasi-inspiration and the "compromise."[143] According to this text balloting itself could produce three forms of results: formal and collective unanimity (in contrast with the informal unanimity of quasi-inspiration); the majority vote pure and simple; or the better (*sanior*) vote, in which all (*omnes*) or the majority (*maior pars*) or the better part (*sanior pars*) of the chapter have agreed. Actual examples of voting by secret ballot have been found as far back as 1159,[144] while there is an instance of election by acclamation to recognize a king of France as late as 1059 (Philip I).[145]

The procedure of accepting a simple majority preference, with or without the technicalities of a secret ballot, probably was used throughout the whole of the medieval period, the number of such instances being of less significance than the fact that this technique was in actual use. There is explicit evidence for the eleventh and twelfth centuries: some kind of voting took place at Tonnerre in 1048–49;[146] an election in 1029 was won by a majority vote, with verification in the traditional twelfth-century form of vote by the *maior et sanior pars*.[147] While there is no earlier evidence from Italian communal law, instances of majority election can be found at Genoa (1143),[148] Parma (1231),[149] and Venice (1326).[150] The contested election of the cardinal-deacon of Saint-Ange in 1130 was achieved by simple majority vote of five of the eight designated members of the election commission, and approved by four of the six supervising cardinals.[151] A general chapter decision of Cîteaux in 1134 declared a majority decision acceptable if,

143. Moulin, "*Sanior et maior pars*," pp. 395–97.
144. Ibid., p. 395, n. 132.
145. Ibid., p. 396, n. 133.
146. Ibid., pp. 507–8.
147. Ibid.
148. Ibid., p. 508, n. 97.
149. Ibid.
150. Ibid.
151. Ibid., p. 509 and n. 99. The successful candidate later became Pope Innocent III.

as was often the case, unanimity proved impossible.[152] An 1179 canonical text speaks of ecclesiastical elections by majority, adding a rider that referred to the *sanior pars*;[153] canon 17 of the Third Lateran Council accepted that a person possessed of the appropriate virtues could be named cardinal by a simple majority; a text predating 1179 speaks of the electors electing a person who has the approval either of all or of the majority;[154] and a 1202 text declares that an emperor can be elected by majority, the other electors not objecting.[155] This last is an example of application of the principle of majority election to a temporal jurisdiction, although the qualification may have been so extreme as to vitiate the principle itself.

The practices and constitutions of the Dominican Order, however, gave greatest impetus to a straightforward majority basis for decision making in medieval ecclesiastical affairs; and the consequences of this fact for both ecclesiastical and temporal decision making is easy to imagine if difficult to document.[156] A system of straightforward majority voting was operating in the Dominican monastic system in the 1220s, covering such matters as admission of a friar to an individual convent, election of provincial and general *diffinitores*, decisions of provincial meetings of *diffinitores*, and election of the Order's master general.[157] In all this Dominic and his fellow friars seem to have been tilling new ground rather than reflecting any existing approved procedures, although the concept of the majority part of a chapter was "in the air" at the time. A canonical text of the period 1227–34 concerning a contested election observed that number is a presumptive sign of superiority, thus giving some basis for explicitly identifying the *maior* with the *sanior pars*.[158] It was in 1274 that Gregory XI extended the two-thirds-majority principle to the explicit statement that such a vote in chapter elections was valid; he extended the majority principle

---

152. Ibid., p. 508 and n. 100.
153. *X* 1.3.11; cited in Moulin, "*Sanior et maior pars*," p. 509, n. 105.
154. Moulin, "*Sanior et maior pars*," p. 509.
155. Ibid.
156. The first effort to connect the Dominican Order with the medieval development of representative decision making was that of Barker, *Dominican Order and Convocation*. Barker's thesis found little acceptance among later scholars: see Post, *Studies*, p. 89 and n. 12; Leclercq, "General Chapters"; Hinnebusch, *Early English Friars*; Tunmore, "Dominican Order and Parliament."
157. Moulin, "*Sanior et maior pars*," p. 510, and n. 116; p. 513.
158. Ibid., p. 512.

without any qualification, although the required majority was actually two-thirds, and not a simple majority of fifty per cent plus one.[159] In fact, ecclesiastical elections involving an absolute majority became much less frequent after the middle of the thirteenth century, although not surprisingly they did not die out entirely. Further, the use of a secret-balloting procedure at the Council of Trent necessarily implied acceptance of the majority principle at the highest level of church decision making.

An interesting medieval example of the use of the concept of *maior pars* in the temporal political sphere reflects the Justinian ideal that any important matter touching the state of the realm touched the king and was his business, as well as the notion that the public business of the king in his public estate was sometimes the business of the *populus* as well (meaning the greater men of the realm) or the *universitas regni*.[160] Innocent IV held that a king could not debase the coinage without "consent of the *populus* or the *maior pars regni*," inasmuch as the business of the king was the business of the *universitas*.[161]

B. *Medieval Monasticism: The Dominican Order*

The significance of electoral procedures employed in the medieval Church in both its secular and monastic forms is underscored by the realization of the virtually universal influence these two forms of ecclesiastical polity exercised in the high and later Middle Ages. Mention has been made of the expansion of ecclesiastical administrative and organizational structure stimulated by the eleventh-century Gregorian reform. A parallel if not greater expansion occurred at the same time in respect of the spirit and institutional establishment of monasticism. It became so widespread in the Middle Ages as to be commonly known and accepted in every corner of western Europe, and its members were generally acceded a respect and veneration that a secular society such as ours is incapable of understanding fully.

The formal origins of medieval Christian monasticism lie in the sixth-century founding of the great monastery at Monte Cassino by St. Benedict, and in the abbot's formulation of his Rule, which became the

159. Ibid.
160. Post, *Studies*, p. 374.
161. In X 2.24.18, p. 118; cited in Post, *Studies*, p. 374 and n. 16.

guide and foundation document for later monastic communities.[162] One of the most noticeable and most important features of Benedict's Rule was the expression it gave to the concept of community, and to the ideal of all members of the religious community living together as equals in perfect harmony and expressing as brothers the loftiest ideals of Christian love. A person of sound practical judgment as well, however, Benedict also formulated procedures to govern the organization and structure of the religious community; someone had to be in charge, and some method for filling the position of leader had to be specified. Concerned too with the practical realities of all his monks sharing and participating in the life of the religious community and thereby achieving perfect harmony with one another, the founder of western monasticism insisted that the abbot of a monastic community must take counsel with all his fellow monks; he also stipulated that all members of the community were to be involved in the election of the abbot.[163]

The establishment by St. Dominic of the Order of Preachers in the early thirteenth century, like the almost contemporaneous establishment of the Order of Friars Minor (Franciscans) by St. Francis of Assisi, shows in a very significant way the expansion of monasticism in the period. The Dominicans, or Friar Preachers as they often were called, were established as canons living according to the Rule of St. Augustine;[164] and the new community drew up constitutions embody-

162. Cf. n. 134. The first Christian monastic grouping in cenobitical form that has left historical traces is the fourth-century establishment made by Saint Pachomius, and there are signs of monastic communities both in the East and in Egypt in the fourth and fifth centuries. There were also monks in the West before the Benedictine establishment of a formal rule, these earlier groups often following one of the known Eastern rules; see Salmon, *Abbot*, pp. 3–17.

163. Benedict *Regula* 3; cf. Lagarde, "Idée de représentation," p. 229, n. 77. Salmon shows that the original Eastern and Egyptian practices favoured the abbot naming his own successor, and that legislative texts stipulating this procedure appear in the West as early as the Council of Chalcedon, between 639 and 654 (canon 12), and that it persisted through the Carolingian period and to the beginning of Cluny. This pseudo-hereditary procedure was rare in the West, however, and was rejected by Gregory the Great, Justinian, and the Council of Carthage as well as by Benedict: Salmon, *Abbot*, p. 17 and n. 9, p. 25 and n. 17, which cites the Gregorian text: *Epistle 1.12*. Benedict did not originate the elective process for an abbot, but he did make it more precise: Salmon, *Abbot*, p. 19.

164. Galbraith, *Constitutions*, p. 1. Salmon provides a very useful though summary, recent account of the flowering of varieties of monastic foundations in the twelfth and thirteenth centuries: Salmon, *Abbot*, pp. 49–86. His primary interest, however, is with the issue of the abbot's permanence of tenure; hence he deals only incidentally with the method by which the monastic leader comes into office. He discusses the founding of the Dominicans at p. 77.

ing their rule that were based on the twelfth-century Institutions of Prémontré, an example of the monastic flowering of the previous century. The first part of the Dominican constitution dealt with the daily life of the religious house, while the second laid down rules for the governance of the Order as a whole.[165] This second section on monastic governance followed a format found in another twelfth-century monastic document, the Charter of Love (*Carta Caritatis*) written by Stephen Harding as second abbot of the Cistercian abbey of Citeaux for the guidance of his monks. The Charter, along with a second treatise known as the *Liber usuum*, formed the basis for the constitutions of Citeaux, which guided the Cistercian monastic foundations of the twelfth and thirteenth centuries. In an effort to standardize the monastic life of the period, Pope Innocent III in 1215 had determined that other regular canonical orders of religious (monks) were to follow the organizational scheme of the Cistercians.[166]

A notable feature of the Cistercian charter had been its insistence on a general chapter, bringing together in a single forum the various individual religious communities living separately under the same constitution and monastic discipline. One result of Innocent's move to standardize monastic organization, then, was the stipulation that monastic orders must have general chapter meetings. The Dominican constitution, accordingly, contained a section outlining rules for the holding of general chapter meetings, one of which rules called for general chapter meetings to take place annually and made attendance by all local abbots mandatory. The constitution adopted by the Dominicans also called for an annual visitation of each associated community; for the election of the abbot of an individual house to be performed by all the monks of that community, as well as by the abbots of all daughter houses; and for the election to be presided over by the abbot of the motherhouse. As well there was a section outlining a procedure for the deposition of an abbot, with judgment of his incompetence or recalcitrance to be made by a congregation of other abbots in council with the monks of the house concerned.[167]

165. Ibid.

166. Galbraith, *Constitutions*, p. 13. Salmon speaks of three redactions of the Charter of Love: the *carta caritatis prior* of 1119, the *summa cartae caritatis* (1123–24) and the revision of 1134–53 that provided the definitive text, the *carta caritatis posterior*: Salmon, *Abbot*, pp. 61–63, with references to modern editions at p. 61, n. 3.

167. Galbraith, *Constitutions*, p. 14; on the role of general chapters among the Cistercians see Mahn, *Ordre Cistercien*; cf. Moulin, "*Sanior et maior pars*," *passim*, and p. 369, n. 1; Salmon, *Abbot*, pp. 60–72.

From the beginning of its existence the Dominican Order was governed by a series of chapters: conventional chapters, for individual houses or convents; provincial chapters, bringing together a number of individual houses themselves interrelated geographically and by way of foundation; general chapters, bringing together all the houses in the Order as a whole. Conventional chapters met as needed for the normal operation of an individual house, while provincial and general chapters met annually. The general principle of structure and authority had the power of the greater bodies deriving from the lesser ones, and the acceptability of this principle rested on the notion that everyone from the ground up, so to speak, was directly involved in the governing structure. The general chapter was made up of representatives from the provinces elected in provincial chapter and invested with plenary powers by that chapter. In this way the Dominicans extended the general prescription of a general chapter, which up to this time had been understood to mean only regular meetings of the abbots of all individual monastic houses: the Dominician constitution called for a general chapter to meet annually, and for it to be composed of elected representatives named by the provincial chapters. It was Dominic's successor as second master general of the Order who introduced in 1228 the practice of individual houses being represented in the annual general chapter. The same innovation was quickly adopted also by the Franciscans, in 1239–40, and by certain congregations of the Benedictines only a few years later in 1248.[168] Similarly, the Dominican provincial chapter included representatives of each individual monastic house in the province, these representatives being elected in conventual chapter. Authority exercised by the general chapter was universal and absolute, there being no right of appeal against general chapter decisions; but the acceptability of this form of authority rested in the fact that its source was from below. One of the distinguishing features of the Dominican constitution was its second degree of election, that is, the election of members of the general chapter by representatives of the provincial chapters.

The methods for electing the various chapters were diverse, and there is some indication of minor variations in different editions of the very early constitutions of the Order. The conventual chapter was

168. Congar, "*Quod omnes tangit*," p. 230. The formalities of an annual general chapter came to the Franciscans because of dissatisfaction with the high-handed manner in which Elias, elected minister general in 1232, energetically implemented his mandate: Salmon, *Abbot*, p. 80 and n. 16.

composed of all the professed friars in a given house, and it elected representatives to go to the provincial chapter. This latter body would have been fairly large, sometimes having as many as two hundred members; its first duty was to elect a small committee of four to act for the whole body, although the responsibility for electing the one representative from a province to the general chapter always remained with the whole provincial chapter. The general chapter was a much smaller body, there being only eighteen provinces in the Order as late as 1360.[169] Membership of the general chapter varied on a three-year-cycle basis; for two consecutive years it was made up of representatives, one from each, elected by the provincial chapters; in the third year the general chapter was constituted of provincial priors *ex officio*. This alternation in form of membership thus gave considerable power to the democratic element in the Order, while ensuring that the "official" point of view of those in authority was heard, and could actually exercise a veto power in certain circumstances. Changes in the constitutions of the Order, for example, required the approval of three consecutive general chapters.[170]

The general chapter elected the master general, the provincial chapter the provincial prior, and the conventual chapter the convent prior; all of these offices were filled for life. Election of the prior in an individual convent was always considered to be very important; accordingly, membership requirements and procedures for establishing the presidency for a chapter were looked to carefully. Dominic had defined the electorate in a conventional chapter as the members of the conventual community. This was soon specified to mean all professed friars with one year of profession, and shortly became those with two years profession; by 1271 four years' religious profession was the requirement. Absentee voting was not permitted. The general procedure confirmed by the Order's general chapter in 1242 called for the prior to be elected by a majority of more than half the friars present in conventional chapter, or by a small committee elected by the whole chapter.[171]

From the beginning the provincial chapter was a novelty in Dominican constitutional practice because it was composed of elected representatives; it was also the major driving force in working out the

169. Galbraith, *Constitutions*, p. 39.
170. Ibid., p. 37.
171. Ibid., p. 46.

Order's constitutions. An ordinary provincial chapter always consisted of three categories of member: the conventual abbot from each convent, who was accompanied by one other friar elected to this role (of *socius*) by conventual chapter, and a third group—the preachers general of the province. This last category was somewhat amorphous in terms of the numbers involved; it has been suggested that there may have been as many as two hundred in the English provinces about 1260. The constitution of 1228 stipulated that the election of a provincial prior, by provincial chapter, required that there be two elected representatives from each convent accompanying their abbot. The special general chapter (*generalissimum caput*) that approved this constitution in Paris was attended by twelve provincial priors, each of them accompanied by two *diffinitores* as deputies of the provincial chapter with full powers. These delegates, it must be understood, were all more than mere representatives of their respective provincial chapters; as elected they were constituted administrators and judges, with the result that the collective entity they formed was a high council and court rather than a representative assembly. Yet it was also a representative assembly in some genuine sense. By 1259, the *socius* had to be elected by at least half his fellow friars voting in conventual chapter. There has been some suggestion that the actual role of the *socius* in provincial chapters was not fully participatory and voting, but merely a supportive and reportive one guaranteeing that full information and the views from each convent would be available to the provincial chapter.[172] But I have not been able to verify the accuracy of this limiting interpretation.

C. Urban Democracy

A historical phenomenon of some currency in medieval Western Europe requiring comment in terms of its possible influence on the notions of popular consent and popular involvement in the exercise of political authority is the city-state. Leaving aside the issue of the theoretical and actual origins of this form of polity in western Europe—an issue perhaps irremediably hidden in the mists of prehistory and certainly still unclear on the basis of currently available data—it is a fact that the Alpine rural cantons of the early thirteenth century in what is modern Switzerland were "pure democracies": tiny

172. Post, *Studies*, p. 89, and n. 112; cf. p. 109. Cf. Galbraith, *Constitutions*, p. 62.

self-governing political entities, employing as an instrument of decision making a form of popular meeting in which every householder had a position of equality with every other.[173] Such political entities, however, were relatively late models of medieval communities, reflecting a basic democratic foundation. Similar developments occurred earlier in northern Italy, Germany, and the northern areas of what are now France, Belgium, and the Netherlands, but the details are difficult to present with precision because written evidence is scanty.[174] The simple and direct type of urban democracy was grounded initially in an identity of economic interests among a relatively small but economically self-sufficient group of individual household units.

In the case of the later Swiss communities, the fact of being largely cut off geographically and climatically from outside contacts and interferences was a further significant factor. Self-sufficiency and relatively complete isolation combined also to foster a strong sense of individual rights and liberties, and independence in judgment. This form of essentially primitive democracy did not survive long, however, social life in these communities soon becoming more complicated with the emergence of conflicting interests, especially as the feature of isolation broke down. Relations with outside interests necessarily provoked a development towards the essential of political sovereignty for the community *vis-à-vis* its neighbors. What came to be needed was a degree of community organization, efficiency, and power that often was to prove antithetical to the values of democracy within the community itself. The history of towns in Italy and Germany in the Middle Ages shows two conflicting elements in their political development: the one internal and directed towards democracy and equality of participation and decision making in communal life, the other external and involving the issue of political sovereignty in respect of outside or foreign interests. These two elements were not reciprocal, except in the very early stages of the lives of the communities. Frequently, the aims of the two elements, inner- and outer-directed, were mutually antipathetic: the determination to achieve or maintain full political sover-

173. Clarke, *Medieval City-State*, p. 3. See also Mundy and Risenberg, *The Medieval Town*; Niccolai, *Citta e signori*; Mayer, *Mittelalterliche Verfassungegenschichte. Deutsche und franzosische Verfassungegenschichte*; Mayer, *Italienische Verfassungegenschichte*; *The Medieval City*, ed. Miskimmin, Herlihy, Udovitch.

174. Pirenne, *Early Democracies*. This is a new edition of part of Pirenne's three-volume *Histoire de Belgique*, published in 1910 and translated into English in 1915 under the title *Belgian Democracy*; cf. Clarke, *Medieval City-State*, p. 5.

eignty often appeared to require a sacrifice of democratic government.[175]

Also, though the original basis of urban life in these communities may have been democratic in a directly participatory way, some social and economic inequality existed from the beginning; and there was a natural and informal delegation of authority that devolved on some type of leader or magistrate, who was usually a person of relative wealth and practical or business experience. Development in organization and administration proceeded in parallel with increasing complexity of social and political life in the communities themselves. There was, nonetheless, a continuing and general acceptance that remained in many communities in the area, and which spread to many cities of Italy and the Holy Roman Empire in the high Middle Ages, that political power and authority rested ultimately in the people as a whole. Even though this democratic "instinct" came to be blocked and thwarted by a variety of political and economic obstacles, it remained a compelling spirit in the medieval free cities, showing itself most strongly in the cities of northern Italy in the eleventh and twelfth centuries, and in central Italy, Germany, and the Netherlands somewhat later, in the period 1200–1500.

In the final analysis, the thrust towards political independence and sovereignty usually proved superior and more enduring than the movement towards democracy; but there can be little doubt that the realities of the forms of polity found in the medieval city-states could not help but have exercised some influence on political thinking at the time. It has been stated often that the fourteenth-century republican views of Marsilius of Padua owed much to their author's upbringing and experience as a citizen of a northern Italian city-state.[176] Potential influences of a similar kind were available to medieval students of politics even earlier. Medieval forms of the democratic city-state ultimately did not survive, however; such types of city-state polity proved a dead end rather than antecedents in the development of the modern democratic nation. But for all that, details of their form and function constitute important data for medieval political history, illustrating what did exist in the way of democratic or popular forms of government and political institutions in the period. The Greek city-states, democratic as some of them clearly were in some stages of

175. Clarke, *Medieval City-State*, p. 4.
176. For Marsilius see Part 4, 1B below.

their existence, did not survive long either. Yet they have not been judged unimportant in the history of western political theory or insignificant for the political theorizing carried out by those who knew of their existence and the details of their operations.

City-states, specifically the current Italian republican models, did exist in the thirteenth century, the period of greatest flowering of medieval political thought and activity. Scarcity of data, however, makes it difficult to be specific about the actual evolution of these interesting and vigorous medieval polities.[177] Owing to the unrelieved tendency of Italian political writers of the twelfth and thirteenth centuries to approach their subject from the side of theory rather than practice, a tradition that continued with only qualified vigour until the early sixteenth century (with Machiavelli), there is almost no discussion of the Italian city-state at the time of its greatest flowering.[178] Further difficulties relate to the informal and improvisatory nature of the institutions that actually functioned in the Italian city-state in this period. For example, it is very difficult to trace the composition and evolution of their municipal councils. Relevant evidence is largely indirect and, until late in the thirteenth century, very fragmentary.[179] It seems, however, that the characteristic organ of the developing Italian commune was the parliament or *arenza* of all citizens. Something of this sort is known to have existed in Orvieto[180] in 1170, but the first reference to town councillors there is in a document from 1203. Even then the citizens' council seems to have been a purely temporary body convened to consent to a treaty with Sienna; and regular permanent councils are known to have been operative only from the 1220s, while specific evidence concerning the election of councillors does not appear in the records until 1295.[181]

177. Recent research on medieval Italian city-states, directed much more to details of the practice, rather than the theory, of governance, has been done by Waley: *Italian City-Republics*; *The Papal State in the Thirteenth Century*.

178. Waley, *Italian City-Republics*, p. 10; but see reference to the Italian city republican form of government in Aegidius of Rome *De regimine principum* 3.2.2 (see nn. 181, 301 and below); cf. Marsilius of Padua *Defensor pacis, passim*.

179. Waley, *Medieval Orvieto*, p. 145.

180. Orvieto was an independent city-republic in the States of the Church, a region controlled by the papacy from the twelfth to the fourteenth century; it fell under a succession of tyrants beginning in 1334: Waley, *Medieval Orvieto*, p. 147.

181. Waley, *Medieval Orvieto*, p. 145. A parallel to the typical (?) elective and temporally limited form of governance in the medieval Italian city-state was the organization of the monastic order known as the Hermits of St. Augustine. Constituted from groups of

It can be accepted, nonetheless, that the late twelfth or early thirteenth century had produced the practical necessities in these communities for them to have formed a type of urban administration that was the successor to the primitive form of town-meeting mode of democracy, the assembly of the entire citizenry being superseded in some fashion by a conciliar type of regular decision making. The characteristic decision-making body in a developing commune or city-state originally was an assembly of all citizens in a kind of parliament (*arengo* or *arenza*) within which, given the primitive character of notions concerned with voting and majorities, decisions were made by the body as a whole; but this large body soon disappeared in favour of a smaller and more efficient council. An illustration of the early, more primitive, form can be seen in the claim by the consul officials of Pisa to have derived their authority from its being "granted by the entire people of Pisa in public gatherings by a cry of *fiat, fiat.*"[182]

A certain amount of caution must be exercised when dealing with this type of data, however, lest a false impression be given concerning the positive features of these forms of early Italian city-state democracies. In the first place, this example of popular decision making indicates an informal, acclamatory type of procedure rather than any formal voting; secondly, there is no indication of how the individuals who were approved came to be chosen in the first place. It should be kept in mind in this latter connection that a selection process for city magistrates and other officials based on a form of lottery was practised in some Italian city-states well into the fourteenth century, this particular method of election being considered the most "democratic" (every candidate for office having an "equal" chance of being selected!).[183] Government of some small towns by a general assembly of the whole people was still occurring in some Italian communities in the thirteenth century, and general assemblies of all citizens continued to meet later than the thirteenth century in such places as Gualdo, Tadino,

---

various hermit communities, mainly in Italy, in the middle of the thirteenth century, the Order was the first to provide specifically for limited tenure for superiors; apparently even the minister general, at least at some point, held office for only one year after election by the annual general chapter: see Salmon, *Abbot*, pp. 83–84 and n. 30. Aegidius of Rome, who makes specific reference in his *De regimine principum* to the elective practices of the Italian city communes, was minister general of the Hermits in the 1290s.

182. Waley, *Italian City-Republics*, p. 61.
183. Moulin, "*Sanior et maior pars*," p. 369, n. 5.

Bassano, and Comacchio, long after this type of gathering could have had any part to play in the government of larger Italian communes.[184]

Even in instances where the general assembly of citizens did function, one of its principal roles was to designate members for the ordinary instrument of regular authority and administration, the consulate. So little is yet known of the actual devolution in the early stages of the history of these communes, however, that it remains a matter for conjecture whether any of these cities ever functioned for any period with only a general assembly and the consulate. Most Italian city-states seem to have evolved a two-tier conciliar system, with a smaller and a larger council, the former, often "secret," being the basic instrument of government. There was constant experimentation concerning the size and functions of both levels of council, so that there was considerable variation in these features from city to city, as well as from time to time in a given community. A "great council" often had 400 members; but sometimes the number was 200 or 300 or 800, even 1000. The "inner" or "secret" council was normally about one-tenth of the size of the larger one, with about 40 members, although it was often smaller: 24 or 16.[185] Methods of conciliar election were equally varied and subject to experiment, as well as often being quite complicated. A meeting of the major guilds at Florence in 1292, for example, considered as many as 24 different methods for electing "priors" (members of the great or general council).[186] At Lucca, a meeting was held in each region of the city, at which lots were drawn by all the citizens of the region; 550 of the lots were inscribed *elector consiliarii*, and everyone drawing one of these lots was required to name one man from his own region to serve as councillor.[187]

Elaborate procedures also were developed for decision making in both the large and small councils, and they were not always identical for the two levels of council. A quorum, often designated as two-thirds of the members, was necessary for the conducting of business. A simple majority of a quorum was usually accepted as sufficient for decisions relating to normal business; but it was quite common for a larger quorum and a larger majority to be required for certain types of important decisions. In some cases as many as ten / elevenths and even

184. Waley, *Italian City-Republics*, p. 61.
185. Ibid., p. 62.
186. Ibid., p. 63.
187. Ibid.

sixteen / seventeenths were stipulated. Voting, especially in the smaller councils, was often by secret ballot, and frequently very careful precautions were taken to protect the secrecy of the ballot. Minutes of council meetings were also normally taken, and carefully preserved by an official notary. Sometimes, too, detailed treatises of advice and procedure were drawn up to guide and limit the performance of those given responsibility for administering conciliar decisions and policy.[188] These documents in some ways resembled the earlier "mirror for princes" treatises, although they also contained technical and legal information concerned with actual procedures for filling an office. It is generally accepted that the late-twelfth- and thirteenth-century canonist and legist theories of corporation and the representation of corporations by way of elected or chosen leaders had considerable influence on the electoral procedures and practices in the Italian city-states; but the conclusion rests more on the certain likelihood that this must have been the case given geographical proximity and the obvious intensity of social and political intercourse between ecclesiastical and temporal spheres, than on documentary evidence, which remains slight.

Mention also should be made of the origins and development of one medieval southern French town, Toulouse, where there is clear evidence of the establishment and exercise of representative institutions. Apparently the Toulousan experience was paralleled in other towns along the Mediterranean coast of France, even though the degree of liberties and privileges achieved there was unique: what appears is an evolution from feudal to autonomous status, from monarchy through aristocracy to some form of democracy.[189] Still under the feudal jurisdiction of its count in the middle of the twelfth century, it seems that Toulouse had some form of elective procedure for providing the administrative and judicial officers who exercised the count's jurisdiction; in any event the count probably did not and could not choose these persons as he saw fit. Even membership in the count's advisory council and court changed frequently, perhaps even yearly, at this time.[190]

There was also a common council for the town. Formally established

188. Ibid., p. 64.

189. See Mundy, *Liberty and Political Power*, pp. xi–xiii; cf. Niccolai, *Citta e signori*; Besta, *Diritto publico italiano*; Mayer, *Mittelalterliche Verfassungegeneschichte*; *Italienische Verfassungegeneschichte*.

190. Mundy, *Toulouse*, pp. 38–39.

in 1152 as the "Common Council of the City and Bourg," it certainly had existed earlier as an informal body of the town's "good men"; and though subordinate to the count it was distinct from him and was not an instrument of his administration. Claiming to represent the whole community and possessing legislative initiative, this council was composed probably from the townfolk themselves by some simple and informal system that gave representation to the notables and family groups through choosing and even voting.[191] And perhaps also the count chose his own administrative and judicial team from the council itself, or from persons who could expect council approval.[192] This loose electoral procedure is reflected in the history of Italian towns of the same period, and reflects the electoral principle employed in the Carolingian tradition for naming judges and advocates.[193]

As the interests of the town's inhabitants diverged strongly from those of the count during the second half of the twelfth century, the Toulouse common council began to assume greater authority, acting for practical purposes through the cadre of administrative and judicial officials with which it had become virtually identical. A kind of consulate was formed—the term was used—representative of the town's common interests and against the count; and in 1188–89 the town's leaders decisively defeated their count, Raymund V, to give concrete expression to their liberties. At the time the so-called consulate was effectively under the electoral control of an oligarchy, but within a few years and without revolution or violence a popular party representing the business interests of Toulouse captured a majority of the elected consular seats (1202).[194] Almost immediately, however, Toulouse, along with other communities in the region, suffered the depradations of the Albigensian crusade, and the town's "age of liberty" came to an end. Some form of elective consulate persisted intermittently and in a variety of forms, but by 1270 Toulouse was reabsorbed under a broader monarchical polity.[195]

Another form of medieval communal democracy developed in the

191. Ibid., p. 32.
192. Ibid., pp. 39–40.
193. Ibid., p. 257, n. 88.
194. Ibid., pp. 66–68.
195. Ibid., pp. 159–71. Nonetheless, Mundy offers a very qualified explanation for this transformation "back" to a more authoritarian political model, pp. 160–67; and he provides considerable detail for the operation of medieval Toulouse's representative institutions, pp. 148–58, 361–76.

towns of the modern Benelux region, where communities developed in the eleventh and twelfth centuries in a way that took them gradually but inevitably outside the existing general orbit of rural feudalism.[196] The growth of these towns was fueled by economic considerations relating to trade and the cloth industry; and the townspeople sought to develop social and economic conditions expressible in legal form and authority in order to separate them from the normal feudal administration of the territory in which they were located. Such towns gradually succeeded in obtaining immunity from the normal laws of the region or territory in which they were located, and the right to develop their own laws. The general features of the growth of towns can be seen throughout western Europe in the twelfth century, but the most clearly defined examples of the phenomenon developed in the basins of the Meuse and Scheldt rivers, where definite forms of independent town organization date from about the middle of the century. As originally established, the medieval town was based on "privilege," that is, formal exemption from normal legal arrangements, with the exemption based on status. Like the feudal noble, the townsman or burgher was privileged: he was "free" from the normal strictures of the law as these applied to rural persons: he was a free man, not a serf.[197]

In the beginning and even later, at least in theory, these communities were democratic when the dominant political concept in practice elsewhere was that of feudal monarchy. Developing informally at first, and with such development having begun by the second half of the eleventh century,[198] the grouping of individuals in city or town was grounded in a community of interest shared by each of the burghers or townsmen, a common interest in maintaining and developing certain advantages deriving from living and working in the town itself. Thus, even though there were obvious and important social and economic interests at issue from the beginning, the form of governance was democratic in the sense that every individual burgher enjoyed the same general rights and obligations. The communes expressed directly, if loosely, the ideal of government of the people by the people themselves, and the authority exercised by the community magistrates came to be delegated directly by the people.[199] This was the theory, insofar as any theory of polity would have been articulated by citizens in these

196. Pirenne, *Early Democracies*, pp. 35–36.
197. Ibid.
198. Ibid., p. 46.
199. Ibid., p. 53.

communities at the time of their coming into being. In practice, however, power in the town was exercised largely by wealthy individuals who embodied quantitatively more of the common interests that had led to the community coming together; this is a normal state of affairs in any democracy where there are only latent conflicts of interest relating to economic life.[200]

By the mid-twelfth century, for example, the burghers of the Belgian town of Huy were electing their own councillors (*jures*), who swore their oath of office in the presence of the assembled burghers and were charged with the care of communal interests. These interests, however, did not encompass the whole range of the town's interests, and thus the town's independence was incomplete. The range of communal interests assigned to the jurisdiction of the *jures* was known as "*la basse justice*," and included such matters as municipal regulations and policing. The "*haute justice*," including such important features as property ownership and jurisdiction and criminal cases, remained in the hands of the territorial lord, who dispensed justice in respect of these matters through justiciaries appointed by him (*échevins*).[201]

A slightly different and more complete form of communal autonomy was established in the latter half of the twelfth century in the largely commercial towns of modern Belgium (Flanders), when Philip of Alsace, Count of Flanders (1168–91), bestowed a form of autonomy on a series of towns in his territorial jurisdiction. The towns were given a separate and independent jurisdiction of the following form: the count chose some twelve or thirteen *échevins* to administer the town, his choices being made exclusively from among the burghers themselves. The responsibilities of these *échevins* required them to act as the count's judges in the town, and to serve as town councillors. In practice, apparently, the count's authority over the town councillors and judges he appointed was slight. Though he nominated them, he could not depose them inasmuch as they served for life; and seemingly he soon did little more than ratify the appointment of new councillors as vacancies through death occurred. By the early thirteenth century the office of *échevins* had become an annual one, at the demand of the burghers; and a system began to develop whereby the individual seats for office of councillor were parcelled out to various districts in the town. This soon became refined further by a more or less complicated

200. Ibid., p. 54.
201. Ibid., p. 63.

form of election to the office. The practice of annual election of *échevins* had been established at Arras in the late twelfth century, spreading from there all over Flanders in the next few years, and thence to Brabant.[202] By this time, however, the actual office holders were drawn exclusively from the wealthy, mercantile class of burgher; and the same situation prevailed generally in other cities in the region: the communes were being governed by the wealthy class and in its interests.

The original state of affairs where office holding was open to all burghers irrespective of economic or social status thus disappeared very early, even though there may not necessarily have been any conscious effort to produce the change. None was needed; and equality disappeared as if by natural evolution. Nor was this change attended by any declaration of principle or change of constitution. Largely as a result of circumstances, power passed irresistibly into the hands of the wealthiest, and the government of towns changed from democracy to plutocracy, and ultimately to oligarchy. These changes had occurred by the twelfth century at the latest, that is, before the technical arrangements were made that saw actual transmission of legal independence to these towns. By the middle of the thirteenth century, for example, there were cases where members of the artisan class were explicitly excluded from holding municipal office.[203]

This state of affairs actually led to instances of artisans' revolts towards the end of the thirteenth century, as the masses of artisans suffered considerably from the exactions of an increasingly unpopular merchant oligarchy. A form of democratic revolution developed in the Low Countries in a number of city-states in Liège, Flanders, and Brabant, at least faint echoes of which can be detected in some of the political writing of the period. The writings of Godfrey of Fontaines are a case in point;[204] and in the midst of the civil disturbances in Liège, John Hocsem produced a political treatise in which he pronounced himself in favour of democracy over aristocracy and oligarchy.[205] Some fourteenth-century political pamphlets reflected similar views,[206] although it seems clear that none of this literary activity had any direct effect on the political realities of the region's communes. In the early

202. Ibid., pp. 72, 116.
203. Ibid., pp. 108–17.
204. See Part 3, 3c below.
205. Pirenne, *Early Democracies*, p. 159; John Hocsem, *Gesta episcoporum leodiensium* 2.283, cited in Lagarde, "Philosophie sociale," p. 121, n. 2.
206. Pirenne, *Early Democracies*, p. 159.

fourteenth century several of the Flemish communes, with the help of several sons of the Count of Flanders, actually succeeded in defeating the French forces of Philip the Fair and for a time established their own brand of artisan democracy.[207]

3. POLITICAL THEORISTS

A. St. Thomas Aquinas

There are three distinguishable types of thirteenth-century texts dealing with political theory: (1) continuing examples of the "mirror for princes" (*speculum principum*) genre; after the enormous success of the exemplar written by Aegidius of Rome about 1280, all later examples tend to be titled after the Aegidean work, *On the governance of princes* (*De regimine principum*); (2) commentaries on the *Politics* of Aristotle, a work that was translated into Latin about 1260 and quickly became a standard text for academic presentation and analysis in the arts faculties of most European universities; (3) occasional works, usually written in connection with the advocacy of one side or another in a contemporary political dispute, and often involving issues of the relationship between church and state.

As he did in many other areas of intellectual concern, Aquinas provided the most comprehensive and systematic thirteenth-century formulation of political thought. He produced examples of the first two types of political writing just mentioned, although his commentary on Aristotle's *Politics* remained unfinished at the time of his death, and covers only the first several books.[208] As well, there are occasional elements in his systematic treatises on theology that can be used to fill out Aquinas's overall views on the nature of polity; the most important of these is the treatise on law in the *Summa theologiae*, which represents his only set piece of political theory, but for all that needs to be supplemented from parts of his treatment of the virtues of prudence and justice.[209] This is not to say, however, that a fully articulated and comprehensive study of politics is found in the writings of Thomas Aquinas. Nor did the most important and influential medieval

---

207. Ibid., p. 136.

208. The *De regimine principum* of Thomas Aquinas is also incomplete and apparently unsystematic in its editing, as well as in the form in which it has come down in the manuscript tradition: see nn. 210, 211 below.

209. Aquinas treats prudence at *S.T.* 2–2.56–66, and justice at *S.T.* 2–2.67–112.

Christian theologian set out to deal directly and in depth with a theory
of polity. He was, however, one of the most rigorously systematic of
intellectuals; hence his efforts at formulating an overall theory of
reality can be expected to offer some views that fall into the category of
our specific interest.

One of the most significant features in the intellectual synthesis
offered by Aquinas is the use to which he puts his broad familiarity with
a wide range of learning in his own time. A particular feature of this is
his authoritative grasp of the philosophy of Aristotle and of the
Stagirite's Arabic commentators, Avicenna and Averroes. Aquinas was
one of the first Christian thinkers seriously to undertake the systematic
analysis of the whole *corpus* of Aristotelian writings, one of whose most
interesting elements is the *Politics*; there is some reason to think that
this document, with which St. Thomas was fully familiar, may have
been translated into Latin in the mid-thirteenth century specifically to
facilitate the Angelic Doctor's work of commenting on it.[210]

Some difficulties arise in attempting to offer a coherent account of
Aquinas's political thought, especially in summary form, because any
such account involves a blending of separate and even disparate
sources. No single *ex professo* Thomistic treatment of politics exists.
There is an incomplete text of the "mirror for princes" type, itself a
fragmented and incompletely formulated piece of advice to a not-fully
identifiable king of Cyprus: the treatise *On Kingship*;[211] an even more
unfinished literal commentary on Aristotle's *Politics*; and a number of
texts from various theological writings, the most complete of which is
the already-mentioned portion of the *Summa theologiae* dealing with
law. The basic principles of a Thomistic theory of polity can be seen,
however, and it is possible to determine at least something of his views
on the notions of consent, coercion, and limit that are of interest to us,
even though he does not deal with any of them either directly or
extensively.

---

210. A Latin translation of the *Politics* is printed along with the Thomistic commentary in *S. Thomae Aquinatis in libros Politicorum Aristotelis expositio*, ed. Raymond M. Spiazzi
(Turin: Marietti, 1951). But Eschmann notes that William of Moerbeke's translation
made for Aquinas is edited by Susemihl Leipzig, 1872: see Eschmann's catalogue of the
works of St. Thomas Aquinas in Gilson, *Christian Philosophy of St. Thomas Aquinas*, p. 465.

211. Eschmann lists several modern editions, none of them critical in the technical
sense, in Gilson, *Christian Philosophy of St. Thomas Aquinas*, p. 415; see also his comments
on the manuscript tradition; ibid., pp. 413–15. The only acceptable English translation,
along with a useful introduction, is Thomas Aquinas, *On Kingship*, trans. Phelan and
Eschmann.

Aquinas followed in the same basic Christian intellectual tradition concerning a theory of polity seen earlier in St. Augustine and John of Salisbury, although his formulation owed much to his reading of Aristotle's *Politics*. Considerable effort has been made to show the distinctiveness of the Thomistic theory of polity, particularly in respect of its basis in Aristotelian thought and in contrast with the earlier Christian political tradition based on Augustine;[212] but this distinction can be overdrawn. Aquinas was greatly influenced by the Aristotelian conception of political society as natural, it is true, and nowhere in his writings does one find the character of authority construed exclusively in terms of punishment for sin. But aside from this clear difference the doctrine of Aquinas continues to reflect the basic elements of the traditional Christian view.

It has been contended that St. Thomas tended to stress the notion of authority rather than that of coercion found in the earlier Augustinian-based tradition. According to this view, the earlier tradition emphasized the ruler's power as something given by God rather than the ruler's authority, and stressed the subject's moral obligation to obey; and even though the element of limit was assumed here, the notion of coercion as power was taken for granted, and consent seemed not to be necessary. But this summary judgment could be made for the most part of the position of Aquinas as well. Some effort has been made recently to stress the "paradoxical" and "dialectical" character of many of Aquinas's views concerning the nature of polity and of authority, acknowledging differences in emphasis and tone, if not in substance, in various texts written at different times and in different contexts of the Thomistic literary corpus.[213] A more plausible if less reverent comment, however, is that the great Dominican theologian was working here with disparate sources, and working in an area that held only moderate interest for him: the Augustinian mode of thinking typical of traditional Christian political views, the significantly different and more philosophical Aristotelian sources whose general attitudes Aquinas found congenial, and the sophisticated jurisprudential positions being developed from Roman legal sources. However possible it might be in theory to construct a coherent

212. On the novelty of interpretation provided for medieval political theorists by Aristotle's thought see Grabmann, "Studien uber den Eingluss"; Gierke, *Political Theories*; Carlyle and Carlyle, *Mediaeval Political Theory*, 5, chap. 3; Lewis, *Medieval Political Ideas*; Rivière, *Problème de l'église et l'état*; cf. Post, *Studies*, pp. 494–561.

213. Gilby, *Political Thought of Thomas Aquinas*.

and fully consistent theory of polity from this variety of sources, it was probably beyond the interest and willingness of Aquinas as a theologian to commit the necessary attention and energy.

St. Thomas follows Cicero rather than Aristotle in his treatment of justice, thus continuing a tradition made respectable by the Church Fathers and Augustine to the extent that after Augustine, Ambrose, and Isidore the Ciceronian definition of justice became a common thread in both Christian philosophy and moral theology; and he employs Ulpian's definition of natural law, probably from Gratian's *Decretum*.[214] It may be most accurate to say of the political thought of Thomas Aquinas that, while it shows significant and explicit influence from Aristotelian sources, a factor not present in earlier Christian material, it exhibits also the traditional elements of earlier Christian political theorizing. Accordingly, the issue of drawing a contrast between Aquinas and the preceding Augustinian tradition in politics must be approached with considerable caution.[215]

Aquinas offers the standard dichotomy between the good ruler and the tyrant, with the basis for the dichotomy, of course, being whether the ruler exercised authority on behalf of the common good or for selfish and arbitrary ends.[216] Thomistic terminology and form of expression on these points consciously follow Aristotle. In his treatise *On Kingship*, he reiterates the emphasis on the moral qualities necessary for a ruler;[217] but he is much more explicit concerning the natural

214. "Natural law is what nature teaches all animals," Ulpian, *Dig.* 1.1.1.3. The difficulties for Aquinas in correlating this Roman legal definition with his general doctrine of natural law are examined in Crowe, "St. Thomas and Ulpian's Natural Law." Aquinas was familiar with Roman law, at least insofar as it was present in Gratian's *Decretum*, and probably more extensively. He cited Roman legal sources, largely from the *Decretum*, more than 150 times: Aubert, *Droit roman dans Saint Thomas*. Cf. Chroust, "Philosophy of Law of St. Thomas Aquinas," pp. 35–38. In a brief and somewhat fulsome article Ernest Barker stated that Aquinas took the Roman conception of law, *lex est quod populus jubet et constituit*, from Ulpian, and taught that inasmuch as a ruler received authority from the people, via the *lex regia*, the people could withdraw this gift if it were abused: Barker, "Elections in the Ancient World."

215. Post minimizes, or at least puts in a more coherent context, the contrast between natural and conventional (Augustinian) views of society in his study "Naturalness of Society," *Studies*, pp. 494–561.

216. Cf. John of Salisbury *Policraticus* 4.1.

217. An earlier thirteenth-century exemplar of the "mirror for princes" genre was Stephen of Tournai's *Eruditio regum et principum*, written about 1259 and addressed to Louis IX of France. The work is almost totally without interest for our purposes, however; it contains little or no theory and only an occasional insight into Stephen's ideas on politics, being unsystematic and largely anecdotal in form.

character of political or civil society than earlier Christian thinkers, again reflecting an Aristotelian influence. With Aristotle and his Arabic commentator Avicenna, Aquinas states explicitly that the human is a social animal, and that to live in society is a necessity of humans insofar as individual human beings have a need for others of their species: this need to live among other humans in order to achieve full human development leads to the necessity of government as a form of social organization, government being concerned with the common good of the group as a whole.[218]

Stimulated by the specifics and the terminology of Aristotelian philosophy, Aquinas is able to express the notion of the common good in terms of the concept of end or final cause, and his particular application of this type of Aristotelian causality leads to a distinction between two levels of final causality for the human: one level, the temporal, is that of the common good to which the individual human is subordinate, as the individual needing other members of a collective group is subordinate to that group as the part is subordinate to the whole; while the other level, the spiritual or heavenly, is that of personal, other-worldly religious salvation.[219] For Aquinas as for any Christian, this world and any form of temporal society does not constitute the ultimate purpose, end, or final cause for human beings; the ultimate locus for a human is not any earthly political society. Man's "proper" place is heaven, where he will live for all eternity as a citizen of heavenly society. While on earth, nonetheless, a human being is necessarily a member of an earthly and temporal society to which in some sense he is subordinated as part to whole, and to which he owes allegiance and obedience. Aquinas in this way gives clear expression to both parts of the Christian directive to "render unto Caesar the things that are Caesar's and to God the things that are God's." He also provides a fuller and more intellectual formulation for this religious exhortation than seen in earlier Christian interpretations. It might also be said that Aquinas here proposes a new, if not novel, notion of what is natural for the human. For Aquinas it seems that one can describe the nature of the human as something to be fulfilled or completed beyond the order of the natural (creation); human nature requires the inter-

---

218. Thomas Aquinas *On Kingship* 1.1. Again, of course, the idea is typical: cf. John of Paris *De potestate regia et papali* 1; Aegidius of Rome *De regimine principum* 3.2.2; Dante *Monarchia* 1.12; James of Viterbo *De regimine christiano* 2.2; John of Jandun, *Questiones in duodecim libros metaphysicos*, 1.18.

219. Cf. Maritain, *Person and Common Good*.

vention of the divine in order to achieve its own purpose, eternal union with God outside the natural order of the universe. Christian theology thus functions to complete the Thomistic philosophical account of human society, and to provide the ground on which personal rights and the illegitimacy of complete subordination to the state or any social institution rest.

Employing Aristotle's theory and terminology for his own purposes, Aquinas expresses the dual directive of the Matthew text in terms of two types of Aristotelian end or purpose, each with its own integrity but with one end subordinated to the other. Temporal political society has a legitimate end or purpose insofar as it is necessary and natural to the fulfillment of individual human beings, who can neither live nor perfect themselves in isolation from other humans. This is why individual humans are legitimately subordinated to the common good of temporal political society and are required to be obedient to directives emanating from the authority necessary to organize and direct such a society. At the same time the individual human also has an end or purpose transcending the temporal limits of political society; and he is required to be obedient to directives emanating from the higher authority necessary to organize and direct this other heavenly or spiritual society. The two ends and societies, moreover, relate to one another in such a way that the temporal is subordinate to the eternal.

Such a formulation of the Christian directive to "render" to different but related authorities is more complex than the original Gospel text, but does not address yet the issue of how to distinguish precisely what things are Caesar's and what God's. Nonetheless, some advance has been made in the articulation of Christian political thought.[220] The thrust of such a theory of politics, however, is still towards a general emphasis on obligations of the individual member of a polity, obligations that reflect his subordinate position as part of a collective whole and the benefits accruing to him from the whole, for which some return is due. An emphasis on rights (in contrast with obligations) of the individual citizen in a polity is not so readily found in Thomistic political theory; and where it does appear it is connected directly with Aquinas's

220. Eschmann considered that in formulating the "thesis that civil society is an institution founded on nature and serving in its own way and at a definite and inalienable place in human affairs, the ultimate end of man, the eternal salvation of his immortal soul . . . [and] for having . . . coined the profoundest and clearest formula of the medieval city of God, the book *On Kingship* rightfully ranks as a classic in the world's political literature": Eschmann, Introduction to *On Kingship*, p. xxxix.

perception of the human person as transcendent in some way (but certainly not entirely!) of the political society of which he is simultaneously a part. In other words, the ground in the Thomistic theory of polity for a doctrine of human rights lies in his perception of a human being as a spiritual entity, something other than a mere material organism, and as such something more than a part of a collective social and political whole.[221] An oversimplification and shallow distortion of this view leads to the insistence that only a religiously based doctrine of the human as a spirit is adequate as a bastion against totalitarian political theory, especially totalitarianism of the "godless" kind.

For Aquinas as for others in the same tradition, the specifics for achieving the purposes of any given society to which individual humans are subordinated are expressed in the law, to which these individuals have obligations and are subject. The laws are in the most basic sense descriptive of reality and prescriptive with respect to how humans are to pattern their behaviour in conformity with their place in it: laws stipulate how humans are to conform themselves to the world in which they live and in respect of their basic relations with one another, thereby conforming to the will of God Who is creator of the totality. This is not to say that Aquinas was unaware of, or would have been unimpressed by, the much-made of modern distinction between prescriptive and descriptive law.[222] He would have accepted the distinction as formulated, but questioned its relevance for the issue at hand, essentially because of his conception of the comprehensive rational orderliness of the universe as a whole.

Aquinas subscribed fully to the view that rulers are subordinate to law in the sense that they are not exempt from its sanctions, and are not permitted to act in an arbitrary or self-serving manner; he specifically rejected the formulation: "What is pleasing to the prince has the strength of law," a principle found in the Justinian Code that was being appealed to by jurists then arguing in favor of the royal prerogative.[223] Of course the position taken by Aquinas here has been seen often enough before and was typical of the Christian moralist. At the same time his theory of law, like his views concerning the purposes of society, embodied a more sophisticated position than any found among earlier Christian writers.

221. Cf. Gilby, *Political Thought*, pp. 237–50.

222. See Schlick, *Problems of Ethics*, chap. 7.

223. *Dig.* 1.4.1; cf. *Inst.* 1.2.6. Aquinas quotes the dictum as an argument against his own definition of law, and responds to it: *S.T.* 1–2.90.1 arg. 3 and *ad* 3. See Gilby, *Political Thought*, pp. 53, 128.

He did not assert nearly as static a notion of law or, indeed, of reality as a whole as that seen in John of Salisbury, for example. Further, reflecting his familiarity with Roman legal dicta as well as a daring not attempted by Salisbury, he accepted the principle that "necessity knows no law."[224] Perhaps influenced by his experience of the political realities of his own day, and certainly inspired by a reading of the *Politics*, Aquinas acknowledged a diversity among forms of political organization and was prepared to legitimize differences in law in terms of diversity of geography, human culture, and custom.[225] Of course, the element of acceptable relativity in law can be seen earlier in Augustine and explicitly in the sixth-century Isidorean definition of law[226] that Aquinas repeated, probably taking it himself from the early part of Gratian's *Decretum*.[227] But there is something more in the Thomistic acceptance of the element of flexibility and variation in law than can be found in earlier Christian writers. He had been influenced by what might be called the more relaxed approach to directives of human behaviour, both ethical and legal, to be found in Aristotle.[228]

Aquinas, for example, expanded directly on Salisbury's distinction between flexible and inflexible law;[229] and his basic conception of natural law—a notoriously slippery concept that appears throughout the history of Greek, Roman, and Christian ethical theory in a variety of guises—takes on the character of an inclination, rather than that of a

224. "Si vero sit subitum periculum, nonpatiens tantum moram ut ad superiorem recurri possit, ipsa necessitas dispensationem habet annexam, quia necessitas non subditur legi": Thomas Aquinas *S.T.* 1–2.96.6; cf. Post, *Studies*, p. 293. Though John of Salisbury makes no reference to the maxim "necessity knows no law," it was a commonplace of his day; it was used by Bernard of Clairvaux, and by canonists and legists generally from the twelfth century onward for almost every need to interpret the letter of the law in terms of equity: see Post, *Studies*, p. 318, n. 22.

225. Thomas Aquinas *S.T.* 1–2.95.3; 97 *ad* 2; John of Paris *De potestate regia et papali* 3; Dante *De monarchia* 1.14; Englebert of Admont *De ortu, progressu et fine Romani imperii* 16.

226. Isidore *Etymologiae* 5.10 and 20. Aquinas cites Isidore's definition of law and explicitly examines its adequacy at *S.T.* 1–2.95.3 and 4.

227. Gratian, D.4 c.1 and c.2; cf. Post, *Studies*, p. 502. Gilby argues that the use of the Isidorean definition illustrates a reflection of Cicero's contention that political liberty implies some share in governance, a view that in turn reflects the ancient notion that the people were the source of political authority: *Political Thought*, p. 133. But see my qualification of Aquinas's treatment of the people as the source of law: section 3A below.

228. Cf. Gilby, *Political Thought*, pp. 170, 178–80, 304–6.

229. John of Salisbury *Policraticus* 4.7.527C.

notion having more fully specified content.[230] Consistent with his acceptance of human legal and institutional diversity, he accepts that there can be different and presumably even contrasting forms of regulating human behaviour where there are real and relevant contrasting factors. He also acknowledges specifically that the law can change, at least in terms of more precise specification and as the result of greater intellectual perception into the meaning of general purposes.[231] Withal, he repeats the basic Augustinian position that human, positive law is an essential extension of natural and eternal law, the order of the universe ordained by God, essential as a structure for and corrective to the nature of humans, which has been damaged by sin. Positive law thus implements and protects natural law.[232]

St. Thomas asserts a preference for monarchy as the most perfect form of polity. Dealing in *On Kingship* with the standard Aristotelian frame of reference for this issue, he opts directly for one-man rule, on the standard theoretical ground that organization of many in a group is best achieved under a single ruler.[233] In a later work, however, he expresses approval for a mixed constitution combining features of monarchy, aristocracy, and democracy: he describes a form of polity in which a single ruler having supreme authority is surrounded by a group of advisors whose credentials are superiority in judgment and virtue, while the ruler himself is elected by the people. This advocacy of a mixed polity showing elements of monarchy, aristocracy, and democracy was repeated by John of Paris. Aquinas actually uses the

230. Thomas Aquinas *S.T.* 1–2.94, 91.2. Literature on the Thomistic conception of natural law is too extensive to enumerate here, but see two recent articles: Crowe, "St. Thomas and Ulpian's Natural Law," and Chroust, "Philosophy of Law of St. Thomas Aquinas."

231. Thomas Aquinas *S.T.* 1–2.94.5, 95.2, 97.1–4. See Chroust's remarks on Aquinas's concern for the legitimate relativity of positive law in Chroust, "Philosophy of Law of St. Thomas Aquinas," pp. 31–33. The view that law could be changed, that is, that new legislation could replace earlier law, was recognized early in the formal development of Roman Law. Jolowicz notes that Livy asserted that the Twelve Tables of republican law admitted of changes according to the principle that later law takes precedence over earlier law in cases of contradiction, a principle connected to the concept of the law having its basis in the popular will: "in XII tabulis legem esse ut, quodcumque populus postremem iussisset, id ius ratumque est" (Tab. 12.5, cited in Jolowicz, *Historical Introduction to Study of Roman Law*, p. 19, n. 10).

232. Thomas Aquinas *S.T.* 1–2.91.3, 95.1 *ad* 2.

233. Thomas Aquinas *De regimine principum* 1.1.

expression: "The election of rulers belongs to the people" (*ad populum pertinet electio principum*);[234] and elsewhere he speaks of the right of a given multitude to provide itself with a king.[235]

Similarly, Aquinas speaks of lawmaking as "the office of the entire people"; but he does not clarify the meaning of this expression, nor comment at all on how this is to be done. He also contends, however, that lawmaking authority does not rest exclusively with the people; it can also reside in "the public personage who has the care of them [the people]."[236] It is not possible to say with exactness what Aquinas has in mind when he speaks of these two sources of lawmaking authority: does he designate the two in either/or terms, contending that either the people themselves have the power to legislate directly, or that this

234. Aquinas asserts that all people should have some share in government, that this is the first principle of a right ordering of the polity inasmuch as it promotes peace: *S.T.* 1–2.105.1 and *ad* 1; Aristotle *Politics* 2.9.1270b17. Cf. John of Paris *De potestate regia et papali* 19 *ad* 36; Marsilius of Padua *Defensor pacis* 1.13.6. The context for the Thomistic doctrine is Aquinas's comment on the fittingness of the Old Testament doctrine concerning rulers. Aquinas's example, like that of John of Paris as well, is the Jewish polity from the time of Moses, that is, before the Jewish monarchy; and he distinguishes the two phases of the Jewish polity before and after the monarchy (ibid., *ad* 2). Aquinas refers to the pre-monarchical model as containing features of all three basic types of polity: monarchical, aristocratic, and democratic. It reflected democracy or popular rule (*democratia, id est potestate populi*) in two ways: (1) its leaders were chosen *from* among the people (*ex popularibus possunt eligi principes*) not another nation; (2) the choice itself pertained to the people (*ad populum pertinet electio principum*). He repeats that the Jewish polity was democratic inasmuch as (1) its leaders were chosen from the whole people (*de omni populi*), citing Exodus 18:21: "Provide wise men from the whole people," and (2) the people chose (*sic*) them (*populus eos eligebat*), citing Deuteronomy 1:13: "Provide wise men from among yourselves." Seemingly, the manner designated here for how the people choose a ruler need not involve any activity on their part. Later in the same text Thomas reiterates that monarchy (of this constitutional type) is the best form of government, and asserts that from the beginning God made certain provisions about how a ruler was to be chosen from the people, but he makes no reference to the choice "pertaining to the people" or to the people "choosing" (ibid., *ad* 2).

235. Thomas Aquinas *De regimine principum* 1.6.49.

236. Thomas Aquinas *S.T.* 1–2.90.4; cf. 90.3; 2–2.57.2; Gilby, *Political Thought*, App. 5, pp. 175–76. Gilby contends that "Aquinas preferred the customs of free people to the prince's initiative as the origin of legislation," citing *S.T.* 1–2.97.3 *ad* 3 (*Political Thought*, p. 133); cf. Regan, "Aquinas on Political Obedience and Disobedience." But this text also offers an option concerning the condition of the people; the human community is either self-governing or under some superior authority. In the latter case the people are not free to make their own law, and it is only in the former case that Aquinas specifies that the people are their own lawmaker. See n. 233.

power rests directly with the ruler, who thus can operate independent-ly of the community he rules; or is there some indication here of an interconnection between ruler and community by which the legislative power directly exercisable by the ruler nonetheless somehow derives from the community as a whole?

The second interpretation is the more probable in Aquinas's case, given the prevalence of the principle that authority and the founda-tions of law in a political community rests ultimately in the people. This principle has been seen in a nugatory form in earlier Christian writers, it existed as a maxim of Roman law, and Aquinas would have seen it again in Aristotle. Such an interpretation is reinforced by the fact that thirteenth-century thinkers generally, though not exclusively, still were inclined to assume that the actual results of lawmaking in a society were to be found in the customs of that society rather than in deliberate and regular activity by the ruler. The prince was seen still largely as an enforcer, interpreter, and implementer of these laws rooted in custom and derivative from the society (the people), rather than as someone who made new law. This attitude was changing, largely as a result of juridical claims being made by advocates of the developing national monarchies, who emphasized the ruler's authority to legislate in virtue of his office as embodying the people as a whole, as well as from the burgeoning legislative activities of the papacy. Aquinas, however, was by no means in the vanguard of the movement in favour of temporal national sovereignty, any more than he was captive of the arguments favouring the centering of some form of power over temporal jurisdictions in the papacy.[237]

There is still a significant element of ambiguity or absence of clear specification here, nonetheless, and it has to do with the question of whether the transmission of authority from the people to a ruling "personage" was complete and permanent, or whether some residual power remained in "the people" or the political community after the community had somehow transmitted its authority to a ruler in the first

237. Gilby, *Political Thought*, p. 191. As the following paragraphs should make clear, Aquinas reflected what Treharne referred to as *the* thirteenth-century constitutional problem, one seen earlier in John of Salisbury but becoming more fraught with practical significance in the later 1200s—the problem of "how to make explicit the implied limitations on royal absolutism": Treharne, "Constitutional Problem," p. 59. For evidence that the notion of the ruler as a lawmaker existed in the early medieval period as well as later, see Brynteson, "Roman Law in the Middle Ages."

place.[238] This issue, as we have seen, was emerging in a rather imprecise way in the twelfth century among canonists concerned about procedures for appointing a bishop. Aware of and interested in preserving the ancient notion that the people of a diocese had rights in the selection of their bishop, they had grappled with the question of how precisely to give procedural expression to this right. And a further issue was perceived, having to do with the possibility of the misuse of authority by a bishop (or pope) once installed in office: was his authority in any way revocable, and if so, how?

The history of canon law in the twelfth and thirteenth centuries shows a continuing interest in and a developing attention to this latter problem, and the emergence of two types of response. One group of canonists, continuing an emphasis on the other basic constitutional principle in medieval Christian theories of polity, namely, that authority comes ultimately from God and *ipso facto* entails the obligation of obedience on the part of subjects, tended to the view that whatever power might be said to have resided in the people as a whole to choose their ruler and formulate their own laws was effectively and completely transmitted to the ruler, so that no power remained in the people. Having relinquished it, they no longer had it; hence, they were effectively powerless in the face of the exercise of authority by their ruler. Only God ultimately had any power remaining with which to deal with a ruler in office. Another group, however, was beginning to take what might be called a more realistic, as well as a more logically sophisticated, view in the face of the potential problem of the misuse of authority, and this group began to urge the thesis that authority was actually revocable in certain circumstances. This thesis was established on the notion that the subjects, over whom and in whose communal interests authority was exercised, retained some rights of control over the authority if it was misused; and hence in these communal "residual" rights and authority rested the justification for revocation of authority.

The whole matter is very imperfectly presented in so brief a summary, but the general frame of reference should be clear. We are

238. Gierke makes reference to the conflicting views concerning the revocable character of the *lex regia*: *Political Theory in the Middle Ages*, pp. 149–50. Two thirteenth-century canonists who held that the people can revoke the transfer of power to the *princeps* were papalist supporters: Godfrey of Trano and Hostiensis. See Ullmann, *Medieval Papalism*, p. 166.

speaking here of *canonical* legal theorizing within the frame of concern for the exercise of ecclesiastical or spiritual authority in the Church. Yet one cannot underestimate the possibilities for transfer of ideology and thought across the jurisdictions of the two laws. Many of the problems were the same in the two jurisdictions: the issue of possible misuse of authority had at least as much reality and as many ramifications in temporal as in ecclesiastical jurisdictions. Any perception of, and reference to, the history of temporal polities placed heavy emphasis on the evils of tyrannical political rule; and it is perfectly plausible to suggest that the legal thinking on such a question among legal experts in the one field of law would be of interest to and known by legal experts in the other. Frequently enough, of course, the experts in the respective fields were the same persons. The question of whether or not the people retained any of their lawmaking authority at least residually, or transferred it wholly and irremediably to the ruler, however, is precisely the question Aquinas failed to address.

Aquinas was equally open-minded and option-offering in respect of the means for establishing temporal authority. Like John of Salisbury, he did not limit to one the legitimate means for placing a ruler in office. He spoke of the right of the people to provide itself with a king, as already noted.[239] But he also held that "a higher authority (God directly? some ecclesiastical authority? or, less dramatically, some higher temporal ruler, such as the emperor?) might also be the establishing instrument; and he presented this two-fold option in two separate works.[240] Again, it is clear that Aquinas did not concern

239. See nn. 234, 236 above.

240. Thomas Aquinas *De regimine principum* 1.6.49–50; 2 *Sent.* 44.2.2 *solutio.* The *On Kingship* text clearly has in mind higher authority of a political type: Aquinas refers to the Jewish people having appealed to Caesar Augustus over the head of Archelaus. But the same text speaks of God as "the King of all," and as such the last recourse for aid "when there is no hope of human aid against tyranny." This remark, however, seems not to intend any juridical interpretation directly applicable to the temporal order. The *Scriptum* text speaks of temporal authority becoming legitimate "either through public consent or by the intervention of a higher authority [*per consensum subditorum, vel per auctoritatem superioris*]," and while Aquinas has a human rather than a divine agency in mind, there is no explicit reference to the higher authority as necessarily a temporal power. A measure of the ambiguity in the use of this "higher authority" concept as one of two sources for legitimate political power, of course, was the force of the claims in current hierarchical theory emphasizing jurisdiction by the spiritual authority as superior over the temporal sphere. Marsilius of Padua was the first explicitly to reject the view that there can be two legitimate causes of temporal authority.

himself with identifying the specific procedure for legitimizing the exercise of political authority. He could afford to be indifferent-seeming in this matter because apparently it held little interest for him. He accepted that there could be a variety of forms of polity and presumably, then, a variety of methods for rulers coming into authority. What did interest him was how a ruler exercised his authority, rather than how he came by it.

Insofar as this was the case, Aquinas's notion of consent by the people did not reflect the element of procedural action by a body of citizens that is an essential in the modern democratic sense of the term. When Aquinas spoke of the people electing or choosing, what he had in mind probably was some form of popular acceptance or acquiescence, with or without a required specific form of expression. He was fully aware of, and concurred in, the principle that the people in some way were a source, if not the origin, of political authority, and that accordingly they had some role in its establishment. But apparently he did not see this role as necessarily anything more than symbolic; certainly he never insisted that it had to be functional and procedural. Nor was his notion of the ruler that of a mere representative. His model was likely that of the traditional Old Testament texts that describe how the Israelites received their king from God, where the primary essential was election by God rather than selection by the people. The people's consent here was neither explicitly nor very clearly described; but it was clearly nothing more than a form of acclamation as a specific procedure.[241] A recent suggestion that Aquinas at least inclined

241. When Aquinas described the benefits of a mixed polity in terms of it having some function for all social classes, he made specific reference to the Israelite polity as the model, wherein the people's consent seems to have been understood generally as acclamatory: see n. 234 above. Gilby is correct, I think, to associate Aquinas's acknowledgment of the basis of political authority in the people with his doctrine of law, rather than with the issue of how a political ruler comes into authority or loses it. Gilby traces this thread back to Cicero through Augustine, but does not clearly specify the channel: see Gilby, *Political Thought*, p. 108, where he cites Cicero *De re publica* 1.25, as a source Aquinas used without naming it via its transmission through Augustine *De civitate Dei* 2.21: *S.T.* 1–2.55.2. It should also be noted in connection with the people as lawmaker that this view reflected the notion that law was not so much made as existed in the customs of the people. The position thus reflects an essentially passive role for the people; they are more a vessel than an agent. Eschmann offers a more formal explanation for Aquinas's silence on what we have been calling the procedural aspects and specifications for expressing a principle of political theory when he says: "The theologian, conscious of both the nature and the limit of his science, knows that a practical order is not set up by

towards a doctrine of residual rights in the people insofar as he taught that the final political test for the legitimacy of power was popular consent seems gratuitous; the evidence for this being his "final test" is not to be found.[242]

While the notion of consent lacks specification in the thought of Thomas Aquinas, his handling of the notions of coercion and limit was more explicit. The latter concept functions regularly in his description of the legitimacy of authority: authority always has limits beyond which its exercise is not legitimate. A comparable and parallel position is taken regarding coercion. Political authority must possess, and is entitled to exercise, such coercive power as is necessary to produce obedience to its laws. Coercive power in a state resides in its authority, which is a social or public corporate reality, not in an individual person. He replies negatively to the question whether any person can make law (legislate) on the grounds that only an entity possessing coercive authority can make law; a private person cannot do so because he lacks the coercive power (*vis coactiva*) needed for law. Such coercive strength (*virtus coactiva*) resides either in the people as a corporate whole or in the public (corporate) figure who personifies them.[243] Aquinas also provided, however, that the laws in whose service force can be used must themselves be genuine laws. He relates coercive power directly and necessarily to the lawmaking authority: a piece of legislation or legal formulation that lacks the backing of coercive authority is simply not a law for Aquinas. But the element of coercion, however necessary, is not in itself a sufficient condition for law; the coercing authority in addition is subject to the further necessity of limit: "Subjects [in a human society with a human authority] are not under their superiors in all regards, but only within fixed limits."[244]

For Aquinas authority, like rationality, is a self-limiting concept; the element of limit is an essential feature in the meaning of the concept

---

deductions but by determinations depending on free will and authority. In other words, St. Thomas knows what a *ratio practica* is ... Aquinas often seems to have irritated, as it were, by his laconic statements in this matter. Their terseness, however, is well founded in an accurately defined theological method from which he never deviated"; "Aquinas on the Two Powers," p. 200.

242. See the Gilby interpretation offered in his translation of Thomas Aquinas *Summa theologiae*, 28:176.

243. Thomas Aquinas *S.T.* 1–2.90.4 *ad* 2.

244. Thomas Aquinas *S.T.* 2–2.104.5 *ad* 2; cf. the contrasting definition of law in Marsilius of Padua.

itself. And coercion, which is integral to the concept of authority as another essential quality, is conditioned necessarily by this element of limit. As noted, St. Thomas even spoke of the coercive strength (*virtus coactiva*) residing in the people or in the public figure who personifies them, showing clearly the essential connection between the notions of authority, coercion, and limit; coercive power resides in a society and its expressed authority by definition.[245] Aquinas also illustrates here the parallel between his notion of coercion and his view of the basics for law.

Aquinas's attitude towards opposition to tyranny provides an opportunity to examine more of the specifications in his doctrine of limited authority. A useful test for any such theory of authority is to enquire what its author proposes in a situation where the theoretical limits of authority, wherever they may be set, are exceeded: what is to happen if and when an authority goes beyond its justifiable limits? Here Aquinas's position is not fully satisfactory, and shows him less than willing to extend the concept of limit to a point logically consistent with the concept itself. This probably reflects the measure of his interest in the subject rather than his capacity for logical analysis. For him, of course, tyranny is not legitimate, nor are tyrannical laws "true" laws. As he puts it: "A tyrannical government is unjust because it is not directed to the common good."[246]

St. Thomas was familiar with the text of John of Salisbury's *Politicraticus* and its justification of tyrannicide; and he addresses this issue specifically in the treatise *On Kingship*. He offers there the following position: inasmuch as it belongs to a group as a whole (*multitudo*) to provide itself with a king, it is not unjust for that king to be deposed or to have his power restricted by the same group when he abuses his royal power and becomes a tyrant. Inasmuch as it pertains to a higher authority to provide a king for a certain group, a remedy against the wickedness of a tyrant is to be sought from that higher

245. Thomas Aquinas *S.T.* 1–2.90.4 *ad* 2. Making coercion a feature of law may indicate that Aquinas saw the use of force as morally positive, something to instil and encourage virtuous behaviour in citizens. This would represent a development of the Augustinian view of coercion as merely repressive and punitive.

246. Thomas Aquinas *S.T.* 2–2.42.2 *ad* 3; cf. *De regimine principum* 1.3. St. Bonaventure, a contemporary of Aquinas, held that Christians were obliged to obey temporal rulers only in such things as are not contrary to God, and then only in respect of matters reasonably ordained to comply with right custom: Bonaventure, 4 *Sent.* 2.54.3.1, cited in Gough, *Social Contract*, p. 37, n. 1.

authority. In the event no human aid whatsoever is forthcoming against a tyrant, recourse must be had to God, the King of all.[247] Access to the means of redress for tyranny seems here to be related to the particular manner by which the tyrant originally came into office, with Aquinas again reflecting his tendency to offer an option regarding the means whereby a ruler comes into office: if the people as a whole put him there, they have the right to remove him (although Aquinas does not specifically identify tyrannicide as a legitimate method for removing a tyrant). Nor is there any blanket approval offered for deposition or restriction of a tyrant's powers. In one place Aquinas even offers an interpretation of a Scriptural text cited by John of Salisbury in order to avoid a forthright acceptance of tyrannicide as authorized by the Old Testament. To the text, "Aioth slew Eglon, king of Moab, who was oppressing the people of God under harsh slavery" (Judges 3:14*ff*), Aquinas comments that Aioth slew a foe rather than assassinated a tyrant.[248]

Another Thomistic text[249] is more forthright in its acceptance of tyrannicide, but the direct comment admitting this form of radical action is in a reply to an objection, and not in the formal body of the text itself, where Aquinas's reply is more circumspect. The issue considered directly is whether there is a necessity to obey a tyrant. Aquinas's response asserts that the obligation to obey political authority rests on the fact that the originating authority (for all authority, including temporal) is God Himself, Who has the power to impose an obligation to obey internally, in conscience, as well as externally through physical coercion. Accordingly, Christians are bound to obey temporal authorities inasmuch as their authority comes from God. He then distinguishes authority by way of acquisition from authority as exercised; and goes on to say that there is no obligation to obey an authority as badly (tyrannically) exercised: such authority as exercised is not lawful authority at all, even though it may have been lawfully acquired in the first instance. He also contends that if the authority is lawfully exercised it must be obeyed, even though it may not have been lawfully acquired. Clearly, the issue of how authority is used is more important for Aquinas than that of how it was acquired in the first place. He adds

247. Thomas Aquinas *De regimine principum* 1.6.49–50.
248. Ibid. In the same text he provided an argument that "apostolic teaching" rejects rather than commends tyrannicide, citing 1 Peter 2:20 and Prov. 20:26.
249. Thomas Aquinas 2 *Sent.* 44.2.2. This text is earlier than *On Kingship*.

that even in a case where a temporal ruler may have acquired his position in an irregular or unacceptable fashion, the usurper of power can have his authority legitimized and become a true ruler either through the consent of the people or in virtue of his position being recognized by a higher authority. Aquinas obviously was repeating here the traditional two options for coming into lawful authority seen in his treatise *On Kingship*, and earlier in John of Salisbury.

On the issue of evil in the exercise of authority Aquinas draws a further distinction: first, authority can be misused insofar as it commands actions directly contrary to the very purpose for which authority is conferred, the common good. Subjects are obliged *not* to obey such commands. Secondly, a misuser of political authority might issue commands that are beyond his legal rights; in these cases subjects are not bound to obey the commands, but neither are they obliged not to obey.[250] Finally, Aquinas is prepared to justify tyrannicide itself in these words: "Where someone has acquired power by violence either against the will of his subjects or by compelling their consent, and in conditions where there is no possibility of appeal to a higher authority for redress, a person who frees his country by killing the tyrant is to be praised and rewarded."[251]

St. Thomas addresses the issue of tyrannicide again, this time more formally, in the *Summa theologiae*, where he offers a typically nuanced view that implicitly qualifies or at least does not directly accept Salisbury's view in even a circumscribed form. He holds here that it is legitimate to kill a malefactor provided that the action is directed to the well-being of the community as a whole, and is performed by someone charged with responsibility for the community as a whole, not by a private individual as such. A private citizen is entitled to perform only those acts directed to the common good that do no harm to any other individual; legitimately to harm another person one must possess judicial authority. Accordingly, a private individual who kills another (presumably, even a tyrant), even in furtherance of the common good, acts beyond his rights as a private individual.[252]

An earlier article also in the *Summa theologiae* amplified Aquinas's position here with regard to what might be done to counter tyranny,

---

250. Ibid., *solutio*.

251. Ibid., *ad* 5. It may be worth noting that this is a relatively early text in the Thomistic *corpus*.

252. Thomas Aquinas *S.T.* 2–2.64.3 *resp.* and *ad* 3.

short of tyrannicide. The question addressed is whether sedition is always a mortal sin? In replying in the affirmative, St. Thomas distinguishes between sedition (always mortally sinful as an act) and an action to depose a tyrant (not sinful because it is not sedition). One of the difficulties Aquinas raises against the view that sedition is sinful is the following: "We praise men who free a people from the rule of a tyrant. But insofar as this is not easily done without some dissension among the people, it would seem that dissension [sedition] is not morally justifiable in these circumstances." His reply to this difficulty runs as follows: a tyrannical government is unjust because it is not directed to the common good. Dissension against such a government, then, is not sedition unless the disturbance against tyrannical rule causes greater suffering among the people than the tyranny itself. Indeed, the tyrant is the more guilty of sedition insofar as he fosters dissension among his own subjects by remaining in power.[253]

In sum, Aquinas seems here not to have rejected categorically the right of revolt against tyranny, even revolt that produces political upheaval. At the same time, however, he qualifies the degree of such upheaval in terms of the degree of tyranny; political revolt legitimately cannot produce greater upheaval than the tyranny it aims to over-throw. In the final analysis, Aquinas authorizes political revolt against an authority that acts seriously and persistently against the public good in terms of either deposition or correction, with the qualification that the dissension caused by such reaction to tyranny must not be so excessive that the people would suffer more from it than from the tyrant. But he does not explicitly approve so extreme an act as tyrannicide; in fact, he denies the right of a private citizen to take the life of a tyrant. But there may be room here for the argument that a person acting to kill a tyrant is not acting solely in the role of a private individual, especially if the theoretical rider is added of there being no other known way to eliminate the tyranny. Cajetan was to interpret this Thomistic text in precisely such a fashion in the sixteenth century and conclude that Aquinas did justify tyrannicide.[254]

253. Ibid., 2–2.42.2; see especially *arg.* 3 and *ad* 3.
254. *Summa theologiae*, vol. 38 of Blackfriars English translation, pp. 26–27, n. a. Eschmann suggested that Aquinas's more mature reluctance to espouse tyrannicide as a direct possibility may have reflected his personal knowledge of the thirteenth-century history of the various Italian communes: Thomas Aquinas *On Kingship*, p. 24, n. 5; cf. *Cambridge Medieval History*, 6:179 *ff*. A recent interpretation of Aquinas's position on

A summary statement of Aquinas's theory of polity must conclude that his views were neither fully comprehensive nor fully coherent, a consequence of them being found in a variety of disparate texts, the major two of which are themselves incomplete, with one of these (the treatise *On Kingship*) apparently somewhat unorganized even in the portions that are complete. The most extensive element in the Thomistic theory of polity, and the most systematic, is the treatise on law from the *Summa theologiae*. Not surprisingly, it has been the most influential as well. All three of our trace elements: consent, coercion, and limit can be found in the political doctrine of Aquinas; but in respect of none of them do we find any genuinely significant new ground being broken. The Thomistic notion of popular consent was the traditional one whose origins are found in the Old Testament precedent of the Jewish polity, and whose importance, though without any procedural specification, was reinforced by the *Politics* of Aristotle. Aquinas's acceptance of the necessity and value of coercion as a feature of legitimate authority echoes the Augustinian tradition on this point, although St. Thomas is much more careful to circumscribe its legitimacy by reference to its limitation in terms of rational ordering to the common good. His overall insistence on rationality as an essential element in the exercise of authority also does much to de-emphasize the notion of coercion.

B. Henry of Ghent

Another theologian of the period whose writings provide information concerning at least some features of political theory was Henry of Ghent (ca. 1217–93). A French secular cleric who spent most of his

---

opposition to tyranny draws very liberal conclusions on his advocacy of this kind of political action, suggesting that St. Thomas was prepared to accept revolt against tyranny even by private citizens. This conclusion is reached by the simple expedient of taking views found in the *Summa theologiae* as Aquinas's last work, and interpreting *S.T.* texts that are silent on qualifications and distinctions made in earlier Thomistic texts as suggesting that Aquinas may have eliminated such notions: Regan, "Aquinas on Political Obedience," pp. 84–85. I am not convinced that this mode of interpretation is acceptable; and on one particular point I think Regan is wrong to suggest that Aquinas accorded the right to a private citizen to engage in revolutionary activity against a tyrant. Aquinas explicitly denies this in *S.T.* 2–2.64 *ad* 3. To be fair to Regan, however, one should note that he is interpreting Aquinas on the legitimacy of revolt against tyranny, not only on the more radical act of tyrannicide.

professional teaching career at the University of Paris, Henry was born in Flanders in an area that had long been one of the most faithful fiefdoms of the king of France; he was also archdeacon of Tournai, a French enclave in Flanders. With whatever deliberate reflection it cannot be said, but Henry has left a doctrine of polity strongly supportive of the type of government he experienced: hereditary monarchy. He offers no formal or extensive treatment on the nature of politics as a whole; but as is so often the case with medieval academics like himself, an examination of his various writings yields a series of comments on the basic elements for a theory of polity.

Like John of Salisbury and St. Thomas Aquinas before him, Henry favours monarchy as the best form of government, stating categorically that "the man who is king and who exercises authority alone in a community is its best chosen ruler."[255] He goes on to say, however, that princes are not feudal lords in respect of the possessions of their subjects as if the subjects were serfs, employing a distinction in use among contemporary Flemish city-states: that between free men (citizens of a city-state) and serfs, who were under ordinary feudal law.[256] Temporal rulers are, rather, protectors and defenders of their subjects who willingly assign to the monarch the office of protector along with the necessary means of exercising it. The prince is representative and chief of the community, whose members extend to him very broad rights; and he in turn extends certain rights and duties to the community.[257] For the good of the state, accordingly, the ruler rightfully can dispose of the goods of his subjects who are parts of the state over which as a whole the prince stands as its embodiment.[258]

There is nothing particularly unique or novel in this position; it is a

255. "Principatus autem in communitate ordinatissimus est ille qui est monarchicus in quo dominatur unus solus": Henry of Ghent *Summae quaestionum ordinarium*, cited in Lagarde, "Philosophie sociale," p. 111.

256. Henry of Ghent *Quodlibeta* 14.9, cited by Lagarde, "Philosophie sociale," p. 110. Henry's distinction, and the identification of citizens as having the status of free men, shows another influence from Aristotle's *Politics* where, of course, the dichotomy was drawn between free man and slave as the most obvious category of non-citizen. Godfrey of Fontaines shows a similar contemporary emphasis on the fact that citizens are free and, accordingly, have a right to expect that their obedience to authority should be voluntary, issuing from agreement and consent. Marsilius of Padua shortly was to give this principle a striking formulation. For Godfrey see section 3C below; for Marsilius, Part 4, 1B.

257. Lagarde, "Philosophie sociale," p. 110.

258. Henry of Ghent *Quodlibeta* 8.22, cited by Lagarde, "Philosophie sociale," p. 111.

standard formulation of the corporation theory of polity typical of the twelfth and thirteenth centuries. The concept of representation or representative does not reflect the procedural feature of explicitly voluntary delegation mentioned earlier. Nor does Henry develop or even present anything bearing directly on the notion of consent; he does not appear even to use the terminology, not speaking directly at all of popular consent or consensus as a feature in the exercise of authority. This is not to say, of course, that he would have denied this notion as a feature of a legitimate polity, merely that he did not express the thought directly. Henry does address directly one of the essential features of any theory of polity, however: namely, the issue of limit in the actual exercise of authority and how, if at all, limit might be imposed on princely power. In a text composed in 1290, he accepts the legitimacy of subjects having an obligation to princely authority, on the grounds that the ruler is supreme in respect of his authority based on pursuit of the common good; but he asks whether subjects are obliged to submit to all orders given by a prince, even those that on the evidence do not seem directed to or inspired by the common good.

Henry responds by noting that two replies can be given. One opinion maintains that a subject cannot judge his ruler under any circumstances and must simply obey: unconditional obedience is the lot of the subject. Others, however, have held that something of a contract exists between ruler and subject, having in mind apparently something involving the general feudal concept of there being some kind of contractual relationship between lord and serf. But consistent with his earlier rejection of a simple feudal relationship between prince and subject and his denial that the ruler exercised a feudal lord's rights over the possessions of a subject, Henry proceeds to develop the notion of the common good and the ruler's connection with it. He maintains that the common good is of absolute primacy in a commonweal—nothing new here!—and that the prince's authority is totally bound up with it. He contends that the prince is obliged to be sufficiently prudent as "to incarnate the common good of the whole community," and to act in such a way as always to command from his subjects only what furthers the common good, without his subjects then having any grounds for protesting against regal actions in terms of their own particular interests. As for the notion of there being some form of contract existing between ruler and subject, Henry submits that even if this were the case, its effect on the subject relates to his being a member of the community in which the contract can be presumed to have force. An individual can either adhere to a community by remaining within its territorial boundaries, or he can move his domicile elsewhere; if he choses to remain, he accepts thereby the authority of the community and of the prince who is its representative or incarnation. Henry thus clearly asserts the concept of continuing tacit consent, according to which the people consent to legislative power even without a verbal promise of obedience; consent originally given in any form cannot be withdrawn thereafter and remains as tacit consent to all laws. He may be reflecting here an interpretation of the *lex regia* current among some jurists.[259]

Henry extends his doctrine of the primacy of the common good explicitly to the nature of corporate communities, urban communes, examples of which he would have been familiar with in the Flemish region. He maintains that there is no escape from the principle that the common good is paramount, even in communities where in some sense the citizens associate themselves freely in the polity. Not only can citizens be asked to contribute the (normal) tenth (*dime*) as a tax contributed to further the common good; they may be required even to contribute half or all, or even life itself; "*non solam decimam, imo medietatem imo totam, imo seipsos.*"

Having stated this formulation in terms of the value of the common good, Henry then returns to the other side of the tension in the thesis: unconditional obedience on the part of the subject relates only to the common good. Accordingly, princes can do nothing except in terms of the common good. Subjects must obey all commands and orders in this respect; and they must be prepared even to concede that in many cases profound implications for the common good can be perceived only by the prince alone, escaping the notice of ordinary subjects. In cases where the relation between a ruler's edict and the common good is not evident to them, subjects in the first instance still should presume good faith on the part of the ruler and obey his commands. The notion of "evident" utility as the basis for public action by the prince goes back to the Roman theory of legislation, to the effect that the emperor when making new law to supersede existing legislation must do so for evident utility (*utilitas evidens*).[261] The concept was cited frequently by medieval

259. Ibid., 14.9 cited by Lagarde, ibid., pp. 113–14.
260. Ibid., 14.8, cited by Lagarde, ibid., p. 113.
261. See Ulpian, *Dig.* 1.4.2. This passage is cited frequently by medieval legists and canonists: *Glossa ordinaria*; Odofredo *Lectura* or *Commentarium* on the *Digesta vetus*, cited in Post, *Studies*, p. 295, n. 114.

legists and canonists, and was being cited regularly at this time by temporal rulers as the basis for their right to special taxes and other forms of exaction of public service. If acts of whose tyrannical character there is no doubt are repeatedly commanded, however, and there is clear evidence of the common good being thwarted, subjects are entitled to appeal to higher authority for redress and correction of their leader, or for his deposition. And in the event that all peaceful attempts at legitimate redress fail, Henry concedes to subjects the right to disobey and to act to depose their ruler themselves, rather than continue to submit to his tyranny: "When no hope of correcting such a ruler [tyrant] any longer exists, subjects should act to depose their ruler rather than submit to him; and they should not obey."[262]

In the last analysis, then, Henry legitimizes and advocates direct action by tyrannized subjects against their ruler; they should serve the common good in ways that can go beyond passive resistance and disobedience to a tyrannical ruler, even if the tyrant is an hereditary prince. In this he takes a more extreme and, it can be said, a more consistently applied and explicit position in extension of the principle of legitimate political authority being limited by the concept of common good than did Thomas Aquinas. It may be that Henry's advocacy of ultimate direct action by citizens against tyranny reflected his familiarity with the circumstances in the Flemish towns in the 1280s when there were serious problems between members of a number of the communes and their leaders or *échevins*, and of the serious reasons leading to actual revolt in that period in the town of Ypres, for example.[263]

C. Godfrey of Fontaines

A contemporary of Henry of Ghent, who would have been equally familiar with political conditions in this region of north-western Europe, took an even more explicit and sophisticated position in relation to citizens' rights and their acceptance of political authority. Godfrey of Fontaines[264] (ca. 1250–1306) was also a secular cleric of the

262. "Quod si non sit omnina spes correctionis in isto, debent subditi agere ad depositionem superioris, potius quam tolerare ipsum et non obedire," Henry of Ghent *Quodlibeta* 14.8, cited in Lagarde, "Philosophie sociale," p. 114.

263. Lagarde, "Philosophie sociale," pp. 116–17.

264. The best single treatment of the political views of Godfrey is still the research of Lagarde: *Naissance de l'esprit laique*, 2, Secteur social de la scolastique, 2nd ed. (Louvain: Nauwelaerts, 1958), pp. 161–213; cf. "Philosophie sociale."

period whose writings contain explicit material dealing with the nature of polity. In particular, he deals in one of his quodlibetal questions (1294) with the same issue raised by Henry of Ghent concerning a temporal ruler's authority to impose an obligation on his subjects. The manner in which Godfrey formulates his question is itself interesting and instructive: "Whether a prince claiming benefit to the state as justification, but without this type of necessity being evident, can impose any form of taxation and require his subjects to be obliged to pay?"[265] Godfrey's extensive reply shows clearly that his acceptance of the general principle that a subject is obliged to support the public interest, merely at the call of the ruler whose responsibility it is to promote it, is solidly and extensively qualified by a realistic assessment of the actual exercise of political authority.

Godfrey first advances a position contrary to his own. A prince can impose a tax on his subjects without there being any manifest reason for so doing, insofar as the prince has the authority to wage war and provide all things necessary for his troops to conduct warfare; accordingly, he can impose any exaction that in his judgment serves this purpose, as St. Augustine established.[266] His own doctrine, however, does not accept that a ruler can impose anything on his subjects arbitrarily. "This kind of activity is not licit in a proper political society (*principatus rectus*) where one person rules over others who are free and not serfs; for a free man has the right to act on his own initiative and not to have his actions totally controlled by someone else."[267] Godfrey accepts that taxation is the legitimate right of a ruler provided it is directed to the fulfilment of the common good. But he contends that imposition of taxes is legitimate only if judged to be in the public interest by the people on whom the burden of tax falls, and is formally accepted by the community as a whole in some way through the consent and knowledge of its superior and more prudent members.

First of all, he points out, subjects or citizens have a right and a duty to examine carefully the issue of public necessity and what is to the benefit of all members of the polity in common; it is proper to inquire whether a given tax measure is fully legal, that is, consistent with reason

265. Godfrey of Fontaines, Quodlibeta 11.17, in *Quatre premiers Quodlibets de Godefroid de Fontaines*, 4:76–78.

266. Augustine *Contra Faustum* 22.75 (*PL* 42:448).

267. "Ubi aliquis principatus aliis ut liberis non ut servis, hoc non licet; quia ad liberum pertinet ut ille sit causa suarum actionum et non ab alio agatur totaliter," Godfrey of Fontaines *Quodlibera* 11.17, p. 76.

and prudence, the foundation stones of good government. Public acts are to be performed by a prudent prince on the advice of a council whose members are true friends of the common good, not merely cronies of the prince who can be expected to agree with their master's wishes and offer little or no objection to the desires of the man whose favour they curry.[268]

Godfrey could also be cynical in his remarks on the actual practices of rulers, observing that everyone knows that princes always claim to be acting with advice from a good and great council (*bono et magno concilio*).[269] His principal contention, however, is that citizens who are free must always be able to evaluate for themselves any demands imposed on them. He is careful, nonetheless, to restrict the process of popular evaluation, and does not extend it in a fully democratic way. Godfrey does not envisage the consultative process as involving literally everyone in the community; like Thomas Aquinas he specifically denies that private persons as such are entitled to deal with public matters. The distinction between an individual as a private person and as a citizen (*civis*) is not in itself sufficient warrant for concluding that Godfrey was less than a complete democrat, of course; the distinction was quite a common one at the time, and can be seen in such quite different political doctrines as those of Thomas Aquinas and Marsilius of Padua. But while there is nothing theoretically impossible in conceding that every individual in a polity could function as a *civis* (as Marsilius of Padua specifically acknowledged), Godfrey in fact did not subscribe to this view. He held that the supervision and evaluation of potential tax legislation, and presumably of other forms of legislation as well, should be carried out by "qualified persons, prudent and faithful, who will concern themselves with government in order to approve measures to be taken for the common good, thereby permitting all in the community to adjudge that what is being imposed on them is reasonable, and that they accept it voluntarily."[270]

In presenting his own position formally, Godfrey begins with the observation that Aristotle held that the best person to provide good and rightful policies as leader of the polity should be one who is himself the best and most prudent of men, a kind of semi-deity in respect of others in the polity. He goes on to comment wryly that what is best does

---

268. Ibid.
269. Ibid., 77–78.
270. Godfrey of Fontaines *Quodlibeta* 11.17, p. 77.

not always produce what is best, however, and proceeds directly to a rejection of hereditary monarchy as the best form of government. It can be taken for granted here that, without mentioning any of them either by name of their authors or other form of designation, Godfrey was taking a conscious stance against contemporary political theories advocating hereditary monarchy as the best form of government. For his part, Godfrey prefers that rulers be chosen "by the people through election (*principes instituerentur a populo per electionem*)";[271] this procedure produces a better result than hereditary succession. For even though common malice sometimes operates among the many and the electorate might thus make a poor choice of ruler, election as a method for selecting a good ruler is still superior to the "natural selection" process of hereditary (*electio secundum se magis est via ad habendum bonum principem quam generatio naturalis*).[272]

These are refreshingly novel views to encounter in the late thirteenth century. For the first time a medieval political theorist is consciously expressing a preference for popularly based political leadership, and specifically rejecting the hereditary principle on the grounds that hereditary succession is inferior because it is less likely than an elective process to produce a good ruler. Godfrey goes on immediately to acknowledge that hereditary succession was the normal method by which the political rulers of his own day came into power; the only exceptions to hereditary succession at that time were the imperial throne of the Holy Roman Empire, where election was by a small group of electors exercising that office in virtue of their own hereditary monarchical position,[273] and a number of city-states, most of which were soon to be transformed in the fourteenth century into hereditary one-ruler states. Godfrey insists, nonetheless, that "normal practice" does not necessarily embody the ideal norm, and that actual hereditary successors to political authority are not necessarily "better and more prudent men." Even when it happens that heredity turns up a good ruler, he continues, such a ruler cannot be expected to be immune totally to personal passions that can affect his judgment for better and for worse, and cause him not to rule principally for the common good but for selfish interests. And here Godfrey inserts the traditional invocation to the necessity that every ruler must exercise his

271. Ibid., p. 76.
272. Ibid.
273. Cf. Heer, *Holy Roman Empire*.

office in accordance with the law, not merely his own conception of what is prudent, citing Aristotle as his authority on the point.[274]

Our author then repeats the principle that when one person rules over other persons who are free men, not serfs, he comes by his right to rule only in virtue of its being given him by the whole community. This time Godfrey mentions a number of options whereby the ruler over free men comes by his authority: the whole community (*tota communitas*) either "elects" (*eligens*), "institutes" (*instituens*), "accepts" (*acceptans*), or "consents" (*consentiens*).[275] He neither defines nor differentiates among these four terms, however, and his text does not make clear whether he actually has a set of differing procedures in mind, or is merely compiling a set of different words to designate one unspecified procedure, although the former seems more likely. What he does go on to state clearly is that the ruler who comes into office through the whole community's choice, however this is to be expressed in detail, cannot impose anything onerous or hurtful on the community he governs except with the consent of the governed (*nisi hoc procedat de consensu subditorum*);[276] and further, that the subjects should obey voluntarily and not as a result of coercion (*debent non coacte sed voluntarie obedire*),[277] knowing the reason for any imposition and approving it as for the community's good.

Godfrey spells out two ways in which a ruler's imposition on his subjects can meet the criterion of being "reasonable" in respect of furthering the common good: (1) it can be a direct extension or

274. Godfrey of Fontaines *Quodlibeta* 11.17, p. 76; cf. Aristotle *Politics* 3.16.1287a. The prospect of a single ruler succumbing to selfish and tyrannical behaviour contrary to the common good echoes another Aristotelian concept: *Nichomachean Ethics* 10.8; cf. Thomas Aquinas *S.T.* 1–2.105.1 *ad* 2.

275. Godfrey of Fontaines *Quodlibeta* 11.17, p. 77. Godfrey does not employ the "normal" medieval formula mentioning the alternative sources of legitimate political authority: the people and some higher authority. Nor, however, does he explicitly reject the latter option, as Marsilius will do.

276. Ibid. In an interesting application of the principle of *q o t* to the ecclesiastical sphere Godfrey indicated that there was some doubt concerning whether the bishop of Paris on his own could condemn a theological opinion as heretical, given that the whole community of the Church and not just its head should be involved in such an action. Godfrey seems here to have had in mind the Tempier great condemnation of 1277 and its inclusion of Thomas Aquinas: Godfrey *Quodlibeta* 3.9; "Quod omnes tangit," p. 239, and n. 114. Godfrey also denied that Celestine V had the right to resign the papacy, arguing that others than the pope himself were involved and ought to have been consulted. *Quodlibeta* 12.4, cited in Congar, "Quod omnes tangit," p. 240 and n. 115.

277. Godfrey *Quodlibeta* 12.4.

application of an already existing statute that itself was established as consonant with the rational and prudent judgement of the discreet men of the community; (2) while formally outside the terms of existing legislation, it can be the result of advice from the prince's council, provided, however, that the advice come from a council made up of just and faithful members who really have considered the measure and its alternatives and have adjudged it to be better and more useful for the common good at issue. And he concludes this section with an admonition: it should be understood, regarding any measure that imposes a heavy burden on the subjects of a polity without there being a clear reason for its imposition in terms of common utility, that the prince himself is not superior to anyone else in prudence, fidelity, and love for the common good, nor is the advice of the members of such a king's council so excellent that it should be accepted as coming from more credible persons than anyone else: the subjects, then, are not legally obliged by any such measure insofar as it is unreasonable.[278]

Godfrey thus directly juxtaposes two of the four elements identified by St. Thomas Aquinas as necessary characteristics for a law,[279] rationality and essential reference to the common good, with the notion that the prince embodies the authority of the state; and he shows them to be limiting conditions on the right to make law. And by connecting this formulation with the practice of imposing new tax legislation, he signals clearly his familiarity with both the form and the reality of the claims being urged in the developing nation-states of the late thirteenth century on behalf of a ruler's right to act for the state as a whole and enjoin obedience to his decisions on his subjects. Godfrey was not unwilling to accept the notion that a ruler embodies the state's full authority; but he objected to its blanket and unqualified application. His aim was to identify some criteria for determining when the principle could be accepted in practice, and when not; and in this respect he was not prepared to concede that agreement by the king's personal advisors was sufficient warrant for acknowledging the rights of a ruler's claim. Even the king's council of advisors could be "in the ruler's back pocket"; hence the need for a more objective and disinterested body of qualified persons. Almost certainly there must be clear echoes here of contemporary political events with which Godfrey was familiar.

278. Ibid.
279. Cf. Thomas Aquinas *S.T.* 1–2.90.1–4.

Godfrey goes on to remark that a prince always maintains that his taxes are being imposed out of state needs and for the advantage of all his subjects, recognizing that otherwise he could not by law impose them. Godfrey insists again that the free subject of a state should do what is in the public interest voluntarily and from choice, not through coercion and violence (*voluntarie et ex electione ... non coacte et per violentiam*).[280] Subjects, therefore, should be shown that it is probable that the tax is appropriate; a mere statement by the ruler that this is so does not suffice; for tyrants and good rulers alike always make such claims, and cannot be distinguished one from the other simply on the basis of what they say.[281]

Godfrey is imprecise concerning the relationship between the group of "qualified prudent and faithful persons" (the representatives) and the people as a whole, and does not discuss any method by which they come to exercise their supervisory and advisory role. However, there are important advances here over anything thus far in medieval political writing. There is some recognition of the need to spell out an actual method for controlling the activities of a given ruler; and the use of the term "voluntarily" to qualify a free subject's obedience to political authority reflects the basis for a newly expressed constitutional doctrine. For Godfrey, someone who governs persons who are free and not slaves holds his right to govern the community as a whole only in virtue of the community having chosen him (*eligit*);[282] the community puts him in the position of authority, accepts him, gives him its consent (*consensus*).[283] In virtue of this fact his rule should be exercised only for the common good, and by way of the authority delegated to him by the people.

As we have seen, Godfrey accepted the legitimacy of hereditary rule, acknowledging it as normal in his own day. But he regretted its prevalence, asserting flatly that while hereditary rule was the norm, very few good rulers were to be found; most rulers were tyrants. His specific suggestion for improvement lacks a certain cogency, however: respect for the law must be fostered in princes; they should be instructed through right reason and submit themselves to the control of prudent men. But Godfrey's realism and cynicism concerning

---

280. Godfrey of Fontaines *Quodlibeta* 11.17, p. 77.
281. Ibid.
282. Ibid. and p. 76.
283. Ibid.

contemporary conditions show clearly when he adds: "When the prince is content to consult his private council, without wishing others to know the reason and necessity for the impositions about which they are deciding, the subjects should resist him if they can until qualified councillors can examine the worth of the measures being proposed. To act otherwise would be to transform the kingdom little by little into a tyranny, and to reduce free men to the condition of serfs. It is to be feared that weakness by some and faithlessness by others is leading us today directly to this."[284] A kind of tired and reluctant acceptance of the inadequacies of the realities of actual governance seems here to accompany Godfrey's expression of the preferred ideal, an ideal that has been described as almost equivalent in formulation to proposition 14 of the *Declaration of the Rights of Man*.[285]

As with Henry of Ghent, Godfrey's views on temporal polity must have been conditioned by his own background and experience. He came from the city of Liège which, unlike neighbouring areas, actually enjoyed a form of quasi-republican constitution at the end of the thirteenth century. It has been called an "ecclesiastical republic" at the time, having been headed for nearly a century by its bishop who "reigned but did not govern." This ecclesiastical and temporal leader was nominated to his spiritual office by the chapter of the episcopal see of St. Lambert and to his temporal authority by three municipal groups: chapter, commune, and nobility, all of whom jealously and vigorously defended their rights to consent to all measures affecting their interests. Godfrey was himself an archdeacon of Liège, and the doctrine advanced in his Quodlibet XI exactly interpreted and reproduced the political realities of his homeland. Like many another political writer, he preferred the conditions of his own community to those he observed elsewhere; and he advocated an extension of these conditions to other constituencies, however skeptical he may have been about such prospects.

D. Aegidius of Rome

Aegidius of Rome, sometimes called Aegidius Colonna or Giles of Rome, was a very prominent theologian and churchman of the late

---

284. Godfrey of Fontaines *Quodlibeta* 11.17, p. 78.
285. Lagarde, "Philosophie sociale," p. 139.

thirteenth century.[286] Born about 1247, he had studied theology at the University of Paris, perhaps under St. Thomas Aquinas during the latter's second tenure at Paris; and in turn Aegidius himself filled a chair in theology in the French capital. Aegidius was also very active politically, in both ecclesiastical and temporal circles; and was to become adviser and confidant to rulers in both. His treatise *On the governance of princes* (*De regimine principum*)[287] may have been written as advice to the youthful Philip IV of France, who succeeded to the French monarchy in 1285, and with whom Aegidius enjoyed something of the status of tutor. The work itself became the standard exemplar of this type of treatise ("mirror of princes") and was enormously popular; it had been translated into Italian as early as 1288, only a few years after its publication, and even earlier into French.[288] In due course, Aegidius became master general of his own religious community, the Hermits of St. Augustine, and as resident in Rome became an advisor to the unfortunate Celestine V, who took but a few months to realize that the public rigours of papal office were ill-suited to his personal inclinations towards solitary piety. When Celestine's resignation from the papacy led to the succession of Boniface VIII in 1294, Aegidius continued as a trusted papal advisor; and Boniface named him cardinal-archbishop of Bourges in 1295.

In response to complaints from both ecclesiastical and temporal quarters concerning the propriety or legality of Boniface's election as pope, Aegidius wrote a treatise justifying papal resignation: *On papal resignation* (*De renuntiatione papali*).[289] Shortly afterwards he was to produce another ecclesiastical political treatise in defence of the papacy of Boniface VIII, *On Ecclesiastical Power* (*De ecclesiastica potestate*),[290] thereby intervening directly in the current controversy between

286. There is no full-scale modern biography or doctrinal treatment of Aegidius. A useful though dated bibliography can be found in Gilson, *History of Christian Philosophy*, 735–36. A recent article is sceptical of the accuracy of much of the conventional biographical data on Aegidius. Referring to Giles of Rome as "an obscure figure," Luscombe makes no reference to any connection between him and the Colonna family: Luscombe, "Lex divinitatis".

287. There is no modern edition of this work, despite its popularity in its own time. I have used the printed edition, Rome: 1556; reprinted Frankfurt: Minerva, 1968.

288. Rubenstein, "Marsilius of Padua," p. 69.

289. Aegidius Romanus *De renuntiatione papae*, ed. Joannis Thomas Rocaberti (Rome, 1698), 2.1. pp. 1–64.

290. Aegidius Romanus *De ecclesiastica potestate*, ed. Richard Scholz (1929; reprinted, Scientia Aalen, 1961). I am preparing an English translation of this work.

Boniface and Aegidius's former pupil, Philip the Fair. Aegidius's treatise on papal power is one of the most extreme, as well as one of the lengthiest, expressions of the medieval theory of papal *plena potestas*, and served as the basis for some of the strongest formulations of this thesis in Boniface's well-known papal bull, *Unam sanctam*, of 1302.[291]

Aegidius's views on the relationship between church and state are expressed at what might seem to some readers as excruciating length in the treatise *On Ecclesiastical Power*. The principal reason for referring to this text is that the work is a graphic illustration, certainly the most sustained and in some ways the most curious because of its extreme emphasis on the superiority of papal authority over temporal rulers, of an earlier statement concerning the general principles underlying a Christian theory of polity. Along with the almost paralysing frequency of Aegidius's insistence that temporal authority is subordinate and inferior to the papacy as the embodiment of spiritual authority, and with his equal insistence that all temporal power derives from spiritual power, Aegidius accepts categorically that there are two distinct and distinguishable spheres of authority, ecclesiastical and temporal, and that temporal political authority enjoys a full integrity at the same time that it is fully subordinate.[292] To state this, of course, is not to suggest that his theory of polity succeeds in its thesis that political authority simultaneously can be possessed of its own integrity and be fully subordinate to ecclesiastical authority. But Aegidius certainly considered that his thesis was defensible, and this fact itself provides a clue to his understanding of the concept of subordination.

For Aegidius, "royal power is established through priestly and papal power,"[293] and "the pope is the source of power among humans."[294] He argues that a ruler born of wrath is not a just ruler except insofar as he is cleansed of his sin by ecclesiastical action. Inasmuch as all rulers require to be cleansed of Original Sin, a cleansing only accomplished through the spiritual activity of the sacrament of baptism, it follows that all rulers are under ecclesiastical authority as dependent on it for their own.[295] Aegidius does not address directly the issue of what happens to a ruler's right of authority when he is "born of wrath"

291. *Extrav. Io.* 1.8.1; English translation in Tierney, *Crisis of Church and State*, pp. 188–89.

292. Aegidius Romanus *De ecclesiastica potestate* 3, esp. 3.1 and 2.

293. Ibid., 3.10.

294. Ibid., 3.9.

295. Ibid., 3.11.

because of the commission of any actual sin (for example, tyrannical behaviour); but the position would be the same. He maintains explicitly that the papal power can intervene when a ruler sins inasmuch as the former is superior to any temporal power, but he contends that such papal intervention should not take place unless the ruler has sinned. And he goes on simply to assert that the papal power shall always "act through a lay person in respect of a judgment of blood,"[296] that is, as regards the use of physical force or coercion. The text is quite without specification, however, as to how the civil authority is to intervene, and no reference is made at all to the people's rights in such a case. Further, it is clear that any such action on the part of the spiritual authority, even though it involved the exercise of physical force on the part of some temporal ruler on the spiritual authority's behalf, would be considered by Aegidius to be a "spiritual action"; its purpose would be spiritual: punishment for sin.

There are several other brief comments in the work *On Ecclesiastical Power* that bear on the elements of our concern with a theory of polity. Aegidius speaks of canons as giving consent and electing a bishop: they function in this respect, he asserts, as secondary efficient causes in the same way that natural things do when they act as causes in this world.[297] His point really has to do with a doctrine of the papal fullness of power, which is such, according to Aegidius, that the pope can do alone and without employing any secondary causes whatever Christ allocated to the power of the Church: the pope can act alone, but under ordinary or natural circumstances he will not do so, just as God Himself can act alone to produce effects in this world, without the operation of secondary efficient causes, but under normal circumstance does not do so. Aegidius insists, for example, that God could make a calf without the secondary efficient activity of a male of the bovine species inseminating a female; however, God does not do so in normal circumstances. Similarly, the pope could perform alone any activity for which the Church has had power allocated to it: for example, he could appoint a bishop without the intervening secondary efficient causal activity of a canonical election. Ordinarily, however, he does not do so. As well, according to Aegidius, the pope can act outside at least certain forms of positive laws: "positive moral laws."[298] His point is that insofar as the

296. Ibid.
297. Ibid., 3.9.
298. Ibid., 3.9 and 10. The distinction between what God can do in the natural order and what He normally does is made use of in a striking formulation of political theory by

pope exercises legitimate authority as head of the Church he can do alone whatever lies in the ecclesiastical jurisdiction, even contravene its "positive" legislation.

Aegidius's views on the nature of temporal polity appear more directly in his treatise on princely rule, however, and in his somewhat polemical work on papal resignation. The latter treatise offers his views on how an authority, in this case the ecclesiastical authority of the pope, relates to other elements of the political community; for example, the people. The work *On the Governance of Princes* is also a very lengthy treatise, and in general contains little to surprise the student of thirteenth-century political theory. Its format of three books follows largely the earlier models of texts devoted to explaining the types of virtues a civil ruler must possess and how they should be exercised to achieve the common good of the realm, the very purpose for which political authority exists.

Like all such treatises of the period, Aegidius's work *On the Governance of Princes* was strongly influenced by Aristotle's *Politics*; and its author, accordingly, takes considerable pains to maintain that humans are by nature civil or social, and that political society (a kingdom or a city-state) is natural.[299] Aegidius also follows the Aristotelian enumeration of the six forms of temporal polity, three good and three "depraved"; and like Thomas Aquinas before him, he opts for monarchy as the best form of government.[300] He also makes reference in this connection to the consent of the people being an ingredient in a form of polity where the people as a whole are somehow engaged in the practice of designating their own political rulers, and acknowledges that such was the contemporary practice in Italian city-states, where the citizens both elect and can depose their rulers.[301]

Marsilius of Padua, who maintains that there is only one "normal" efficient cause or origin for temporal power: the human legislator, the people. The source of this doctrine of the general principles of nature, of course, as well as of their application to the order of politics, is Aristotle.

299. Aegidius *De regimine principum* 3.1.4; cf. 3.2.2.

300. Ibid., 7.1.1.

301. Ibid,. 3.2.2; cf. the remarks on the possible influence on Marsilius of Padua in Rubenstein, "Marsilius and Italian Political Theory," pp. 69–70 and p. 70, n. 1. Rubenstein also identifies Ptolemy of Lucca as oe of the most vigorous contemporary advocates of the Italian communal theory (p. 54). Aegidius did acknowledge the traditional concept that consent of the people was involved in the legitimacy of political authority in a text arguing for justifiable grounds for papal resignation: *De renuntiatione*

In dealing with monarchy as the best form of government, Aegidius raises a specific issue not seen in any earlier medieval treatise of the genre, an issue that probably occurred to him because of his knowledge of current practices in some Italian city-states and also, perhaps, because of accepted procedures in the Holy Roman Empire, although in the work there is no explicit reference to the empire. Aegidius directly considers the question whether a monarchy should be hereditary or elective,[302] and his instructive reply is as follows: the question itself arises because of the realization that what happens by design, deliberately, is superior to what occurs by chance. Accordingly, appointment of a temporal ruler by election, inasmuch as it precisely involves the deliberation of electors and is not, therefore, a matter of mere chance, seems to be a better method for acquiring a new ruler than accepting succession through heredity, wherein the element of chance functions with respect to the necessary qualities and virtues of governance; the hereditary successor may or may not be possessed of the essential features: "If succession is by heredity, the kingdom is greatly exposed to the elements of chance and fortune, inasmuch as there is uncertainty about how the [succeeding] son will reflect the needed virtues of royalty and dignity." Continuing, Aegidius accepts that, absolutely speaking, it is better for a prince to succeed to office through election than by way of heredity. However, he adds immediately: "Inasmuch as people in the main (*plurimum homines*) possess corrupt appetites in respect of human affairs and conditions, as experience shows, it seems that hereditary succession rather than election is to be considered preferable in a kingdom or city-state."[303]

Aegidius goes on to provide three points of view from which a consideration of the actual condition of humans shows that heredity is preferable to election: from consideration of the nature of the king who has ruled; from consideration of the son who will succeed; from

---

papae 16; cf. also 5.11.24. But it is impossible to see anything specific here; and in the context of his rejection of an elected monarchy it is implausible that he could have envisaged anything more than some unspecified type of acclamatory consent.

302. Aegidius *De regimine principum* 3.2.5.

303. "Sed si per haeriditatem hoc fiat, exponitur regnum quasi forti, casui et fortunae; nam incertum est qualis debeat esse filius, ad quem spectabit habere regiam et dignitatem ... quia ut plurimum homines habent corruptum habitum consideratis gestis et conditionibus hominum, quas experimentaliter videmus, videtur esse censendum magis expedire regno vel civitati, ut dominus praeficiatur per haeriditatem quam per electionem"; Aegidius *De regimine principum* 3.2.5.

consideration of the people to be ruled. In this last connection, Aegidius offers the totally damning judgment that the people (*plebs*) are naturally fitted to obey a ruler rather than exercise political authority; the latter sort of activity leads to dissension and conflict in a political society, features precisely opposed to the virtues of peace and tranquillity essential in any realm. Further, persons elected to temporal office are less inclined to seek the common good than those who succeed by heredity.[304]

Aegidius's views regarding temporal rule thus are seen to be equally as conservative as his views on papal authority. For all that, he never denied the principle that legitimate authority, both ecclesiastical and temporal, must function within limits; and regardless of the abstractness with which he expressed it, he also accepted the principle that an ecclesiastical leader, and *mutatis mutandis* presumably a temporal leader as well, should resign and could be deposed when this legitimate limit was exceeded. At the same time and as already noted, Aegidius was prepared to acknowledge the integrity and legitimacy of political authority. As well he asserted categorically the right of a political authority to act in forthright fashion in pursuit of its proper responsibilities in respect of the common good. He maintained that a king could levy taxes on the clergy of his country without waiting for papal consent, on condition that the ruler judged the circumstances to be of sufficient urgency to require such action.[305] Aegidius also accepted that in some way the "consent of man" was involved in the exercise of spiritual authority, but this did not mean that he accepted the principle that papal authority derived from the people.

E. John of Paris

John of Paris (John Quidort) was a Dominican theologian who taught at the University of Paris at the turn of the fourteenth century.[306] He may have studied under St. Thomas Aquinas; and he produced a

---

304. Ibid., 3.2.5.

305. Aegidius "Tractatus quomodo reges et principes possunt possessiones et bona regna peculiaria ecclesiis elargiri," in *Opera*, 1.37, cited in Post, *Studies*, p. 289 and n. 99. Post states that he consulted this work in manuscript form: Paris, BN,MS Lat. 6786, fols. 22–41.

306. See biographical data on John in *Royal and Papal Power*, ed. Monahan, pp. xv–xvii; and a fuller account of the dispute between Boniface and Philip in another recent translation of the same treatise: *Royal and Papal Power*, ed. Watt, pp. 14–32.

treatise on church/state relations precisely at the time of the great conflict on this issue between Pope Boniface VIII and Philip the Fair, king of France. John's treatise *On Royal and Papal Power* is one of the most significant treatments of the issue of church/state relations written in the medieval period; it also contains explicit, if not comprehensively specified, views on the issue of consent.[307] Quidort's ideas were clearly influenced by his reading of Aristotle's *Politics*, as well as by Thomas Aquinas; but he also shows himself thoroughly familiar with earlier and contemporary Christian writings on the general topic of political theory, including both civil and canonical law.

John maintained categorically that kingship was the preferred form of polity, one-man rule,[308] but he maintained equally that this form of government is "from God and the people electing";[309] that "a king exists by the will of the people";[310] and that "kingly power is from . . . the people who give their consent and choice."[311] He makes similar statements concerning the basis for imperial, as opposed to individual national monarchical, authority.[312] He also draws a correlative conclusion concerning withdrawal of the people's consent from a temporal ruler: such withdrawal constitutes deposition from office.[313] He is not sufficiently specific, however, about any procedure whereby the people express their consent or opposition to a political ruler, although he does assign the function of expressing the popular will in both establishing and deposing a king to "the barons and peers" of the realm.[314] But John again fails to spell out either the precise manner in which the people exercise their rights in these two matters, or even the precise relationship between "barons and peers" and the people.

The attention John devotes to the issue of an individual ceding or being deposed from authority had been stimulated by the consequences flowing from the recent resignation of Pope Celestine V, the incident that led to the enthronement of Boniface VIII. Boniface was a

---

307. John of Paris *De potestate regia et papali* 10; 19 *ad* 33; 17 *ad* 21; 15 *ad* 9; 13; 12; 14 *ad* 5; 25 *ad* 3. Cf. Renna, "Populus in John of Paris."

308. John of Paris *De potestate* 1.

309. Ibid., 10.

310. Ibid., 19 *ad* 33, where he cites Averroes as an advocate of this position, an interesting reference I have not been able to locate.

311. Ibid., 17 *ad* 21.

312. Ibid., 17 *ad* 33; 15 *ad* 9.

313. Ibid., 13.

314. Ibid., 12; 14 *ad* 5.

much more formidable figure on the European political stage than his other-worldly predecessor; and the new pope quickly gave evidence of holding strong views on the nature and extent of papal authority. A number of persons, both lay and ecclesiastical, had been surprised and disappointed by Celestine's departure after only a few months in the papal office; and a number of these, especially among the supporters of Philip the Fair, quickly became apprehensive about the stronger papalist line being adopted by Boniface. The novelty of anyone actually resigning the see of Peter thus afforded an opportunity to question the legitimacy of Boniface's authority by raising the issue of whether a pope could resign. The issue came to be much debated among contemporary canonists and theologians and, as already noted, the indefatigable Aegidius of Rome produced a formal academic treatise on the question. John of Paris's work *On Royal and Papal Power* has a section devoted to the question of a pope leaving office that is obviously and strongly influenced by the Aegidean text.[315] Quidort's concurrent treatment of the deposition of a temporal ruler is an illustration of his practice of dealing in parallel fashion with the spheres of ecclesiastical and temporal authority.

John's views of papal resignation and deposition, and on the attainment and exercise of ecclesiastical office in general, follow the lines already seen in his comments on temporal authority. He states that "the power of prelates is ... from the people choosing and consenting,"[316] and that "the relationship between a prelate and the church can be dissolved when there is dissension between the person elected and the electors, the elements through whose consent the relationship is established."[317] Again, details of procedure for expressing the people's consent and / or dissent are missing, and for this reason it is difficult to appreciate precisely how Quidort understands the principle of consent to operate. He does address this issue partly in the case of the papal office, however, when he assigns to the college of cardinals a role similar to that of the barons and peers in respect of a temporal ruler: the cardinals "act in place of the whole clergy and the whole people."[318] They can compel the resignation of a pope who has

315. John treats the issue of papal resignation and deposition at the end of his treatise, chap. 23–25; the contents of his treatment are based largely on Aegidius *De reuntiatione papae*.

316. John of Paris *De potestate* 10.

317. Ibid., 25 *ad* 3.

318. Ibid., 13.

acted in such a way as to have lost the people's consent for his holding papal office. John is able here to ground any specifics of procedure on the fact that the college of cardinals actually functioned as the body that elected a pope. In the temporal sphere, however, the only comparably functioning group of electors to political office with which he would likely have been familiar directly was that which named the Holy Roman Emperor.

John is rather cryptic in giving details on how loss of popular support might occur, referring in respect of both temporal and papal (and other ecclesiastical?) rulers only to circumstances in which persons holding office have committed wrongs and remain incorrigible. He speaks of how "the people actually would depose [an incorrigibly criminal temporal ruler]"[319] by their obedience to a papal edict of excommunication; but a number of distinctions have to be introduced here. First, John is speaking of the limited character of ecclesiastical (in this case, papal) authority: he explicitly limits the legitimate exercise of spiritual or ecclesiastical authority to the declaration of excommunication as the maximum spiritual penalty that can be imposed, and explicitly denies the exercise of any temporal, physical coercive power to a spiritual authority.

In this Quidort simply continues the expression of a doctrine found in Gratian and Hugh of St. Victor, quoting Bernard of Clairvaux's advice to Pope Eugene III not to employ physical coercion for spiritual purposes.[320] Further, however, John is speaking in this text of specific instances of "spiritually criminal" and incorrigible behaviour on the part of a temporal ruler. He maintains that the Church (any church authority, papal or other) "has no jurisdiction over any crime except insofar as the crime relates to what is spiritual and ecclesiastical."[321] Even further, the only ecclesiastical crime John mentions specifically, and for which the ultimate spiritual penalty of excommunication is legitimate, is heresy.[322] It seems clear that John would not restrict his doctrine of legitimate excommunication for an incorrigible, spiritually criminal temporal ruler to this one category of crime, since he spoke also of a king being excommunicable because "derelict in spiritual matters such as faith, marriage and things of this kind";[323] but the full

319. Ibid.
320. Bernard of Clairvaux *De consideratione* 3.4.17.
321. John of Paris *De potestate* 13.
322. Ibid.
323. Ibid.

range of these other categories is not clear, and John does not amplify his remarks.

Nor does he say anything directly about how the spiritual penalty of excommunication translates into the act of deposition of a ruler "by the people." Presumably, the spiritual act of excommunicating a temporal ruler has the direct "spiritual" effect of depriving him of his moral or "spiritual" right to hold and exercise political authority; straightforward recognition of this "fact" by the people, the ruler's subjects, then results in the subjects ceasing to obey him insofar as their obligation to obey has been dissolved or, rather, shown to exist no longer: the obedience of his subjects, the correlative for them of the authority a ruler must possess to command obedience, simply has ceased to exist. This is all very unsatisfactory from a procedural point of view, of course, however solid the argument may appear as a deduction employing abstract principles, or psychologically persuasive for those who give a high priority to moral concerns. John does attribute some function in deposing a temporal ruler for spiritual crimes to the barons and peers, as we have seen. But the formulation here is also very abstract and unsatisfactory, indicating how little interested Quidort, like so many other medieval political theorists, was in the mechanics or procedures of political theory. A similar absence of detail surrounds his description of the role of the cardinals in deposing an incorrigibly criminal pope in terms of the specification of how the sacred college would function in expressing the people's dissent (or withdrawal of consent).

However, John did address the same problem at some length in another text where he held that, while a wilfully and incorrigibly criminal pontiff could be deposed by the college of cardinals, he would be put out of office most fittingly by action of a general church council. John cites canon law on the point, while referring again to "agreement of the people" and "deposition by the people."[324] The context suggests that John saw the functioning of the college of cardinals and / or general council in such matters as somehow expressive of a judgment by "the people"; but the position is still enigmatic and unclear. John refers to the role of the cardinals again, using the expression "They represent the whole clergy";[325] but once more what the specific form of

---

324. Ibid., 24; John cites Gratian, D.21 c.7. John also asserts that a seriously errant pope could be deposed by the emperor, acting perforce on the request of the college of cardinals, "who represent the whole clergy," but are unable by use of their own spiritual resources "to eliminate the scandal to the Church": *De potestate* 13.

325. John of Paris *De potestate* 13.

representation is or how precisely the cardinals come by their mandate is not spelled out. Towards the end of his treatise Quidort speaks of an incompetent pope being "expected" to seek a release from his office from the people, or from the assembly of cardinals who act in the place of the whole clergy and the whole people in such a case.[326] But how exactly a pope was to go about seeking his release from office, and how exactly the cardinals were to act in place of either the whole clergy or the whole people or both—what instrumentalities were to be brought into play and by whom—were questions that he neither answers nor even addresses directly.

John goes on to say that a seriously errant pontiff "is bound to yield office whether or not he obtains permission,"[327] a remark that may contain a clue as to why John was seemingly so indifferent to issues of procedure ("The man is gone, anyway"). What is clear is that, for Quidort, the function of representing does not require any formal action on the part of those who are to be represented. In the first instance, representatives fill a symbolic role; and they do no need to be put into office, so to speak, because a symbol is not an office or an office holder. Yet, John perceives a value in having office holders exercise an active and not a purely symbolic role in their office. He does not insist on prior action by those represented and served by office holders, however, because he does not make the issue of how a person comes into office an essential prerequisite for that person having the authority of the office; at least he does not do so with respect to the people as a whole being represented.

Another reference to consent in the instance of papal resignation throws further light on John's understanding of this concept. John contends that "where a clear and reasonable cause (for papal resignation) is apparent, just as where there is a clear defect, the consent and authority of God to renounce and depose are supposed ... just as divine agreement is supposed in his confirmation."[328] If God's "consent" to deposition (and election) can be assumed to be present and supposed to be absent on the evidence of sin or defect, might not the consent of the people required in the process also be assumed, and thus

326. Ibid., 24.

327. John of Paris *De potestate* 24. The permission John is speaking of here is specified as follows: "He [the pope] ought to seek a release from his office from the people or from the assembly of cardinals who act in place of the whole clergy and the whole people in such a case."

328. Ibid., 25 *ad* 3.

there be no need to check with them in any specific way? John's doctrine reflects the principle of *q o t*, but only in an inchoate fashion as regards procedure; he is much less hard-headedly functional than Marsilius of Padua or William of Ockham several decades later, or even than his contemporary Godfrey of Fontaines.

John expressed views on the value of popular consent as he understood this concept in yet another feature of his political theory: he accepted the element of consent as a general principle in both temporal and ecclesiastical governmental structures. Considering the standard issue of what is the best form of government, Quidort chose monarchy over the alternative forms of aristocracy and democracy; but what he had in mind was something close to what might be called a constitutional monarchy. An interesting formulation occurs in the context of a reply to an objection that there should be only one form of authority, spiritual, insofar as God's establishment of a kingship among the Israelites came about as a result of God being offended by them for having rejected Him.[329] John replies by pointing out that the relevant Old Testament texts do not show monarchy to be absolutely displeasing to God as an evil, but only that God had chosen for His People a purer form of polity than that of kingship, namely, a mixed form of governance.

Quidort goes on to assert that there are two reasons why the form of government God chose for the Jews was superior to monarchy. While citing Aristotle[330] as a reason for accepting that one-man rule is best insofar as a single ruler in theory can be the most suitable ruling agent because the most virtuous, he goes on to state that a mixed form of rule is superior on practical grounds. Citing Aristotle on this point as well, Quidort argues that a form that affords some role in the governing process to everyone in the community is the best form on practical grounds, in that it offers the best guarantee for stability (peace) because everyone likes it. This is the type of government God provided for the Jews when he established their original form of governance: their polity was monarchic insofar as one man such as Moses or Joshua was pre-eminent absolutely; but it was also aristocratic inasmuch as the seventy-two elders exercised a form of leadership according to virtue in serving as a council under the single ruler; it was also democratic to the extent that the seventy-two elders were elected from and by the

---

329. Ibid., 19 *ad* 35.
330. Aristotle *Politics* 3.16.1287a30.

whole people. Hence, "everyone had something to do with, some role to play in, governing." John goes on to remark that "certainly this form of rule would be best for the Church, with several men being elected by every province and from every province under one pope. In this way everyone would have some role to play in the rule of the Church."[331] John of Paris thus advocates a governing procedure for the Church as a whole patterned on the constitutional practice of his own Dominican order,[332] whose master general was elected by a general chapter, itself composed of persons chosen from each of the Order's provinces. He does not go further, however, in the details of how such a polity might be implemented or how it would function.

The second reason John advances for favouring a mixed form of polity over a pure kingly rule relates again to a practical consideration. He raises the difficulty of the single monarch becoming corrupted in office: one-person rule is best in itself if the ruler is not corrupt; but centering all power in a king "makes it easy for a monarchy to degenerate into tyranny unless there is perfect virtue in the man to whom this power is given."[333] Again quoting Aristotle, John remarks that persons of perfect virtue are rare; accordingly, there are advantages to a mixed polity both in its provision for some form of checks and balances against tyranny on the part of the single leader and in its accessability to virtue from others in the community who have some function in its governance.[334]

It is somewhat curious that John's advocacy of a mixed polity is not to be found in the early chapters of his treatise that deal directly with the issue of the best form of government in typically Aristotelian fashion. Here John opts without qualification for kingship, offering only theoretical arguments favouring one-man rule as the best form of government, "if there were any such person possessed of pre-eminent virtue."[335] There does not seem to be any inconsistency between this and Quidort's later, more practical views, however, if one accepts that in the early texts he was simply following the sequence of Aristotle's *Politics*, where the Stagirite, in the beginning, definitional part of the *Politics*, also offered a theoretical and "conditional" justification (a

---

331. John of Paris *De potestate* 19 *ad* 35.
332. Cf. section 2B above. Cf. Thomas Aquinas *S.T.* 1–2.105.1 *ad* 1.
333. John of Paris *De potestate* 19 *ad* 35.
334. Ibid. John cites Aristotle *Politics* 3.15.1285a34.
335. John of Paris *De potestate* 1.

contrary-to-expected-fact-conditional!) for monarchy as the best form
of government. A different formulation emerges later, when Aristotle
also expresses a preference for a mixed form of government based on
law,[336] this preference being based on a practical judgment rather than
on a theoretical and conditional postulate. Of course, John never set
himself the task of formulating a comprehensive theory of polity; his
efforts at definition and assessment of the various forms of secular
polity occur within the context of his primary purpose, which was to
define the role and limits of ecclesiastical and temporal authority. St.
Thomas Aquinas also expressed a favourable judgment on a mixed
form of polity, as has been noted; and there is good reason to think that
Quidort would have been aware of the Thomistic view and was simply
subscribing to it himself, adding some slight specification. Both the
Thomistic text and that of Quidort make explicit reference to the Old
Testament model for the mixed form.

John of Paris also referred to the element of coercion in *On Royal and
Papal Power*; and again the manner of his treatment is of interest. The
issue arises within Quidort's general examination of the nature and
limits of the two types of authority, spiritual and temporal. He is at
great pains to distinguish between the two, and to insist that those in
authority in either of the two spheres are entitled to use only the type of
authority appropriate to the sphere in which their authority exists:
spiritual authority has the use of spiritual power, temporal authority
the use of temporal or physical power, and neither can invoke any form
of power other than what is appropriate to his own sphere.[337] It is clear
that the whole thrust of Quidort's thesis in this respect, the thesis that
the Church has only "indirect" power over temporal affairs, is to limit
ecclesiastical power in the sphere of the secular or temporal. The
specific issue of coercion arises in John's discussion of the authority
appropriate to the exercise of spiritual power. The text, then, requires
application to the area of secular or temporal power; it speaks to this
area only indirectly.

John contends that the whole difficulty surrounding the proper
exercise of the authority given by God to the leaders of His Church
turns around what he calls "judicial power in the external forum."[338]

336. Aristotle *Politics* 4.11.1295a25 *ff*.
337. This is the essence of John's so-called doctrine of conditional and accidental
(indirect) power that one sphere can exercise over the other: *De potestate* 12 and 13.
338. Ibid., 12 and 13.

He says that there are two things involved here: first, authority to exercise jurisdiction and intervene; secondly, the power to coerce(!), a power Quidort also designates as the power of correction or censure. In respect of the power to coerce, John asserted flatly that the spiritual authority can exercise only spiritual power to coerce, correct, or censure; and he specifies that the maximum form of spiritual coercion or force is excommunication,[339] permanent separation of a member from the spiritual community of the Church and from spiritual fellowship with other members of the society of the faithful. Other lesser forms of spiritual coercion, of course, were envisaged. Power to employ physical coercion, correction, or censure is forbidden to the Church; this type of coercion rests for use in the hands of temporal authority.[340] It follows, then, that secular political authority does possess the power of physical coercion; indeed, it is one of its essential distinguishing marks.

An interesting aspect of John's theory of polity in which the notion of physical coercion as an essential of temporal authority operates explicitly is his rejection of the concept of universal or world government. He agrees that it is natural for humans to come together in a political society for their individual development and mutual benefit; but he contends that it is neither from natural inclination nor natural law that all persons be subject to one supreme authority in temporal matters. John is careful to distinguish between his negative view on universal temporal government and his acceptance of one supreme authority over the universal Church. He asserts that the latter is acceptable both in theory and in practice, inasmuch as it is comparatively easy for a single spiritual authority to exercise spiritual coercive power on a broad basis; the exercise of this form involves only the use of words to convey it, and rests on voluntary acceptance by its subjects. Temporal political authority, on the other hand, requires application of the material sword as coercive power; and the necessary use of physical force to ensure the obedience of subjects is not easy to do from a great physical distance.[341]

Corresponding to the view that efficient exercise of temporal authority entails a feature of geographical limit, John accepted that there would be a variety of different political communities in which

339. Ibid., 13.
340. Ibid.
341. Ibid., 3.

humans would live together according to natural law and natural inclination, and that these different political societies could be expected to choose different forms of polity and ruler, conforming to differences in geography, climate, language, and conditions of men; and he acknowledged that what is suitable for one polity is not so for another.[342] This view has been seen expressed earlier in very similar terms in St. Thomas Aquinas.[343]

John's treatise provides no separate or explicit treatment of the notion of limit, but obviously there was no need for him to have done so. The concept of limit was at work throughout his efforts to distinguish the spiritual and temporal spheres of authority from one another, and to delineate their respective responsibilities. Each sphere has its limits, and the authorities in each are required to exercise their powers within these limits; even the types of power to be exercised in each sphere are limited.

342. Ibid.
343. See nn. 225, 226 above.

PART FOUR

The Fourteenth Century

1. POLITICAL THEORISTS

A. Dante Alighieri

THE FIRST REPRESENTATIVE of fourteenth-century political theorists will be considered briefly, because there is little of theoretical or doctrinal interest in his position. Nonetheless, the significance of the political views of Dante Alighieri is not negligible; for they illustrate the traditional medieval approach to popular consent in a particularly concrete and unreflective manner unique among other medieval thinkers. Of course, Dante was not primarily a political theorist, nor was he a medieval academic, as in some sense were most of the other writers examined. Dante was a poet of genius and an impassioned advocate of strongly held and changing personal political views. Comments on his political doctrine will be restricted to a single political treatise, the *Monarchia*, although this is not to deny that political attitudes and even theory are to be found in his other writings.[1]

Dante Alighieri was born in 1265, the son of a small businessman whose support for the Guelph faction in the municipal conflicts of medieval Florence resulted more than once in exile from his home city

---

1. The standard modern edition is Dante Alighieri *Monarchia*, ed. G. Vinay (Florence: 1950); a recent English translation is *Monarchy and Three Political Letters by Dante Alighieri*, trans. Donald Nicholl, new introduction by Walter F. Bense (New York: Garland, 1972). A comparison between *Monarchy* and the political ideas expressed in Dante's other writings can be found in d'Entrèves, *Dante as a Political Thinker*; see also Goudet, *Dante et la politique*, which has an extensive bibliography.

when the Ghibelline faction gained ascendancy there. Dante himself took part in 1289 in the Battle of Campaldino, which saw the permanent destruction of the political power of the Florentine Ghibellines; subsequently he became active in local Florentine politics and was for a short time in 1300 one of the seven members making up Florence's governing council. He soon found himself on the wrong side of a division among the Florentine Guelphs, however, and left the city in 1301, only to be convicted and sentenced to death *in absentia* for malfeasance in office and treason. The 1303 death sentence was reconfirmed in 1311 and again in 1315, and Dante never returned to Florence. After some twenty years in exile he died in 1321.

His treatise *Monarchy* was probably written during the period 1309–13 when Henry VII, who had been crowned Holy Roman Emperor in 1308, was manoeuvering in an ultimately unsuccessful campaign to bring the whole of the Italian peninsula under his control. Dante was an enthusiastic supporter of Henry, and saw him as the political saviour of Florence and Italy as a whole. *Monarchy* is literally an apologia for Henry's territorial ambitions as Holy Roman Emperor, and constitutes a straightforward advocacy for re-establishing the Roman Empire as a universal polity to establish peace and good order for the whole world. As already noted, it does not represent by any means the only literary expression of its author's political views— Dante had always been deeply interested in politics and the twenty years of exile stimulated him to frequent political outbursts and expressions of view. But the *Monarchy* is the only item in the Dantean literary corpus to treat exclusively, and in the formal, *ex professo* manner of a reasoned scholastic treatise, a single political topic: the legitimacy and value of a unitary, universal temporal power. This is why the work can be examined on its own. For all that, its value with respect to the concept of popular consent is modest.

Dante sets himself three questions at the beginning of the work, the second of which is: "Whether it was by right that the Roman people [sic] took upon itself the office of monarch?"[2] His response makes clear immediately that Dante was simply not interested in the whys or hows of any connection between the Roman people and their emperor. For practical purposes, as well as on theoretical grounds, he simply accepts the equation: Roman emperor equals Roman people; and he assumes that any actual Roman emperor, including the current Henry VII, can

2. Dante *Monarchia* 1.2.

be presumed to reflect the authority of the Roman people. When asking again, at the point where he presents his answer, whether the Roman people function legitimately as a monarch, he reformulates the question's original terms and inquires whether the Roman people acquired the imperial dignity by right. And his reply merely stipulates that history shows that the Roman empire was ordained by God; the issue of how the Roman people might have given expression to their "rights" in terms of confiding them to an emperor is not raised. God's will is the instrument Dante invokes to explain and justify how "the Roman people acquired their imperial office over other persons."[3]

While Dante undoubtedly would have expected his readers to understand that he considered the exercise of political authority by a Roman emperor to entail and express the consent of the Roman people, he shows absolutely no concern for the procedure or mechanism for expressing popular consent. In a fashion not found expressed in such a blunt and straightforward a manner in other medieval political texts (though one suspects frequently a parallel attitude), Dante shows clearly that for him the concept of popular consent has almost no functional meaning at all; so great is the abstract character of the concept that it is not even employed specifically, and what is implied is a notion almost without content. A further telling point concerning Dante's indifference to the reality of popular consent in the exercise of political authority is the fact that he makes no reference to whether other peoples than the Romans do or should consent to fall under the empire. Dante on this issue is disarmingly succinct: "The Roman people were ordained by nature to rule others."[4]

An argument against papal claims to the right to appoint the emperor (and other temporal rulers) shows once more how little interested Dante was in the relationship between legitimate political authority and any specific expression of popular consent. Denying the contention that the people should appoint and depose secular rulers because Samuel, acting on God's command, named and deposed Israel's first king, Dante asserted that it was not Samuel but God who chose and deposed Saul.[5] No role, not even an acclamatory one, is mentioned for the people. It is fair to say, however, that Dante likely would not have denied that the Israelites consented to receive their first

3. Ibid., 2.3.
4. Ibid., 2.6. William of Ockham makes the same point.
5. Ibid,. 3.6.

king; nor likely would he have denied some such role to the Romans of his own day, although what he might have said about the functional efficacy or necessity of their role probably would not be very significant for a positive view on popular consent. Of course, Dante was arguing strenuously at this point for the divine foundation and authority of an empire. That for Dante it is God alone, and no human agency, who chooses the emperor is understood again when he categorically denies authority to elect the Holy Roman Emperor even to the persons who functioned traditionally in that role: "God alone elects and confirms the Emperor ... the title of elector should not be accorded either to those now described as electors, or to any others. Properly speaking, their office is to proclaim what God has providentially decided."[6]

Another argument in the *Monarchy* involving popular consent can be mentioned. Arguing that the Church does not have the right to confer authority on the Roman emperor, Dante contends that it would only have acquired this right from one of four possible sources: God, the Church itself, some earlier emperor, or "the universal consent of men."[7] He denied that any of these sources provided such authority to the Church, and rejected the notion that there could be universal popular consent for such a situation with the contemptuous remark that "not only everyone in Africa and Asia but even most inhabitants of Europe revolt at the suggestion [that the papacy give authority to temporal rulers]. It is wearisome, indeed, to develop arguments in support of a perfectly obvious truth."[8] A reader looking for some expression of appreciation for the procedural aspects of consent necessary to give the concept functional significance again is disappointed. Dante's treatise on monarchy thus provides no basis for judging whether its author had anything but a traditional and traditionally inadequate perception of the notion that political authority somehow involves popular consent.

B. Marsilius of Padua

Marsilius of Padua is a medieval political thinker whose views require examination in some detail. A cleric of the northern Italian city-state of

6. Ibid., 3.16.
7. Ibid., 3.14.
8. Ibid., 3.14.

Padua, he was the son of a notary employed by the University of Padua, and may himself have studied there.[9] He became one of the most notorious critics of the early-fourteenth-century papacy, his reputation in this respect resting basically on the writing of one book, a political treatise whose explicit and consistently sustained purpose was to show the contemporary papacy as the major cause of civil unrest and political instability in western Europe. The *Defensor pacis* of Marsilius has been seen by many interpreters across the centuries since its publication about 1323 as one of the most significant treatises in the history of western political theory, as well as one of the most influential.[10] It also has been hailed as one of the first serious advocacies for modern democracy. The Paduan's single work, accordingly, has been the object of considerable interest in modern investigations into medieval politics, having been edited twice and translated at least four times in the past fifty years.[11]

The principal reason for the modern historian's interest in the political thought of Marsilius is that he asserts categorically that the basis for good government is the popular will,[12] a statement often taken as capsulizing the whole of the Paduan's political theory. Such a view certainly can be expected to attract the interest and admiration of contemporary students of politics who may be inclined to see reflections of modern democratic theory in Marsilius's late-medieval text, and accordingly be inclined to perceive the author of the *Defender of Peace* as a political theorist who succeeded in throwing off the medieval shackles of ecclesiastical domination of temporal authority and thought in general.[13] The fact that Marsilius was an implacable foe of ecclesias-

9. For biographical data on Marsilius see the Gewirth treatment of the *Defensor pacis*, 1:20–31; cf. n. 10 below.

10. A recent extensive interpretation of the *Defensor pacis* is Alan Gewirth, *Marsilius of Padua, The Defendor of Peace*, vol. 1, Marsilius of Padua and Medieval Political Philosophy (New York: Columbia University Press, 1951); vol. 2, *Defensor pacis*. See also Lagarde, *La naissance de l'esprit laïque au moyen âge*, 3, Marsile de Padoue, 3rd ed. (Louvain: 1965); Wilks, "Coronation and representation"; Rubenstein, "Marsilius and Italian Political Thought"; Lagarde, "Marsile de Padoue et Guillaume d'Ockham"; Lewis, "'Positivism' of Marsiglio of Padua"; and the brief introduction and useful notes to the recent French translation: Marsile de Padoue, *Défenseur de la paix*. Trans. Jeannine Quillet (Paris: Vrin, 1968).

11. Lagarde, "Marsile de Padoue," p. 593, n. 17.

12. Wilks, "Coronation and Representation," p. 254; cf. Marsilius *Defensor pacis* 1.12.3, 1.12.5; cf. n. 33 below.

13. Gewirth, *Marsilius of Padua*, 1:167–225, 303–17.

tical, particularly papal, efforts to exercise jurisdiction over lay rulers, and devoted a major portion of his not inconsiderable literary talents to excoriating the medieval church, only provides further encouragement to those who would interpret Marsilius as an enlightened political thinker. His rigorous "secularist" insistence on making the Church and its clergy completely subordinate to the temporal authority of the state, which was to have ultimate control over ecclesiastical appointments,[14] is but another piece of evidence favouring a radical modern interpretation of Marsilius.

There is a sense in which this interpretation is sound and genuinely instructive with regard to Marsilius's views; but it is also true that a careful examination of his political theory shows Marsilius to have been distinctly a man of his own time, and in some ways less politically advanced by modern standards than some of the medieval figures examined earlier. It is significant in this connection to point out, for example, that Marsilius's views that the people are at the base of good government is a reflection of a traditional medieval political attitude that was itself grounded in classical Roman law.[15] It has been asserted often, and correctly, that Marsilius exhibits in the *Defender of Peace* massive influence from Aristotle's *Politics*; but it was from the Romano-Christian tradition grounded in Cicero and the Roman law, rather than from the *Politics*, that the Paduan derived his basic conception of the nature of political society. His definition of law, for example, reflects Azo's *Summa institutionum*;[16] and the basic terminology Marsilius employs reflects an outlook distinctively medieval in its presentation of a very familiar corporation theory of polity.

The *Defensor pacis* is in three parts, the most important of which for our purposes is Part One. Here, basically, Marsilius presents in both

14. Marsilius *Defensor pacis* 2.4.

15. Marsilius was the son of a notary, and it has been suggested that he himself once had considered studying law; cf. Wilks, "Coronation and Representation," p. 254, and n. 5.

16. See Lewis, "'Positivism' of Marsiglio," pp. 545–48, 552–55. This is a valuable corrective to recent interpretations of the Marsilian theory of law that associate it with modern positivism in legal philosophy; it shows the theory's reflection of traditional medieval legal thinking found among the canonists and civilians, and even in Thomas Aquinas, with whom Marsilius is often contrasted on this point. Nevertheless, the Paduan does place special emphasis on coercion as an essential feature of law and this emphasis, along with his consistent tendency to describe human behaviour from its darker, more competitive and pugnacious side, sets a new tone to the formulation of political and legal theory.

outline and considerable detail the first *ex professo* treatment of political theory we have seen since the twelfth-century *Policraticus* of John of Salisbury. Following a schema based on the scientific method of Aristotle and using basic Aristotelian terminology, especially the Aristotelian schema of the four types of causality,[17] Marsilius offers a pungent description of his ideal of a temporal society, the most obvious feature of which is the total subordination of church to state. His views on consent, coercion, and limit are set out reasonably explicitly, so that it is possible to determine with some precision what meaning these elements have in his theory of polity.

Marsilius conceived of the people (*populus*) as a corporate entity, as did thinkers like John of Paris, Thomas Aquinas, and John of Salisbury before him. Not that Marsilius agreed on all points with these earlier thinkers any more than they did with one another; however, he did reflect the basic medieval corporate view of the people considered as a whole. What makes the position of Marsilius apparently so different from earlier medieval theories of polity is his elimination of another standard ingredient found in the earlier medieval formulations: namely, the expression of options concerning the immediate source of a given ruler's authority. The normal medieval view on this issue was that a ruler's authority derives either from the people as a whole or from some higher authority, and usually no preference between the two options was expressed. The traditional theory accepted that the ultimate source of political authority, as of all authority, was God; accordingly, the correlative options of authority coming directly to a ruler either through the people or through some higher authority can be interpreted in terms of the transmission of authority to a temporal ruler by way of some human agency. In this case the "higher authority" option would entail reference to some higher form of humanly exercised instrumentality, presumably either temporal or ecclesiastical. But this is not precisely how Marsilius construed the matter.

As a medieval schoolman and sometime theologian he was familiar with and accepted the view that God ultimately is the source of all authority. His concern, however, was to foreclose the position that ecclesiastical authorities had jurisdiction over temporal rulers, and specifically over their selection. He interprets the traditional doctrine concerning the source of political authority to mean that the immediate source was either God, who intervened directly in the selection of a

17. Aristotle *Physics* 1; *Metaphysics* 1.

ruler, or the people themselves as human legislator. And Marsilius is quite explicit that the normal and natural method of instituting political authority is the second way: "There is another method of establishing governments which proceeds immediately from the human mind, although perhaps remotely from God as remote cause ... God does not always act immediately ... ; indeed in most cases, nearly everywhere, he establishes governments by means of human minds, to which he had granted the discretionary will for such establishment."[18] Marsilius goes further in this respect, using language that strikes an immediately responsive chord among modern readers: not only are the people, the human legislator, the origin of political authority, but they are to function as the cause of political authority by way of election of the ruler. For the Paduan, "the absolutely better method of establishing governments is election."[19]

Traditional medieval political theory, of course, also had connected the element of popular consent with the first of the two options, the people as origin of authority. But insofar as there had normally been no preference expressed for this option over the other, the importance attached to the notion of popular consent must be considered problematic, as indeed it was for almost all the medieval thinkers examined thus far. When Marsilius eliminates the statement of alternatives, then, and asserts plainly and without qualification that the basis of temporal authority lies with the whole people, the contemporary reader is likely to perceive a modern rather than a medieval perspective. Such a perception might yet be problematic, however, because the medieval political theorist typically accepted the concept of popular consent, but understood it to entail nothing more than acclamation or concurrence for an otherwise already designated ruler. The modern democratic understanding of consent as involving an essential operating procedure whereby all individual citizens express their approval cannot be assumed to be part of Marsilius's theory.

The perception of Marsilius as a modern thinker, then, is both accurate and inaccurate. Marsilius does not repeat the view that either

18. Marsilius *Defensor pacis* 1.9.2, 12.1, 15.2, 7.3. The Marsilian position is not as qualified in identifying the only source of legitimate political authority as it might seem from the literal reading: "in most cases, nearly everywhere"; these qualifications reflect what Aristotle says about the character of scientific knowledge of nature, whose principles hold "for the most part": Aristotle *Physics* 2.5.196b10–1. Cf. *Défenseur de la paix*, trans. Quillet, p. 89, n. 1.

19. Marsilius *Defensor pacis* 1.9.11.

the people or some higher authority can be the legitimate source of a temporal ruler's power. But in order to see what significant differences, if any, there are in Marsilius on this point it is essential to understand more fully what he means by "the people," and how the people, the human legislator, transfer authority to the ruler who exercises it. The first thing to be noted in this connection, a point mentioned already, is that Marsilius retains the medieval corporation theory's view of the people: according to this view the people are seen as an abstract entity, the character of which is theoretically functional as a whole but is not identified with the simple aggregate number of the individuals making up the whole. For Marsilius the people, society as a whole, is a collective concept rather than a notion of an aggregate collection of the individuals who make it up.

There is nothing new in this, of course; we have tried to show earlier how the notion of corporate entity developed in medieval legal theory and practice, and how this development was transferred into the domain of public law and, to some extent, began to appear in the actual procedures of both courts and parliaments in the thirteenth century. Specific issues began to emerge about how corporations were to function through representatives and how these functional procedures might be used to limit the actual power of a ruler. The emergence of these practical issues, especially on the English political scene, was to result in the fourteenth century in genuine progress towards the development of modern parliamentary democracy, although it was to be centuries before the reality approximated today's norms for this mode of governance. Somewhat parallel practical issues in the area of ecclesiastical governance were to give a stimulus in this arena as well to thought about how the corporation as a whole, in this case the community of the Church, was to exercise some control to limit the authority of the ruler: the issues of the Avignon papacy and the contested papal elections leading to the several schisms of the fourteenth and early fifteenth centuries were the practical problems stimulating the thinking among theologians and canonists that led to the development of the conciliar movement.[20]

To be fair to him, Marsilius was an innovative political theorist; but he was also a man of his time and reflected typically medieval views. A

---

20. See Tierney, *Foundations of Conciliar Theory*. The conciliar theory and its use in resolving the ecclesiastical scandal of the Great Schism lie outside the limits of this study. See Conclusion, nn. 3 and 4, below.

balance has to be struck between these two elements in an interpretation of his thought. If we seem here to be denigrating his contributions as an innovator, the intention is not to deprive him of his rightful claims as an important political theorist. But some earlier interpretations have laid too much stress on these aspects of his thought, failing to interpret them in the total context of his doctrine; hence, some righting of the balance is in order. Wilks puts the issue squarely when he asserts that "the mere use of corporation theory by a fourteenth century writer is very far from being a guarantee that he espoused popular sovereignty in any modern sense of that expression."[21]

A genuine test of Marsilius's meaning for the view that the people are the base for political sovereignty is the position he presents concerning the manner in which the people express their views, his theory of popular consent. In this area Marsilius expresses typically medieval notions, the most obvious feature of which is the doctrine of the people's will being expressed through the *maior et sanior pars*.[22] A first reading of the *Defensor pacis* usually has this feature of Marsilius's text strike the modern reader as a curious expression whose meaning is not immediately clear; even as understood it seems anachronistic and out of phase with the otherwise "modern" Marsilian theory of popular sovereignty. There is a failure in perspective here, however; Marsilius

21. Wilks, "Coronation and Representation," p. 256.

22. We have seen already an examination of this concept from the perspective of the modern notion of majority as expressed in numerical terms (50 per cent plus one!): see Moulin, "Sanior et maior pars," and Part 3, 2A above. Marsilius employs the expression *valentior pars* first at *Defensor pacis* 1.12.3: "civium universitas aut eius pars valentior." Wilks notes that the term *valentior pars* derives from William of Moerbeke's translation of Aristotle's *Politics* at 4.12.1296b: "The part of the state which wishes the state to remain should be weightier [*valentiorem*] than that which does not." Cf. Wilks, "Coronation and Representation," p. 266, and n. 43, 44. While Marsilius probably did take the expression *valentior pars* from the Moerbeke translation of the *Politics*—the fact that Marsilius cites Aristotle at the point where he introduces the term seems conclusive—it is not stretching credibility too far to suggest further that the Paduan blended the Aristotelian concept of *valentior pars* with the traditional canonical and ecclesiastico-legal concept of *sanior pars*. Wilks notes Marsilius's use of the traditional medieval corporation theory in which this term features prominently, and himself applies the term *sanior pars* to an interpretation of the Paduan's position: Wilks, "Coronation and Representation," p. 276; cf. pp. 277–78. Gewirth mentions also the use Marsilius makes of the notion of "*maior et sanior pars*, noting that the concept functioned in the statutes of Padua governing the election of the *gastaldiones* of the guild of notaries to which Marsilius's father probably belonged, as well as in the election of officials elected by the Norman "Nation" at the University of Paris: Gewirth, *Marsilius of Padua*, 1:143–44, and references in n. 91.

really does not exhibit a modern theory of popular sovereignty, but only some of the ingredients for one. The idea of the *populus* as a corporate or juristic entity; its government by laws perceived to be the expression of the will of the corporate personality itself; the determination of laws by a majority principle in which the view of the *maior pars* is considered the equivalent to unanimity; the assumption that dissenters should be disregarded as anti-social—these were all common features of Roman corporation law; and they had been employed in ecclesiastical jurisdictions by medieval canonists, as well in thirteenth-century political thought. They are also to be found in the *Defensor pacis*. The interesting one for our purposes is the notion of *maior pars*.

Marsilius explicitly indicates that his theory of polity for governing temporal states is applicable to ecclesiastical communities as well;[23] and this is because he conceived of the principles and structures of the two spheres as identical: each was a corporate entity whose ruler incorporated the collective entity as a whole. The notion of the comparability of the ideal structure in the two spheres of authority, temporal and spiritual, has been seen earlier in John of Paris; and in a way Quidort seems more modern in this connection than Marsilius, perhaps because the Paduan was much more explicit in detailing his polity than Quidort, sufficiently explicit in fact that it is possible to see that the real basis for comparison between the spheres in the Marsilian doctrine is a conception of both church and state as medieval corporations that noticeably lack any specific emphasis on the elective rights of individual members.

Quidort normally seems medieval to the modern reader; we applaud him then when we hear him sounding modern. Marsilius, on the other hand, sounds very modern in his basic emphasis on the people; consequently, we tend to be surprised and ultimately disappointed when we are forced to acknowledge that he too was a man of his own time. But what views did he actually hold?

Like Cicero and Augustine long before him, and many Christian thinkers after them, Marsilius held that the state, the human legislator, is the people conceived as a whole engaged in a joint enterprise of collective well-being.[24] It is an abstract thing, a corporate entity, rather

23. Wilks, "Coronation and Representation," p. 255.

24. Cicero *De re publica* 1.25.39, 1.26.41; Augustine *De civitate Dei* 19.21; *Epistolae* 138.2. Cf. Wilks, "Roman Empire and Christian State"; "Coronation and Representation," pp. 257–58.

than the collection of its individual parts, a public thing rather than the general public. Marsilius would have found the notion of a political society as a collective whole in Aristotle's *Politics*,[25] as well as in normal medieval corporation theory; and it is probable that for the Paduan, as indeed for other medieval theorists such as John of Paris, Aegidius of Rome, and Thomas Aquinas, the two sources for the same general view reinforced one another. Marsilius makes his basic position very clear in the description of political society he offers; it is directed to the common good, whose unity is the collective entity itself.[26] Its ruler, accordingly, is the embodiment or personification of the social entity, all of whose efforts are to be directed to achieving the end of this society.

The very purpose of a political society, the reason for its individual members coming together as a whole, is the establishment of a collective unity needed to effect the common good, a collective form of right living to which the individual citizen is subordinate. Borrowing the terminology from Aristotle's *Politics*, perhaps, but the basic notion from the Romano-Christian tradition that goes back to Cicero, Marsilius stressed the rational character of this emphasis on political society as united under the aim of achieving the common good: the common good itself is a rational goal in the sense that it can be understood rationally, and rational thought is the means of discovering its specifications.[27] Further, the organization and direction of political society will also reflect this essential element of rationality. All of this sounds familiar enough to the student of medieval political theory, without for all that, perhaps, sounding particularly clear.

However, when one turns to an examination of what Marsilius proposes as the method by which the people (*populus*), the human legislator, give expression to the rationality of achieving the common good, matters become somewhat more pointed as well as more coherent. Marsilius speaks of the multitude of subjects or the human legislator as having a will of its own "by which the men of one city or province are said to be one state (*civitas*) or kingdom (*regnum*) insofar as they will be numerically one political entity (*principatum*)";[28] "the power (*virtus*) and authority (*auctoritas*) of a state (*principatus*) consist in the

---

25. Aristotle *Politics* 3.9.11.1281a–82a, esp. 1281b; 4.4.1292a; 8.1.1337a.

26. Marsilius *Defensor pacis* 1.4.5, 1.12.5; cf. Gewirth, 1:203.

27. Marsilius *Defensor pacis* 1.2.3, 1.3.4, and 1.11.4, which quotes Aristotle's definition of law as reason without passion, citing Aristotle's *Politics* 3.16.1281a; cf. Wilks, "Coronation and Representation," p. 260, and n. 25.

28. Marsilius *Defensor pacis* 1.17.11.

expressed will of the multitude of subjects or legislator."[29] Marsilius refers to Aristotle's *Politics* and to the notions of the people as a whole and popular election as cause of the authority in a political society. It is clear, however, that what he has in mind is the collective unanimity of a rational view about how a polity should operate, not any *de facto* political society in which divergent and conflicting opinions are normally present, and for whose expression and accommodation an adequate theory of popular sovereignty must provide. Marsilius asserts further that "we maintain in accordance with the truth as well as the advice of Aristotle *Politics 3.6* that the legislator or the first and proper efficient cause of law is the people or the corporation of citizens (*civium universitas*) or of its weightier part (*valentior pars*) decreeing or determining through its own choice (*electio*) or will (*voluntas*) in a general gathering of citizens by way of explicit statement what is to be done or not done concerning civil human behaviour under temporal penalty or punishment."[30]

Marsilius speaks here of the first and proper efficient cause of law being the people *or* its weightier part, just as earlier he had spoken of the people being the first and proper efficient cause of the authority of the ruler, having in mind the issue of how the ruler comes into power. He distinguishes between the cause of the ruler's authority in general acquired from the people, and the cause of the ruler's authority as exercised in office. The efficient cause of both is the same, however: the legislator, the people, *or* the *valentior pars*. The precise meaning of the latter alternative, and why it is as legitimate a cause of authority and law as the whole people, are matters that require careful examination. So, too, does the mentioned element of unanimity of collective will and choice, which appears here alongside an explicit reference to election,[31] and is reflected again in Marsilius's approval for the Aristotelian

29. Ibid., 3.3: "Quoniam in ipsius (i.e. multitudinis subiectae seu legislatoris) expressa voluntate consisti virtus et auctoritas principatus." Cf. "Sic quoque unius civitatis aut provinciae homines dicuntur una civitas aut regnum, quia volunt unum numero principatum," *Defensor pacis* 1.18.11.

30. Ibid., 1.12.3, 1.16.11, 1.16.19; cf. Gewirth, *Marsilius of Padua*, 1:57–58; Wilks, "Coronation and Representation," 261, and n. 29. Marsilius unquestionably had in mind a direct-participation republican form of government like that of Padua and other northern Italian cities of the time, where all citizens came together in a great council to approve legislation formulated by the ruler and small executive body. It might be argued further that his emphasis on the whole people as the seat of sovereignty had a practical as well as theoretical basis: it was a response to the factional rivalry between the two political groups in Padua.

31. See n. 33.

temperate form of government, wherein authority is exercised for the common good in accordance with the will of the subjects (*ad commune conferens secundum voluntatem subditorum*).[32] What emerges from inter-relating these various elements is the realization that the most important single element is the people's involvement through a single will, which seems itself necessarily expressive of the common good, rather than the involvement of the citizenry as a whole.

Marsilius also indicates clearly that he agrees with the Augustinian thesis that the primary feature of good government is peace, the tranquillity of order, concord among the citizenry.[33] There is nothing startling in this view except perhaps that, like so many other medieval writers, Marsilius subscribed to it. But after all, like so many of these other writers, Marsilius was himself something of a theologian. The Paduan was to give this feature of traditional Christian political theory a particular twist, however, anticipating the positivistic theory of law that rests its validity exclusively on the power to coerce. Certainly there is a sense in which this theory of law and coercion is modern, but not for all that attractive.

For Marsilius, the will of the human legislator is expressible either through the people as a whole or through the *valentior pars*; thereby he accepts at a theoretical level the idea of there being a variety of forms through which the human legislator, the political society acting as a corporate whole in its common interests, might act to achieve its purposes. On personal and practical grounds, however, he expressed preference in his own actions for the monarchical imperial administration under Ludwig of Bavaria, with whom Marsilius cast his lot in Ludwig's dispute with the papacy.[34] The Paduan continued this support for many years and over the reigns of three fourteenth-century pontiffs. Support for Ludwig is offered traditionally as the reason for Marsilius having composed the *Defender of Peace*; and it has even been contended recently that Marsilius's real intention in the work was to promote the Aristotelian model of the well-tempered monarch, the ideal prince from whom the totality of political prudence

32. Marsilius *Defensor pacis* 1.8.2; cf. the terminology *voluntas sive consensus* in 1.8.3; cf. Wilks, "Coronation and Representation," p. 262, and n. 30.

33. Marsilius *Defensor pacis* 1.2.3, 1.19.2.

34. Marsilius held that the prime reason for temporal discord was the refusal of Pope John XXII to recognize the emperor (who was Ludwig at the time), and Ludwig was the "defender of peace" of the title of the Paduan's·work. See the references to Ludwig, direct and indirect, noted by Wilks, "Coronation and Representation," p. 285, and nn. 102, 103.

flows, as the paradigm of which Ludwig of Bavaria could be seen to be the historical embodiment.[35]

In fact, as just mentioned, Marsilius is not dogmatic in identifying the best form of government from among the various well-tempered forms of monarchy, aristocracy, and polity, but he does indicate some preference for the monarchical form: "One of the well-tempered types of governance, and perhaps the more perfect, is kingly monarchy."[36] He also insists that, absolutely speaking, the best form of any government must reflect the elective principle;[37] and he calls specifically for an elected monarchy.[38] The general thrust of much of the Paduan's discussion of the qualities of the perfect ruler and of the best method for establishing a government imply that he is thinking primarily of a ruler elected for life. Further, and crucial for our interests, he refuses to identify any single mechanism for the election procedure: "The method of coming together to effect the aforesaid establishment or election of the ruler may perhaps vary according to the variety of provinces."[39] Marsilius pushed harder than any medieval political theorist yet seen the concept of popular consent, and expanded its meaning and importance by insisting that the people's consent, as expressed via election, is an essential in every instance of legitimate political authority; but he did not stipulate any specific procedure or mechanism whereby this election or choice should be expressed. For this reason it might be better to use the expression "choosing" rather than "election" or "electing," inasmuch as these latter terms when used of the people tend in modern usage to have a democratic flavour and the connotation of a specific action performed (by the people) that are simply lacking in the *Defensor pacis*.

It has been noted that when Marsilius speaks of the people as the source of political authority he is speaking of an abstraction. When he speaks of political authority as exercisable in a variety of forms, then, he always has in mind a specific operative form that embodies the moral authority of the collective whole in given circumstances; the specific form is the best embodiment for the individuals who actually

---

35. Wilks, "Coronation and Representation," pp. 285–87, 292. Marsilius, of course, exhibits a preference for elected monarchy as perhaps the best form of government (nn. 40, 41).

36. Marsilius *Defensor pacis* 1.9.5.

37. Ibid., 1.9.11, 1.9.7.

38. Ibid., 1.16.11.

39. Ibid., 1.15.2.

constitute the corporation in those circumstances. Thus, a qualitative feature appears alongside the quantitative one in the meaning of collective good. This qualitative element is particularly noticeable when Marsilius describes the people as cause in the activity of lawmaking; he makes explicit reference to the need to "take into consideration the quantity and the quality of the persons in that community over which the law is made."[40] What is paramount is the human legislator's capacity to perceive the common good rationally, because the legislator's capacity to make proper laws depends necessarily on this rational perception. For Marsilius, as for his medieval predecessors, lawmaking is essentially an activity of the polity itself, of the people as a collective whole, rather than of the individuals who constitute it. Accordingly, his regular use of the terms "the people," "the human legislator," "the majority" should not be understood as connoting anything of the essentially numerical sense they have in much of modern democratic theory. Given the nature of his understanding of the people as a corporation, the issue of how the people give expression to the functioning human legislator is not specified in terms of the number of individuals in the collective who make it up. Rather, what interests Marsilius—and again here he reflects earlier medieval attitudes—is the issue of who represents best in practice the will of the abstract entity that is the state; who gives this abstraction its best physical expression. The Paduan's answer is straightforward: the weightier part (*valentior pars*). The weightier part speaks for the collective whole, legislates for it because, in a word, the weightier part is the state; it embodies the state in the same way as John of Salisbury's prince embodies the state. Both are abstract embodiments of an abstract entity. Yet both must have a physical form; and both do!

Certain ambiguities in the Marsilian position can begin to appear at this point. There can be no doubt about what John of Salisbury understands as the concrete realization of the abstraction he calls the prince (or ruler); it can only be the real individual male human who actually occupies the monarchical position of supreme temporal authority in a state. Who else could it be? Any difficulties in interpretation of the Salisbury doctrine only appear when John begins to talk about the prince being bound by the law and also being above it: how can he be both? The answer, as we have seen, is that the individual occupant of the seat of temporal authority must recognize his position

40. Ibid., 1.12.3.

itself to be circumscribed in abstract terms by the limits of its own specifications, while at the same time his position cannot be circumscribed in its authority to make law insofar as the position itself is the very seat of lawmaking activity. It is in the latter sense that the prince as an abstraction for the lawmaking authority of the society itself is "above the law." Nevertheless, the lawmaking function is circumscribed by the moral requirement to act for the common good in a manner consistent with the laws of nature and of God. At the same time, the prince's function cannot be circumscribed completely by actually existing legislation that is the product of any previous exercise of the function. To limit the function of the prince as legislator to following only existing legislation would effectively deny the legislator's lawmaking function, a contradiction in terms. The prince as legislator is limited, but not in that way. It is the prince as administrator who is bound to follow the laws already produced by the prince as legislator, inasmuch as he is the one and same authority that produced them in the first instance.

And so, the prince is "above the law" in two senses. First, there is no set of legislated rules formulated by any legislator superior to him: as the supreme legislator he has no one superior in his sphere of jurisdiction. Secondly, as legislator he is not bound by the specific limits of the existing legislation in his own jurisdiction: he possesses the power to make new law and thereby, as appropriate, to set aside existing law. In neither sense, however, can the legislator be said to act arbitrarily; he is still bound by the limits of the rational specification of his responsibilities, by what can be called the moral law.

Similarly for Marsilius: the human legislator is the abstract instrument of authority for the political society as a whole; in this sense the human legislator is synonymous with the polity, just as was Salisbury's prince. Marsilius made a significant move, however, when he transformed the traditional medieval concept of the prince as legislator into the concept of the people as legislator. But what he means by the people is just as much an abstraction as what earlier thinkers had meant by prince or ruler. However, because he uses the terms "people" and "human legislator," Marsilius is sometimes interpreted as more modern than he was. The Paduan recognized that from a theoretical point of view the state, the human legislator, could best be represented in some circumstances by all the individual persons who constituted a political society directly participating in its governance; it has been suggested that in such circumstances the people, the aggregate of individual citizens, would be identical with the People, the state as a collective whole.[41] Marsilius never denied the possibility that in given circumstances all the individual members of a polity could function as elements in the human legislator; in which case, of course, each individual would function as a citizen (*civis*) rather than merely as a person (*homo*). When speaking in this fashion Marsilius can sound very democratic; but there are important qualifications to be kept in mind. The functioning of all members of a political society is not what is essential for Marsilius; it is the functioning of the *valentior pars* of that society that is crucial. When the individual members of an aggregate actually constitute the *valentior pars*, then they should so function. But there are other forms the *valentior pars* can take; and these other forms are equally valid modes of governance. And it seems that for Marsilius other such forms are preferable to that of direct democracy, the form he apparently has in mind when he speaks of all the people participating individually as elements in the human legislator as lawmaker.[42]

Marsilius does speak strongly concerning the advantages of popular participation in government[43] and these texts, taken with his specific willingness to afford the right to any community to rid itself of a poor government,[44] seem to place him in the forefront of democraic constitutional thinking. Many of his most forthright statements concerning the role of the people in government relate to their function in the activity of lawmaking; and it is noteworthy that he is much more specific about the people as efficient cause in the ruler's function as lawmaker than as efficient cause of a ruler coming into office. Marsilius maintained that each individual is more likely to observe a law he has had a hand in making, and contends that this fact justifies action by the whole multitude: "A law is better kept when it is seen to have been imposed by all the citizens on themselves than by one of them; this is the type of law [made] with the understanding [*auditu*] and

---

41. Wilks, "Coronation and Representation," p. 267.

42. Marsilius *Defensor pacis* 1.12.5. Marsilius has been interpreted and complimented frequently enough for his advocacy of a republican form of government; and earlier advocates of polity have been identified as forerunners of this view: Ptolemy of Lucca and Remigio de Girolami (see Davis, "An Early Florentine Political Theorist"; "Ptolemy of Lucca"). For a careful examination of the political realities of Marsilius's home town see Hyde, *Padua in the Age of Dante*. See n. 30 above.

43. Marsilius *Defensor pacis* 1.13.6, 1.13.3–5, 1.12.8, 2.17.14, 2.17.11–12; cf. Wilks, "Coronation and Representation," pp. 269–70.

44. Marsilius of Padua *Defensor pacis* 1.15.2.

involvement of the whole multitude."[45] Here the Paduan is making shrewd use of a notion found in Aristotle's *Politics*: "the multitude is dominant in the more important matters."[46] He also speaks of the abilities of the many to recognize possible defects in legislation in respect of the common good, and argues against their exclusion from lawmaking activities on the grounds that legislative authority in the hands of a few will encourage that minority to pursue its own interests to the disadvantage of the community as a whole. He even advocates the calling of assemblies of "the whole body of citizens for their approval or disapproval [of future laws]."[47]

In the final analysis, however, the role in lawmaking that Marsilius assigns to the multitude is rather like that seen earlier for the multitude in a religious community choosing a bishop; it is the function of consenting in an auxiliary and acclamatory way. Laws are largely formulated by the knowledgeable and expert members of the community, whose background and position best fit them for such technical chores;[48] and the ordinary folk have the right of approval by way of acclamation. While Marsilius concedes to the multitude as a whole the right to reject, amend, and improve legislative proposals, and comments that the whole *universitas* often can detect significant defects in draft legislation that the wiser formulators have managed to overlook or ignore,[49] he seems to have envisaged the community's actual involvement as little more than "additions made by men of humbler mind" (*adinventes autem addere possunt etiam humilioris ingenii homines*).[50] There is an emphasis on the limited capacity of the ordinary citizen, and the role accorded to the multitude reflects this limited capacity. It can be difficult to see this interpretation in the Marsilian text, particularly when the most trenchant expressions of the limited capacities of ordinary people are noted in objections to the author's

45. "Quoniam lex illa melius observatur a quocumque civium quam sibi quilibet imposuisse videtur: talis est lex lata ex auditu et praecepta universae multitudinis civium": Marsilius *Defensor pacis* 1.12.6.

46. Ibid., 1.13.4, 1.15.2; Aristotle *Politics* 3.6.1282a38.

47. Marsilius *Defensor pacis* 1.13.8.

48. Ibid., 1.13.8.

49. Ibid., 1.13.3–7, 1.12.8; cf. 2.6.13, where the same argument is directed against clergy using their powers of excommunication; and 2.17.14 and 2.17.11–12, where Marsilius advocated ecclesiastical appointments being made by the *universitas civium* through the lay ruler. Cf. Wilks, "Coronation and Representation," p. 268, n. 49.

50. Marsilius *Defensor pacis* 1.13.7; Wilks, "Coronation and Representation," p. 271.

own position that the people are the efficient cause of law. But in the final analysis Marsilius shares with his objectors this negative view of the general population's capacity as individuals to have either the time, ability, or inclination to function as rational beings in the determination of complex matters such as lawmaking. The right and ability of the people so to function ultimately are the right and ability of an abstraction; accordingly, some function must logically be accorded to all. But the actual role accorded to the masses as a functioning part of the abstract collective, even though by far the numerically superior, need not be very significant in practice. A modern echo of this attitude is to be seen in Rousseau's views on the voting and election rights of all the citizens.[51]

While Marsilius counters the objection that denies any rightful role to all the people in the activity of lawmaking, he is careful to do so in terms of an abstraction and without denying the adverse judgment on the actual capacities of ordinary uncultivated persons. Lawmaking is to be accomplished by those few who actually possess the requisite quality of rationality and right-willing mind. Even the few are brought to agreement by a still smaller group of *prudentes* especially endowed by nature to be more astute politically; these are the *valentior pars*, a portion of the *prudentes*. This portion of a portion of the whole multitude provides the necessary expertise in legal and political matters through their superior rationality or right-mindedness. From them the aristocracy as a whole (the *prudentes*) are taught how to give specification to their own natural gifts of rationality, gifts that in turn place the *prudentes* in a loftier position than the vulgar multitudes of the labouring classes, whose natural mental abilities are so low as to keep them only in "vile and defiling" positions. Marsilius acknowledges Aristotle as his authority for this stratified view of society and denigrating attitude towards the mental and moral capacities of the masses.[52]

The general character of the *valentior pars* for Marsilius should now be clear. Yet, as mentioned earlier, Marsilius maintains that in theory the multitude can rule as a whole in a mode of governance that is truly democratic. His comments on actual instances of this form of polity, however, reinforce the view that the *valentior pars* is given more perfect

51. Marsilius *Defensor pacis* 1.14; cf. Rousseau, *Contrat social*, 4:2 and 3.

52. Marsilius *Defensor pacis* 1.5.1, 1.5.13. Marsilius quotes Aristotle: see *Politics* 7.8.1328b; 4.4.1290b–91b; but he cites *Politics* 7.7 at *Defensor pacis* 1.5.1.

expression when embodied in a minority. Some communities, he states, were so primitive as to lack persons qualified as *prudentes*; in such cases a different form of social contract was adopted, reflecting the household model of polity wherein the single best-informed person, the father, exercises authority.[53] A case in point, he indicates, was seen in the early Church where there was a marked deficiency in both quantity and quality of leadership ability; the multitude of the faithful had been so few and of such lack of cultivation in many areas that it had been difficult even to find a suitable candidate for bishop, not to speak of a group of electors; in such cases a single Apostle had had to make the appointment.[54]

In particular Marsilius emphasizes the contributions all citizens can make to the formulation of laws for a given community; he speaks of the people as the efficient cause or source of law in a society, as well as cause of the agency of authority (the ruler). And the remarks he makes concerning the role of the people in respect of lawmaking activity show him proceeding further in the direction of spelling out the details of how this should be done than he does when he describes the role of the people in putting a ruler in place. Procedural specification in the latter case is missing and, indeed, deliberately so inasmuch as Marsilius accepted that the people as legislator could "speak" (express their collective authority and reality) in a variety of ways in conferring authority on a ruler. The specification of how they were to do so, however, was not a significant issue for him, inasmuch as his designation of the people as the efficient cause of political authority conceives of them essentially as an abstraction. Marsilius does speak of an original coming together of individuals "to establish the civil community and civil law" (*ad civilem communitatem et legem ordinandum convenerunt homines a principio*),[55] something of a forerunner to the Hobbesian and Lockean

---

53. "Multiplicatis autem vicis et facta communitate quod oportuit crescente propagatione, adhuc regebantur uno, vel propter defectum pluralitatis aut aliam quandam alteratam causam": Marsilius *Defensor pacis* 1.3.4; Marsilius cites Aristotle *Politics* 2.15.1286b.

54. Marsilius *Defensor pacis* 2.17.7, cited by Wilks, "Coronation and Representation," p. 276, n. 73. Marsilius's statement about the limited abilities of early Christian communities to function by way of collective action contrasts with the traditional perception of the value of exercising authority via common consent or consensus, a perception that had some favour among medieval Christian writers because of their view that it was the method employed by the original Christian groups. Wilks traces Marsilius's comment about how the uncultivated multitude contribute to society's formation to Cicero, who refers to the people's condition as one of *imbecillitas*: *De re publica* 1.25.39.

55. Marsilius *Defensor pacis* 2.22.15; cf. 2.16.19.

descriptions of the original social contract. And the details he provides are of interest: the *valentior pars* (of the whole multitude) either assumes or is given the task of "agreeing on matters pertaining to sufficiency of life"; initiative in summoning all to come together is taken by "the prudent and able men exceptionally endowed by nature with an inclination for this task of guiding others"; and the multitude as a whole "readily [heed] the persuasion of the prudent and able to form a community to which all [are] naturally inclined."[56]

In the case of the people as lawmaker he is more explicit, though still not sufficiently so to show adequate evidence of a modern theory of democratic constitutionalism. Again Marsilius makes explicit and shrewd use of concepts and principles he has found in Aristotle's *Politics*, the principal one being that "the multitude is dominant in the more important matters"; but like Aristotle himself the Paduan falls well short of anything approximating a modern theory of representative democracy.

Marsilius includes both quantitative and qualitative elements in his notion of the *valentior* or *maior pars*, but they correlate in an inverso ratio. An increase in quantity is necessary where the quality level is low; correspondingly, any appreciable level of quality in a minority of the community signifies that the *valentior pars* can and should be that minority; the numerical or quantitative level of those involved in government need not be high. Marsilius's notion of majority, the *maior pars*, is equated with the weightier part (*valentior pars*), and is not based on number (quantity) at all. Seemingly numerical terms such as "majority," "plurality," "most," and "weightier part" thus do not have an exclusively numerical connotation for the Paduan; they are simply synonymous with representation by the right-willing portion of the polity. Marsilius reflects here an attitude to be found in Cicero; and it had a very respectable history in medieval thought. His definition of *valentior pars* is a virtual restatement of the definition of *universitas* found in Isidore of Seville's *Differentiae*,[57] where the distinction is drawn between the People (*populus*) and the people (*plebs*). Gregory I used the latter term to designate the element of the community to be involved in consent to the election of a bishop,[58] while Marsilius draws a

---

56. Ibid.

57. Cicero *De re publica* 2.22.39; cf. Aristotle *Constitution of Athens* 26.1 and 3; Isidore *Differentiae* 1.445 and 472 (*PL* 83:55 and 58), *Etymologiae* 9.4.5–6; cited and quoted in Wilks, "Coronation and Representation," p. 279, n. 84; cf. n. 83.

58. Leo *Epistle* 167, cited in Gratian, D.63, c.26.

seemingly exact parallel between the temporal (political) and the spiritual (ecclesiastical) spheres with respect to the function assigned to the masses.[59]

Marsilius repeats the Christian patristic and later feudal view, itself reflective of the classical Roman view of the Senate, that a given political society should possess a relatively small group of men who were considered to be the "image" of the state, that is, the people as a whole. This is his *valentior pars*, whose virtues are in such contrast with the deformed character of the numerically large multitude. Marsilius's position is well illustrated by his remark that, quite aside from the practical difficulties of assembling all the citizens in a physically large state, it would not be desirable to include in decision making those whose natural irrationality would preclude a rightful unanimity.[60] Such a numerical majority is better provided for through being represented by those who know better the nature of polity and the mind of the political community as such. Nor is there any need even to elect these "superior political minds"; the aristocracy already existing is self-evidently fitted for the positions of political authority. And fully consistent with this general theory, Marsilius extends his concept of the *valentior pars* to identify at least in theory with one person. The *pars principans*, the functional part of the human legislator, not only can be a small part of the highly qualified, "rational," members of the multitude as a numerical whole, but can even be a single individual. Marsilius speaks of the Roman emperor as *pars principans, pars valentior*, and *legislator humanus* all combined.[61]

Exhibiting his understanding and familiarity with Roman law in a clear reference to the Roman *lex regia*,[62] he interprets this well-known legal maxim to mean that the people (*populus*) mentioned in the law as having transferred *imperium* to the prince is really the state itself.[63] Accordingly, the person to whom the *imperium* of the *populus* has been

59. Wilks, "Coronation and Representation," p. 281.

60. "Quoniam non est facile aut non possibile omnes personas in unum convenire sententiam, propter quorundam esse naturam orbatam, malitia vel ignorantia singulari discordantem a communi sententia; propter quorum irrationabilem reclamationem seu contradictionem non debent communia conferentia impediri vel omitti. Pertinet igitur ad universitatem civium aut eius valentiorem partem tantummodo legum lationis seu institutionis auctoritas": Marsilius *Defensor pacis* 1.12.5.

61. Ibid., 1.12.3, 1.13.8, and 1.12.8, cited by Wilks, "Coronation and Representation," p. 283, n. 95.

62. *Inst.* 1.2.6; *Dig.* 1.4.1.

63. Wilks, "Coronation and Representation," p. 284.

transferred *is* the state in human form, and is possessed of the full authority of the corporation of the state: he *is* the human legislator. In advancing this position the author of the *Defensor pacis* cannot be seen as an advocate for democratic sovereignty. However novel and modern his political theory may appear, it does not go this far.

Marsilius accepts the theoretical possibility and legitimacy of a form of popular sovereignty in which all citizens participate directly in governmental activities and thereby are each a part of the human legislator, which itself is identical *de facto* with the aggregate of all individual citizens. But other medieval political theorists also accepted at least implicitly that this could be a possible mode of legitimate polity; indeed I know of no medieval thinker who rules out such a form of governance as unacceptable in theory. Moreover, the whole thrust of the Paduan's thesis concerning an ideal polity seems to have been towards the practical embodiment of the essentials of the *valentior pars* in a relatively small group of rational individuals, and even in some form of Aristotle's temperate monarchy by a heroic individual whom Marsilius may have been willing to identify with the embattled Ludwig of Bavaria, although he never said as much explicitly in the *Defensor pacis*. Nor could he be expected to do so in a treatise that aimed at being a disinterested examination of the nature and best form of temporal polity. His description of the imperial mode of governance also showed that he was prepared to concede an essential function to the imperial electors of the emperor,[64] and that as well he had serious reservations about mere heredity as a qualification for holding the office that wielded the supreme power of human legislator.[65] The *Defensor pacis* propounds general rules for governing a polity and was intended, therefore, to apply to all forms of political society, great and small; and its author also accepted the view that there could, and perhaps ordinarily should, be variant forms of polity existing throughout the universe. It has been contended, nonetheless, that Marsilius probably would have argued for a single person as *valentior pars* in a truly universal political community had such been in existence, a *valentior* and *maior pars* in one human being just as there is one embodiment of divine authority in God Himself. His actual text, however, does not show him doing this.[66]

64. Marsilius *Defensor pacis* 2.26.9. Cf. Bayley, *Formation of German College of Electors*.
65. Marsilius *Defensor pacis* 1.16.
66. Wilks, "Coronation and Representation," pp. 290–91.

C. William of Ockham

The last medieval thinker to be considered is William of Ockham (ca. 1280–1348). A contemporary of Marsilius of Padua and, like Marsilius, a supporter of Ludwig of Bavaria's claims to the Holy Roman Empire William was, however, a much different sort of person and a much different type of political thinker than the Paduan. Where Marsilius had been reared in the heady and politically active environment of a late-thirteenth-century northern Italian city-state, William was an Englishman brought up in the rural countryside of Edward I. Marsilius was a secular cleric and physician who had taught theology briefly before throwing in his lot with Ludwig and producing the *Defensor pacis*, thereby earning the undying enmity of the contemporary papacy: further, he took his position against the papacy as a comparatively young man, and spent the rest of his days in Ludwig's service. Ockham, on the other hand, had joined the Franciscans as a young man and spent many years teaching theology at Oxford, enjoying an international reputation as an authoritative and subtle thinker; he became involved with the papacy when his theological views were made the object of ecclesiastical investigation and, concurrently, his status as a ranking Franciscan thinker probably made him a butt of criticism revolving around the dispute between the leaders of his order and Pope John XXII over the meaning of monastic poverty.[67]

Marsilius came to the defence of Ludwig of Bavaria and the Holy Roman Empire from essentially Ghibelline political views imbibed in the Padua of his youth, and wrote the *Defensor pacis* as a programmatic means of focusing opposition on the papacy, which he saw as the chief source of discord in the Italy of his time and in western Europe generally. William of Ockham, on the other hand, found himself defending personal theological doctrines and the position of his order

---

67. William of Ockham has become a figure of considerable interest in recent years, although scholars had tended for centuries to avoid research in the extensive Ockhamite corpus that remained in large part in manuscript and non-critical editions. His political writings are now in critical edition in *Guillelmi de Ockham Opera Politica*, 1, ed. J. G. Sikes et al. (Manchester: Manchester University Press, 1940); 2, ed. H. S. Offler (Manchester: 1963); 3, ed. H. S. Offler (Manchester; 1956). A fine monograph on William's political doctrine is McGrade, *Political Thought of William of Ockham* which has a good bibliography; see also Leff, *William of Ockham*, which has an extensive bibliography; Lagarde, *Naissance de l'esprit laique au déclin du moyen âge*, 3rd ed., vols. 4 and 5; Boehner, *Collected Articles on Ockham*; Leff, *Heresy in the Later Middle Ages*, 2 vols.

during the first phase of his quarrel with the papacy. Initially he seems not to have joined the camp of Ludwig for political reasons at all, but simply took refuge there in company with the master general of the Franciscans, Michael of Cesena, after having fled from the prospect of papal incarceration at Avignon. For his part, Marsilius was essentially a one-book author, a pungent and brilliant polemicist whose text "in defence of the peace" exhibited little concern for the subtleties of speculative scholastic thought. Ockham, however, was one of the most renowned and influential academic thinkers of his day, the author of magisterial treatises in a variety of intellectual disciplines before being thrown into the arena of political polemics relatively late in life. And even when committed to what may well have been an unpalatable task of writing political tracts, he retained a somewhat ponderous and impersonal scholastic style, considering the various options on a given issue and making careful distinctions in the manner of his earlier theological and philosophical texts. He produced several massive volumes and a number of smaller ones in the category of political writings, and in general they do not make easy reading, especially the lengthy ones, which are so prolix and often so self-effacing as to appear sometimes ambiguous concerning their author's own position. Yet they are capable of yielding up an accuracy and clarity that many apparently straightforward texts often do not achieve. Ockham was a Franciscan theologian who became a political polemicist in defence of his order's interests against the early-fourteenth-century papacy. Having committed himself to this task, he persisted in it for nearly two decades and against three occupants of the Holy See.

William's doctrine of polity, still only incompletely available in fully systematic terms[68] and the subject of varying if not contradictory interpretations,[69] contains specific views on the issue of popular consent. Accordingly, it is possible to provide some focus on this element even if a comprehensive interpretation of Ockham's political writings as a whole may not yet be possible. Beginning with the *Opus nonaginta dierum* of 1332, where he subjected certain bulls of John XXII to an exhaustive critique, through the massive but incomplete *Dialogus inter militem et clericum*, the first part of which dates from 1334 and the third part from 1338, to later less substantial political tracts

68. See Leff, *William of Ockham*, pp. xi–xii for a list of Ockham's works and their status in terms of modern editions; cf. pp. xii–xxiv; Lagarde, *Défense de l'empire*, pp. 15–43.
69. See McGrade, *Political Thought*, pp. 28–46.

produced more or less steadily until his death in 1348, Ockham proffers a sustained attack on the functioning ecclesiastical polity of his day, especially the papacy. In doing so he provides a wealth of material from which to formulate a theory of polity. For all the material available, however, there still are difficulties in establishing a fully coherent and systematic Ockhamite doctrine, especially in terms of a careful correlation between his theological and philosophical views and the later diffuse political writings.[70] A further difficulty, and an especially frustrating one because of the large quantity of Ockhamite political material, is that for all his writing on political matters having to do with the authority of the papacy and with the relationship between temporal and ecclesiastical authorities, in the final analysis he was really not interested in producing a comprehensive and systematic investigation of the whole range of the political order. Like so many medieval writers in the general field of political theory, Ockham was primarily a theologian who wrote on political questions; his perspective was never either directly or exclusively that of a political thinker as such. Thus, what he does say so often requires interpretation and application to issues he does not address directly.

One useful approach to Ockham's theory of polity is to try and see it in contrast with the doctrine of Marsilius of Padua. For despite contemporary medieval as well as some recent modern efforts to identify with one another the views of these fourteenth-century opponents of the papacy,[71] they did not agree on many fundamental points of political doctrine. Moreover, the two authors consciously recognized each other as being opposed on important elements of theory, and they subjected one another's writings to specific criticism: whole sections of William's *Dialogue* are explicit and careful criticisms of the *Defensor pacis*,[72] and Marsilius replied to these criticisms in his own *Defensor minor*.[73]

Unlike Marsilius, who was always forthright in insisting that the

70. Leff, *William of Ockham*, p. 614; it is of some interest that in his massive treatment of Ockham's thought Professor Leff devotes only 29 of 643 pages to William's views on society; McGrade, *Political Thought*, pp. 44–46, 207–9.

71. Lagarde, "Marsile de Padoue," p. 593, where Lagarde notes that William and Marsilius were associated as early as 1331 by John XXII's accusation that Ockham was repeating already condemned errors found in the *Defensor pacis*.

72. Lagarde, "Marsile de Padoue," p. 593. Offler lists a number of references to Marsilius's *Defensor pacis*, though not mentioned by name, in *Octo quaestiones* 1.7.19–29, 3.93–120, 3.2.5–13, 3.3.5–28, and 8.6.147, cited in *Opera politica*, 1:9 (2nd ed.).

73. Marsilius *Defensor minor* 11.31–4, cited in Lagarde, "Marsile de Padoue," p. 599, and n. 37.

foundation of political authority was the people—popular sovereignty of a specific medieval type—Ockham seems to have been more cautious and more traditional in his examination of the source and base of political authority. He repeated the conventional notion that political authority originates in the people,[74] but the context for his statement indicates a less than rigorous commitment to this position despite a clear presentation of the traditional formula. He seems to have regarded popular consent as the normal original ground for legitimate political authority, and offered an interesting thesis in this respect that reformulates the Augustinian position that the emergence of civil authority was a consequence of Original Sin.[75] According to Ockham, neither political authority nor private property existed before the Fall; both came afterwards, when God conferred on humans power to appropriate material things to specific persons and to set up rulers—powers conferred on the human race as a whole rather than on particular individuals. Consequently, establishing actual political authority is achieved by positive action involving the whole body of those affected; dominion and jurisdiction are introduced by human law as the joint exercise of a common power.

When explaining how the Romans came to be rulers of an empire, however, Ockham asserted that "it was necessary for the common utility of the whole world that one emperor rule over all mortals, ... hence the Romans could licitly subjugate opponents."[76] Here, of course, William was reflecting a common view, found not only in traditional Christian writings as well as in Aristotle's *Politics*,[77] but reflecting also an attitude grounded in the acceptance of the ages-old

74. William of Ockham *Dialogus* 1.8 (Goldast 2:514), 1.84 (Goldast 2:603), 1.97 (Goldast 2:613), 3.2.1.28 (Goldast 2:901), 3.2.3.6 (Goldast 2:934). References to the *Dialogus* give page references to Goldast, *Monarchia*. Cf. Lagarde, *Naissance*, 4:228, n. 153; *Breviloquium* 4.10 (Scholz, p. 161); *Octo quaestiones de potestate papae* 2.9 (*Opera politica*, 1:87). Lagarde considers that Ockham's emphasis on popular consent was used only to support the existing order: see Lagarde, *Naissance*, 4:230. Lagarde also makes an issue of the exceptions William noted to the principle of popular consent, pointing out further that Ockham cites popular consent as only one among several methods for establishing legitimate political authority: *Naissance*, 4:231–32. On this score William was more comprehensive than his medieval predecessors, most of whom identified only two methods: popular consent and some higher authority.

75. William of Ockham *Breviloquium* 3.7–11 (Scholz, pp. 125–32); cf. *Opus nonaginta dierum* 88 (*Opera politica*, 2:655–63); Boehner, "Ockham's Political Ideas," pp. 454–58.

76. William of Ockham *Dialogus* 3.2.1.27 (Goldast 2:899). However, cf. *Breviloquium* 4.10 (Scholz, pp. 161–62) for possible alternative forms.

77. Aristotle *Politics* 8.14.1333a39; 3.2.

and common practice of military conquest. It is another telling illustration, nonetheless, of the tendency on the part of the typical medieval political theorist to offer a purely abstract form of acceptance to the principle of popular consent as the basis for political authority; the principle could be articulated explicitly while at the same time, seemingly, being accommodated to an apparently opposed mode of achieving political jurisdiction. Nothing shows more clearly the lack of interest in giving the concept of popular consent any specific form of procedural expression. Further, the issue of how, if at all, consent was to be shown to their new rulers by conquered people was not even addressed directly by Ockham. Nor was it, for that matter, by any of his medieval predecessors as far as I have been able to determine. Also, Ockham's claim for the legitimacy of Ludwig of Bavaria as Holy Roman Emperor rested on the simple contention that the Gospels recognized the pagan empire of Rome, and not on any theoretical appeal to popular consent.[78] As has been seen with many if not all his medieval predecessors, Ockham was relatively indifferent to the specific mode of governance practised by legitimate political authority in any jurisdiction; he mentions without any expression of preference lords, princes, kings, free cities and, above all, emperor.[79] Even when he does urge the case for the legitimacy of Ludwig's occupancy of the imperial throne, the argument made is simply that Ludwig was properly elected to a position for which there is clear historical warrant and ecclesiastical acceptance.[80] There is no suggestion from William that this is the only acceptable mode of governance, or that it is indispensable for any reason; it just happens to be one among many legitimate forms.

Ockham expressed unwillingness to make popular consent the only basis for political legitimacy in still another way, declining specifically to accept that a Holy Roman Emperor might hold office only at the pleasure of his electors and be subject to removal without cause by the same electors.[81] By extension, presumably, he would deny also that

78. William of Ockham *Contra Benedictum* 6.5 (*Opera politica*, 3:277–78), where William lists a number of Scriptural references attesting the legitimacy of the Roman Empire based on de facto recognition; cf. *Breviloquium* 74–78; *Octo quaestiones* 129–30; cf. Lagarde, *Défense de l'empire*, 1:248–53.

79. See McGrade, *Political Thought*, pp. 122–25.

80. William of Ockham *Octo quaestiones* 4.3 (*Opera politica*, 1:129–30), cited by McGrade, *Political Thought*, p. 97, and n. 46.

81. William of Ockham *Breviloquium* 4.12–13 (Scholz, pp. 165–66).

temporal rulers of any sort could be deposed validly by the people or anyone else, except for cause. The view that a practical and valuable method for expressing the concept of limit in the exercise of political authority could be the limitation of tenure in office was not common in the medieval period. The specific issue of whether a ruler could be deposed by the people for cause was not addressed directly by Ockham either, but his texts do show a clear affirmative answer at least by implication. Much of his political writing was designed specifically to show that the contemporary occupant of the papal throne was a pertinacious heretic who was failing signally to exercise authority properly and who should be removed if he could not be persuaded to renounce his heresies.[82] William made major literary efforts to establish that the reigning pope could be challenged as a heretic, even though his views on how to further the challenge successfully by way of specific procedure are not sufficiently explicit.

Ockham's position here concerning the circumstantial necessity of papal resignation or deposition suffers from the very traditional approach he took towards the authority of the papacy and the institutional church as a whole. His traditionalism seems to have inhibited him from producing any theory on how to give procedural expression to actual political necessities. William specifically rejected the view that either an ecumenical council or the college of cardinals could be said to embody a higher authority than the pope in terms of representing the Church as a corporate whole; for all that, however, he did not specifically deny that either or both of these agencies might function to achieve a papal deposition. But neither did he specifically assign papal deposition as a proper function to either. Nonetheless, as we shall see, he had very specific views concerning the authority of a general council in circumstances where no one occupied the papal throne, and presumably, one such set of circumstances for Ockham was the vacancy created by papal heresy. He had specific views as well concerning the relative authority of a general council and a heretically errant pope. Hence, much like Gratian almost two centuries earlier, Ockham gave expression to a general theory of limitation for papal (and any) authority without addressing adequately the critical issue of how to give procedural expression to such limitation even in serious

---

82. As already noted, William extended his judgment concerning the heretical state of the incumbent of the papal throne to three consecutive occupants: John XXII, Benedict XII, and Clement IV.

circumstances. He faced the concrete issue of dealing with a seriously malevolent misuse of ecclesiastical authority at the highest level, and still failed to respond directly to the procedural problem.

It may be that the contingent character of the concrete need to deal with papal heresy, however urgent and practically necessary it may have been in William's judgment, led Ockham not to raise in academic treatises examining the generalities of a question the issue of precisely how to depose; but this is only conjecture. Other grounds having to do with philosophical and logical principles have been suggested, grounds that correlate with Ockham's refusal to identify the Church with any of its parts or institutional forms. This may be why, for Ockham, no part of the Church could lay claim to the right to speak infallibly against an errant pope, and why there could be no fail-safe ecclesiastical constitution or constititional solution for papal heresy.[83] It has been suggested further that, perhaps independently of any connection between Ockham's nominalistic bias and the possibility of a constitutional provision for dealing with papal heresy, William's theology conditioned him against spelling out constitutional procedures for expressing the limits of ecclesiastical authority or for evaluating persons expected to exercise spiritual power within such limits.[84] What Ockham must have had in mind as a solution to the perceived case of papal heresy, however, was the possibility if not the likelihood that on a contingency basis (*casualiter*) a sufficiently powerful temporal power such as the emperor could be persuaded to act in some not specified way against a heretical pope. Ockham held that even though a pope "does not regularly have from Christ the power to dispose and order temporal matters accepted as pertaining to kings and other temporal rulers," he could act *casualiter*: "If there is a proven crisis in temporal affairs and no layman can or will act [in such circumstances], the pope would have by divine right power to intervene to do whatever reason dictated as necessary."[85] Similarly,

---

83. See McGrade, *Political Thought*, p. 73. A measure of the difficulty some medieval thinkers had in coming to grips with the problem of papal abuse of authority can be seen in the position taken by Guido Terreni, that God simply would not permit a pope to become a heretic: Tierney, *Origins of Papal Infallibility*, pp. 238–69, esp. pp. 245–52.

84. McGrade, *Political Thought*, p. 171.

85. William of Ockham *Dialogus* 3.1.1.16 (Goldast 2:786). McGrade notes, however, that the position taken by Ockham in an early political tract, *Opus nonaginta dierum* (1332), shows only a very mild limitation on the papal right to intervene and depose secular rulers ("in a case of crime [*ratione crimine*])": *Opus nonaginta dierum* 93 (*Opera politica*, 2:688); later he was more cautious about the papal right of intervention and placed more

the pope is normally exempt from the exercise of power and jurisdiction by the supreme secular ruler (the emperor); but the supreme temporal ruler can intervene in circumstances where the pope is seriously in error, especially if he persists in his error. The calling of an ecumenical council by the emperor might well have been seen by William as a reasonable method for dealing with a heretical pope; either that or some more direct action with sufficient temporal and ecclesiastical support simply to force a pope's resignation.

Certainly William called frequently for lay rulers to intervene in the case of papal heresy; but even in the tension of his efforts to unseat John XXII Ockham was careful to restrict the secular judge's right to intervene casually in ecclesiastical matters. In the first place, the issue seemingly had to be one of papal heresy; and he distinguished carefully between heresy that was explicitly condemned in some clear fashion and cases where the pope's views might be seen as not certainly heretical because they had not been previously condemned by the Church. A secular ruler could act to depose only in the former case, while the latter sort pertain to the universal Church and a general council and are not appropriate for disposition before a secular tribunal.[86] In later writings William was less generous in attributing the right of intervention for papal heresy to the secular authority. In *Dialogus* 3.2 and in his last significant writing, the *De imperatorum et pontificum potestate*, he reversed his earlier position and denied that the emperor as such could intervene in a case of papal heresy; he argued, rather, that intervention would be legitimate in virtue of the emperor being a Christian, not in virtue of his possessing secular authority.[87]

If Ockham was neither as forthright nor as explicit as Marsilius on the issue of popular consent as the basis for political authority, there are several points on which his concern for the people as individuals in

---

stress on lay persons having responsibility to correct and depose criminal secular authorities: McGrade, *Political Thought*, p. 92. The concept of the legitimacy of occasional intervention (*casualiter*) by one power into the legitimate sphere of activity of the other, principally of spiritual intervention into the temporal order, of course, was very common: see the references given by Post, *Studies*, p. 269, n. 57; p. 301, n. 130; and pp. 241–309, *passim*.

86. William of Ockham *Dialogus* 1.6.2.100 (Goldast 2:633): The distinction noted is at *Dialogus* 1.2.17–24: McGrade, *Political Thought*, p. 132 and n. 149.

87. William of Ockham *De imperatorem et pontificum potestate* 12 (Scholz, p. 403); *Dialogus* 3.2.3.4 (Goldast 2:929–30); but cf. *Octo quaestiones* 3.12 (*Opera politica*, 1:123), cited by McGrade, *Political Thought*, p. 132 and n. 152.

a community goes well beyond what Marsilius urged in this respect. Ockham explicitly accepted the maxim *q o t*, that all who are touched by a given issue are to be consulted and give their consent; and he applied the dictum in the spheres of both spiritual and temporal authority in a fashion not hitherto seen among medieval political theorists.[88] In effect, Ockham called for the application of *q o t* in terms of the rights of each individual affected, specifically rejecting the traditional medieval concept of corporation and the earlier medieval notion of representation as image. In this way, curiously perhaps, he came closer to formulating one of the essential features in a modern theory of democratic polity than has been seen in any other medieval political thinker: emphasis on the rights of individual citizens to participate somehow in the governing process. An irony is immediately apparent here: Ockham's views gave an impetus to the concept of the legitimacy of popular participation in the activity of governing at the same time as he declined himself either to give clear specification to the expression of popular consent or to advocate any constitutional form for its regular expression.

An interesting example of the Ockhamite position on *q o t* occurs in a passage dealing with the convocation of a general Church council. Ockham addresses the issue of whether such a council can be called without papal authority, having replied negatively to the question previously and citing the traditional Decretalist view on the matter.[89] The possibility of the pope being heretical, Ockham suggests, poses the question in different circumstances; and he offers two comments: "A general council has power principally from the universal Church, whose power it embodies [*cujus vicem gerit*] and by whose authority it is convoked, even though in the immediate instance it is convoked by the pope provided he be catholic and seeks to follow justice. Accordingly, [members of a general council] can be convoked and convened in certain circumstances [*in casu*] without the pope."[90] William's second comment is as follows: The people as a whole, the whole community, the whole body can in its own right make law and choose persons to exercise the authority of the whole community or body without either

88. Lagarde asserts that William gave a very individualistic interpretation to *q o t*, stressing the role of every individual in a group, the very stress commonly assumed and understood in contemporary democratic theory: Lagarde, "Idée de réprésentation," p. 499.

89. William of Ockham *Dialogus* 1.6.64 (Goldast 2:571) and 83 (Goldast 2:601).

90. Ibid., 1.6.83 (Goldast 2:602).

the consent of or authority from anyone who is not a member of the body (and, presumably, this would be the case for a pope who is a heretic: he would not be a member of the body of the Church) and without the need for any higher authority. All the faithful taken together are one body—one people and one community; accordingly, they can elect persons to act for the whole body. Persons so chosen constitute a general council when they convene, inasmuch as a general council is nothing other than a gathering (*congregatio*) of those persons who act for the whole of Christendom. A general council, therefore, can be convened without the authority of a heretical pope.[91]

Ockham affords the same authority to a general council in circumstances where the papal throne is vacant and the size of the entire Church community is such that it is not practical to convene all Christians to conduct essential ecclesiastical business. In such circumstances, he contends, "whatever the whole Church [*universitatis ecclesia*: literally, the Church of the whole, meaning the aggregate of individual members] can do itself can be done through a calling together of those chosen [*electus*] by various parts of the Church. Hence, assuming that in the absence of any true pope the various parts of the whole Church were to choose persons to convene as a unity to make decisions for God's Church, such a gathering of elected persons could be termed a general council, and a general council could be convened in these circumstances."[92]

The roots of Ockham's theory of qot have been traced to his philosophical stance as a nominalist,[93] and his views illustrate at two levels the subsidiary character of political theory: one, his political doctrine was in fact a function of more basic philosophical and theological principles; secondly, it expressly reflected Ockham's judgment concerning the concrete political realities of his day, as well as his religious order's unacceptable relations with the papacy.

91. Ibid.
92. Ibid.
93. In an earlier article Lagarde stressed a nominalist metaphysics and theory of knowledge as a basis for Ockham's doctrine of representation: Lagarde, "Idée de réprésentation," pp. 435, 437, esp. 441–42 and 442, n. 2. Subsequently he became more cautious in interpreting Ockhamist political theory in terms of more fundamental philosophical and theological positions, and criticized William's writings as lacking any coherent philosophical or theological basis for politics: *Naissance*, 4:193, 234, 254 (2nd ed.); cf. McGrade, *Political Thought*, p. 31. Lagarde's third edition of *La naissance* offers a complete reworking of the material on Ockham and is even less doctrinaire in explaining William's theory of politics.

For Ockham, the only realities are individual existing things. Only individuals exist, and groups are really nothing more than the aggregate of their individual real parts. This is as true for the individuals in a political society as it is for a collection of stones that may constitute simply a pile or the walls and roof of a building. In a commentary on the *Physics* of Aristotle, Ockham flatly rejects the Aristotelian distinction between the unity of individuation (*unum numero*) and the unity of order (*unum per se*). If a people (*populus*) is an aggregation of many distinct persons (*aggregatio multorum distinctorum*), the term "one people" in the expression "many persons are said to be one people" does not designate a true unity: "For many persons are said to be a people in the same way matter and form are said to be part of a composite, and a house a collection (*achevus*) of stones."[94]

Here Ockham directly and rigorously applied a nominalistic theory of unity to the order of politics, and rejected the corporation theory of the medieval legists attributing some kind of juristic reality to a collective whole, *corporatio* or *universitas*, on the same grounds as he rejected a realist epistemology attributing some form of reality to abstract concepts.[95] And Ockham made the application directly to the concepts of both church and state. There is no such thing as a real corporation viewed as some kind of collective entity. Accordingly, legists were correct in describing the corporate entity as a fiction, but they ought to have been consistent and accepted that fictions, images, representations cannot be said to have rights.[96] Only real persons, real individuals, have rights. The rights present in any grouping of individuals, then, are simply the aggregate, the actual collection, of the rights of the individuals who make up the group. Ockham did not deny the existence of rights and interests in a grouping of humans; but what he did was to insist that such rights and interests are not the property, so to speak, of some fictional abstraction that stands for the group conceived of as a whole: the only real rights are those belonging to the real individuals who make up the group, and they cannot be alienated to a non-existent corporation or representative, neither of which in effect has the real capacity to receive them.

Obviously, there are profound implications for a theory of represen-

94. William of Ockham *Summulae in libros physicorum*, introductio, cited on Lagarde, "Idée de représentation," p. 437, n. 1.

95. Cf. Leff, *William of Ockham* pp. 78–123 for a recent, nuanced, and sympathetic treatment of Ockham's nominalism.

96. Lagarde, "Idée de représentation," p. 437.

tation in this attitude, implications that Ockham did not hesitate to draw and that he drew consciously with respect to positions expressed by Marsilius of Padua from which he differed seriously. According to Ockham, in a text containing a direct reply to papal criticism concerning the Franciscan theory of property that William was defending, "the Order of Friars Minor, like the Church and any community, has a real existence and, thus, can exercise rights and act. But these communities are not a unique real person; they are a sum of real persons. The people is not an individual, it is an aggregate of individuals."[97] It follows evidently that neither is the order an imaginary or representative person: "the Order is the sum of true, real persons. Actions [*facta*] do not always require one [*sic*] true person, but sometimes they require several true persons . . . It is true that the Order is not a unique person, but is true persons, just as the people is not one human but several . . . and the Church is true persons."[98] Elsewhere Ockham was equally insistent that the Church is a sum of its members, a simple aggregate number of individuals, the congregation of Christian men and women it includes;[99] and he saw absolutely no difference in the two formulas: the Church is *either* the sum of actually living Christians *or* the Church is the sum of all those who have been, are, or will be Christians. The only essential element in these two forms of his definition of Church is the plurality of individual members.[100]

Inasmuch as for Ockham there is no reality corresponding to the corporate entity of the community, state, or church, there is no other way such an entity can be said to exist in, or be represented by, any of its office holders as such. In themselves they are not, they cannot be, representative of (be the embodiment of) the *universitas* of the corporate community; there simply is no reality there to be represented or embodied. In taking this negative position on the medieval concepts of corporation and representation, Ockham was well aware of what he was doing with respect to the contemporary political theory found in Marsilius of Padua's *Defensor pacis*[101] and earlier expressions

97. William of Ockham *Opus nonaginta dierum* 62 (*Opera politica*, 2:568).

98. "Ordo non est unica persona sed est verae personae, sicut populus non est unus homo sed est plures homines . . . sicut ecclesia est verae personae": ibid.

99. "Congregatio christianorum fidelium quae tam viros quam mulieres comprehendit," *Dialogus* 1.1.4 (Goldast 2:402), 1.5.3 (Goldast 2:471), 1.5.8 (Goldast 2:479), 1.5.30 (Goldast 2:501); *Contra Joannem XXII* (*Opera politica*, 3:116).

100. Lagarde, "Idée de représentation," p. 440.

101. Marsilius *Defensor pacis* 2.19.

of the medieval theory of corporation. He cited long passages from the Marsilian work, and criticized them with devastating effect. He rejected the Paduan's conception of the nature of both church and state as corporate entities, a conception not unique to Marsilius, of course, but reflecting the longstanding, Christian view of both ecclesiastical and political societies as some form of communal entity. Twelfth- and thirteenth-century legists had given greater precision in applying the concept of corporation to juristic and administrative procedures, as has been noted earlier; so too had thirteenth-century theologians and other writers of political treatises in virtue of their reading of Aristotle.

The basis for Ockham's rejection of any notion of representation of a community conceived of as a corporate entity, as already stated, was disarmingly simple; there was nothing real to represent. A particularly interesting form in which Ockham urged this criticism had to do with his rejection of the Marsilian position that the pope could be disciplined by a general Church council insofar as this form of council represented the corporate community of the Church as a whole. William was just as keen as Marsilius to provide a sound basis for directing criticism at the current papacy; he was prepared as well to concede this task to a general Church council. But he took specific issue with the theoretical justification offered by Marsilius in the *Defensor pacis*. Marsilius had contended that the principal cause of current evil in the world was the overweening claims for plenitude of power by the papacy, claims given a particularly noxious expression in the doctrine of papal infallibility that was based on the Gospel text wherein Christ guaranteed to His Church that it would always be free from error. The assertion by Marsilius, moreover, and by William as well it should be noted, that the reigning pontiff was in fact heretical was dismissed by papal supporters on the grounds that the papacy was the very vessel of Christian truth: an infallible vessel and possessed of authority that was inalienable.[102] It was to this view that Marsilius opposed the contention that the ultimate repository of Christian truth and vessel of infallibility was a general Church council rather than the papacy, inasmuch as the former was the ultimate formal embodiment of the corporate entity of

102. This may overstate the historical record somewhat; I know of no such comment actually being used to reject the anti-papal position of Marsilius and William. It is the case, rather, that the onus was on them to establish that the pope was *not* the infallible vessel of Christian truth; if he were not, then his formal pronouncements as such need not be accepted as identical with Christian truth.

the Church. The Paduan based his views on the authority of a general Church council squarely on the notion that popular sovereignty reflected the will of a corporate whole.

William begged leave to demur. As anxious as Marsilius to deny infallibility to the papacy as such as well as to any of its individual occupants, he did not agree that the characteristic of infallibility lay with a general Church council. For Ockham, Marsilius was wrong to attribute infallibility to a general Church council because he was mistaken to think that any institutional form of the Church could embody its corporate reality. The Church simply had no corporate reality; its only reality as a community was the aggregate reality of its individual members. Any guarantee provided to the Church by Christ its founder, then—and Ockham acknowledged that infallibility had been guaranteed to the Church—rested with the whole Church perceived as a simple aggregate of its members. Accordingly, no portion or administrative element in the Church as a whole could presume to speak infallibly for the whole Church, neither pope nor general council nor any other institutional form or office. The Church was indeed infallible; but evidence of this infallibility would show only in absolute unanimity among all its members. Marsilius, who attributed infallibility to a general council on the grounds that such a council was composed of "persons representing the authority of the corporation [*universitas*] of the faithful,"[103] was as much in error as anyone who attributed infallibility to the pope alone. Nothing, neither general Church council nor papacy, can represent something that has no reality. The reality of the Church is the aggregate of all its members. The attribute of infallibility was given to this aggregate; thus the sign of this attribute can only be absolute unanimity among all Church members.[104]

Ockham was very clear on this point, and with typical logical rigour took the argument in the opposite direction as well. Not only was absolute unanimity among members of the Church the only acceptable evidence of a concrete instance of the guarantee of infallibility, but it was logically possible that the truth of faith might rest with a few or even with only a single member of the Church.[105] As far as Ockham was

---

103. Marsilius *Defensor pacis* 2:20; cf. 2.19, cited in Lagarde, "Idée de représentation," p. 447, n. 1.

104. William of Ockham *Dialogus* 1.2.25 (Goldast 2:429).

105. Ibid., 3.3.1 (Goldast 2:819), 3.3.10 and 11 (Goldast 2:827–28), cited in Lagarde, "Idée de représentation," p. 442, n. 2.

concerned, any individual member of the Church—a real part of the only reality, as an aggregate of individuals, that the Church has—might be the vessel of its infallible truth. Certainly, a real part of this real aggregated whole had more reality than any fictive corporate entity, and was entitled to be taken into account just as much as any other real individual member, though the account to be taken of each was in respect of the status of each in the Church.[106]

Unsurprisingly, Ockham was thorough also in considering the forms of corporation theory as applied to political authority that he rejected when dealing with the problem of infallible truth in the Church. Never in any doubt that the quality of infallibility resided in the ecclesiastical polity in some manner, his location of it and his rejection of alternative views favouring a general council (including the views of his own religious superior, Michael of Cesena)[107] simply reflected his conception of the Church as a whole. He rejected the view that a *maior pars*—as understood by Marsilius who, as has been seen, identified the majority with the weightier part (*valentior aut sanior pars*)—or any other mode of majority, could embody the Church or that the pope as successor to Peter *ipso facto* could do so either. Nothing could represent a fiction. Criticism of representation of the Church as a corporate fiction also extended to rejection of the concept of corporation itself, and of the term "representative" meaning image—the older, less sophisticated view of community current before the legists developed the concept of corporation.[108] Further, it extended to the notion of representation by way of succession, a view also advanced by Marsilius in the *Defensor pacis*.[109] According to this notion, even if one failed to accept that a general council was representative of the corporate community of the whole Church, it should still be acknowledged as the supreme authority in the Church insofar as it represented by succession the Apostles and ancients of the early Church.[110] Ockham's criticism extended finally to the notion that a general council was representative of the corporate Church by way of delegated consent from the members of the ecclesiastical community, a position of some significance inasmuch as what Ockham is seen to criticize here seems to be a modern

---

106. Cf. Lagarde, "Idée de représentation," pp. 446–69, esp. 449, n. 3.
107. Ibid., p. 443, and n. 2.
108. William of Ockham *Dialogus* 1.5.25 (Goldast 2:494).
109. Marsilius *Defensor pacis* 2.19.
110. William of Ockham *Dialogus* 3.1.3.9 (Goldast 2:926).

form of the notion of representation of which there was no extant medieval expression. It was typical of Ockham's logical rigour that he would identify all the possibile forms of a given position and then deal explicitly with each of them.[111]

With all this criticism of the opponent's views on representation, Ockham might be thought to have rejected utterly any acceptable meaning for this notion as an instrument and procedure for social action. This, however, is not the case. Turning from the positions and procedures he rejects as irrational, he subscribes to a position that appears quite congenial to modern theories of democratic polity, showing that his criticisms are directed only to the rational justifications offered by his contemporaries for the concept of representation. Ockham's own views are found in what he says about the real character of a general Church council and about its potential value in curbing the powers of a heretical pope. In presenting this position he also presents his views concerning the rights of an individual in an actual community, thereby clarifying certain essentials of his theory of popular consent.

Ockham's case for practising representation is as follows: to contend that infallibility lies with the universal Church does not deny validity to general Church council decisions, any more than the view that general council decisions are superior to papal decisions means that infallibility rests with a general council rather than with the pope. To deny the characteristic of infallibility to a general council is not to deny all significance to such a council.[112] Neither pope nor general council possesses the characteristic of infallibility bestowed on the Church, because neither is a valid corporate expression of the Church. But this is not to say that what is expressed in a general Church council is of no significance or of lesser significance than what the pope expresses on his own authority; it may well be of greater significance. A general council should be surrounded with the greatest publicity so that all Christians might be called to give their views on the conciliar matters to be dealt with and on the delegates charged to represent them.[113]

111. Ibid., 3.1.3.13 (Goldast 2:830); cf. Lagarde, "Idée de représentation," p. 446.

112. Ockham frequently invokes the notion of public power for both temporal and ecclesiastical jurisdictions: see *Dialogus* 1.6.92 (Goldast 2:611); 1.6.83 (Goldast 2:601); 1.6.99 (Goldast 2:621, 622, 624); cf. 1.6.64 and 83 for his notion of representation involving public power, in these instances having to do with the rights of a general council in the absence of a pope. Cf. Lagarde, "Idée de représentation," p. 447, n. 3.

113. William of Ockham *Dialogus* 3.1.3.13 (Goldast 2:830).

Christians, however, cannot place everything a priori in the hands of these delegates. They only give their consent to these persons under a reserved form, the reservation being that the representative delegates will do nothing contrary to the faith and to sound morals. Even when they delegate, individual Christians always reserve to themselves the possibility of rejecting any errors the council might formulate. Decisions of the council, then, are valid only if no Christian rises to challenge them. Only in the case of absence of challenge from any individual Christian can one assert that the universal Church has spoken.[114]

Some curious consequences follow from Ockham's doctrine of representation and delegation, however. For one thing, the question can be raised as to whether there really is any theory of representation here at all.[115] If the representative does not have full powers to commit, in the sense that those he represents always retain as individuals the right to reject the acts and agreements of their representative, what meaning remains in the notions of representation and delegation? Without making an explicit statement to this effect, William's categorical rejection of the concept of *plena potestas* for any representative or delegate to a general Church council seems thereby to reject the view that individual members of the Church are bound by conciliar decisions. Such a reservation might be seen even to extend to views concerning the obligations of an individual Christian *vis-à-vis* any form of obedience to ecclesiastical authority. Yet in the same text Ockham acknowledges that representation can and does function in general councils. He certainly accepts the idea that councils will be convened, and clearly considers them useful instruments of the ecclesiastical polity: he even speaks directly of delegates to general council as "representatives of all Christians."[116]

Ockham was not totally opposed to the concept of representation. In fact, he speaks of it in several different forms: delegates to a general

114. "Postquam acta generalis concilii per universos catholicos populos fuerunt promulgata, si nullius contradicens aut impugnans apparet, sunt putanda ab universali ecclesia approbata et de talibus consiliis loquuntur Gregorius et Gelasius. Si autem acta generalis concilii non fuerunt apud omnes catholicos diligenter exposita non est dicendum quod tale concilium generale sit explicite ab universali ecclesia approbatum"; ibid.

115. Lagarde calls William's position on representation "completely metaphorical": Lagarde, "Idée de représentation," p. 447.

116. William of Ockham *Dialogus* 1.6.50 (Goldast 2:552–55), 64 (Goldast 2:571), and 83 (Goldast 2:602).

Church council represent and direct the universal Church;[117] so, too, though in a different fashion does the pope represent the universal Church and function as its head, insofar as he is the public person standing for the whole community and having its direction as his responsibility.[118] Similarly, the prince electors are representative of the whole empire in their function of electing the Holy Roman Emperor.[119] Ockham seems to have borrowed this language directly from another contemporary imperialist publicist, Lupold of Bebenburg, although he would have been just as capable of formulating the point himself.[120]

What William rejected was any logical or rational connection between the notion of representation and the concept of corporate entity. Delegates can represent, but they cannot embody the total authority of a corporate entity because, again, there is no such real thing as a corporation. Delegates can represent others provided representation not be construed as representation of a corporate fiction. A representative can only represent something real: namely, the individuals or some portion of them who make up the whole group. Yet another qualification must be accepted, moreover: even in cases of valid and actual representation the individual(s) being represented do not cede total a priori authority to their representative to deal for them. Apparently this is impossible. Ockham rejects categorically the pure and simple assimilation of the representative organ to the community it represents, even in the case where representation is of real individuals. Yet he is quite satisfied to accept the notion that public power can be exercised in fact by administrative organs and personnel in both ecclesiastical and temporal spheres. He also accepts the possibility of a certain delegation of sovereignty to the benefit of one or other organ or assembly acting in the name of the universal Church or other such

117. Ibid.

118. Ibid.

119. William of Ockham *Octo quaestiones* 8.1–8 and 4.8–9 (*Opera politica*, 1:177–217 and 144–51), where he responds directly to the views of Lupold of Bebenburg; cf. Gierke, *Political Thought*, p. 104, and n. 72.

120. Cf. William of Ockham *Octo quaestiones* 8.3 (*Opera politica*, 1:180–81), cited in Lagarde, "Idée de représentation," p. 447, n. 1. However, William did not agree with Lupold on all aspects of support for the empire. Lupold distinguished between the emperor's national and his universal authority in an effort to separate the imperial lands in Germany and Italy from papal claims. Ockham examines Lupold's views in *Octo quaestiones* 8.3–5 and 4 (*Opera politica*, 1:184–202 and 126–27). Cf. McGrade, *Political Thought*, p. 97, n. 46.

community; and in these senses his political doctrine can be seen to accept the notion of representation, and with a meaning that strikes a more modern note than has been struck explicitly by an earlier medieval political thinker.

Ockham's strictures in respect of the authority of a general Church council, the papacy, the college of cardinals, or any other juristic or administrative church organ, are not to the effect that they lack authority in all conceivable circumstances, but simply that none of these is identical with the community of the Church as a whole and never can be. Hence he can be completely sanguine concerning the value of representation, even though his notion of this mechanism has lost the feature of collective delegation given it by Marsilius of Padua and other medieval political thinkers. For Ockham, representation involves individual delegation by members of the community, nothing more. A representative body, then, is essentially a consultative grouping, and the larger in scale its consultative character the more significant its authority. Seemingly, however, no level of authority is functionally absolute. Can we say that such a judgment applies equally to the spheres of the spiritual and the temporal? Presumably, if William was prepared to deny functionally absolute authority in the Church to any organ of church administration, including pope and general council, and to reserve the reality of infallibility to the circumstances of complete unanimity among all Christians, he would take a similar stand in the case of temporal political authority. Thus no organ of government, emperor, king, or representative assembly of any kind, could be said to embody a priori the authority of the entire community; the rights and authority of the temporal polity would reside always in the individuals, the aggregate of which constitutes the only reality the polity possesses. I know of no Ockhamite text, however, that puts this issue in such succinct, or even comparable, terms. Ockham does not reject the authority of large-scale representative gatherings, then, even though he does not lay down explicitly the nature and limits of their authority. One other point is also clear, however: he conceives of such gatherings only as occasional instruments for the expression of the community's views and not as regular or fully institutionalized gatherings. Further, William does not even consider democracy as a regular form of temporal governance, restricting himself to a consideration of only monarchy and aristocracy.[121]

121. McGrade, *Political Thought*, p. 107, and n. 79.

Ockham does not reject the authority of large-scale representative gatherings, even though he does not specify clearly the nature and limits of their authority. When the issues of the community as a whole are at stake, he insists that such representative gatherings as general Church councils might meet and should be as broadly based as possible in their representation of their universal constituency. He accepts and invokes the principle of *q o t* in this connection, while declining, naturally, to give it a collective or corporate sense. He accepts *q o t* in a manner that appears very advanced; indeed, he rejects precisely the feature of its use in earlier medieval thought that strikes a modern student as unreasonably narrow. Ockham tells us that the issue of papal deposition and, *omnibus ceteris paribus* presumably, imperial or monarchical deposition as well is something that affects everyone without, for all that, lying with some corporate collective community. It touches each member of the Church individually; and each must be consulted on matters that affect each.

Ockham's position here is genuinely different from previous medieval views precisely because of its logical consistency in applying the maxim *q o t*. A key to understanding this difference is the idea of personal liberty, the liberty of the individual Christian in respect to the Church.[122] The individual Christian is an active member in the Church as a whole. In expressing this view Ockham is presenting a position not unlike Luther's sense of Christian liberty, which makes it impossible for the individual Christian to place his faith completely in the operation of any human institution, even the institution of the Church.[123] Ockham advocates the element of individual liberty and postulates the right of all to be consulted and to be heard, clergy and laity, princes and prelates, man and woman. He even maintains that if the need arises, everyone should be able to convene a general council (*quilibet debet paratus esse si expedit ad concilium generale convenire*).[124] Ockham's appeal

122. Lagarde, "Idée de représentation," p. 449.
123. Ibid.
124. William of Ockham *Dialogus* 1.6.83 (Goldast 2:602). Ockham's text offers the following enumeration of those entitled to status at a general Church council: "Verumtamen spectat principalius ad prelatos et in divina lege peritos. Secundo spectat ad reges et principes et alias publicas potestates. Tertio, autem spectat ad omnes catholicos viros et mulieres. Unde etiam mulieres catholicae scientes papam esse haereticum, et electores circa electionem summi pontificis negligentis debent si expedit catholicos exhortari, ut ad generale concilium pro ecclesia ordinanda concurrant. Ipsaemet ire debent si poterint bono communi prodesse."

to the *lex libertatis* is the principal argument he advances in criticism of
the concept of papal *plenitudo potestatis*. It is not to be found in Part 1
of the *Dialogue*; but beginning with the treatise against Benedict XII
written in May 1237, Ockham makes large-scale use of it, developing it
and invoking it frequently in Part 3 of the *Dialogue*; it is used regularly
also in the *Octo quaestionum decisiones* and in the *De imperatorum et
pontificium potestate*.[125]

Still speaking of the involvement of all Christians in the activities of a
general Church council, Ockham invokes a second principle in support
of his *q o t*: the need to defend the rights and liberties (by which latter
term he means "exemptions") of actual individuals and bodies existing
in both church and state. The pope, he contends, can only govern "by
safeguarding the rights and liberties of others."[126] Thus, for Ockham,
the presence of the laity is necessary at Church councils, to make it
possible to offer exemptions and liberties to the clergy that they can
only enjoy with the consent of the secular authorities. So also, persons
called to consent to any limitations on their rights or property should
come themselves or be specifically represented.[127]

Ockham's notion of delegation here is very precise: it is individual
delegation. Representatives in this sense are procurators for the
various members and groups of members of the community. One of
many texts on the point puts this matter as follows: the rule *q o t* should
be understood in the sense that no one is to be deprived of consultation
without a good reason. This does not mean, however, that all need to be
present and take part in person in the council. All who wish to do so
should be allowed to designate procurators or other delegates to
handle their rights either directly or indirectly, and either individually
or in groups. For example, kings, princes, and other important lay
personnages could attend in person unless a serious reason existed to
exclude any of them (and Ockham considered it useless for such
persons to send procurators, apparently because their authority was so

---

125. Lagarde, "Idée de représentation," p. 449, n. 1. Personal liberty is identified
here as an essential element for the first time in a medieval political theory, the individual
being accorded a status that was developed later into a modern theory of rights. Villey
considers Ockham's *Quia vir reprobus* as fundamental in the evolution of rights theories:
Villey, "Origins de la notion du droit subjectif"; "Genèse du droit subjectif," cited in
Tuck, *Natural Rights Theories*, p. 22, n. 43; cf. McGrade, *Political Thought*, p. 16. See
Conclusion, n. 9, below.

126. Lagarde, "Idée de représentation," p. 449.

127. Ibid.

great that it did not admit of being delegated). Other communities that do not have a king (*aliae communitates quae regibus non subsunt*) could, if they so wish, send procurators, agents, delegates to whom they have given authority to negotiate in their name. Ockham accepts further that secondary groupings could have their representatives selected by the authorities that are the instruments of authority for the groups.[128] In this way he outlines a much more specific method for representation in large-scale ecclesiastical gatherings, quite different from the abstract conceptions of earlier jurists and theologians that reflect the medieval corporation theory, and closer to the model of some representative political institutions developing at the time, particularly the English model.

In fact the details of how the various states (or estates) of the community of the Church are to be present in William's general Church council bear a striking resemblance to the actual practice in late-thirteenth- and early-fourteenth-century English parliamentary convocation. Edward I, for example, in respect of raising a subsidy for defence of the realm in the late thirteenth century summoned "the whole community of the realm." By this was meant that he called together all his subjects who, because of recognized legal rights based on jurisdiction, property, or franchise, were seen to be members of the fictive corporation of the kingdom (*q o t*). Excluded, seemingly, were freeholders and even the well-to-do twenty-pound (£20) men, who probably were represented in some fashion by the knights of the shires; as well as villeins and serfs, who were not represented at all as a class (state) except through their lords whose land they cultivated, these lords in their own right being knights, magnates, prelates, and ecclesiastical corporations. The entities that were included were the prelates and lower clergy, who met in a separate convocation, and the great nobles, the knights of the shires, and burgesses and citizens of enfranchised towns. The king summoned all these members to parliament, the greater ones being summoned individually and the lesser ones to appear by way of representation with full powers.[129]

The procedure in early-fourteenth-century France for calling the estates general was somewhat analogous, although subsequent developments in England and France showed continuing and increasing divergence with respect to the concentration of royal authority. Like

128. William of Ockham *Dialogus* 1.6.83 (Goldast 2:601–2).
129. Post, *Studies*, p. 327.

the late medieval English parliament, the French estates general of Philip the Fair (1302), for example, did not include representatives from all the people. The nobles and clergy, including prelates and representatives of ecclesiastical corporations, were summoned, as well as representatives from the privileged towns, but the lords spoke for the peasantry and unincorporated villagers, who had no representation of their own. The medieval French jurist Jean Faure addressed the issue of whether or not all individuals from a given region or an order (religious or lay, presumably) must be summoned to an assembly of the realm, consistent with the principle *q o t* and in recognition of the fact that the assembly's business touched many. His reply was that the principle required all to be summoned, but the practical difficulties entailed in a literal application of the principle admitted of the various corporations being represented by their administrators, and of the individuals in rural communities and villages being represented by the prelates and barons who exercised jurisdiction over them.[130]

Ockham actually used the term *status* (state, *état*) employed in France for the convening of estates general, and accepted as well the connotation of a category or class of individual or corporation being called to such general assemblies. He does not seem to have understood there to be any element of geography in the term's meaning, however; at the same time, the notion retained the feature of quality. Accordingly, his doctrine concerning the nature of a general Church council likely was not greatly, if at all, in advance of the views of some contemporary canonists. Similar views on the notion of status can be found at the time of the Great Schism in the definition of general council offered by Conrad of Geldnhauser.[131]

Ockham's strictures concerning the non-reality of corporate fictions notwithstanding, then, his theory of polity concerning representative assemblies accepts them as useful institutions and reflects the actual practices of the contemporary English and French monarchies, but as applied to the Church. Like Marsilius of Padua whose personal political experience was that of the city-republic of Padua, like Henry of Ghent and Godfrey of Fontaines whose personal experience in

---

130. Esmein, *Cours élémentaire d'histoire du droit français*, p. 475, n. 2; cited in Post, *Studies*, p. 327, n. 45. Cf. a more recent view dealing with local assemblies and local groupings representing them in Cheyette, "Procurations by Large Scale Communitis."

131. Cited in Lagarde, "Idée de représentation," p. 450, n. 2. Conrad of Geldnhaussen *Tractatus de congregando concilio tempore schismatos* 3.

politics was gained in the free cities of the Benelux region, William of Ockham tended to express in his theory of polity personal familiarity with the institutions and practices of his homeland. This, with two major qualifications, however. First, his position is descriptive of an ecclesiastical polity, not a temporal one; secondly, he makes specific reference to the place of women in the community as a whole: women are all equally individuals in the community as a whole and have the same status as men.

One other similarity can be mentioned in conclusion regarding William's theory of general Church councils and contemporary parliaments: both seem to have been conceived of, and actually were employed, as occasional and extraordinary instruments of political jurisdiction. William did not advocate an ecclesiastical polity in which general councils were regular, ordinary, and institutionalized features of a kind of spiritual constitutionalism; indeed, the idea that the truth of Christianity could be the subject of automatic institutional determination by such means as agreement by a majority or wiser part speaking for the Church as a whole was anathema to him. The norm for Ockham was the traditional form wherein the pope represented the whole Church and individual bishops were the authorities in individual dioceses, and so on; the views expressed in *Dialogus* 1 concerning the role of universal Church councils were designed to deal with the extraordinary case of papal heresy. Accordingly, these views ought not to lead to Ockham being interpreted as expressing approbation of representative bodies that had an integral function in the general affairs of governance, either ecclesiastical or temporal.[132]

There are problems with this interpretation of Ockham's view, particularly with respect to the ultimate coherence of his overall theory of polity. For obviously, the theoretical correlation between what he advocated in the extreme circumstances of papal heresy and his apparent acceptance of traditional theories of feudal and papal monarchy is difficult if not impossible. Perhaps the most realistic comment is that William, like all the other medieval commentators on political theory, failed to develop a fully coherent doctrine of polity simply because he never set out deliberately to do so. His failure, then, and the term "failure" may be too strong, reflecting more than anything else a limitation in focus of attention and intellectual energy.

132. McGrade, *Political Thought*, p. 107.

Conclusion

THERE IS NO NEED to review or summarize the data showing medieval interest in the concepts of consent, coercion, and limit. Several points deserve mention, however, in bringing this investigation to a close. History is a continuum exhibiting few if any gaps in its intellectual fabric, and fewer genuinely creative and novel concepts in the identification and elaboration of basic social forms and institutions. Primordial notions tend to appear early in political theory as basic building blocks for later and more elaborate rational constructions. Often expressed originally in lapidary form, they tend to persist even as they undergo a variety of specification and application. The focus of their meaning shifts with the stimulus of concrete circumstances and problems, and these shifts can set in train profound changes in social and legal institutions. Such changes usually reflect either an expansion of meaning through more careful analysis, or application to hitherto unrecognized areas of practice, or both.

This is what occurred with the concepts of consent, coercion, and limit in the Middle Ages. Evidence of their existence is unmistakable; evidence for their imaginative development and application, particularly at the hands of twelfth- and thirteenth-century canonists, conclusive. In fact, so great is the evidence that it is impossible to gainsay their acceptance in this period. What might seem to require stressing, rather, is that medieval political thinkers did not recognize features in these notions readily understood in modern thought.

Their understanding, it is true, did not correspond to contemporary political thought. But undue emphasis on this point can produce a lack of balance in interpreting medieval thought by undervaluing the element of continuity in political theory. Consent, coercion, and limit are primary concepts in any coherent theory of polity, a fact much more significant than the difference in specification between their medieval and modern understanding. Such a claim may seem comparable to insisting that a bottle is half full when someone else wants to call it half empty. But accentuating the positive provides a more comprehensive frame of reference; it stresses continuity and the view that intellectual progress begins with an intuitive grasp of basic general concepts and is made over time by way of an analysis of these concepts that recognizes implications for the conditions and problems of real human experience.

A balance must be struck, however, between the notion that these concepts enjoyed medieval currency and the fact that the way they were employed does not reflect their modern understanding. This requires reiterating a distinction mentioned in the Preface between active and passive connotations for a term like "consent." Medieval writers often were completely indifferent about the mechanisms and procedures needed to implement their own concepts and principles, an attitude not likely to win many marks from contemporary critics. A political thinker apparently insensitive to the order of practice, and seemingly prepared to rationalize the status quo as a coherent expression of their own political theory, may be dismissed as a serious proponent of the concept or principle itself. Such a reading can be defective, however, by failing to account for how the medieval mind reflected its own perception of reality.

The most significant point in this connection is the close correlation in medieval consciousness between morality and law. However confusing and simplistic such an attitude may seem to some modern western theorists of law, the medieval thinkers assumed a direct and essential relation between virtue in a person and that individual's ability to act well. Hence, details for specifying how a given principle should be implemented, how a specific value or good should be given expression, frequently attract little interest. What needs to be described and advocated is the good itself, the given concept or principle; how precisely to implement it lies entirely with the virtuous individual. The function of the theorist, even the theorist as advocate, then, is to identify and enumerate the value concepts and principles. Such a limited conception of political theorizing scants issues of implementation and institutional procedure. Examples of medieval political thinking that are little more than moral exhortation for a ruler to develop and employ a range of personal moral virtues illustrate this attitude clearly.

Similarly, the difficulties that medieval canonists and theologians had in detailing how to deal with an errant pope reflect the same inadequacy. Nonetheless, these same groups, particularly the canonists, developed over time a formulation of the principle of popular consent that resolved the greatest ecclesiastical scandal of the Middle Ages, the Great Schism.[1] And in doing so, they formulated and applied for the first time in western political thought a doctrine that formally expressed the necessity for all members of a political community, including the individual legitimately holding the office of highest authority (indeed, supreme authority in that community) to acknowledge that ultimate authority rested with the community of members as a whole represented by a discrete group of individuals.

With its claim that the whole Christian church, represented by the delegates to a general Church council, could exercise authority superior to the papacy, the conciliar theory expressed in a remarkable yet altogether medieval way the concepts of consent and limit. The notion of limit, and the entailment that it could be exceeded, were expressed in practical and procedural terms by the conciliar "representatives" of "the people" (= the community of the Christian church) when they declared that none of the three proclaimed popes actually possessed or continued legitimately to exercise the papal office. The theory articulated at the Council of Constance (1415) by major participants like Jean Gerson, Pierre d'Ailly, and Cardinal Zabarella,[2]

---

1. I do not extend this inquiry fully into the fourteenth century, a task for a second, companion volume. But some basic references are in order. See Francis Oakley's bibliographical article "Religious and Ecclesiastical Life on the Eve of the Reformation." Oakley rightly identifies the Delaruelle / Labande / Ourliac contribution to the Fliche and Martin *Histoire de l'église* as a landmark contribution: E. Delaruelle, E.-R. Labande, and Paul Ourliac, *L'Eglise au temps du Grand Schisme et de la crise conciliare.* 2 vols. (Paris: Bloud & Gay, 1962–64). This work has an extensive bibliography. A number of other Oakley writings deal with the Council of Constance from both a historical and ideological point of view: *Council over Pope*; "Figgis, Constance and the Divines of Paris"; "Gerson and d'Ailly: An Admonition"; "Natural Law, Corpus Mysticum, and Consent in Conciliar Thought from John of Paris to Matthias Ugonius"; "On the Road from Constance to 1688: The Political Thought of John Major and George Buchanan"; all articles reprinted in Oakley, *Natural Law*; Crowder, *Unity, Heresy and Reform*; Tierney, *Foundations of the Conciliar Theory*; Ullmann, *Origins of the Great Schism*; see also Skinner, *Foundations of Modern Political Thought*, esp. 2:113–65.

2. For Gerson see: Morrall, *Gerson and the Great Schism*; Pascoe, *Jean Gerson: Principles of Church Reform*; Oakley, "Gerson and d'Ailly"; for d'Ailly: Oakley, *Political Thought of Pierre d'Ailly*; "Gerson and d'Ailly"; Bernstein, *Pierre d'Ailly and the Blanchard Affair*; for Zabarella: Ullmann, *Origins of the Great Schism*, pp. 191–231.

and authoritatively expressed in the conciliar text *Haec sancta*,[3] graphically and concretely conveyed the concepts we have been investigating —in the instant, of course, in the spiritual or ecclesiastical sphere. This conclusion represents a judgment beyond the historical limits of the present study, but it also reinforces conclusions expressed in earlier pages.[4]

To suggest that the position taken at Constance is at best only an instance of resistance theory,[5] a doctrine expressed in the Middle Ages in inchoate form at least as early as John of Salisbury, again would overemphasize a modern distinction and interpretation. Several more centuries would pass before adequate expression was given to the modern theory and procedure whereby the people as a whole are given authority to install (as well as remove) persons in positions of political authority. Yet both activities, installing and removing, derive their legitimacy and necessity from the same theoretical principle, namely, that the ultimate source of authority in a polity is the people who constitute it. And traces of how the people might give procedural expression to placing an individual in jurisdictional authority are also found in the medieval era, much of this evidence deriving again from the spiritual sphere.

Medieval texts showing formal reference to the concept of popular consent reflect influences from a variety of sources: classical Roman law; Aristotle's *Politics*; the practices of community involvement in decision making among early Christian community groups and in the medieval political communes of the northern Italian cities; the tribal practices and customs of western and northern Europe, and most particularly the common-law background in England; the organization and practices of an institutional church staffed and dominated by a male celibate clergy, and particularly of its male religious communities. All contributed to a developing sense of the meaning of consent in

---

3. There has been a controversy recently concerning the authoritative character of *Haec sancta*: a good review of the opposing views with the appropriate bibliographical references, is in Oakley, "New Conciliarism"; cf. *Council over Pope*.

4. It is my intention to extend this study into the sixteenth century in a second volume.

5. Oakley shows the clear implications for resistance theory found in both continental and English critics of fifteenth- and sixteenth-century forms of absolute monarchy: "On the Road from Constance"; "Almain and Major"; "Conciliarism in the Sixteenth Century"; "Figgis, Constance"; cf. Skinner, *Foundations*, 2, *passim*.

various, even conflicting ways, the development being anything but linear.[6]

Yet issues of political theory held no very high priority for medieval thinkers; and many of their efforts in this area were repetitive and of no great originality. Augustine is a case in point, notwithstanding the authority accorded his views by later Christian writers like Henry of Ghent, Godfrey of Fontaines, and Thomas Aquinas. The relative terseness and summary style with which these late-thirteenth-century theologians expressed their political theories may also reflect their recognition that the science of politics was the province of jurists and legislators. But this does not account fully for the limited attention they paid to political thought. Nor does it account for thinkers like John of Salisbury and Marsilius of Padua, not to speak of the legal theorists, both civilian and canonical.

The real difficulty for a medieval articulation of a theory of polity lay with the perception that the notion of limit is essentially, if not exclusively, ethical in connotation. This attitude produced a tendency to express the legal almost totally in terms of the ethical. Further, the ethical or spiritual was conceived of as the province of the divine; hence its formal essence is the divinity, God Himself, and its expression and application are through God's will and God's laws. Interpretation and implementation of God's laws, moreover, were seen as the prerogative of God's spiritual representatives, the clergy of the Christian church. Even advocates of temporal power in the Middle Ages, as well as those who exercised it, typically accepted that their authority did not extend to ethical matters.[7]

The dilemma for political theorizing posed by this type of perception, a dilemma that persisted through the medieval period and is still reflected in the more strident late-nineteenth- and twentieth-century

6. Oakley holds that, on the narrower issue of constitutional limitations on papal authority advocated by the conciliar development, two elements were in operation: canonical thinking from decretist sources and a current from the natural law tradition via John of Paris: Oakley, "Natural Law, Corpus Mysticum and Consent," pp. 794–806.

7. A typical example from the twelfth century is Henry II's decision that an appeal to the king's court regarding a matrimonial dispute should be referred to an episcopal court because questions of marriage should be resolved according to canon law: noted in Cheney, *From Becket to Langton*, pp. 54–58. Cheney asserts that "the study of canon law was then [12th century] and remained for long intimately connected with that of theology, and the two had techniques in common ... for even if theology seemed to be concerned with dogmas and the law with discipline, these presented two sides of the same problem": p. 43.

reaction to legal positivism,[8] is only resolved when full integrity in making moral judgments in the temporal order is conceded directly to individuals as personal moral agents. What is needed to bring doctrinal clarity and coherence to this issue is a theory of personal political rights.[9] Such a theory rests in turn, however, on a logically prior feature of ethical theory: articulation of the notion of the individual's inalienable integrity when making a moral judgment. Once more, then, interpretation of medieval political thought turns on the balance between the issue of how far a concept or principle can be said to be present in a given theory and the adequacy of its specification.

No medieval political thinker illustrates this point more clearly than Marsilius of Padua. His doctrine of the people as legislator seems to reflect a theory of popular sovereignty when he speaks of the people as efficient cause of both ruling and lawmaking authority, and calls election the best way to establish political authority. Yet ambiguity in his use of "popular consent" (is it to be active or passive?) and in the meaning of the term "elect," as well as confusion from a failure to distinguish between moral and procedural requirements, are all present in his position. He states that "the best ruler is obtained only by the method of election; for it is expedient that the ruler be the best man in the polity inasmuch as he must regulate the civil acts of all the rest."[10]

8. Pressing an analysis of some literal descriptions of legal positivism can lead to the conclusion that the validation of legal authority rests exclusively on the sovereign's power, and that the entailed obligation on the subject to obey is equally grounded, and that no element of the ethical is in play inasmuch as the order of the legal is completely distinct from that of the moral. See the dramatic formulations of this theory of jurisprudence in Austin, *Province of Jurisprudence Determined*, Lectures 1 and 6, reproduced in selection in Feinberg and Gross, eds., *Philosophy of Law*, 2nd ed., pp. 26–37; and even in H. L. A. Hart, "Positivism and Separation of Law and Morals." The real issue is only joined, however, when the question is asked whether a subject always has a moral obligation to obey a positive law?—to which Hart replies: "We say that laws may be laws but too evil to be obeyed," and he contends that "Austin and, of course, Bentham [held] that if laws reached a certain degree of iniquity then there would be a plain moral obligation to resist them and to withhold obedience": ibid.

9. A valuable examination of the transition from medieval to modern political theorizing in respect of the extremely complex and controversial notion of rights is: Tuck, *Natural Rights Theories*; cf. also Villey, *Formation de la pensée juridique moderne*. Villey's thesis that the essential element in modern juridical thought, namely, the idea of a "subjective" right, was entirely absent from classical Roman law is developed in two important articles: Villey, "Idée du droit subjectif et les systèmes juridiques romains"; "Origines de la notion du droit subjectif."

10. Marsilius *Defensor pacis* 1.9.7.

But two questions occur immediately: (1) What precisely is the meaning of "best" in the term "best ruler"; (2) Why is the best ruler produced by election rather than any other procedure? The text does not respond adequately to either issue, although "best" seems to have a primarily moral connotation. For his conclusion that election produces the best ruler Marsilius provides a deductive argument employing two Aristotelian principles. He cites the *Politics* for the view that "the multitude is dominant in more important matters,"[11] and rests this principle on a second from the *Physics*: "What generates a form determines the subject in which that form inheres."[12] Arguing that this second principle holds for both natural and artificial bodies (such as a polity), he presents the following position: as the thing generating the specific form of political authority, the people as a whole determine the subject (ruler) to whom the authority is given: we might say that the people have the power to designate the person(s) to exercise authority over them.

If this is so, however, the next step should be to specify how the people are to exercise their power. But Marsilius shows no great concern for this issue. He states that "the method of coming together to effect election of the ruler may vary."[13] Apparently the question of what precise action is necessary to give actual specification to the people's consent is not crucial for him. Nor, in the final analysis, does he explain why an elected ruler is best. The text seems to imply that either the person elected is best, by definition so to speak, insofar as the people do not err in this function—surely a gratuitously optimistic assumption if "best" has a moral connotation; or that the people's choice for ruler is the best person simply in virtue of having been chosen by the people—again an exercise in pure definition, but with a different definition of "best" that is descriptive rather than normative. And neither implication provides adequate rational ground for a modern theory of popular sovereignty. Marsilius's position shows further weakness moreover, inasmuch as the popular sovereignty he seems to have had in mind was the republican variety of Padua and other northern Italian city communes of his day. The Marsilian notion of popular consent is typical of medieval political thinking in reflecting the absence of any active aspect to this notion.

11. Aristotle *Politics* 3.2.1282a38, cited by Marsilius *Defensor pacis* 1.15.3.
12. Aristotle *Physics* 2.2.194122, cited by Marsilius, ibid.
13. Ibid.

Aegidius of Rome was the only major medieval writer to have addressed directly the question of how best to implement the concept of popular consent in the selection of a political ruler. He actually asked whether a ruler should be elected or succeed to office through heredity. He even drew the proper logical conclusion that subscribing to popular consent as a principle entails accepting the practice of electing a ruler. Yet he rejected his own logical conclusion because he was not prepared to put faith in ordinary people's judgments about such a crucial matter.

Only William of Ockham made a sustained and concrete claim for individuals to exercise their own judgment in a matter of genuine political substance. He held that every individual in the Church community possesses an equal quantum of authority when judging the legitimacy of papal behaviour in the context of a general Church council, and explicitly rejected the typical medieval corporate theory of community. The novelty of Ockham's emphasis on the basic value of individual action within a polity calls for careful interpretation and explanation, and both the nominalism in William's theory of knowledge[14] and his voluntarism in ethics and theology[15] have been suggested as a basis for his political position here. Though plausible at first glance, these interpretations lack sufficient textual basis to be much more than authoritative guesses. Much more investigation into Ockham's thought is needed to make its intricacies fully comprehensible. His writings are prolix and tortuous in expression, and often exceedingly circumspect in presenting their author's views. This is especially true of his political treatises, which can also reflect a polemical tone not always consonant with a thinker's best efforts.

There is also the problem of how to correlate Ockham's ecclesiology with his theory of temporal polity: his views on the place of the individual in a community are part of his criticism of current papal notions of the Church as a corporation and of the authority of the pope. Nevertheless, William did accord the individual in a community, including women as he notes specifically, equal status with every other individual, even the person in highest office. He seems thereby to

14. Lagarde identified William's nominalism as the basis for his theory of the individual, but revised his view later. Cf. Courtenay, "Nominalism and Late Medieval Thought"; "Mysticism, Nominalism and Dissent" and "Pierre d'Ailly."
15. Oakley, "Medieval Theories of Natural Law."

accord the individual a more substantial basis for what modern political and legal theory calls "rights" than any medieval contemporary or predecessor. Rejection of the simple corporate theory of community and a view of community as a collection of discrete individuals whose status is more than a fraction of the whole, are two necessary ingredients for a theory of personal political rights.

Ockham does not express his position in these terms, however, but remained typically medieval when he held that the individual Church member is theoretically equal in authority to any other. His contention was that an individual in whom the truth resides possesses authority greater than even the totality of all opposing individuals, all of whose views would thus be false. Not the nature and status of the individual as such, then, but truth is the critical element in William's doctrine. The value attributed to the individual is located in an accidental quality that may or may not be present in a given person. Ockham does not locate it in the moral integrity of the person, where it must be located to have a doctrine of personal rights on which a modern theory of popular election properly must rest.

Analysis of consent in more modern terms is required to clarify why an individual member of a polity has a right based on personal moral worth and integrity to participate in conferring public authority. This more complete understanding of the concept fractures the simple medieval corporate theory of community; and its blending with some specific procedural implementation will produce a rational theory of representative democracy.

Conclusions from this study are, in sum, not very dramatic. They reflect a constant shifting from positive to negative when assessing the medieval contribution to the development of the concepts under examination. No single writer emerges as a winner in terms of formulating either a modern or an adequate political theory. The notion of limit received the most careful analysis and development in medieval political thinking; and its impact on the other concepts of consent and coercion typified and advanced theories of politics in the Middle Ages. It was the primary and controlling feature. Legitimacy in exercising medieval political authority, both temporal and ecclesiastical—especially when either physical or moral coercion was involved—was always construed in terms of the limits circumscribing the purpose for which authority was exercised. Moreover, these limits were never conceived of as something for arbitrary declaration by the ruler, never something self-validated automatically by ruler or pope.

Rational justification was necessary to support coercive action, although how to establish and verify this essential condition was seldom addressed directly. Even when it was conceded that the ruler could judge in virtue of his office what was necessary for the good of the realm, he was expected to have a reason relating to this good.

Similarly in the case of consent: when a medieval thinker identified popular consent as a feature of legitimate political authority, temporal or spiritual, he always connected it to the notion of limit. Thus, the most significant medieval references to consent occur in texts dealing with tyranny; for it is the condition wherein a ruler exceeds the limits of his authority. For a political thinker in the Middle Ages the theoretical problem of tyranny was almost as difficult as its reality is for those who suffer from it in practice in any age.

Bibliography

Adam, chaplain of St. Hugh. *The Life of St. Hugh of Lincoln*. Edited by Decima L. Doccie and Dom Hugh Farmer. 2 vols. London: Nelson, 1962–62.

Adams, George Burton. *Constitutional History of England*. Revisd by Robert L. Schuyler. London: Jonathan Cape, 1963.

Adams, J. du Q. *The Populus of Augustine and Jerome*. New Haven: Yale University Press, 1971.

Aegidius Romanus. *De ecclesiastica potestate*. Edited by Richard Scholz. Leipzig: 1929. Reprint Scientia Aalen, 1961.

– *De regimine principum*. Rome: 1556. Reprint. Frankfort: Minerva, 1968.

– *De renuntiatione papae*. Edited by J. T. Rocaberti and Joannus Thomas. Biblioteca Maxima Pontificia. Rome: 1698. Vol. 2, pt. 1.

Albright, William Foxwell. *The Biblical Period from Abraham to Ezra*. New York: Harper Torchbooks, 1972.

Alexander III. *Die summa magistri Rolandi, nachmals Papstes Alexander III*. Edited by Friedrich Thaner. Innsbruck: 1874.

Alexander of Roes. *Die Schriften des Alexander von Roes*. Edited by Herbert Grundmann and Hermann Heimpel. *MGH. Auctorum* 4.

Ambrose. *De officiis ministrorum*. Edited by P. Domenic Bassi. Siena: E. Cantagalli, 1936.

Amman, A. *La doctrine de l'église et de l'état: Etude sur le Breviloquium*. Paris: Vrin, 1942.

Anderson, M. W. *Kings and Kingship in Early Scotland*. Edinburgh: Scottish Academic Press, 1973.

Anselm of Lucca. *Anselmi Lucensis collectio canonum una cum collectione minori*. Edited by F. Thaner. 2 vols. Innsbruck: Wagner, 1906–15.

Aristotle. *Nicomachean Ethics*. Translated by David Ross, revised by J. L. Ackrill and J. O. Urmson. Oxford: Oxford University Press, 1980.

– *The Politics of Aristotle*. Translated by Ernest Barker. New York: Oxford University Press, 1958.

– *Prior and Posterior Analytics*. Edited and translated by W. D. Ross. Oxford: Clarendon Press, 1957.

Arnold, F. "Die Rechtslehre des Magisters Gratians." *Studia Gratiana* 1 (1953): 451–82.

Arquillière, H.-X. *L'Augustinisme politique: Essai sur la formation des théories politiques du moyen âge.* 2nd ed. Paris: Vrin, 1955.

– "Origines de la théorie des deux glaives." *Studi Gregoriani* 1 (1947): 501–21.

– *Le plus ancien traité de l'église. Jacques de Viterbo De regimine christiano (1301–1302)* . . . Etude des sources et édition critique. Etudes de Théologie Historique. Paris: Bariel Beauchesne, 1926.

– "Réflexions sur l'essence de l'augustinisme politique." In *Augustine magister: Actes du congrès augustinien international de Paris*, 1954. Vol. 2: 991–99.

– *Saint Grégoire VII. Essai sur sa conception du pouvoir pontifical.* L'église et l'état au moyen âge, no. 4. Paris: Vrin, 1934.

– "La signification théologique du pontificat de Grégoire VII." *Revue de l'Université d'Ottawa* 20 (1950): 140–61.

– "Sur la formation de la théocratie pontificale." In *Mélanges Ferdinand Lot.* Paris: 1925.

Artz, Frederick B. *The Mind of the Middle Ages A.D. 200–1500: An Historical Survey.* 2nd ed. New York: Knopf, 1954.

Aubenas, R. "De quelques problèmes concernant la renaissance du droit romain au moyen âge." *Recueil Montpellier* 6 (1967): 51–53.

Aubert, Jean-Marie. *Le droit romain dans l'oeuvre de Saint Thomas.* Paris: Vrin, 1955.

Augustine. *The City of God.* Translated by Demetrius B. Zema and Gerald G. Walsh. 3 vols. New York: Fathers of the Church, 1950–54.

– *De civitate Dei.* Edited by B. Dombart. Leipzig: Teubner, 1928.

– *De Genesi ad litteram libri duodecim.* Edited by Josephus Zucha. Prague: F. Tempsky, 1893.

– *The Trinity.* Translated by Stephen McKenna. Fathers of the Church, vol. 45. Washington, D.C.: Catholic University of America Press, 1963.

Augustinus Triumphus. "Tractatus contra articulos inventos ad diffamandum sanctissimum patrem dominum Bonifacium papam sancte memorie et de commendatione eiusdem." In *Aus den Tagen Bonifaz VIII, Funde und Forschungen*, edited by Heinrich Finke. Munster: 1902.

Ault, Warren L. "Manor Court and Parish Church in Fifteenth century England: a Study of Village By-laws." *Speculum* 42 (1967): 53–67.

– "Open-field Husbandry and the Village Community: A Study of Agrarian By-laws in Medieval England." *Transactions of the American Philosophical Society* 55, no. 7 (1965).

– "Village Assemblies in Medieval England." In *Album Helen Maud Cam.* Studies Presented to the International Commission for the History of Representative and Parliamentary Institutions, no. 23. Louvain: Beatrice-Nauwalaerts, 1960. Vol. 1: 13–35.

– "Village By-laws by Common Consent." *Speculum* 29 (1954): 378–94.

Azo. *Select Passages from the Works of Bracton and Azo.* Edited by Frederick William Maitland. London: 1895.

Baldwin, John W. *Masters, Princes and Merchants: The Social Views of Peter the Chanter and His Circle.* 2 vols. Princeton: Princeton University Press, 1970.

Balon, Joseph. *Ius Medii aevi, II Lex iurisdictio: Recherches sur des assemblées judiciares et législatives sur les droits et sur les obligations communitaires dans l'Europe des Francs.* 3 vols. Namur: Anciennes études Godenne, 1960–72.

Barclay, William. *De regno et regali postestate.* Paris: 1600.

Barker, Ernest. *The Dominican Order and Convocation: A Study of the Growth of Representation in the Church during the Thirteenth Century.* Oxford: Clarendon Press, 1913.

– "Elections in the Ancient World." *Diogenes* 8 (Autumn 1954): 1–13.

– *Social and Political Thought in Byzantium from Justinian I to the Last Palaeologus: Passages from Byzantine Writers and Documents.* Oxford: Clarendon Press, 1957.

Barraclough, Geoffrey. *The Medieval Papacy.* London: Thames and Hudson, 1968.

Barrow, G. W. S. *The Kingdom of the Scots: Government, Church and Society from the Eleventh to the Fourteenth Century.* New York: St. Martin's Press, 1973.

Bartolus de Sassoferrato. *On the Conflicts of Laws.* Translated by Joseph Henry Beale. Cambridge: Cambridge University Press, 1914.

– *Opera quae nunc extant omnia.* 5 vols. Basel: 1558–59.

Battaglia, F. *Marsilio de Padova e la filosofia politica del medio evo.* Florence: F. Le Monnier, 1928.

Beaudry, Léon. *Guillaume d'Occam. Sa vie, ses oeuvres, ses idées sociales et politiques.* Paris: Vrin, 1949.

– "Le philosophe et le politique dans Guillaume d'Occam." *Archives d'histoire doctrinale et litéraire du moyen âge.* 12 (1939): 209–30.

Bayley, Charles Calvert. *The Formation of the German College of Electors in the Mid-thirteenth Century.* Toronto: University of Toronto Press, 1949.

– "Pivotal Concepts in the Political Philosophy of William of Ockham." *Journal of the History of Ideas* 10 (1949): 199–218.

Benedict. *Sancte Benedicti regula monasteriorum.* Edited by Cuthbert Butler. Fribourg: Herder, 1935.

Benson, Robert Louis. *The Bishop-elect: A Study in Medieval Ecclesiastical Office.* Princeton: Princeton University Press, 1968.

– "Plenitudo potestatis; Evolution of a Formula from Gregory IV to Gratian." *Studia Gratiana* 14 (1967): 193–217.

– ed. *Imperial Lives and Letters of the Eleventh Century.* Translated by Theodor E. Mommsen and Karl F. Morrison, with a historical introduction by Karl F. Morrison. Records of Civilization series: Sources & Studies, no. 67. New York: Columbia University Press, 1967.

Berges, S. "Die Fürstenspiegel des hohen und spaten Mittelalters." *MGH. Scriptores* 2.

Berlière, V. *Les élections abbatiales au moyen âge.* In Academie royale de Belgique, *Lettres. Mémoires.* 2nd ser. Vol. 20, fasc. 3. Brussels: 1927.

Berlin, Isaiah. *Two Concepts of Liberty.* Oxford: Clarendon Press, 1958.

Berman, Harold Joseph. *Law and Revolution: The Formation of the Western Legal Tradition.* Cambridge, Mass.: Harvard University Press, 1983.

Bernard of Clairvaux. *Five Books on Consideration: Advice to a Pope.* Translated by John D. Anderson and Elizabeth T. Kennan. *The Works of Bernard of Clairvaux,* vol. 13. Kalamazoo: Cistercian Publications, 1975.

– *Opera.* Edited by J. Leclercq, C. H. Talbot, H. M. Rochais. 8 vols. Rome: Editiones Cistercienses, 1957–77.

Bernard of Pavia. *Summa decretalium.* Edited by T. Laspeyres. Leipzig: 1860.

– *Summa de Electione.* Edited by T. Laspeyres. Ratisbon: 1860.

Bernstein, Alan E. *Pierre d'Ailly and the Blanchard Affair. University and Chancellor of Paris at the Beginning of the Great Schism.* Studies in Medieval and Reformation Thought, no. 24. Leiden: Brill, 1978.

Beskow, P. *Rex Gloriae: the Kingship of Christ in the Early Church.* Stockholm: Almquist and Wiksell, 1962.

Besta, Enrico. *Il dirito pubblico italiano.* 4 vols. Padua: A. Milani, 1927–31.

Bettenson, Harold. *Documents of the Christian Church.* New York: Oxford University Press, 1963.

Biel, Gabriel. *Defensorium obedientiae apostolicae et alia documenta.* Edited and translated by Hecko A. Oberman, Daniel E. Zerfos, and William J. Courtenay. Cambridge: Belknap Press of Harvard University Press, 1968.

Binchy, Daniel Anthony. *Celtic and Anglo-Saxon Kingship.* Oxford: Clarendon Press, 1970.

Biondo, B. *Il dirito romano cristiano.* 3 vols. Milan: Guiffrè, 1952–54.

Bisson, Thomas N. "An Early Provincial Assembly." *Speculum* 36 (1961): 254–81.

– "The General Assemblies of Philip the Fair." *Studia Gratiana* 15 (1972): 537–64.

Black, Antony J. *Council and Commune: The Conciliar Movement and the Fifteenth Century Heritage.* London: Burnes and Oates, 1979.

– *Monarchy and Community, Political Ideas in the Later Conciliar Controversy, 1430–1450.* Cambridge: Cambridge University Press, 1970.

– "Panormitanus on the *Decretum.*" *Traditio* 26 (1970): 440–44.

– "The Political Ideas of Conciliarism and Papalism, 1430–1450." *Journal of Ecclesiastical History* 20 (1969): 45–65.

Bloch, Marc. *Feudal Society.* Translated by L. A. Manyon. 2 vols. London: Routledge & Kegan Paul, 1961.

– *La France sous les derniers Capétiens, 1223–1328.* Paris: A. Colin, 1958.

– *Les rois thaumaturges: Études sur le caractère surnaturel attribué à la puissance royale particulièrement en France et en Angleterre.* Paris: A. Colin, 1961.

– *La société féodale: La formation des liens de dépendance.* 2 vols. Paris: A. Michel, 1939–40.

Bodet, Gerald P., ed. *Early English Parliaments: High Courts, Royal Councils, or Representative Assemblies?* Boston: Heath, 1960.

Boehner, Philotheus. *Collected Articles on Ockham.* Edited by E. M. Buytaert. Philosophy Series 12, St. Bonaventure, N.Y.: Franciscan Institute Publications, 1958.

– "Ockham's Political Ideas." *Review of Politics* 5 (1943): 462–87. Reprinted in Boehner, *Collected Articles.*

Boniface VIII. *De concordantia sacerdotii et imperii.* Edited by P. Barluze. Paris: 1669.

Borchert, Ernst. *Der Einfluss des Nominalismus auf die Christologie du Spätscholastik.* Münster: Oschendorff, 1940.

Born, Lester Kruger. "The Perfect Prince: A Study in Thirteenth and Fourteenth Century Ideas." *Speculum* 3 (1928): 470–504.

Boulet-Sautel, Marguerite. "Les paleaes empruntées au Droit Romain dans quelques manuscrits du Décret de Gratien conservés en France." *Studia Gratiana* 1 (1953): 149–58.

– "Le princeps de Guillaume Durand." In *Etudes d'histoire du droit canonique dédiées à Gabriel le Bras,* 803–14. Paris: Sirey, 1965.

Bouman, C. A. *Sacring and Crowning: The Development of the Latin Ritual for the Anointing of Kings and Crowning of an Emperor before the Eleventh Century.* Groningen: J. B. Walters, 1957.

Boutaric, E. "Notices et extraits de documents inédits relatifs à l'histoire de France sous Philippe le Bel." *Notices et Extraits des manuscrits* 20 (1862): 82–237.

Bourke, Vernon. *Augustine's Quest of Wisdom: Life and Philosophy of the Bishop of Hippo.* Milwaukee: Bruce, 1945.

Bowe, G. *The Origin of Political Authority: An Essay in Catholic Political Philosophy.* Dublin: Clonmore and Reynolds, 1955.

Boyle, Leonard E. "The *De Regno* and the Two Powers." In *Essays in Honour of Anton Charles Regis,* edited by J. Reginald O'Donnell, pp. 237–247. Toronto: Pontifical Institute of Mediaeval Studies, 1974. Reprinted in Boyle, *Pastoral Care.*

– *Pastoral Care, Clerical Education and Canon Law, 1200–1400.* London: Variorum, 1981.

– *A Survey of the Vatican Archives and its Medieval Holdings.* Toronto: Pontifical Institute of Mediaeval Studies, 1972.

– "William of Pagula and the *Speculum regis.*" *Mediaeval Studies* 32 (1970): 329–36. Reprinted in Boyle, *Pastoral Care.*

Brachmann, Albert. "The Beginnings of the National State in Medieval Germany and the Norman Monarchies." In *Medieval Germany,* edited and translated by G. Barraclough. Oxford: Clarendon Press, 1948.

Bracton, Henry de. *On the Laws and Customs of England.* Edited by George E. Woodbine. Translated and revised by Samuel E. Thorne. 4 vols. Cambridge: Belknap Press of Harvard University Press, 1968–77.

– *Select Passages from the Works of Bracton and Azo.* Edited by Frederick William Maitland. Publications of the Selden Society, no. 8. London: 1895.

Brentano, Robert. *The Early Middle Ages, 500–1000.* New York: Free Press of Glencoe, 1964.

– *Two Churches: England and Italy in the Thirteenth Century.* Princeton: Princeton University Press, 1968.

Bright, John. *A History of Israel.* 2nd ed. Philadelphia: Westminster Press, 1972.

Brooke, Christopher N. L. *Medieval Church and Society: Collected Essays by Christopher Brooke.* London: Sedgewick and Jackson, 1971.

– *The Saxon and Norman Kings.* London: Batsford, 1963.

– *The Twelfth Century Renaissance.* London: Thames and Hudson, 1969.

Brooke, Zachary Nugent. *The English Church and the Papacy from the Conquest to the Reign of John.* Cambridge: Cambridge University Press, 1931. Reprinted 1969.

Bross, Stanislaw. *Gilles de Rome et son traité du "De ecclesiastica potestate."* Paris: Beauchesne, 1930.

Browne, Elizabeth A. R. "Assemblies of French Towns in 1316: Some New Texts." *Speculum* 6 (1971): 282–301.

– "Royal Salvation and Needs of State in Late Capetian France." In *Order and Innovation in the Middle Ages: Essays in Honor of Joseph R. Strayer*, edited by William C. Jordan, Bruce McNab, and Teofilo F. Ruiz, pp. 103–10. Princeton: Princeton University Press, 1976.

– "Subsidy and Reform in 1321: The Accounts of Najac and the Policies of Philip V." *Traditio* 27 (1971): 399–430.

– "Taxation and Morality in the Thirteenth and Fourteenth Centuries: Conscience and Political Power and the Kings of France." *French Historical Studies* 8 (1973): 3–8.

Brown, M. A. "John of Salisbury." *Franciscan Studies* 19 (1959): 241–97.

Brown, Peter Robert. *Augustine of Hippo: A Biography.* London: Faber and Faber, 1967.

Brunetto Latini. *Li Livres dou tresor.* Edited by F. T. Carmody. Berkeley: University of California Press, 1948.

Brynteson, William E. "Roman Law and Legislation in the Middle Ages." *Speculum* 41 (1966): 420–37.

– "Roman Law and New Law: The Development of a Legal Idea." *Revue internationale des droits de l'antiquité*, 3rd ser., 12 (1965): 61–81.

Brys, J. *De dispensatione in iure canonico praesentim apud decretistas et decretalistas usque ad medium saeculum decimum quartum.* Bruges: Beyaert, Witteren, 1925.

Buisson, Ludwig. *Konig Ludwig IX der Heilige und das Recht. Studie zur Gestaltung der Lebensordnung Frankreischs im hohen Mittelalter.* Frieburg: Herder, 1954.

– *Potestas und caritas: Die Papstlichen Gewalt im Spätmittelalter.* Forschungen zur kirchlichen Rechtsgeschichte und zum Kierkenrecht, vol. 2. Cologne: Graz, 1958.

Burchard of Worms. *Decretum. PL* 140: 537–1090.

The Burgundian Code: Book of Constitutions or Law of Gundobad. Translated by K. F. Drew. Reprinted Philadelphia: University of Pennsylvania Press, 1972.

Burhill, Robert. *De potestate regia et usurpatione papali*. Oxford: 1613.

Byrne, Francis John. *Irish Kings and High Kings*. London: Batsford, 1973.

Caenegem, Raoul van. *The Birth of the English Common Law*. London: Quaritch, 1959.

– "L'histoire du droit et la chronologie. Réflexions sur la formation du "common law" et la procédure romano-canonique." *Etude d'histoire du droit canonique dédiées à Gabriel le Bras*, 2: 1459–66. Paris: Sirey, 1965.

– *Royal Writs in England from the Conquest to Glanvill: Studies in the Early History of the Common Law*. Seldon Society 77. London: Quaritch, 1959.

Caird, C. B. *Principalities and Powers: A Study of Pauline Theology*. Oxford: Oxford University Press, 1956.

Calasso, Francesco. *I Glossatori e la teoria della sovranita*. 2nd ed. Milan: Guiffrè, 1951.

Calisse, C. *Storia del parlemento in Sicilia*. Turin: 1887.

Cam, Helen Maud. "The Community of the Vill." In *Medieval Studies Presented to Rose Graham*, edited by V. Ruffer and A. J. Taylor, pp. 1–14. London: Oxford University Press, 1950.

– "The Evolution of the Medieval English Franchise." *Speculum* 26 (1957): 427–42. Reprinted in Cam, *Law-Finders and Law-Makers*.

– *Law-Finders and Law-Makers in Medieval England: Collected Studies in Legal and Constitutional History*. London: Merlin Press, 1962.

– *Liberties and Communities in Medieval England: Collected Studies in Local Administration and Topography*. London: Merlin Press, 1963.

– "Recent Books in English on the Parliamentary Institutions of the British Isles in the Middle Ages." *Bulletin of the International Committee for the Historical Sciences* 9, pt. 4, no. 37 (1944): 413–18.

– "The Relation of English Members of Parliament to the Constituencies in the Fourteenth Century." In *L'organization corporative du moyen âge à la fin de l'ancien régime*. Louvain: Bureau de Recueil, Bibliothèque de l'Université, 1939.

– "Stubbs Seventy Years After." In *Cambridge Historical Journal* 1948. Reprinted in Cam, *Law-Finders and Law-Makers*.

– "The Theory and Practice of Representation in Medieval England." *History* 1 (1953): 11–26. Reprinted with revisions, in Cam, *Law-Finders and Law-Makers*, pp. 159–75.

– Marongiu, R., and Stockl, G. "Recent Work and Present Views on the Origin and Development of the Representative Assemblies." In *Relazioni del X Congresso Internazionale di Storiche* 1: 3–101. Florence: 1955.

Cantor, Norman Frank. *Church, Kingship and Lay Investiture in England, 1089–1135*. Princeton Studies in History 10. Princeton: Princeton University Press, 1958.

Carlyle, Alexander James. "The Development of the Theory of the Authority of the Spiritual over the Temporal Power from Gregory VII to Innocent III." *Tijdschift voor Rechtsgeschiedensis* 5 (1923): 33–44.

— *Political Liberty: A History of the Conception in the Middle Ages and Modern Times.* London: Cass, 1963.

— "The Theory of Political Sovereignty in the Medieval Civilians to the Time of Accursius." In *Mélanges Fitting* 1: 183–93. Montpellier: 1907.

— and Carlyle, Robert Warrand. *A History of Mediaeval Political Theory in the West.* 6 vols. New York: Barnes & Noble, 1936.

Carter, Barbara Barclay. "Dante's Political Ideas." *Review of Politics* 5 (1943): 339–55.

Catalano, G. "Contributo alla biografia di Uguccio da Pisa." *Il diritto ecclesiastico* 65 (1954): 3–67.

— *Impero, regni e sacerdozio nel pensiero di Uguccio da Pisa.* Milan: Guiffrè, 1959.

Cerfaux, L. *The Church in the Theology of St. Paul.* Translated by Lilian Soiron. London: G. Chapman, 1967.

Chabod, Federico. *Machiavelli and the Renaissance.* Translated by David Moore. London: Bowes and Bowes, 1958.

Chadwick, Hector Munro. *The Heroic Age.* Cambridge: Cambridge University Press, 1926.

— *Studies on Anglo-Saxon Institutions.* New York: Russell, 1963. Original edition 1905.

Chaney, William A. *The Cult of Kingship in Anglo-Saxon England: The Transition from Paganism to Christianity.* Manchester: Manchester University Press, 1970.

Chatillon, Jean. "Une ecclésiologie médiévale: L'idée de l'église dans la théologie de l'école de St. Victor au XII siècle." *Irenikon* 2 (1949): 115–38; 395–411.

Cheney, C. R. *From Becket to Langton: English Church Government, 1170–1213.* Manchester: Manchester University Press, 1956.

— and Cheney, M. G. *The Letters of Innocent III Concerning England and Wales. Calendar with an Appendix of Texts.* Oxford: Clarendon Press, 1967.

Chenon, Emile. *Histoire générale de droit français public et privé des origines à 1815.* 2 vols. Paris: Recueil Sirey, 1926–29.

Chevrier, Georges. "Les critères de la distinction du droit privé et du droit public dans la pensée savante médiévale." In *Etudes d'histoire du droit canonique dédiées à Gabriel le Bras,* 2: 841–60. Paris: Sirey, 1965.

Cheyette, Fredric L., ed. *Lordship and Community in Medieval Europe.* New York: Holt, Rinehart & Winston, 1968.

— "The Sovereign and the Pirates, 1332." *Speculum* 45 (1970): 40–68.

Chodorow, Stanley. *Christian Political Theory and Church Politics in the Mid-twelfth Century: The Ecclesiology of Gratian's Decretum.* Berkeley: University of California Press, 1972.

— "Magister Gratian and the Problem of *regnum* and *sacerdotium*." *Traditio* 26 (1970): 364–81.

Chrimes, S. B. *English Constitutional Ideas in the Fifteenth Century.* Cambridge: Cambridge University Press, 1936.
– *An Introduction to the Administrative History of Medieval England.* Oxford: Clarendon Press, 1959.
Chroust, Anton-Hermann. "The Corporate Idea and the Body Politic in the Middle Ages." *Review of Politics* 9 (1947): 423–52.
– "The Fundamental Ideas of St. Augustine's Philosophy of Law." *The American Journal of Jurisprudence* 18 (1973): 57–79.
– "Natural Law and 'according to nature' in Ancient Philosophy." *The American Journal of Jurisprudence* 23 (1978): 73–87.
– "The Philosophy of Law of St. Augustine." *Philosophical Review* 53 (1944): 195–202.
– "The Philosophy of Law of St. Thomas Aquinas: His Fundamental Ideas and Some of His Historical Precursors." *The American Journal of Jurisprudence* 19 (1974): 1–38.
Church, William F. *Constitutional Thought in Sixteenth-Century France: A Study in the Evolution of Ideas.* Cambridge: Harvard University Press, 1941.
– "The Problem of Constitutional Thought in France from the End of the Middle Ages to the Revolution." In *IXe Congrès internationale des sciences historiques, Paris, 1950, IXth International Congress for Historical Sciences,* pp. 173–86. Louvain: 1952.
Church and Government in the Middle Ages: Essays Presented to C. R. Cheney. Edited by C. N. L. Brooke et al. Cambridge: Cambridge University Press, 1976.
Cicero. *Offices.* Translated by Thomas Cockman. Everyman's Library. London: J. M. Dent, 1953.
Clagett, Marshall; Post, Gaines; and Reynolds, Robert L., eds. *Twelfth Century Europe and the Foundations of Modern Society.* Madison: University of Wisconsin Press, 1961.
Clark, David W. "William of Ockham on Right Reason." *Speculum* 40 (1973): 13–36.
Clarke, Maude V. *Fourteenth Century Studies.* Edited by L. S. Sutherland and M. McKisack. Oxford: Clarendon Press, 1968.
– *The Medieval City-State: An Essay on Tyranny and Federation in the Later Middle Ages.* New York: Barnes and Noble, 1966.
Medieval Representation and Consent: A Study of Early Parliaments in England and Ireland, with Special Reference to the Modus tenendi parlementum. London: Becker & Warburg, 1958.
Cohn, Norman. *The Pursuit of the Millennium: Revolutionary Millenarians and Mystical Anarchists of the Middle Ages.* London: Secker and Warburg, 1957.
Combes, Gustave. *La doctrine politique de Saint Augustin.* Paris: Petit-fils de Plon et Nourrit, 1927.
Conciliorum oecumenicorum Decreta. Edited by J. Alberigio, P. P. Joannow, C. Leonardi, and P. Prodi. Frieburg: Herder, 1962.

Congar, Yves, M.-J. "Aspects ecclésiologiques de la quérelle entre mendicants et séculiers dans le séconde moitié du XIIIᵉ siècle et le début du XIVᵉ." *Archive d'histoire doctrinale et littéraire* 36 (1961): 35–151.

– *Droit ancien et structures ecclésiales.* London: Variorum, 1982.

– *L'ecclésiologie du haut moyen âge de Saint Grégoire le Grand à la désunion entre Byzance et Rome.* Paris: Cerf, 1968.

– *L'église: De Saint Augustin à l'époque moderne.* Paris: Cerf, 1970.

– "L'église et l'état sous le règne de Saint Louis." In Septième centenaire de la mort de Saint Louis. *Actes des colloques de Royaumont et de Paris, 1970,* pp. 257–71. Paris: Les Belles Lettres, 1976. Reprinted in Congar, *Droit ancien.*

– *Etudes d'ecclésiologie médiévale.* London: Variorum, 1983.

– "Maître Rufin et son De bono pacis." *Recherches des sciences philosophiques et théologiques* 12 (1975): 428–44.

– "Quod omnes tangit, ab omnibus tractari et approbari debet." *Revue historique de droit français et étranger,* 4th ser., 36 (1958): 210–59. Reprinted in Congar, *Droit ancien.*

– "Status ecclesiae." *Studia Gratiana* 15 (1972): 1–31. Reprinted in Congar, *Droit ancien.*

– "Un témoignage des désaccords entre canonistes et théologiens. In *Etudes d'histoire du droit canonique dédiées à Gabriel le Bras,* 2: 861–85. Paris: Sirey, 1965.

Constable, Giles. "The Alleged Disgrace of John of Salisbury in 1159." *English Historical Review* 69 (1954): 67–76.

– *Religious Life and Thought (11th–12th Centuries).* London: Variorum, 1979.

– "The Structure of Medieval Society according to the *Dictatores* of the Twelfth Century." In *Law, Church and Society: Essays in Honor of Stephan Kuttner,* edited by Kenneth Pennington and Robert Summerville, pp. 253–67. Philadelphia: University of Pennsylvania Press, 1977. Reprinted in Constable, *Religious Life and Thought.*

Corpus iuris canonici. Edited by Aemilius Friedberg. 2 vols. Leipzig: 1879. Reprinted Graz: Akademischen Druck-u. Verlagsanstall, 1959.

Corpus iuris civilis. Edited by T. Mommsen, P. Kruger, R. Schoell, and E. Knoll. 3 vols. 12th ed. 1911. Reprinted Berlin: 1954.

Corpus juris Romani: A Translation, with Commentary of the Source Material of Roman Law. Edited by Clyde Phair. Vol. 1. Princeton: Princeton University Press, 1952.

Costa, Pietro. *Iurisdictio Semantica del potere politica nella publicistica medievale (1100–1433).* Milan: Guiffrè, 1969.

Councils and Synods, with Other Documents relating to the English Church. Edited by F. M. Powicke and C. R. Cheney. Oxford: Clarendon Press, 1964.

Courtenay, W. J. "Nominalism and Late Medieval Religion." In *The Pursuit of Holiness in the Late Middle Ages and the Renaissance,* edited by C. Trinkaus and H. A. Oberman, pp. 26–59. Leiden: Brill, 1974.

– "Nominalism and Late Medieval Thought: A Bibliographical Essay." *Theological Studies* 33 (1972): 716–34.

Courtois, Christian. *Les Vandales et l'Afrique*. Paris: Arts et métiers graphiques, 1955.

Cowdrie, H. E. J. *The Cluniacs and the Gregorian Reform*. Oxford: Clarendon Press, 1970.

– ed. and trans. *The Epistolae vagantes of Gregory VII*. Oxford: Clarendon Press, 1972.

Cox, R. F. *A Study of the Juridic Status of Laymen in the Writings of the Medieval Canonists*. Canon Law Studies 395. Washington: Catholic University of America Press, 1950.

Cranz, F. E. "The Development of Augustine's Ideas on Society before the Donatist Controversy." *Harvard Theological Review* 47 (1954): 253–316.

Creation: The Impact of an Idea. Edited by Daniel O'Connor and Francis Oakley. New York: Scribner, 1969.

Crosara, F. "Respublica e respublicae: cenni terminologici dall' età romana all' XI secolo." *Atti del congresso internazionale di diritto romano e di storia del diritto, Verona, 1948* 4. Milan: 1953.

Crowder, C. M. D. *Unity, Heresy and Reform, 1378–1460. The Conciliar Response to the Great Schism*. London: Edward Arnold, 1977.

Crowe, Michael Bertram. "St. Thomas and Ulpian's Natural Law." In *St. Thomas Aquinas 1274–1974: Commemorative Studies*, pp. 261–82. Toronto: Pontifical Institute of Mediaeval Studies, 1974.

Cullman, Oscar. *The State in the New Testament*. London: SCM, 1957.

Cunningham, S. B. "Albertus Magnus on Natural Law." *Journal of the History of Ideas* 28 (1967): 479–502.

Cuttino, G. P. "Mediaeval Parliament Reinterpreted." *Speculum* 12 (1966): 681–87.

– "A Reconsideration of the *Modus tenendi parliamentum*." In *The Forward Movement of the Fourteenth Century*, edited by F. L. Utley, pp. 31–60. Columbus, Ohio: Ohio State University Press, 1960.

Dabin, Pierre. *Le Sacerdoce royal des fidèles dans les Livres Saints*. Brussels and Paris: Bloud & Gay, 1950.

Dannenbauer, H. *Herrschaft und Staat im Mittelalters*. Darmstadt: Wissenschaftliche Buchgesellschaft, 1960.

Dante Alighieri. *Monarchia*. Edited by P. G. Ricci. Milan: Mondadori, 1965.

Darquennes, A. *De juridische structuur van der Kark volgens Saint Thomas van Aquino*. Louvain: Universiteits biblioteek, 1949.

Daube, David. "'Princeps legibus solutus.'" In *Europa e il diritto romano; studi in memoria di Paolo Koschaker*, 2: 401–22.

– *Roman Law, Linguistic, Social and Philosophical Aspects*. Edinburgh: Edinburgh University Press, 1969.

– *Studies in Biblical Law*. Cambridge: Cambridge University Press, 1947.

David, Marcel. "Le serment du sacré du IXe au XVe siècle." *Revue du moyen âge latin* 6 (1950): 5–212.

– *La souveraineté et les limites juridiques du pouvoir monarchique du IXe au XVe siècle.* Paris: Librairie Dalloz, 1954.

Davies, J. C. *The Baronial Opposition to Edward II. Its Character and Policy.* Cambridge: Cambridge University Press, 1918.

Davies, R. G., and Denton, J. H., eds. *The English Parliament in the Middle Ages.* Manchester: Manchester University Press, 1981.

Davis, Charles T. "An Early Florentine Political Theorist: fra Remigio de Girolami." *Proceedings of the American Philosophical Society* 104 (1960): 662–76.

– "Ptolemy of Lucca and the Roman Republic." *Proceedings of the American Philosophy Society* 118 (1974): 30–56.

– "Remigio de Girolami and Dante." *Studi Danteschi* 36 (1959): 105–36.

Dawson, John P. *A History of Lay Judges.* Cambridge: Harvard University Press, 1960.

Deane, Herbert Andrew. *The Political and Social Ideas of St. Augustine.* New York: Columbia University Press, 1963.

Decretales Pseudo-Isidorianae. Edited by P. Hinschius. Leipzig: Bernhard Tauchniz, 1863. Reprinted 1963.

De laudibus legum Anglie. Edited and translated by S. B. Chrimes. Cambridge: Cambridge University Press, 1942.

Deighton, H. S. "Clerical Taxation by Consent, 1279–1301." *English Historical Review* 68 (1953): 161–92.

Delhaye, Philippe. "Le Bien commun suprème d'après le *Policraticus* de Jean de Salisbury." *Recherches de théologie ancienne et médiévale* 20 (1953): 203–21.

– "L'enseignement de la philosophie morale au XIIe siècle." *Mediaeval Studies* 11 (1949): 77–99.

Dempf, Alois. *Sacrum imperium Geschichts-und Staatsphilosophie der politischen Renaissance.* Munich: Oldenbourg, 1962.

Deniel, R. "*Omnis potestas a deo* (Rm. 13, 1–7): L'origine du pouvoir civil et sa relation à l'église." *Recherches de science religieuse* 56 (1968): 43–85.

Denifle, Heinrich. "Die Denkschriften du Colonna gegen Bonifaz VIII und der Cardinale gegen die Colonna." *Archiv für Literatur-und Kirchengeschichte des Mittelalters* 5 (1889): 493–529.

Depoorter, A. "De argumento duorum gladiorum apud S. Bernardum." *Collationes Brugenses* 48 (1952): 22–26; 95–99.

De potestate ecclesiae. Edited by Jean Leclercq in "Textes contemporains de Dante sur des sujets qu'il a traités." *Studi Medievali*, 3rd ser., 6, no. 2 (1965): 507–17.

Determinatio compendiosa de jurisdictione imperii. Edited by M. Krammer. Berlin: 1909.

Devisse, J. "Essai sur l'histoire d'une expression qui fait fortune au IX siècle." *Moyen Age* 23 (1968): 179–205.

– *Hincmar et la loi.* Dakar: Université de Dakar, 1963.

Dialogus de Scaccario. Edited by C. Johnson. Nelson Medieval Texts. London: Nelson, 1950.

Dickinson, John. "The Mediaeval Conception of Kingship as Developed in the *Policraticus* of John of Salisbury." *Speculum* 1 (1926): 307–37.

Digard, Georges. *Philippe le Bel et le sainte-siège de 1285 à 1304.* 2 vols. Paris: Sirey, 1936.

Documents relatifs aux Etats généraux et assemblées réunis sous Philippe le Bel. Edited by Georges Picot. Paris: 1901.

Douie, Decima L. *The Conflict between the Seculars and Mendicants at the University of Paris in the Thirteenth Century.* London: Blackfriars, 1954.

Dubois, Pierre. *De recuperatione terrae sancti, traité de politique générale par Pierre Dubois.* Edited by C. V. Langlois. Paris: A. Picard, 1891.

Duggan, Charles. *Canon Law in Medieval England: The Becket Dispute and Decretal Collections.* London: Variorum, 1982.

– "The Reception of Canon Law in England in the Later Twelfth Century." *Proceedings of the Second International Congress of Medieval Canon Law,* edited by S. Kuttner and J. J. Ryan, pp. 159–390. Monumenta Iuris Canonici ser. C, sub. 1. Vatican City: Biblioteca Apostolica Vaticana, 1965. Reprinted in Duggan, *Canon Law in Medieval England.*

– *Twelfth-Century Decretal Collections and Their Importance in English History.* London: Athlone Press, 1965.

Dunbabin, J. "Aristotle in the Schools." In *Trends in Medieval Political Thought,* edited by Beryl Smalley, pp. 65–85. Oxford: Clarendon Press, 1965.

Dunn, J. "Consent in the Political Theory of John Locke." *Historical Journal* 10 (1967): 153–82.

Dupré, Theseider Eugenio. *L'idea imperiali di Roma nella tradizione del medioevo.* Milan: Instituto per gli studi di politica internazionalei, 1942.

Dupuy, Pierre. *Histoire du différend d'entre le pape Boniface VIII et Philippe le bel.* Paris: 1655.

Durandus, Gulielmus, the Elder. *Speculum iuris.* Frankfurt: 1668.

Durandus, [Gulielmus], Bishop of Mende, the Younger. *Tractatus de modo generalis concilii celebrandi.* Paris: 1672. Reprinted London: Gregg, 1964.

Dvornik, Francis. "Emperors, Popes and General Councils." *Dumbarton Oaks Papers* 6 (1951): 1–23.

Edwards, John Goronwy. *The Commons in Medieval Parliaments.* London: Athlone Press, 1958.

– "*Confirmatio cartorum* and Baronial Grievances in 1297, Part 1." *English Historical Review* 58 (1943): 147–71.

– "The Emergence of Majority Rule in the Procedure of the House of

Commons." *Transactions of the Royal Historical Society*, 5th ser., 15 (1965): 165–87.

– *Historians and the Medieval English Parliament.* Glasgow: Jackson, 1960.

– "The *Plena potestas* of English Parliamentary Representatives." In *Oxford Essays in Medieval History Presented to H. E. Salter*, pp. 141–54. Oxford: Clarendon Press, 1934.

– *The Principality of Wales, 1267–1967: A Study in Constitutional History.* Caernarvon: Caernarvonshire Historical Society, 1969.

– "Taxation and Consent in the Court of Common Pleas, 1338." *English Historical Review* 57 (1942): 473–82.

Ehler, S. Z. "On Applying the Modern Word 'State' to the Middle Ages." In *Medieval Studies Presented to Aubrey Gwynn, S. J.*, edited by J. A. Watt, J. B. Morrall, and F. X. Martin. pp. 143–501. Dublin: C. O. Lochlainn, 1961.

– and Morrall, J. B., eds. *Church and State through the Centuries* London: Burns, Oates and Washbourne, 1954.

Ehrlich, L. *Proceedings against the Crown.* Oxford Studies in Social and Legal History. Oxford: Clarendon Press, 1921.

Ejerfeldt, L. "Myths of the State in the West-European Middle Ages." In *Myth of the State*, edited by H. Biezais, Scripta instituti Donneriani Aboensis, 7: 160–69. Stockholm: Almquist & Wiksell, 1972.

Elsener, Ferdinand. "Zur Geschichte der Majoritätsprinzips (Pars maior und pars sanior) inbesondere nach schweizerischen Quellen." *Zeitschrift der Savigny Stiftung*, Kanonische Abteilung (1956): 73–116, 560–73.

Engelbert of Admont. "Engelbert of Admont's *Tractatus de officiis et abusionibus eorum.* Edited by George B. Fowler. In *Essays in Medieval Life and Thought*, edited by John H. Meindy et al., 109–22. New York: Columbia University Press, 1955.

The English Government at Work, 1327–1336. 3 vols. Edited by J. F. Wellard, W. A. Morris, J. R. Strayer, and W. H. Dunhan, Jr. Cambridge: Harvard University Press, 1940–50.

Ensslin, W. "Der Kaiser in der Spatantike." *Historische Zeitschrift* 177 (1954): 449–65.

Entrèves, A. Passerin d'. *Dante as a Political Thinker.* Oxford: Oxford University Press, 1952.

– *La filosofia politica medievale.* Turin: 1934.

– *The Medieval Contribution to Political Thought.* Oxford: Oxford University Press, 1939.

Epistolae pontificum Romanorum genuinae. Edited by A. Thiel. Brunsberg: Edward Peter, 1862.

Epistolae Romanorum pontificum, et quae ad eos scriptae sunt a S. Clementis I usque ad Innocentium III. Edited by P. Constant. Reprinted Farnborough: Gregg, 1967.

Erickson, Norma N. "A Dispute between a Priest and a Knight." *American Philosophical Society: Proceedings* 3, no. 5 (1967): 288–309.

Eschmann, Ignatius T. "St. Thomas and the Decretal of Innocent IV. Romana ecclesia: A New Argumentation in Innocent IV's Apparatus." *Mediaeval Studies* 20 (1958): 177–205.

– "St. Thomas on the Two Powers." *Mediaeval Studies* 20 (1958): 177–205.

– "Studies on the Notion of Society in St. Thomas Aquinas, 1. St. Thomas and the Decretal of Innocent IV, *Romana ecclesia: aeternum.*" *Mediaeval Studies* 8 (1946): 1–42.

– "A Thomistic Glossary on the Principle of the Preeminence of a Common Good." *Mediaeval Studies* 5 (1943): 123–66.

Esmein, A. "La Maxime *Princeps legibus solutus est* dans l'ancien droit public français." In *Essays in Legal History*, edited by P. Vinogradoff, pp. 102–14. Oxford: Oxford University Press, 1913.

Espinar, G. "Le droit d'association dans les villes de l'Artois et de la Flandre française depuis les origines jusqu'au début du XVI siècle." In *L'organization corporative du moyen âge à la fin de l'ancien régime*, pp. 179–230. Louvain: Bureau de Recueil, Bibliothèque de l'Université, 1943.

Essays in Medieval History Presented to Bertie Wilkinson. Edited by T. A. Sandquist and M. R. Powicke. Toronto: University of Toronto Press, 1969.

Essays in Medieval History Presented to Thomas Frederick Tout. Edited by A. E. Little and F. M. Powicke. Freeport, N.Y.: Books for Libraries Press, 1967.

Essays in Medieval History, Selected from the Transactions of the Royal Historical Society on the Occasion of Its Centenary. Edited by R. W. Southern. London: Macmillan, 1968.

Essays in Medieval Life and Thought, Presented in Honor of Austin Patterson Evans. Edited by John Hine Mundy, Richard W. Emery, and Benjamin N. Nelson. New York: Columbia University Press, 1955.

Etudes d'histoire du droit canonique dédiées à Gabriel le Bras. 2 vols. Paris: Sirey, 1965.

Etudes sur l'histoire des assemblées d'état. Paris: 1966. Publication de la section française de la Commission internationale pour l'histoire des assemblées d'états et du Centre international d'études d'histoire comparée du droit de la Faculté de droit et des sciences économique de Paris.

Europe in the Late Middle Ages. Edited by John Hale, Roger Highfield, and Beryl Smalley. Evanston, Ill.: University of Illinois Press, 1965.

Fawtier, Robert. *The Capetian Kings of France: Monarchy and Nation 987–1328.* Translated by Lionel Butler and R. J. Adam. New York: St. Martin's Press, 1960.

– "Le conflit entre le pape et le roi." In *Histoire générale*, edited by G. Glotz. Moyen âge, vol. 2. Paris: Presses universitaires de France, 1940.

Feenstra, Robert. "Jean de Blanot et le formule *Rex franciae in regno suo princeps est.*" In *Etudes d'histoire du droit canonique dédiées à Gabriel le Bras*, 2: 885–95. Paris: Sirey, 1965.

– "Quelques remarques sur le texte de la glose sur le D. V." *Atti II Congresso internazionali ... di storia del diritto* (1972): 205–13.

Fesefeldt, W. *Englische staatstheorie des 13 Jahrhunderts: Henry de Bracton und sein Werk.* Gottingen sur Geschechtswissenschaft 33. Gottingen: Musterschmidt, 1962.

Figgis, John Neville. *The Political Aspects of St. Augustine's City of God.* London: Longmans, Green, 1921.

Filmer, Sir Robert. *Patriarcha and Other Political Works of Sir Robert Filmer.* Edited by Peter Laslett. Oxford: Clarendon Press, 1949.

Fliche, Augustin. "Bernard et la société civile de son temps." in *Bernard de Clairvaux,* edited by Commission d'histoire de l'ordre de Citeaux, pp. 355–78. Paris: Abbaye N. D. d'Aiguebeel, 1953.

– and Martin, J., eds. *La Chrétienté romaine (1198–1274).* Histoire de l'église, vol. 10. Paris: Bloud & Gay, 1950.

Flint, Valerie I. J. "The *Historia regum britanniae* of Geoffrey of Monmouth: Parody and its Purpose. A Suggestion." *Speculum* 54 (1979): 447–78.

Foreville, Raymonde. *Gouvernement et vie de l'Eglise au Moyen Age.* London: Variorum, 1979.

– "Le recours aux sources scripturaires. A quel moment de l'histoire l'Ecriture a-t-elle cessé d'être source directe du droit de l'Eglise?" *L'Année canonique* 12 (1977): 49–55. Reprinted in Foreville, *Gouvernement et vie.*

– "Le régime monocratique en Angleterre au Moyen Age des origines anglo-saxonnes à la mort d'Edouard I." In *Recueils Jean Bodin* 21 (1969): 119–38.

– "Représentation et taxation du clergé au IVe concile du Latéran (1215)." In *Etudes présentées à la Commission internationale pour les Assemblées d'états* 31 (12e Congrès internationale des sciences historiques). Paris, Louvain: Nauwelaerts, 1966. Reprinted in Foreville, *Gouvernement et vie.*

Fortescue, Sir John. *The Governance of England, Otherwise Called the Difference between an Absolute and a Limited Monarchy.* Revised text edited by Charles Plummer. London: Oxford University Press, 1926.

Fournier, Paul. *L'église et le droit romain au XIIIe siècle.* Paris: 1921.

Fowler, George Bingham. *Intellectual Interests of Engelbert of Admont.* Studies in History, Economics and Public Law, no. 530. New York: Columbia University Press, 1947.

François de Meyronnes. *De praelatura dominii spiritualis ad dominium temporale.* Edited by F. Baethgen in "Dante und Franz von Mayronis." *Deutsches Archiv für Erforschung des Mittelalters* 15 (1959): 120–36.

– *Quaestio de subiectione.* Edited by P. de Lepparent in "L'oeuvre politique de François de Meyronnes." *Archives d'histoire doctrinale et littéraire du moyen âge* 13 (1940–42): 75–92.

– *Tractatus de principatu regni Sicilae.* Edited by P. de Lapparent in *Archives d'histoire doctrinale et littéraire du moyen âge* 13 (1940): 93–116.

Franklin, Julian Harold. *Jean Bodin and the Rise of the Absolutist Theory.* London: Cambridge University Press, 1973.

Fransen, Gerard. "Une suite de recherches sur le Décret de Burchard de Worms." *Traditio* 25 (1969): 514–15.

Friedrich, Carl. *Constitutional Reasons of State: The Survival of the Constitutional Order*. Providence: Brown University Press, 1957.

Fryde, E. B. and Miller, Edward, eds. *Historical Studies of the English Parliament*. 2 vols. Cambridge: Cambridge University Press, 1970.

Gagner, Sten. *Studien zur Ideengeschichte der Gesetzgebung*. Acta universitatis Upsaliensis, Studia iuridica Upsaliensia 1. Uppsala: 1960.

Galbraith, Georgina Rosalie. *The Constitution of the Dominican Order, 1216–1360*. Manchester: Manchester University Press, 1925.

– "The Modus tenendi parliamentum." *Journal of the Warburg and Courtauld Institutes* 16 (1953): 81–99.

– *Roger Wendover and Mathew Paris*. Glasgow: Jackson, 1944.

– "The St. Edmundsburg Chronicle, 1296–1301." *English Historical Review* 58 (1943): 51–78.

Gallacher, S. A. "Vox populi vox dei." *Philological Quarterly 24* (1945): 12–19.

Gandillac, M. Patronnier de. "De l'usage et de la valeur des arguments probables dans les Questions du Cardinal Pierre d'Ailly sur le 'Livre des Sentences.'" *Archives d'histoire doctrinale et littéraire du moyen âge* 8 (1933): 43–91.

Ganshof, François Louis. *Feudalism*. Translated by Philip Grierson. London: Longmans, Green, 1952.

– "Note sur l'élection des évêques dans l'empire romain au IVe et pendant la première moitié du Ve siècle." *Revue internationale des droits de l'antiquité 4* (1950): 467–98.

Gaudemet, Jean. "Aspects de la législation conciliare française au XIIIe siècle." *Revue de droit canonique* 9 (1959) 319–40. Reprinted in Gaudemet, *La formation du droit canonique médiéval* (below).

– "Collections canoniques et primauté pontificale." *Revue de droit canonique* 16 (1966): 105–17. Reprinted in Gaudemet, *La société ecclésiastique* (below).

– "Contributions à l'étude da la loi dans le droit canonique du XIIe siècle." Etudes de droit contemporain (nouvelle série). Contributions françaises au VIIe congrès international de droit comparé. Uppsala, 1966. Paris: 1966. Reprinted in Gaudemet, *La formation du droit canonique médiéval*.

– "La doctrine des sources du droit dans le Décret de Gratien." *Revue de droit canonique* 1 (1950): 5–31: Reprinted in Gaudemet, *La formation du droit canonique médiévial*.

– Le droit roman dans la pratique et chez les docteurs au XIe et XIIe siècles. "*Cahiers de civilization médiévale* 8 (1965): 365–80.

– "Equité et droit chez Gratien et les premiers décrétistes." In *La storia del diritto nel quadro della scienze storiche*, pp. 269–90. Atti del I congresso internazionale della Societa italiana di storia del diritto. Florence: 1966. Reprinted in Gaudemet, *La formation du droit canonique médiévale*.

– *La formation du droit canonique médiéval*. London: Variorum, 1980.
– *La formation de droit séculier et droit de l'église au IVe et Ve siècles*. Paris: Sirey, 1957.
– "La participation de la communauté au choix de ses pasteurs dans l'Eglise latine. Esquisse historique." *Ius canonicum* 14, no. 28 (1974): 308–36. Reprinted in Gaudemet, *La société ecclésiastique* (below).
– "Le role de la papauté dans le règlement des conflits entre états au XIIIe et XIVe siècles." Recueils de la Société Jean Bodin, no. 15, pp. 79–106. Brussels: La Paix, 1961. Reprinted in Gaudemet, *La société ecclésiastique*.
– "Das romische Recht in Gratians Dekret." *Osterreichisches Archiv für Kirchenrecht* 12 (1961): 177–91.
– *La Société ecclésiastique dans l'Occident médiéval*. London: Variorum, 1980.
– "Survivances romaines dans le droit de la monarchie franque du Ve au Xe siècle." *Tijdschrift voor Rechtsgeschiedenis* 23 (1955): 149–206. Reprinted in Gaudemet, *La formation du droit canonique médiéval*.
– "Unanimité et majorité (observations sur quelques études récentes)." In *Etudes historiques à la mémoire de Noel Didier, Faculté de droit de Grenoble*, pp. 149–162. Paris: 1960. Reprinted in Gaudemet, *La société ecclésiastique*.
Gaven, Frank. *Seven Centuries of the Problem of Church and State*. Princeton: Princeton University Press, 1938. Reprinted New York: Howard Festig, 1971.
Genet, Jean-Philippe, ed. *Four English Political Tracts of the Later Middle Ages*. Camden Fourth Series, no. 18. London: Royal Historical Society, 1977.
Génicot, L. *Les lignes de faîte du moyen âge*. Tournai: Casterman, 1951.
Genzmer, E. "Kodification und die Glossatoren." In *Atti del Congresso internationale di Diritto Romano*, 1: 345–430. Bologna and Rome: 1933; Pavia: Tipografia successori Fusi, 1934.
Gerald of Wales (Geraldus Cambrensis). "De principis instructione liber." In *Opera*, edited by J. S. Brewer. 8 vols. London: 1861–91.
Gewirth, Allan. *Marsilius of Padua: The Defender of Peace. 1: Marsilius of Padua and Medieval Political Philosophy*. New York: Columbia University Press, 1951; 2: see Marsilius of Padua, *Defensor pacis*, below.
Ghellinck, Jean de. *Le mouvement théologique du XIIe siècle*. 2nd ed. Brussels: Editions De Tempel, 1948.
Giacchi, Orio. "La regola 'quod omnes tangit' nel dirito canonico." In *Studi in onore di Vincenzo del Guidice*, pp. 353–72. Milan: Guiffrè, 1953.
Gierke, Otto von. *Das deutsche Genossenschaftrecht*. Vol. 3: Die Staats-und Korporationslehre des Alterums und des Mittelalters und ihre Aufnahme in Deutschland. Berlin: 1881.
– *Political Theories of the Middle Age*. Translated by F. W. Maitland. Cambridge: Cambridge University Press, 1938.
Gilbert, Allan H. *Machiavelli's Prince and its Forerunners*. Durham, N.C.: University of North Carolina Press, 1938.

Gilbert, Felix. "Sir John Fortescue's Dominion regale et politicum." *Medievalia et Humanistica* 2 (1943): 88–99.

Gilby, Thomas. *The Political Thought of Thomas Aquinas*. Chicago: University of Chicago Press, 1958.

— *Principality and Polity: Aquinas and the Rise of State Theory in the West*. London: Longmans, Green, 1958.

Gilchrist, J. T. "Canon Law Aspects of the Eleventh Century Gregorian Reform Programme." *Journal of Ecclesiastical History* 13 (1962): 21–38.

— "Gregory VII and the Juristic Sources of His Ideology." *Studia Gratiana* 12 (1967): 1–37.

— "The Social Doctrines of John Wyclif." *Historical Papers of the Canadian Historical Association for 1969*, pp. 157–65.

Giles, John Allen. *William of Malmesbury's Chronicle of the Kings of England*. London: 1847. Reprinted 1904, 1968.

Gillet, P. *La personnalité juridique en droit ecclésiastique spécialement chez les Décrétistes et les Décrétalistes et dans le Code de droit canonique*. Molines: W. Godenne, 1927.

Gilmore, Myron. *The Argument from Roman Law in Political Thought, 1200–1600*. Cambridge: Harvard University Press, 1941.

Gilson, Etienne. *History of Christian Philosophy in the Middle Ages*. New York: Random House, 1955.

— *Les Métamorphoses de la cité de Dieu*. Louvain: Publications Universitaires de Louvain, 1952.

Giocarnini, K. "An Unpublished Late Thirteenth Century Commentary on the Nicomachean Ethics of Aristotle." *Traditio* 15 (1959): 299–326.

Glanvil, Randolphus de. *De legibus Angliae*. Edited and translated by E. D. G. Hall. Nelson Medieval Texts. London: Nelson, 1965.

— *De legibus et consuetudinibus regni angliae*. Edited by George E. Woodbine. Yale Historical Publications, Manuscripts and Edited Texts, 13. New Haven: Yale University Press, 1932.

— *See* Hall, G. D. G.

Glorieux-Patemon. *Répertoire des maîtres en théologie de Paris au XIIIe siècle*. 2 vols. Paris: Vrin, 1932–33.

Godfrey of Fontaines. *Les quatre premiers Quodlibets de Godefroid de Fontaines*. Edited by M. de Wulf et al. 5 vols. Louvain: Institut supérieur de philosophie de l'Université, 1904–37.

Goffart, W. *The Le Mans Forgeries: A Chapter in the History of Church Property in the Ninth Century*. Cambridge: Harvard University Press, 1966.

Goldast, Melchoir, ed. *Monarchia s. Romani imperii sive tractatus de iurisdictione imperiali seu regia, et pontifica seu sacerdotali*. 3 vols. Frankfurt: 1614. Reprinted Graz: Akademische Druck-u. Verlagsanstalt, 1960.

Goodhart, A. L. *English Law and the Moral Law*. The Hamlyn Lectures. London: Stevens, 1953.

Goudet, Jacques. *Dante et la politique*. Paris: Aubier-Montaigne, 1969.

Gough, John Wiedhofft. *Fundamental Law in English Constitutional History*. Oxford: Clarendon Press, 1955.

– *John Locke's Political Philosophy*. Oxford: Clarendon Press, 1956.

– *The Social Contract: A Critical Study of Its Development*. 2nd ed. Oxford: Clarendon Press, 1957.

Grabmann, Martin. "Studien über den Einfluss der aristotelischen Philosophie auf die mittelalterlichen theorien über das verhaltnis von Kirsche und Staat." *Sizungsberichte bayrischen Akademie der Wissenschaften*. Philosophische-Historische Abteilung. Munich: 1934. Part 2.

– *Studien zur Joannes Quidort von Paris, O.P.* Verlag der bayrischen Akademie der Wissenschaften. Munich: 1922.

Grant, F.C. "The Idea of the Kingdom of God in the New Testament." In *The Sacral Kingship. Contributions to the Central Theme of the VIIIth International Congress for the History of Religions*, pp. 437–46. Leiden: Brill, 1959.

Gratian. *Concordantia discordantium canonium (= Decretum)*. Edited by E. Friedberg. *Corpus iuris canonici*, vol. 1. Leipzig: 1879. Reprinted Graz: Akademische Druck-u. Verlagsanstalt, 1959.

Gray, J. W. "Canon Law in England: Some Reflections on the Stubbs-Maitland Controversy." *Studies in Church History* 3 (1966): 48–68.

Greenleaf, W. H. *Order, Empiricism and Politics: Two Traditions of English Political Thought 1500–1700*. Oxford: Oxford University Press, 1964.

Gregory the Great. *Opera*. Edited by Werner Jaeger. 9 vols. Leiden: Brill, 1957–67.

– *The Pastoral Care*. Edited by Ingvar Carlson. Stockholm: Almquist & Wiksell, 1975.

Griesbach, Marc. "John of Paris as a Representative of Thomistic Political Philosophy." In *An Etienne Gilson Tribute*, edited by Charles J. O'Neil. Milwaukee: Marquette University Press, 1959.

Griffiths, Q. "Origines et carrières de Pierre de Fontaines." *Revue historique de droit français et étranger* 48 (1970): 544–67.

Grignaschi, M. "L'interprétation de la 'politique' dans le Dialogue de Guillaume d'Ockham." In *Liber memorialis Georges de Lagarde*, pp. 57–72. Paris: Beatrice-Nauwelaerts, 1970.

– "Nicolas Orèsme et son Commentaire à la *Politique* d'Aristote." In *Album Helen Maud Cam*. Studies Presented to the International Commission for the History of Representative and Parliamentary Institutions, no. 23. Louvain and Paris: Beatrice-Nauwelaerts, 1960–61. Vol. 1: 95–151.

– "Le rôle de l'aristotelisme dans le *Defensor pacis* de Marsile de Padoue." *Revue d'histoire et de philosophie religieuses* 35 (1955): 301–40.

Grossi, Paolo. "Unanimitas, Alle origini del concetto di persona giuridica nel diritto canonico." *Annali di Storia del Diritto* 2 (1958): 1–103.

Gryson, H. "Les elections ecclésiastiques au IIIe siècle." *Revue d'histoire ecclésiastique* 68 (1973): 353–404.

Guido Vernani. *De reprobatio Monarchiae composita a Dante*. Edited by Thomas Kappeli. In *Der Dantegegner Guido Vernani O. P. von Rimini*. Quellen und Forschungen aus italienischen Archiven und Bibliotheken 28, pp. 123–46. Rome: Halle, 1938.

Guillelmus de Sarzano. *Tractatus de potestate summi pontificis*. Edited by R. del Ponti. *Studi Medievali*, 3rd ser., 12 (1971): 1020–94.

Guitierrez, D. *De Jacobi Viterbiensis vita operibus et doctrina theologica*. Analecta Augustiniana, Rome: 1939.

Haahr, Joan Gluckauf. "The Concept of Kingship in William of Malmesbury's *Gesta regum* and *Historia novella*." *Medieval Studies* 38 (1976): 351–71.

Hackett, J. H. "State of the Church: A Concept of the Medieval Canonists." *The Jurist* 23 (1963): 259–90.

Haines, Roy Martin. *The Church and Politics in Fourteenth-Century England: The Career of Adam Orleton, c. 1275–1345*. Cambridge Studies in Medieval Life and Thought, 3rd ser., 10. Cambridge and New York: Cambridge University Press, 1978.

Hall, G. D. G., ed. *Tractatus de legibus et consuetudinibus regni Anglie qui Glanvilla vocatur: The Treatise on the Laws of the Realm of England Commonly Called Glanville*. With introduction, notes, and translation. Selden Society. London, Edinburgh: 1965.

Halphen, Louis. *Peuples et civilisations: Histoire générale*. Vol. 6: L'Essor de l'Europe. Paris: Alcan, 1932.

Hamburger, Max. *Morals and Law: The Growth of Aristotle's Legal Theory*. New Haven: Yale University Press, 1951.

Hamman, A. *La doctrine de l'église et de l'état chez Occam. Etude sur le "Breviloquium."* Paris: Aux Editions franciscaines, 1942.

Harding, Alan. "Political Liberty in the Middle Ages." *Speculum* 55 (1980): 423–43.

Harriss, G. L. *King, Parliament, and Public Finance in England to 1369*. Oxford: Clarendon Press, 1975.

Hartmann, L. M. *The Early Medieval State: Byzantium, Italy and the West*. Translated by H. Liebeschutz. London: Philip, 1949.

Hartmann, W. "Manegold von Lautenbach und die Arfange der Fruhscholastik." *Deutsches Archiv* 26 (1970): 47–62.

Haskins, George L. "Executive Justice and the Rule of Law: Some Reflections on Thirteenth-Century England." *Speculum* 30 (1955): 529–38.

– "Francis Accursius: A New Document." *Speculum* 13 (1938): 76–77.

– *The Growth of English Representative Government*. Philadelphia: University of Pennsylvania Press, 1948.

– *The Statute of York and the Interest of the Commons*. Cambridge: Cambridge University Press, 1935.

Hauck, Albert. *Kirchengeschichte Deutschlands.* 5 vols. in 6. Leipzig: J. C. Heinrichs, 1900–11.

Hazeltine, H. D. "The Early History of English Equity." In *Essays in Legal History,* edited by P. Vinogradoff. Oxford: Oxford University Press, 1913.

Heer, Friedrich. *The Holy Roman Empire.* Translated by Janet Sondheimer. New York: Praeger, 1968.

Heintschel, D. E. *The Medieval Concept of an Ecclesiastical Office.* Washington: Catholic University of America Press, 1956.

Hendrix, Scott H. "In Quest of the *vera ecclesia*: The Crises of Late Medieval Ecclesiology." *Viator* 7 (1976): 437–78.

Henry of Ghent. *Quodlibetales Magistri Henrici Gehals.* 2 vols. Paris: 1518. Reprinted Louvain: 1961.

– *Summae questionum ordinarum.* Franciscan Institute Publications Text Series 5. Louvain, Paderborn: St. Bonaventure, N.Y.: 1953. Reprint of 1520 edition.

Herde, Peter. "Romisches und kanonisches Rect bei der Verfolgung des Falschungsdelikts im Mittelalter." *Traditio* 21 (1965): 291–362.

Herlihy, David. *Cities and Society in Medieval Italy.* London: Variorum, 1980.

– *Medieval and Renaissance Pistoia. The Social History of an Italian Tour, 1200–1430.* New Haven: Yale University Press, 1967.

– ed. *The History of Feudalism.* New York: Harper and Row, 1970.

– et al., eds. *Economy, Society and Government in Medieval Italy: Essays in Memory of Robert L. Reynolds.* Kent, Ohio: Kent State University Press, 1969.

Hermannus de Scildis. *Tractatus contra haereticos negante immunitatem et iurisdictionum sanctae ecclesiae et Tractatus de conceptione gloriosae virginis Mariae.* Edited by A. Zumkeller. Wurzburg: Augustinus-Verlag, 1970.

Hervieu, H. *Recherches sur les premiers états-généraux et les assemblées représentatives pendant la première moitié du quatorzième siècle.* Paris: 1879.

Heuston, R. F. V. *Essays in Constitutional Law.* London: Stevens, 1961.

Heydte, F. A. E., von der. *Die Geburtstunde des souveranen Staates.* Regensburg: J. Habbel, 1952.

Hincmar of Rheims. *De ordine palatie.* In *MGH. Legum* 2.2.

Hinnebusch, William A. *The Early English Friars Preachers.* Rome: Ad. S. Sabinae, 1951.

Hinschius, Paul. *Das Kirchenrecht der Katholiken und Protestanten in Deutschland.* 6 vols. Berlin: 1869–97.

Hinton, R. W. K. "English Constitutional Theories from Sir John Fortescue to Sir John Eliot." *English Historical Review* 75 (1960): 410–17.

– "Government and Liberty under James I." *Cambridge Historical Johrnal* 11 (1953): 48–64.

Hochsemius, Joannes. *Liber primus complectens gesta pontificum Leodiensium ab Henrico Guelrensi, usque ad Adolphum a Marcka; liber secundus complectens gesta pontificum Leodiensium Adolphi et Engelbert a Marcka.* Edited by J. Chapearillus. 2 vols. 1612.

Hodl, I. *Johannes Quidort von Paris O.P. (†1306) De Confessionibus audiendis (Quaestio disputata Parisius de potestate papae)*. Mitteilungen des Grabmann Instituts 6. Munich: 1962.

Hocsem, Jean de. *La chronique de Jean de Hocsem*. Edited by Godefroid Kurth. Brussels: Kiessling, 1927.

Hoffman, Hartmut. "Die beiden Schwerter im hohen Mittelalter." *Deutsches Archiv für Erforschung des Mittelalters* 20 (1964): 78–114.

Hoffmann, J. "Droit canonique et théologie du droit." *Revue de droit canonique* 20 (1970): 289 *ff*.

Hofler, O. "Das Sakralcharakter des germanischen Konigtums." In *Das Konigtum seine geistegen und rechtlichen Gundlagen*, edited by T. Mayer, pp. 75–104. Vortrage und Forschungen 3. Konstanz: 1954.

Holt, J. C. *Magna Carta*. Cambridge: Cambridge University Press, 1965.

– "The Prehistory of Parliament." In *The English Parliament in the Middle Ages*, edited by R. G. Davies and J. H. Denton, pp. 23–24. Manchester: Manchester University Press, 1981.

– "Rights and Liberties in *Magna Carta*." In *Album Helen Maud Cam*. Studies Presented to the International Commission for the History of Representative and Parliamentary Institutions, no. 23. Louvain: Béatrice-Nauwelaerts, 1960. Vol. 1: 56–69.

Homo, Léon. *Les institutions politiques des Romains; de la cité à l'état*. Paris: Renaissance du livre, 1927.

– *Roman Political Institutions from City to State*. Translated by M. R. Dobie. London: Routledge & Kegan Paul, 1962.

Horn, N. "Philosophie in der Jurisprudenz der Kommentatoren: Baldus Philosophus." *Ius commune* 1 (1968): 104–27.

Hoyt, Robert S. "The Coronation Oath of 1308: The Background of 'les leys et les custumes'." *Traditio* 11 (1955): 234–57.

– "Recent Publications in the United States and Canada on the History of Representative Institutions before the French Revolution." *Speculum* 29 (1954): 356–77.

– "Representation in the Administrative Practice of Anglo-Norman England." In *Album Helen Maud Cam*. Studies Presented to the International Commission for the History of Representative and Parliamentary Institutions, no. 24. Louvain: Béatrice-Nauwelaerts, 1961. Vol. 2: 15–26.

– "Royal Taxation and the Growth of the Realm in Medieval England." *Speculum* 25 (1950): 36–48.

Huebner, R. *A History of Germanic Private Law*. Translated by F. Philbrick. Boston: Little, Brown, 1914.

Hugh of St. Victor. *De sacramentis Christianae fidei. PL* 176: 183–618.

– *On the Sacraments of the Christian Faith*. Translated by Roy J. Deferrari. Cambridge, Mass.: Mediaeval Academy of America, 1951.

Hughes, Philip. *The Church in Crisis: A History of the General Council, 325–1870*. Garden City, N.Y.: Hanover House, 1961.

Huillard-Breholles, Jean Louis Alphonse, ed. *Historia diplomatica Friederici Secundi*. 7 vols. Paris: 1859.

Hunt, N., ed. *Cluniac Monasticism in the Central Middle Ages*. London: Macmillan, 1972.

Hunt, R. D. "The Library of Robert Grosseteste." In *Robert Grosseteste, Bishop and Scholar*, edited by D. A. Callus. Oxford: Oxford University Press, 1955.

Hyde, J. K. "Contemporary Views on Faction and Civil Strife in Thirteenth and Fourteenth Century Italy." In *Violence and Civil Strife in Italian Cities, 1200–1500*, edited by Lauro Marines, pp. 273–307. Berkeley: University of California Press, 1972.

– *Padua in the Age of Dante*. Manchester: Manchester University Press, 1966.

– *Society and Politics in Medieval Italy: The Evolution of Civil Life, 1000–1350*. New York: St. Martin's Press, 1973.

Ibach, H. *Leben und Schriften des Konrad von Megenburg*. Berlin: Junker und Kunnhaupt. 1938.

Immink, P. W. A. *At the Roots of Medieval Society*. Vol. 1: The Western Empire. Oslo: H. Aschehoug & Co., 1958.

Irenaeus. *Adversus haereses*. Edited by Joseph Martin. Bonn: Peter Hanstein, 1930.

– *Writings*. Translated by Alexander Roberts and W. H. Rambaut. Ante-Nicene Fathers 5. Edinburgh: T. & T. Clark, 1910.

Isidore of Seville. *Etymologiae*. Edited by W. M. Lindsay. 2 vols. Oxford: Clarendon Press, 1910.

Ivo of Chartres. *Decretum*. PL 161: 47–1022.

Izbicki, Thomas M. "Infallibility and the Erring Pope: Guido Terreni and Johannes de Turrecremata." In *Law, Church and Society: Essays in Honor of Stephan Kuttner*, edited by Kenneth Pennington and Robert Somerville, pp. 97–112. Philadelphia: University of Pennsylvania Press, 1977.

Jacob, Ernest Fraser. "The Conciliar Movement in Recent Study." *Bulletin of John Rylands Library* 41, no. 1 (1958–59): 26–53.

– *Essays in the Conciliar Epoch*. 2nd ed. Manchester: Manchester University Press, 1953.

– "John of Salisbury and the *Policraticus*." In *The Social and Political Ideas of Some Great Medieval Thinkers*, edited by F. J. C. Hearnshaw, pp. 53–84. London: Dawson, 1923.

– "Panormitanus and the Council of Basle." In *Proceedings of the Third International Congress of Medieval Canon Law*, edited by Stephan Kuttner, pp. 205–21. Vatican City: Biblioteca Apostolica Vaticana, 1971.

– *Some Notes on Occam as a Political Thinker*. Manchester: Manchester University Press, 1936.

Jacqueline, Bernard. "A propos des 'dictatus papae': Les 'auctoritates apostolicae sedis' d'Avranches." *Revue historique de droit français et étranger*. 4th ser. 34 (1956): 568–74.

– *Papauté et episcopat selon saint Bernard de Clairvaux*. Saint-Lo: Editions du centurion, 1963.

James of Vitterbo. *Le plus ancien traité de l'église: Jacques de Viterbo De regimine christiano (1301–1302): Étude des sources et édition critique*. Edited by H.-X. Arquillière. Paris: Gabriel Beauchesne, 1926.

Jarrett, Dom Bede. "Friar Confessors of English Kings." *Home Counties Magazine* 12 (1910): 100–12.

Jedin, Hubert. *A History of the Council of Trent*. Translated by Ernest Graf. London: Nelson, 1957.

Johannes Andreae. *In quinque decretalium libris novella Commentaria*. Venice, 1504. Reprinted, with introduction by Stephan Kuttner. Turin: Bottega d'Erasmo, 1963–66.

Johannes Quidort von Paris [John of Paris]. *Uber konigliche and papstliche Gewalt: Text Kritische Edition mit deutscher Ubersetzung*. Edited by F. Bleienstein. Frankfurter Studien zur Wissenschaft von der Politik 4. Stuttgart: Ernst Klett Verlag, 1969.

Johannes de Viterbo. *Liber de regimine civitatum*. In *Biblioteca juridica medii aevi*. Edited by G. Salvemini. Vol. 3. Bologna: 1901.

John Chrysostom. *Commentary on Saint John the Apostle and Evangelist. Homilies 1–47*. Translated by Sr. Thomas Aquinas Goggin. Fathers of the Church 33. New York: Fathers of the Church, 1957.

John of Naples. *Quaestiones variae Parisiensis disputatae*. Naples: 1618.

John of Paris. *Le Corruptorium correctorii "circa" de Jean Quidort de Paris*. Edited by J-P. Muller. Studia Anselmiana 9. Rome: Herder, 1941.

– See also Johannes Quidort von Paris.

John of Paris on Royal and Papal Power. Translation, with introduction, of the *De potestate regia et papali* of John of Paris. Arthur P. Monahan. Records of Civilization Sources and Studies, no. 90. New York: Columbia University Press, 1974.

John of Salisbury. *Frivolities of Courtiers and Footprints of Philosophers, Being a Translation of the First, Second and Third Books and Selections from the Seventh and Eighth Books of the Policraticus of John of Salisbury*. Translated by Joseph B. Pike. New York: Octagon, 1972.

– *The Letters of John of Salisbury*. Vol. 1. *The Early Letters (1153–1161)*. Edited by W. J. Miller and H. E. Butki; revised C. N. L. Brooke. London: Nelson, 1955.

– *Policraticus*. Edited by C. C. I. Webb. 2 vols. London: 1909. Reprinted Frankfurt: Minerva, 1965.

– *The Statesman's Book of John of Salisbury, Being the Fourth, Fifth, and Sixth Books, and Selections from the Seventh and Eighth Books of the Policraticus*. Translated by John Dickinson. New York: Russell & Russell, 1963.

Jolliffe, John Edward Austin. *Angevin Kingship*. London: Adam and Charles Black, 1955; 2nd ed. 1963.

– *The Constitutional History of England from the English Settlement to 1485.* London: Adam and Charles Black, 1937.

Jolowicz, Herbert Felix. *Historical Introduction to the Study of Roman Law.* Cambridge: Cambridge University Press, 1954; 3rd ed., B. Nicholas, 1972.

– "The Stone That the Builders Rejected: Adventures of Some Civil Law Texts." *Seminar* 12 (1954): 34–50.

Jordan, E. *L'Allemagne et l'Italie aux XIIe et XIIIe siècles.* Paris: Presse universitaire de France, 1939.

Jordan of Osnabruck. *Die Schriften de Alexander von Roes.* Edited by Herbert Grundmann and Hermann Heimpel. In *MGH. Auctorum* 4.

Journet, Charles. *La juridiction de l'église sur la cité.* Paris: Desclée de Brouwer, 1931.

Jouvenel, Edouard Bertrand de. *The Pure Theory of Politics.* Cambridge: Cambridge University Press, 1963.

– *Sovereignty: An Inquiry into the Political Good.* Translated by J. F. Huntington. Chicago: Chicago University Press, 1957.

Judson, Margaret Atwood. *The Crisis of the Constitution: An Essay in Constitutional and Political Thought in England 1603–1645.* New Brunswick, N.J.: Rutgers University Press, 1949.

Justin Martyr. *The First Apology.* Translated by Thomas B. Falls. Fathers of the Church 6. Washington, D.C.: Catholic University of America Press, 1943.

Kantorowicz, Ernst H. "Deus per naturam, deus per gratiam." *Harvard Theological Review* 45 (1952): 253–77.

– "Inalienability: A Note on Canonical Practice and the English Coronation Oath in the Thirteenth Century." *Speculum* 29 (1954): 488–502.

– *Kaiser Friedrich der Zweite.* 2nd ed. Berlin: G. Bondi, 1928. Translated by E. O. Lorimer. London: Constable, 1917.

– *King Frederick II.* Translated E. O. Lorimer. London: Constable, 1957.

– "Kingship under the Impact of Scientific Jurisprudence." In *Twelfth-Century Europe and the Foundations of Modern Society,* edited by Gaines Post, M. Clagett, and R. Reynolds, pp. 89–111. Madison: University of Wisconsin Press, 1961.

– *The King's Two Bodies: A Study in Mediaeval Political Theory.* Princeton: Princeton University Press, 1957.

– *Laudes regiae. A Study in Liturgical Acclamations and Medieval Ruler Worship.* Berkeley: University of California Press, 1958.

– "The Prologue to *Fleta* and the School of Petrus de Vinea." *Speculum* 32 (1957): 231–49.

– "*Pro patria mori* in Medieval Political Thought." *American Historical Review* 57 (1951): 472–92.

– *Selected Studies.* Locust Valley, N.Y.: J. J. Augustin, 1965.

– "The Sovereignty of the Artist: A Note on Legal Maxims and Renaissance Theories of Art." In *De Artibus opuscula XL: Essays in Honor of Erwin Panofsky,* edited by M. Meiss, 1: 267–79. New York: New York University Press, 1961.

Kantorowicz, Herman U. "The Quaestiones disputatae of the Glossators." In *Rechts historische Schriften*. Edited by H. Coing and G. Immel. Karlsruhe: C. F. Müller, 1970.

— ed. *Studies in Glossators of the Roman Law. Newly Discovered Writings of the Twelfth Century*. Cambridge: Cambridge University Press, 1938.

— and Smalley, Beryl. "An English Theologian's View of Roman Law: Pepo, Irnerius, Ralph Niger." *Medieval and Renaissance Studies* 1 (1941): 237–52.

Kay, Richard. "'Ad nostram praesentiam evocamus': Boniface VIII and the Roman Convocation of 1302." In *Proceedings of the Third International Congress of Medieval Canon Law*, edited by Stephan Kuttner, pp. 165–89. Vatican City: Biblioteca Apostolica Vaticana, 1971.

Keen, M. H., and Hugh, Maurice. "The Political Thought of the Fourteenth Century Civilians." In *Trends in Medieval Political Thought*, edited by Beryl Smalley. Oxford: Clarendon Press, 1965.

Kemp. Eric Waldram. *Counsel and Consent: Aspects of the Government of the Church as Exemplified in the History of English Provincial Synods*. The Bampton Lectures for 1960. London: S.P.C., 1961.

Kempf, Friedrich. "Die Katholische Lehre von Vorrang der Kirche und ihrer Gewalt über das Zeitliche in ihrer geschichtlichen Entwicklung seit dem Investitutstreit." *Catholica* 12 (1958).

— "Die papstliche Gewalt in der mittelalterlichen Welt." *Miscellanea Historiae Pontificalis* 21 (1959): 153–66.

— *Papsttum und Kaisertum bei Innocens III*. Miscellanea historiae pontificalis 19. Rome: 1954.

— "Das problem der Christianitas im 12. und 13. jahrhundert." *Historisches Jahrbuch* 70 (1960): 104–23.

Kennan, E. "The 'de consideratione' of St. Bernard of Clairvaux and the Papacy in the Mid-twelfth Century: A Review of Scholarship." *Traditio* 23 (1967): 73–115.

Kenney, Barnaby C. *Judgement by Peers*. Harvard Historical Monographs 20. Cambridge: Harvard University Press, 1948.

Kerchkhove, M. Van de. "La notion de jurisdiction dans la doctrine des décrétistes et des premiers décrétalistes." *Etudes franciscaines* 49 (1937): 420–55.

Kern, Fritz. *Kingship and Law in the Middle Ages*. Translated by S. B. Chrimes. Oxford: Blackwell, 1956.

Kilga, Klemens. *Der Kirchenbegriff der hl. Bernard von Clairvaux*. Sonderbruck: Cistercienser Chroniker, 1947–48.

King, Paul David. *Law and Society in the Visigothic Kingdom*. Cambridge Studies in Medieval Life and Thought, 3rd ser., vol. 5. London: Cambridge University Press, 1972.

Kirshner, Julius. "*Civitas sibi faciat civem*: Bartolus of Sassoferrato's Doctrine on the Making of a Citizen." *Speculum* 48 (1973): 694–713.

Knowles, David. *The Evolution of Medieval Thought.* Baltimore: Helicon Press, 1962.

– *The Monastic Order in England.* Cambridge: Cambridge University Press, 1950.

Koch, Joseph. *Durandus de S. Portiano, O.P. Forschungen zum Streit um Thomas von Aquino zu Beginn des 14. Jahrhunderts.* Beiträge zur Geschichte der Philosophie des Mittelalters, vol. 26. Munster: Aschendorff, 1927.

Koht, Halvdan. "The Dawn of Nationalism in Europe." *American Historical Review* 52 (1947): 265–80.

Kölmel, Wilhelm. "Paupertas und potestas: Kirche und Welt in der Sicht des Alvarus Pelagius." *Franziskanische Studien* 46 (1964): 57–101.

– *Regimen Christianum: Weg and Ergebnisse des Gewaltemverhaltnisses (8 bis 14, Jahrhundert).* Berlin: Walter & Gruyter & Co., 1970.

– "Uber spirituale und temporale Ordnung." *Franziskanische Studien,* 36 (1954): 171–95.

– *Wilhelm Ockham und seine kirchenpolitischen Schriften.* Essen: Ludgerus Verlag, 1962.

Konvitz, M. *The Jews: Their History, Culture and Religion.* 2 vols. London: 1961.

Korn, J. B. *La justice primitive et le péché original d'après saint Thomas.* Paris: Vrin, 1932.

Kraus, H. J. *Worship in Israel: A Cultic History of the Old Testament.* Translated by Geoffrey Bushwell. Oxford: Blackwell, 1966.

Kuiters, R. "Aegidius Romanus and the Authorship of *In utramque partem* and *De ecclesiastica potestate.*" *Augustiniana* 20 (1947): 146–214.

– "De ecclesiastica sive de summi pontificis potestate secundum Aegidium Romanum." *Analecta Augustiniana* 20 (1947): 146–214.

Kunkel, Wolfgang. *An Introduction to Roman Legal and Constitutional Law.* Translated by J. M. Kelley. 2nd ed. Oxford: Clarendon Press, 1973.

Kuttner, Stephan. "Additional Notes on the Roman Law in Gratian." *Seminar* 12 (1954): 68–74.

– "The Father of the Science of Canon Law." *The Jurist* 1 (1941): 2–19.

– "Gratian and Plato." In *Church and Government in the Middle Ages: Essays Presented to C. R. Cheney,* edited by C. N. L. Brooke et al., pp. 93–118. Cambridge: Cambridge University Press, 1976.

– *Harmony from Dissonance: An Interpretation of Medieval Canon Law.* Wimmer Lecture 10, St. Vincent College, Latrobe, Pa.: Archabbey Press, 1960. Reprinted in Kuttner, *History of Ideas.*

– *The History of Ideas and Doctrines of Canon Law in the Middle Ages.* London: Variorum, 1981.

– *Medieval Councils, Decretals and Collections of Canon Law: Selected Essays.* London: Variorum, 1980.

– "New Studies in the Roman Law in Gratian's *Decretum.*" *Seminar* 13 (1955–56): 51–55.

– "Papst Honorius III und des Studium des Zivilrechs." In *Festschrift für Martin Wolff*, pp. 79–101. Tubingen: 1952.
– *Repertorium der Kanonistik (1140–1234)*. Citta del Vaticano: Biblioteca Apostolica Vaticana, 1937.
– "Some Considerations on the Role of Secular Law and Institutions in the History of Canon Law." In *Scritti di sociologia e politica in honore di Luigi Sturzo* Bologna: N. Zanichelli, 1953–54.
– "Urban II and the Doctrine of Interpretation: A Turning Point?" *Studia Gratiana* 15 (1972): 55–86.
– and Rathborne, E. "Anglo-Norman Canonists of the Twelfth Century." *Traditio* 7 (1949–51): 270–358.
Lachance, L. *Le concept de droit selon Aristote et Saint Thomas d'Aquin*. Ottawa: University of Ottawa Press, 1948.
– *L'humanisme de Saint Thomas d'Aquin: Individu et état*. 2nd ed. Montreal: Editions du Lévrier, 1965.
Lactantius. *Divine Institutes. Books I–VII*. Translated by Sr. Mary Francis McDonald. Fathers of the Church 49. Washington, D.C.: Catholic University of America Press, 1964.
Ladner, Gerhart B. "Aspects of Medieval Thought on Church and State." *Review of Politics* 9 (1947): 403–22.
– "Bibliographical Survey: The History of Ideas in the Christian Middle Ages from the Fathers to Dante in American and Canadian Publications of the Years 1940–1952." *Traditio* 9 (1953): 439–514.
– "The Concepts of ecclesia and christianitas and their Relation to the Idea of Papal 'plenitudo potestatis' from Gregory VII to Boniface VIII." in *Sacerdotio e regno du VII a Bonifacio VIII*, pp. 49–77. Miscellanea Historiae Pontificalis 18. Rome: 1954.
Lagarde, Georges de. "L'idée de représentation dans les oeuvres de Guillaume d'Occam." *Bulletin of the International Committee of Historical Sciences* 9. Pt. IV, no. 37 (1937) 425–51.
– "Individualisme et corporatisme au moyen âge." In *L'organisation corporative du moyen âge*, pp. 1–60. Etudes . . . pour l'histoire des assemblées d'états, no. 2. Louvain: Nauwelaerts, 1937.
– "Marsile de Padoue et Guillaume d'Occam." *Etudes d'histoire du droit canonique dédiées à Gabriel le Bras*, 2: 593–605. Paris: Sirey, 1965.
– *Marsile de Padoue ou le premier théoricien de l'état laïque*. La naissance de l'esprit laïque, 1st ed., vol. 3. Paris: Béatrice-Nauwelaerts, 1948.
– *La naissance de l'esprit laïque au déclin du moyen âge*. 5 vols. 1. Bilan du XIIIe siècle. 3rd ed. Louvain / Paris: Nauwelaerts, 1965. 2. Secteur social de la scolastique, 2nd ed. Louvain / Paris: Nauwelaerts, 1958. 3. Le Defensor pacis. 4. Guillaume d'Occam: Défense de l'empire. 5. Guillaume d'Occam: Critique des structures ecclésiales. Louvain / Paris: Nauwelaerts, 1962.
– "Occam et le concile général." In *Album Helen Maud Cam*, 1: 83–94. Louvain: Beatrice-Nauwelaerts, 1960.

- "La philosophie social d'Henri de Gand et Godefroid de Fontaines." *Archives d'histoire doctrinal et littéraire du moyen âge* 18 (1943–45): 73–142.
- "Rapports entre Marsile de Padoue et Guillaume d'Occam." *Revue des sciences religieuses* 17 (1937): 168–85, 428–45.
- "Les théories représentatives des XIVe–XVe siècles et l'église." In *Studies Presented to the International Commission for the History of Representative and Parliamentary Institutions* 18: 63–76. Louvain: Béatrice-Nauwelaerts, 1958.

Landolfus of Colonna. *De pontificali officio.* Edited by Richard Scholz. In *Unbekannte,* 2: 530–39.

Langlois, Charles Victor. *De recuperatione terre sancte.* Paris: C. V. Langlois, 1891.

Langmuir, Gavin I. "Consilia and Capetian Assemblies, 1179–1230." In *Album Helen Maud Cam.* Studies Presented to the International Commission for the History of Representative and Parliamentary Institutions, 24, Vol. 2: 27–63. Louvain: Béatrice-Nauwelaerts, 1961.
- "Counsel and Capetian Assemblies." In *Studies Presented to the International Commission for the History of Representative and Parliamentary Institutions,* no. 18, pp. 19–34. Louvain: Béatrice-Nauwelaerts, 1958.
- "'Judei nostri' and the Beginning of Capetian Legislation." *Traditio* 16 (1960): 203–39.
- "*Per communem consilium regni* in magna carta." *Studia Gratiana* 15 (1972): 465–85.
- "Politics and Parliaments in the Early Thirteenth Century." In *Etudes sur l'histoire d'états,* pp. 47–62. Aix-en-Provence: 1964.

Lapsley, Gaillard T. "Bracton and the Authorship of the 'addicio de cartis.'" *English Historical Review* 62 (1947): 1–19.
- *Crown, Community and Parliament in the Later Middle Ages: Studies in English Constitutional History.* Edited by Helen M. Cam and Geoffrey Barraclough. Oxford: Blackwell, 1951.

Laski, Harold J. ed. *Natural Law: A Defence of Liberty against Tyrants. A Translation of the Vindiciae contra tyrannos by Junius Brutus.* London: G. Bell and Sons, 1924.

Law, Church and Society: Essays in Honour of Stephan Kuttner. Edited by Kenneth Pennington and Robert Somerville. Philadelphia: University of Pennsylvania Press, 1977.

Le Bras, Gabriel. "Accurse et le droit canon." *Atti accursiani* 1: 217–31.
- "Le droit canon dans la litérature quodlibétique." *Zeitschrift du Savigny-Stuftung für Rechtgeschichte, Kanonistische (Romanistische) Abteilung* 46 (1960): 62–80.
- "Le droit romain dans la littérature quodlibétique." *Mélanges Julien,* pp. 166–73.
- "L'église médiévale au service du droit romain." *Revue historique de droit français et étranger,* 4th ser., 44 (1966): 193–209.
- *Institutions ecclésiastiques de la chrétienté médiévale.* 2 vols. Paris: Bloud & Gay, 1959–64.

– "Naissance et croissance du droit privé de l'église." In *Etudes Petot*, pp. 329–45.

– "Notes pour l'histoire littéraire du droit canonique." *Revue de droit canonique* 5 (1955): 131–46.

– *Prolégomènes. Histoire du droit et des institutions de l'église en occident.* Paris: Sirey, 1955.

– ; Lefebvre, Charles; and Rambaud, Jacqueline, eds. *L'âge classique (1140– 1378). Histoire du droit et des institutions de l'église en occident*, vol. 7. Paris: Sirey, 1965.

Lecler, Joseph. "L'argument des deux glaives dans les controverses politiques du moyen-âge." *Recherches de science religieuse* 21 (1931): 299–339.

– *Histoire de la tolérance au siècle de la Réforme.* 2 vols. Paris: Aubier, 1955.

– "Pars corporis papae . . . le sacré collège dans l'ecclésiologie médiévale." In *L'homme devant Dieu: Mélanges offerts au père Henri de Lubac*, 2: 183–98. Paris: Faculté de Théologie S.J. de Lyon-Pourvière, 1964.

– "Les théories démocratiques au moyen âge." *Etudes* 225 (1935): 5–26, 168–89.

Leclercq, Jean. "The General Chapters of the Cistercians, Cluny and the Dominicans." *Concilium* 7 (1972): 86–93.

– *L'idée de la royauté du Christ au moyen âge.* Paris: Editions du Cerf, 1959.

– *Jean de Paris et l'ecclésiologie du XIIIe siècle.* Paris: Vrin, 1942.

– "Modern Psychology and the Interpretation of Medieval Texts." *Speculum* 48 (1973): 476–90.

– "Questiones des XIIIe et XIVe siècles sur la jurisdiction de l'église et le pouvoir séculier." *Studia Gratiana* 12 (1967): 309–24.

Leff, Gordon. "The Apostolic Ideal in Later Medieval Ecclesiology." *Journal of Theological Studies*, n.s., 18 (1967): 58–82.

– *Heresy in the Later Middle Ages: The Relation of Heterodoxy to Dissent c. 1250 – c. 1450.* 2 vols. Manchester: Manchester University Press, 1967.

– "The Making of a Myth of a True Church in the Later Middle Ages." *Journal of Medieval and Renaissance Studies* 1 (1971): 1–15.

– *Paris and Oxford Universities in the Thirteenth and Fourteenth Centuries: An Institutional and Intellectual History.* New York: Wiley, 1968.

Legendre, P. "Accurse chez les canonistes." *Atti accursiani* 1: 233–245.

– *La pénétration du droit romain dans le droit canonique de Gratien à Innocent IV.* Paris: Imprimerie Jouve, 1964.

– "Recherches sur les commentaires pré-accursiens." *Revue d'histoire du droit* 33 (1965): 353–428.

Leges Alamannorum. Edited by Karl August Eckhardt. 2 vols. Germanenrechte Neue Folge. Gottingen: Musterschmidt, 1958–62.

Legrand, Hervé-Marie. "Theology and the Election of Bishops in the Early Church." *Concilium* 7 (1972): 31–42.

Lehane, Brendan. *The Quest of Three Abbots.* New York: Viking Press, 1968.

Leicht, P. S. *Parlamento Friulano*. Vol. 1 (1228–1420), pt. 1. Bologna: N. Zanichelli, 1917; vol. 2 (1420–50), pt. 1. Bologna: 1956.

– "Un principio medievale." *Rendiconti della Reale Accademia Nazionale dei Lincei. Classe di Scienze morali storiche*, 5th ser., 19 (1920).

– "Un principio politico medievale." *Rendiconti della Reale Accademia Nazionale dei Lincei. Classe di Scienze morali storiche*, 5th ser, 30 (1931) 232–45.

Lemaire, A. *Les lois fondamentales de la monarchie française d'après les théories de l'ancien régime*. Paris: A. Fontemoing, 1907.

Leone, G. "De juribus singulorum jure proprio et non jure collegii." *Ephemerides juris canonici* (1955).

Lerner, Ralph, and Mahdi, Mushin, eds. *Medieval Political Philosophy: A Sourcebook*. New York: Free Press of Glencoe, 1963.

Lerner, Robert E. "Joachim of Fiore as a Link between St. Bernard and Innocent III on the Figural Significance of Melchisedech." *Mediaeval Studies* 42 (1980): 471–76.

Lévis-Mirepoix, le duc de. *Philippe le Bel*. Paris: Editions de France, 1936.

Levison, Wilhelm. "Die mittelalterliche Lehre von den beiden Shwerten." *Deutsche Archiv* 9 (1951): 14–42.

Levy, Ernst. "Natural Law in Roman Thought." In *Studia et documenta historiae et iuris* 15. Rome: Apollinaris, 1949.

– *West Roman Vulgar Law: The Law of Property*. American Philosophical Society Memoirs 29: 1–18. Philadelphia: 1951.

Lewis, Ewart (Mrs.) "King above Law?" 'Quod principi placuit' in Bracton." *Speculum* 39 (1964): 240–69.

– *Medieval Political Ideas*. 2 vols. London: Routledge & Kegan Paul, 1954.

– "Organic Tendencies in Medieval Political Thought." *American Political Science Review* 32 (1938): 849–76.

– "The 'Positivism' of Marsiglio of Padua." *Speculum* 38 (1963): 541–82.

Lewis, P. S. *Later Medieval France: The Polity*. London: Macmillan, 1968.

Lex Burgundiorum (Gesetze der Burgunden). Edited by Franz Beyerle. Germanenrechte: Texte und Ubersetzungen. Weimar: Herm. Bohlaus, 1936.

Lex Lombardorum (Gesetze der Langobarden). Edited by Franz Beyerle. Germanenrechte: Texte und Ubersetzungen. Witzenhausen: Deutschrechtlicher Institut, 1963.

Lex Ribuaria. Edited by Karl August Eckhardt. Germanenrechte Neue Folge. Gottingen: Musterschmidt, 1959.

Lex et sacramentum im Mittelalter. Edited by Paul Wilpert. Miscellanea medievalia 6. Berlin: Walter de Gruyter, 1969.

Leyden, W. von. "Aristotle and the Concept of Law." *Philosophy* 47 (1967): 1–19.

Liber augustalis. Edited by A. Cervone (Constitutionum regni Siciliarum libri III. Sumptibus Antonii Cervoni). Naples: 1773.

Liebeschutz, Hans. "John of Salisbury and Pseudo-Plutarch." *Journal of the Warburg and Courtauld Institutes* 6 (1943): 33–39.

— *Medieval Humanism in the Life and Writings of John of Salisbury*. Studies of the Warburg Institutes, no. 17. London: 1950. Reprinted with new bibliography. Nendeln: Kraus, 1968.

Lohr, Charles H. "Aristotle in the West: Some Recent Books." *Traditio* 25 (1969): 416–31.

Lohrmann, D. *Das Register Papst Johannes VIII*. Tubingen: M. Niemeyer, 1968.

The Lombard Laws. Translated by K. F. Drew. Philadelphia: University of Pennsylvania Press, 1973.

Long, R. James. "Utrum iurista vel theologus plus perficiat ad regimen ecclesie." A Quaestio Disputata of Francis Caraccioli. Edition and Study." *Mediaeval Studies* 30 (1968): 134–62.

Lot, Ferdinand, and Fawtier, Robert. *Histoire des institutions françaises au Moyen Age*. 3 vols. Vol. 1: Institutions seigneuriales; vol. 2: Institutions royales; vol. 3: Institutions ecclésiastiques. Paris: Presses universitaires de France, 1957–62.

Lottin, O. *Le droit naturel chez St. Thomas d'Aquin et ses prédécesseurs*. 2nd ed. Bruges: C. Buyaert, 1931.

— "Les vertus morales acquises sont-elles de vraies vertus? La réponse des théologiens de Pierre Abelard à Saint Thomas d'Aquin." *Recherches de théologie ancienne et médiévale* (1953): 13–39; 21 (1954): 101–29.

Louis IV of Germany. *Die Appellation Konig Ludwigs des Baiern von 1324*. Edited by J. Schwalm. Weimar: Herman Bohlaus Nachfolger, 1906.

Lousse, Emile. "Les caractères essentiels de l'état corporatif médiéval." In *Bulletin of the International Committee of Historical Sciences* 9, fasc. 4, no. 37 (1937): 452–67.

— Les origines des assemblées d'état." *Revue historique de droit français et étranger*, 4th ser., 14 (1935): 683–706.

— *La société d'ancien régime: organisation et représentation corporatives*. Vol. 1, 2nd ed. Louvain: Béatrice-Nauwelaerts, 1952.

Loyne, H. R. *Anglo-Saxon England and the Norman Conquest*. London: Longmans, 1962.

Lubac, Henri de. *Corpus mysticum: L'eucharistie et l'église au moyen âge*. 2nd ed., rev. Paris: Aubier, 1949.

— *Exégèse médiévale: Les quatre sens de l'Ecriture*. 4 vols. Paris: Aubier, 1959–64.

deLucca, L. "L'accetazione popolare della legge canonica nel pensiero di Graziano e dei suoi interpreti." *Studia Gratiana* 3 (1955): 194–276.

Lunt, W. E. "The Consent of the English Lower Clergy to Taxation during the Reign of Henry III." In *Persecution and Liberty: Essays in Honor of George Lincoln Burr*, pp. 126–32. New York: Century, 1932.

— *Financial Relations of the Papacy with England in 1327*. Cambridge: Harvard University Press, 1939.

Luscombe, David. "The *lex divinitatis* in the Bull *Unam Sanctum* of Pope Boniface VIII." In *Church and Government in the Middle Ages: Essays Presented to C. R. Cheney on His 70th Birthday*, edited by C. N. L. Brooke, D. E.

Luscombe, G. H. Martin, and Dorothy Owen, pp. 205–21. Cambridge: Cambridge University Press, 1976.

Lyon, Bryce. "Medieval Constitutionalism: A Balance of Power." In *Album Helen Maud Cam*. Studies Presented to the International Commission for the History of Representative and Parliamentary Institutions. Louvain: Béatrice-Nauwelaerts, 1961. Vol. 1. 155–83.

– *Studies of West European Medieval Institutions*: London: Variorum, 1978.

– "What Made a Medieval King Constitutional." In *Essays in Medieval History Presented to Bertie Wilkinson*, edited by T. A. Sandquist and M. R. Powicke, pp. 157–75. Toronto: University of Toronto Press, 1969.

Maassen, Friedrich. *Geschichte der Quellen und Literatur des Canonischen Rechts in Aberlande*. Reprinted Graz: Akademicien Druck-u. Verlagsanstalt, 1956.

Maccarrone, Michele. *Chiesa e stato nella dottrina di papa Innocenzo III*. Lateranum n.s. 6. Rome: Facultas theologica pontificii Athenaei lateranensis, 1940.

– "Il Papa 'Vicarius Christi.' Testi e dottiena dal sec XIII al principio de XIV." In *Miscellane Pio Paschini*, vol. 1.

– *Papato e Impero dalle elezione di Frederico I alla mort di Adriano IV*. Lateranum n.s. 25. Rome: Facultas theologica pontificii Athenaei lateranensis, 1959.

– "Potestas directa e potestas indirecta nei teologi del xii e xiii secolo." In *Sacerdozio e Regno da Gregorio VII a Bonifacio VIII*, pp. 27–47.

– "Una questione inedita dell' Olivi sull' infallibilita del papa." *Rivista di Storia della Chiesa in Italia* 3 (1949): 309–43.

– *Vicarius Christi: Storia del titolo papali*. Lateranum 18. Rome: Facultas theologica pontificii Athenaei lateranensis, 1952.

Machiavelli, Niccolo. *The Discourses of Niccolo Machiavelli*. Edited by Leslie J. Walker. 2 vols. London: Routledge & Kegan Paul, 1950.

Maddicott, J. R. "Magna Carta and the Local Community 1215–1259." *Past and Present* 102 (1984): 25–65.

Maffei, Domenico. *La donazione di Constantino nei giuristi medievali*. Milan: Guiffrè, 1964.

Mahn, J. B. *L'ordre Cistercien et son gouvernement des origines au milieu du XIIIe siècle*. Paris: E. de Boccard, 1945.

Mahoney, Edward P., ed. *Philosophy and Humanism: Renaissance Essays in Honor of Paul Oskar Kristeller*. Leiden: Brill, 1976.

Maitland, Frederick W. "Introduction to *memoranda de parliamento*, 1305." In *Selected Historical Essays of F. W. Maitland*, edited by Helen M. Cam, pp. 52–96. Cambridge: Cambridge University Press, 1957.

– *Roman Canon Law in the Church of England*. London: 1898.

Major, James Russell. "The French Renaissance Monarchy as Seen through the Estates General." *Studies in the Renaissance* 9 (1962): 113–25.

– *Representative Institutions in Renaissance France, 1421–1559*. Madison: University of Wisconsin Press, 1960.

Mansi, Giovanni Domenico, ed. *Sacrorum conciliorum nova et amplissima collectio*. 53 vols. Paris: H. Welter, 1901–27.

Mariani, U. *Chiesa e stato nei teologi agostiani del secolo XIV*. Rome: Editione di Storia e letteratura, 1957.

Maritain, Jacques. *An Essay on Christian Philosophy*. Translated by Edward H. Flannery. New York: Philosophical Library, 1955.

Markus, R. A. "Two Conceptions of Political Authority: Augustine, *De civitate dei* XIX, 14–15, and some Thirteenth-century Interpretations." *Journal of Theological Studies* 16 (1965): 68–100.

Marongiu Antonio. *Byzantine, Norman, Swabean and Later Institutions in Southern Italy: Collected Studies*. London: Variorum, 1972.

– *L'istituto parlamentare in Italia dalle origini al 1500*. Rome: Guiffre, 1948.

– *Medieval Parliaments: A Comparative Study*. Translated and adapted by S. J. Woolf. Studies Presented to the International Commission for the History of Representative and Parliamentary Institutions, no. 32. London: Eyre & Spottiswoode, 1968.

– *Mélanges Antonio Marongiu*. Studies Presented to the International Commission for the History of Representative and Parliamentary Institutions. Brussels: Librairie Encyclopédique, 1968.

– *Il parlamento in Italia nel medio evo e nell 'eta' moderna: Contributa alla storia della instituzione parlamentari del l'Europa occidentale*. Milan: Guiffrè, 1962.

– "Il principo fondamentale della democrazia nel XIII secolo." *Paideia*, 1946.

– "Q.o.t., principe fondamental de la démocratie et du consentement au XIVe siècle." In *Album Helen Maud Cam*. Studies Presented to the International Commission for the History of Representative and Parliamentary Institutions, no. 24. Louvain: Béatrice-Nauwelaerts, 1961. Vol. 2: 101–15.

– "Le 'quod omnes tangit' et une légende dure à mourir." *Revue historique de droit français et étranger*, 4th ser., 48 (1970): 183–84.

– ; Cam, Helen; et al. *Recent Work and Present Views on the Origin and Development of Representative Assemblies*. Rome: 1955.

Marsile de Padoue. *Le Défenseur de la paix*. Translated by Jeannine Quillet. L'église et l'état au moyen âge, no. 12. Paris: Vrin, 1968.

Marsilius of Padua. *Defensor pacis*. Edited by C. W. Previté-Orton. Cambridge: Cambridge University Press, 1928.

– *Defensor pacis*. Translated by Alan Gewirth. 2 vols. New York: Columbia University Press, 1951.

Martin of Braga. *Martini episcopi Bracarensis opera omnia*. Edited by C. W. Barlow. New Haven: Yale University Press, 1950.

Martin, Conor. "The Commentaries on the Politics of Aristotle in the Late Thirteenth and Early Fourteenth Century." Ph. D. diss., Oxford: 1949.

– "Some Medieval Commentaries on Aristotle's *Politics*." *History* 36 (1951): 29–44.

Martin, R. M. *La controverse sur le péché original au début du XIVe siècle*. Textes inédits. Louvain: Spicilegium sacrum, 1930.

Martin, V. *Les origines du gallicanisme*. 2 vols. Paris: Bloud & Gay, 1939.

Martines, Lauro. *Power and Imagination: City-states in Renaissance Italy.* New York: Knopf, 1979.

— *Violence and Civil Disorder in Italian Communes 1200–1500.* Berkeley & Los Angeles: University of California Press, 1972.

Mathew, Donald. *The Medieval European Community.* London: Batsford, 1977.

Mayer, Ernst. *Italienische Verfassungegenschichte von der Gothenzeit bis zur Zunftherrschaft.* 2 vols. Leipzig: Deichert, 1909.

— *Mittelalterliche Verfassungegenschichte: Deutsche und französische Verfassungegeschichte von 9. bis zum 14 Jahrhundert.* Leipzig: Deichert, 1899.

McCready, William C. "Papalists and Anti-papalists: Aspects of the Church-State Contoversy in the Later Middle Ages." *Viator* 6 (1975): 241–73.

— "Papal *plenitudo potestatis* and the Source of Temporal Authority in Late Medieval Papal Hierocratic Theory." *Speculum* 48 (1973): 654–74.

— "The Papal Sovereign in the Ecclesiology of Augustinus Triumphus." *Medieval Studies* 39 (1977): 177–205.

— "The Problem of the Empire in Augustinus Triumphus and Late Medieval Papal Hierocratic Theory." *Traditio* 30 (1974): 325–49.

McGrade, Arthur Stephen. *The Political Thought of William of Ockham: Personal and Institutional Principles.* Cambridge: Cambridge University Press, 1974.

— "Two Fifth-Century Conceptions of Papal Primacy." In *Studies in Medieval and Renaissance History,* edited by William M. Bowskey, 7: 1–45. Lincoln, Neb.: University of Nebraska Press, 1970.

McIlwain, Charles Howard. *Constitutionalism, Ancient and Modern.* Ithaca: Cornell University Press, 1947.

— *Constitutionalism and the Changing World.* New York: Macmillan, 1939.

— *The Growth of Political Thought in the West.* New York: Macmillan, 1939.

— *The High Court of Parliament and Its Supremacy: An Historical Essay on the Boundaries between Legislation and Adjudication in England.* New Haven: Yale University Press, 1910.

McKechnie, William Sharp. *Magna Carta. A Commentary on the Great Charter of King John, with an Historical Introduction.* 2nd ed. New York: Burt Franklin, 1958.

McKisack, May. *The Fourteenth Century (1307–1399).* Oxford: Clarendon Press, 1959.

— *The Parliamentary Representation of the English Boroughs during the Middle Ages.* London: Oxford University Press, 1932.

McKittrick, Rosamund. "Some Carolingian Lawbooks and Their Functions." In *Authority and Power: Studies in Medieval Law and Government,* edited by Brian Tierney and Peter Linchen, pp. 13–28. Cambridge: Cambridge University Press, 1980.

The Medieval City. Edited by Harry A. Miskimmin, David Herlihy, and A. L. Udovitch. New Haven and London: Yale University Press, 1977.

Meijers, E. M. *Etudes d'histoire du droit.* Edited by R. Feenstra & H. F. W. D.

Fescher. Vol. 3: Le droit romain au moyen âge. Leiden: Presse Universitaire, 1959.

Meinecke, Friedrich. *Machiavellism: The Doctrine of Raison d'état and Its Place in Modern History*. Translated by Douglas Scott. New Haven: Yale University Press, 1962.

Mercati, John Angelo. "La prima relazione del cardinale Nicolo de Romanis sulla sua legazione in Inghilterra." In *Essays in History Presented to Reginald Lane Poole*, edited by H. W. C. Davis. Oxford: Oxford University Press, 1927.

Meyjes, G. H. M. Posthumus. *Jean Gerson et l'Assemblée de Vincennes (1329): Ses conceptions de la jurisdiction temporelle de l'église accompagné d'une édition critique du De jurisdictione spirituali et temporali*. Leiden: Brill, 1978.

Meynial, E. "Notes sur la formation de la théorie du domaine de vise du xiiie au xive siècle dans les Romanistes." *Mélanges Fitting* 2: 411–61. Montpellier: 1908.

Michalski, K. "La philosophie au XIVe siècle." Edited by K. Flasch. In *Opuscula philosophica, Abhandlungen zur Philosophie und ihrer Geschichte*. Frankfurt: 1969.

Michaud-Quantin, P. "Collectivités médiévales et institutions antiques." In *Miscellanea medievalia*, edited by P. Wilpert, 1: 239–62. Berlin: 1966.

– *Universitas: Expression du mouvement communautaire dans le moyen âge latin*. Paris: Vrin, 1970.

Miethke, J. "Zu Wilhelm Ockhams Tod." *Archivum franciscanum historicum* 61 (1968): 79–98.

Migne, J.-P. *Patrologia cursus completus. Series graeca*. 161 vols. Paris: J.-P. Migne, 1857–87.

– *Patrologia cursus completus. Series latina*. 227 vols. Paris: Garnier Fratres, 1879–90.

Miller, Edward. *The Origins of Parliament*. The Historical Association General Series, no. 44. London: Routledge & Kegan Paul, 1960.

Miller, G. J. T. "The Position of the King in Bracton and Beaumanoir." *Speculum* 21 (1956): 269–96.

Minio-Paluello, L. "Remigio Girolami's *De bono Communi*." *Italian Studies* 11 (1956): 56–71.

Mitchell, S. K. *Taxation in Medieval England*. New Haven: Yale University Press, 1951.

Mitteis, Heinrich. *Der Staat des hohen Mittelalters: Grundlinien einer vergleichenden Verfassungegeschichte des Lehnzeitalters*. 4th ed. Weimar: H. Bohlaus Nachfolger, 1953. Translated by H. F. Orton: *The State in the Middle Ages: A Comparative Constitutional History of Feudal Europe*. Amsterdam: North Holland Pub. Co., 1975.

Mochi Onory, Sergio. *Fonti canonistiche dell'idae moderna dello stato*. Pubblicazioni dell 'universita' del Sacro Cuore, no. 38. Milan: Guiffrè, 1951.

Monumenta Germaniae historica.

- *Auciorum.* 15 vols. Berlin: Weidmann, 1877–1919.
- *Fontes.* Hanover: Hahnian, 1933–.
- *Legum.* 5 vols. New York: Kraus Reprint, 1965.
- *Libelli.* 3 vols. Hanover: Hahnian, 1891–1917.
- *Scriptores.* 30 vols. New York: Kraus Reprint, 1963–64.

Moody, Ernest A. "Ockham and Aegidius of Rome." *Franciscan Studies* 9 (1949): 414–42.

Mordek, H. "Une nouvelle source de Benoit le Levite." *Revue de droit canonique* 20 (1970): 241–51.

Morrall, John B. *Gerson and the Great Schism.* Manchester: Manchester University Press, 1960.
- *Political Thought in Medieval Times.* 2nd ed. London: Hutchinson, 1960.
- "Some Notes on a Recent Interpretation of William of Ockham's Political Philosophy." *Franciscan Studies* 9 (1949): 335–69.

Morris, Colin. *The Discovery of the Individual, 1050–1200.* London: SPCK for the Historical Society, 1972.

Morrison, Karl F. *Tradition and Authority in the Western Church 300–1140.* Princeton: Princeton University Press, 1969.
- *The Two Kingdoms: Ecclesiology in Carolingian Political Thought.* Princeton: Princeton University Press, 1964.
- *Western Canon Law.* London: Adam and Charles Black, 1953.

Moulin, L. "Aux sources des libertés européennes. Réflexions sur quinze siècles de gouvernement des religieux." *Les Cahiers de Bruges,* July 1956.
- "Le gouvernement des communautés religieuses comme type de gouvernement mixte." *Revue française de science politique* 2, no. 2 (1952): 335–55.
- "Les origines religieuses des techniques électorales et délibératives modernes." *Revue internationale d'histoire politique et constitutionnelle* 3 (April-June 1953): 106–48.
- "Sanior et maior pars: Notes sur l'évolution des techniques électorales dans les ordres religieuses du VIe siècle." *Revue historique de droit français et étranger,* 4th ser., 36 (1958): 368–97, 491–530.
- "La science politique et le gouvernement des communautés religieuses." *Revue internatinale des sciences administratives* 6 (1951): 42–67.
- *Socialism in the West: An Attempt to Lay the Foundation of a New Socialist Humanism.* Translated and edited by Alfred Heron. London: Gollancz, 1948.

Moynihan, James M. *Papal Immunity and Liability in the Writings of the Medieval Canonists.* Rome: Gregorian University Press, 1961.

Muckle, J. T. "The *De Officiis ministrorum* of St. Ambrose: An Example of the Process of the Christianization of the Latin Language." *Mediaeval Studies* 1 (1939): 63–80.
- "Greek Works Translated Directly into Latin Before 1350. Part I—Before 1000." *Mediaeval Studies* 4 (1942): 33–42; Part II—Continuation." *Mediaeval Studies* 5 (1943): 102–14.

Mulcahy, D. G. "The Hands of St. Augustine but the Voice of Marsilius." *Augustiniana* 18 (1972): 475 *ff*.

– "Marsilius's Use of St. Augustine." *Revue des études Augustiniennes* 18 (1972): 180–90.

Muldoon, J. "The Contribution of the Medieval Canon Lawyers to the Formation of International Law." *Traditio* 28 (1972): 483–97.

– *"Extra ecclesiam non est imperium*: The Canonists and the Legitimacy of Secular Power." *Studia Gratiana* 9 (1966): 551–80.

Mundy, John Hine. *Liberty and Political Power in Toulouse 1050–1230*. New York: Columbia University Press, 1954.

– and Riesenberg, Peter. *The Medieval Town*. Princeton: Van Nostrand, 1958.

Munier, C. "Droit canonique et droit romain d'après Gratien et les décrétistes." In *Etudes d'histoire du droit canonique dédiées à Gabriel le Bras*, pp. 943–54. 2 vols. Paris: Sirey, 1965.

– *Les sources patristiques du droit de l'église du VIIIe au XIIIe siècle*. Strasbourg: Mulhouse, 1957.

Munz, P. *The Place of Hooker in the History of Thought*. London: Routledge & Kegan Paul, 1952.

Murray, Alexander. *Reason and Society in the Middle Ages*. Oxford: Clarendon Press, 1978.

Murray, John Courtney. "Contemporary Orientations of Catholic Thought on Church and State in the Light of History." *Theological Studies* 10 (1949): 177–235.

Myers, Alex Reginald. "The English Parliament and the French Estates-General in the Middle Ages." In *Album Helen Maud Cam*. Studies Presented to the International Commission for the History of Representative and Parliamentary Institutions, no. 24. Louvain: Béatrice-Nauwelaerts, 1961. Vol. 1: 139–53.

– "Parliaments in Europe: The Representative Tradition." *History Today* 5 (1955): 383–90, 446–54.

Myers, Henry A. "The Concept of Kingship in the Book of Emperors ('Kaiserchronik')." *Traditio* 27 (1971): 205–230.

– *The Myth of State*. Edited by H. Biezais. Scripta instituti Donneriani Aboensis 6. Stockholm: Almquist & Wiksell, 1972.

Narki, Bruno. *Sigieri di Brabante nel pensiero del rinascimento italiano*. Rome: Edizione italiane, 1945.

Nelson, Janet L. "Inauguration Rituals." In *Early Medieval Kingship*, edited by Peter H. Sawyer and Ian N. Woods, pp. 50–71. Leeds: University of Leeds School of History, 1978.

– "Kingship, Law and Liturgy in the Political Thought of Hincmar of Rheims." *English Historical Review* 92 (1977): 241–79.

– "The Problem of Alfred's Anointing." *Journal of Ecclesiastical History* 18 (1967): 145–63.

Niccolai, Franco. *Citta e signori*. Bologna: Zanichelli, 1941.

Nicholas d'Orèsme. *The De moneta of Nicholas d'Orèsme and English Mint Documents*. Edited and translated by Charles Johnson. Nelson Medieval Texts. London: Nelson, 1956.

Nineham, R. "The So-called *Anonymous of York*." *Journal of Ecclesiastical History* 14 (1963): 31–45.

Noonan, John T. "Gratian Slept Here: The Changing Identity of the Father of the Systematic Study of Canon Law." *Traditio* 35 (1979): 145–72.

— "Who was Rolandus?" In *Law, Church and Society: Essays in Honor of Stephan Kuttner*, edited by Kenneth Pennington and Robert Somerville, pp. 21–48. Philadelphia: University of Pennsylvania Press, 1977.

Norman Anonymous of 1100 A.D. Edited by George Huntingdon Williams. Harvard Theological Studies 8. Cambridge: Harvard University Press, 1951.

Oakley, Francis. "Almain and Major: Conciliar Theory on the Eve of the Reformation." *American Historical Review* 70 (1965): 675–90. Reprinted in Oakley, *Natural Law* (below).

— "Celestial Hierarchies Revisited: Walter Ullmann's Vision of Medieval Politics." *Past and Present, a Journal of Historical Studies* 60 (August 1973): 3–48.

— "Conciliarism in the Sixteenth Century: Jacques Almain Again." *Archiv für Reformationsgeschichte* 68 (1977): 111–32. Reprinted in Oakley, *Natural Law*.

— *Council over Pope? Towards a Provisional Ecclesiology*. New York: Herder and Herder, 1969.

— *The Crucial Centuries: The Medieval Experience*. Rev. ed. London: Terra Nova, 1979.

— "Figgis, Constance, and the Divines of Paris." *American Historical Review* 75 (1969): 368–86. Reprinted in Oakley, *Natural Law*.

— "Gerson and d'Ailly: An Admonition." *Speculum* 40 (1965): 674–83. Reprinted in Oakley, *Natural Law*.

— "Jacobean Political Theology: The Absolute and Ordinary Powers of the King." *Journal of the History of Ideas* 29 (1968): 323–46.

— "Medieval Theories of Natural Law. William of Ockham and the Significance of the Voluntarist Tradition." *Natural Law Forum* 6 (1961): 65–83. Reprinted in Oakley, *Natural Law*.

— *Natural Law, Conciliarism and Consent in the Late Middle Ages*. London: Variorum, 1984.

— "Natural Law, the *Corpus Mysticum*, and Consent in Conciliar Thought from John of Paris to Matthias Ugonis." *Speculum* 56 (1981): 786–810. Reprinted in Oakley, *Natural Law*.

— "On the Road from Constance to 1688: The Political Thought of John Major and George Buchanan." *Journal of British Studies* 1 (1962): 1–31. Reprinted in Oakley, *Natural Law*.

— *The Political Thought of Pierre d'Ailly: The Voluntarist Tradition*. Yale Historical

Publications, Miscellany 81. New Haven and London: Yale University Press, 1964.

– *The Western Church in the Later Middle Ages*. London: Cornell University Press, 1979.

Oberman, Heiko Augustus. "From Ockham to Luther—Recent Studies." *Consilium* 7, no. 2 (1966): 63–68.

– *The Harvest of Medieval Theology: Gabriel Biel and Late Medieval Nominalism*. Cambridge: Harvard University Press, 1963.

O'Callaghan, Joseph F. "The Beginnings of the Cortes of Leon-Castile." *American Historical Review* 74 (1969): 1503–37.

– "The Cortes and Royal Taxation during the Reign of Alfonso X of Castile." *Traditio* 27 (1971): 379–98.

Odegaard, C. E. *Vassi and Fideles in the Carolingian Empire*. Cambridge: Harvard University Press, 1945.

Odenheimer, M. J. *Der christliche-kirchliche Anteil an der Verdrangung der mittelalterlichen Rechstructur und an der Entstelung der Vorherrschaft des staatslich gesetzten Rechte im deutschen und franzosischen Rechtsgebiet: Ein Beitrag zur historischen Strukturanalyse der Modernen kontinental – europais-Rechtsordnungen*. Basel: Helbing & Lichtenhahn, 1957.

O'Donoghue, Noel Dermot. "The Law beyond the Law." *The American Journal of Jurisprudence* 18 (1973): 150–64.

Offler, H. S. "Aspects of Government in the Late Medieval Empire." In *Europe in the Late Middle Ages*, edited by J. R. Hale, J. R. L. Highfield, and B. Smalley, pp. 217–47. Evanston, Ill.: Northwestern University Press, 1965.

Oleson, Tryggvi J. *The Wittenagemot in the Reign of Edward the Confessor*. Toronto: University of Toronto Press, 1955.

Olivier, Martin F. *Histoire du droit français des origines à la Revolution*. Paris: Domas Montchrestien, 1948.

Olsen, Glenn. "The Idea of the *ecclesia primitiva* in the Writings of the Twelfth century Canonists." *Traditio* 25 (1969): 62–86.

O'Malley, John W. *Giles of Viterbo on Church and Reform: A Study in Renaissance Thought*. Leiden: Brill, 1968.

Onclin. W. "Le droit naturel selon les romanistes des XIIe et XIIIe siècles." In *Miscellanea moralia A. Janssen*. Louvain: E. Nauwelaerts, 1948.

Order and Innovation in the Middle Ages. Edited by William C. Jordan, Bruce McNab, and Teofilo F. Ruiz. Princeton: Princeton University Press, 1976.

Origen. *Origenes Werke*. 12 vols. Leipzig: J. C. Hinricks, 1899–1910.

Otway-Ruthven, A. J. "The Constitutional Position of the Great Lordships of South Wales." *Transactions of the Royal Historical Society*, 5th ser., 8 (1958): 1–20.

Ovid. *Metamorphoses*. Translated by Frank Justus Miller. Cambridge: Harvard University Press, 1946.

Owen, D. *Herod and Pilate Reconciled*. London: 1663.

Ozment, Steven E. "Mysticism, Nominalism and Dissent." In *The Pursuit of Holiness in Late Medieval and Renaissance Religion*, edited by Charles Trinkaus and Heido Oberman, pp. 67–92. Studies in Medieval and Reformation Thought, no. 10. Leiden: Brill, 1974.

Pacaut, Marcel. *Alexandre III: Etude sur la conception du pouvoir pontifical dans sa pensée et dans son oeuvre*. Paris: Vrin, 1956.

– "L'autorité pontificale selon Innocent IV." *Le Moyen Age* 66 (1960): 85–119.

– *Louis VII et les élections épiscopales dans le royaume de France*. Paris: Vrin, 1957.

– *La théocratie: L'église et le pouvoir au moyen âge*. Paris: Vrin, 1957.

Pantin, W. A. "Grosseteste's Relations with Papacy and Crown." In *Robert Grosseteste, Bishop and Scholar*, edited by D. A. Callus. Oxford: Oxford University Press, 1955.

Parkinson, G. H. R. "Ethics and Politics in Machiavelli." *Philosophical Quarterly* 5 (1953): 37–44.

Parsons, Anscar. *Canonical Election: An Historical Synopsis and Commentary*. Washington, D.C.: Catholic University of America Press, 1939.

Parsons, Wilfrid. "The Influence of Romans XIII on Christian Political Thought. II. Augustine to Hincmar." *Theological Studies* 2 (1949): 325–46.

– "The Influence of Romans XIII on Preaugustinian Christian Political Thought." *Theological Studies* 1 (1940): 337–54.

– "The Medieval Theory of the Tyrant." *Review of Politics* 4 (1942): 129–43.

– "St. Thomas Aquinas and Popular Sovereignty." *Theology* 16 (1941): 473–92.

Partee, C. "Peter John Olivi: Historical and Doctrinal Study." *Franciscan Studies* 20 (1960): 215–60.

Pascoe, Louis B. "Jean Gerson: The 'ecclesia primitiva' and Reform." *Traditio* 30 (1974): 379–409.

– *Jean Gerson: Principles of Church Reform*. Leiden: Brill, 1973.

Pasquet, D. *Essai sur les origines de la chambre de communes*. Paris: Librairie Armand Colin, 1914.

– *An Essay on the Origins of the House of Commons*. Translated by R. E. D. Laffan. Cambridge: Cambridge University Press, 1925. Reissue, London: Merlin Press, 1964.

Paucapalea. *Die Summa des Paucapalea über das Decretum Gratiani*. Edited by Johanne Freidrich von Schutle, Giessen: 1890.

Pegues, F. J. *The Lawyers of the Last Capetians*. Princeton: Princeton University Press, 1962.

Pennington, K. F., Jr. [Kenneth James]. "Bartoleme de Las Casas and the Tradition of Medieval Law." *Church History* 39 (1970): 149–61.

– "Pope Innovent III's Views on Church and State: A Gloss to *per venerabilem*." In *Law, Church and Society: Essays in Honor of Stephan Kuttner*, pp. 49–68. Philadelphia: University of Pennsylvania Press, 1977.

Perrin, John W. "Azo, Roman Law and Sovereign European States." *Studia Gregoriana* 15 (1972): 97–101.

– "'Legatus' in Medieval Roman Law." *Traditio* 29 (1973): 357–78.
– "*Legatus*, the Lawyers and the Terminology of Power in Roman Law." *Studia Gratiana* 11 (1967): 461–89.
Peter John Olivi. "De renuntiatione papae." Edited by P. Livarius Oligen. In *Archivum franciscanun historicum* 11 (1918): 341–66.
Peter of Auvergne. "Questiones in Politicam Aristotelis." In Paris, Bibliothèque Nationale, Latinus, 16089, fol. 274r–319r.
Peters, Edward. "Dante and an Urban Contribution to Political Thought." In *The Medieval City*, edited by Harry A. Miskimmin, David Herlihy, and A. L. Udovitch, pp. 113–40. New Haven, London: Yale University Press, 1977.
– "Rex inutilis: Sancho II of Portugal and Thirteenth century Deposition Theory." *Studia Gratiana* 14 (1967): 253–305.
– *The Shadow King: Rex inutilis in Medieval Law and Literature, 751–1327*. New Haven, London: Yale University Press, 1970.
Petit-Dutaillis, Charles, and Lefebre, Georges, eds. *Studies and Notes Supplementary to Stubbs' Constitutional History*. Manchester: Manchester University Press, 1930.
Petrani, A. "Genèse de la majorité qualifiée." *Apollonaris* 30 (1957): 430–36.
Petrau-Gay, J. "La notion de 'lex' dans la côutume selienne et ses transformations dans les capitulaires." Ph.D. diss., University of Lyons, 1920.
Philip of Leyden. *De cura rei publicae et sorte principantis*. Edited by R. Fruin and P. C. Molhuysin. Gravenhage: Martinus Nijhoff, 1900. Reprinted and revised 1971.
Pilati, G. *Chiesa e stato nei primi quindici secoli*. Rome: Desclée, 1961.
Pincin, C. *Marsilio*. Turin: Giappichelli, 1967.
Pinckers, G. "L'église et l'état au sein de la chrétienté médiévale." *Revue ecclésiastique de Liège* 49 (1963); 50 (1964): 164–79.
Pirenne, Henri. *Les anciennes démocraties des Pays-Bas*. Paris: Flammarion, 1910.
– *Belgian Democracy: Its Early History*. Translated by J. V. Saunders. Manchester University Pub'ns. Historical Series, no. 27. Manchester: Manchester University Press, 1915.
– *Early Democracies in the Low Countries: Urban Society and Political Conflict in the Middle Ages and the Renaissance*. Translated by J. V. Saunders. New York, London: Harper and Row, 1963.
– *Medieval Cities, Their Origins and the Revival of Trade*. Translated by F. D. Halsey. Princeton: Princeton University Press, 1935.
– *Les villes du moyen âge. Essai d'histoire économique et sociale*. Brussels: Lamertin, 1927.
– ; Cohen, G.; and Fouillon, H. *La civilization occidentale au moyen âge du XIe milieu du XVe siècle*. Histoire générale de Glotz. Vol. 8. Paris: Presses universitaires de France, 1933.
Pitkin, H. F. *The Concept of Representation*. Berkeley: University of California Press, 1967.

Plamenatz, John. "The Use of Political Theory." *Political Studies* 8 (1960):
   37–47.
Plato. *Phaedo*. Translated by David Gallop. Oxford: Clarendon Press, 1975.
– *Republic*. Translated by G. M. A. Grube. Indianapolis: Hackett, 1974.
Plucknett, R. G. T. *A Concise History of the Common Law*. 5th ed. London:
   Butterworth, 1956.
– *Edward I and Criminal Law*. Cambridge: Cambridge University Press, 1960.
– *Legislation of Edward I*. Oxford: Clarendon Press, 1949.
– "Parliament." In *The English Government at Work, 1327–1336*, edited by J. F.
   Wallard and W. A. Morris, vol. 1. Cambridge: Harvard University Press,
   1940.
– "The Relations between Roman Law and the English Common Law."
   University of Toronto Law Journal 3 (1939): 24–50.
Pocock, John G. H. *The Machiavellian Moment*. Princeton: Princeton University
   Press, 1975.
Pognet du Haut Jusse, B. A. "Le sécond différend entre Boniface VIII et
   Philippe le Bel, Note sur l'une de ses causes." In *Mélanges Albert Dufourcq,
   études d'histoire religieuse*. Paris: Plon, 1932.
Pollard, A. F. *The Evolution of Parliament*. 2nd ed. London: Longmans, Green,
   1926.
Pollock, (Sir) Frederick. "The History of the Law of Nature." In *Essays in the
   Law*, pp. 31–79. London: Macmillan, 1922.
Ponte, R. de. "Il tractatus de potestate pontificis de Gugliemo da Sarzano."
   Studi Medievale 12 (1971): 997 *ff*.
Posch, Andreas. *Die Staats- und Kirchenpolitische Stellung Engelberts von Admont*.
   Paderborn: Ferdinand Schöningh, 1920.
Post, Gaines. "'Blessed Lady Spain'—Vincentius Hispanus and Spanish
   National Imperialism in the Thirteenth Century." *Speculum* 29 (1954):
   198–209. Reprinted in Post, *Studies*, pp. 482–93.
– "Bracton as Jurist and Theologian on Kingship." In *Proceedings of the Third
   International Congress of Medieval Canon Law*, edited by Stephan Kuttner, pp.
   113–30. Vatican City: Biblioteca Apostolica Vaticana, 1971.
– "Bracton on Kingship." *Tulane Law Review* 42 (1968): 519–54.
– "Copyists' Errors and the Problem of Papal Dispensation, *contra statutum
   generale ecclesiae* or *contra statum generalem ecclesiae* according to the Decretists
   and Decretalists ca. 1150–1254." *Studia Gratiana* 9 (1966): 357–405.
– "Early Medieval Ecclesiastical and Secular Sources of *iura illibata-illaesa* in
   the Inalienability Clause of the Coronation Oath." *Studia Gratiana* 11
   (1967):491–512.
– "The Medieval Heritage of a Humanistic Ideal. 'Scientia donum dei est unde
   vendi non potest.'" *Traditio* 11 (1955): 195–234.
– "Philosophantes and philosophi in Roman and Canon Law." *Archives
   d'histoire doctrinale et littéraire du moyen âge* 29 (1954): 135–38.

– "Philosophy and Citizenship in the Thirteenth Century—Laicization, the Two Laws and Aristotle." In *Order and Innovation in the Middle Ages: Essays in Honor of Joseph R. Strayer*, edited by William C. Jordan, Bruce McNab, and Teofilo F. F. Ruiz, pp. 401–8. Princeton: Princeton University Press, 1976.

– *"Plena potestas* and Consent in Medieval Assemblies: A Study in Romano-Canonical Procedure and the Rise of Representation, 1150–1325. *Traditio* 1 (1943): 355–408. Reprinted in Post, *Studies*, pp. 91–162.

– "'Ratio publicae utilitatis, ratio status' and 'Staatsrason' (1110–1300)." *Die Welt als Geschichte* 21 (1961): 8–28, 71–99. Reprinted in Post, *Studies*, pp. 241–309.

– "Roman Law and Early Representation in Spain and Italy." *Speculum* 18 (1943) 211–32. Reprinted in Post, *Studies*, pp. 61–90.

– "A Roman Legal Theory of Consent, 'quod omnes tangit,' in Medieval Representation." *Wisconsin Law Review* 1950, pp. 66–78.

– "A Romano-Canonical Maxim, 'quod omnes tangit,' in Bracton and in Early Parliaments." *Traditio* 4 (1946): 197–225. Reprinted in Post, *Studies*, pp. 163–238.

– "Some Unpublished Glosses (ca. 1210–1214) on the translatio imperii and the Two Swords." *Archiv für katholisches Kirchenrecht* 117 (1937).

– "Status regis." In *Studies in Medieval and Renaissance History*, edited by W. M. Bowsky, pp. 1–103. Lincoln, Neb.: University of Nebraska Press, 1964.

– *Studies in Medieval Legal Thought: Public Law and the State, 1100–1322.* Princeton: Princeton University Press, 1964.

– "The Theory of Public Law and the State in the Thirteenth Century." *Seminar (The Jurist)* 6 (1948): 42–59.

– "The Two Laws and the Statute of York." *Speculum* 29 (1953): 417–32.

– "Two Notes on Nationalism in the Middle Ages." *Traditio* 9 (1953): 281–320.

– "Vincentius Hispanus, Pro ratione voluntas, and Medieval and Early Modern Theories of Sovereignty." *Traditio* 28 (1972): 159–84.

– Review of Walter Ullmann, *The Medieval Idea of Law as Represented by Lucas de Penna* (London: Methuen, 1946), in *Traditio* 5 (1947): 402–9.

Post Scripta: Essays on Medieval Law and the Emergence of the European State in Honor of Gaines Post. Studia Gratiana, vol. 15. Rome: 1972.

Powell, John Enoch, and Wallis, K. *The House of Lords in the Later Middle Ages: A History of the English House of Lords to 1540.* London: Weidenfeld and Nicolson, 1968.

Powicke, F. M. *King Henry III and the Lord Edward: The Community of the Realm in the Thirteenth Century.* Oxford: Clarendon Press, 1947.

– "Recent Work on the Origin of the English Parliament." In *L'Organization corporative du moyen âge à la fin de l'ancien régime*, pp. 131–40. Recueil de travaux publiées par les membres des conférences d'histoire et de philologie, 2nd ser., 50th fasc. Louvain: Nauwelaerts, 1939.

– *The Thirteenth Century, 1206–1307.* Oxford: Clarendon Press, 1953.

Prestwick, M. C. *War, Politics and Finance under Edward I*. London: 1972.

Previté-Orton, C. W. "The Authors Cited in the *Defensor pacis*." In *Essays in History Presented to R. L. Poole*, edited by H. W. C. Davis, pp. 405–20. Oxford: Clarendon Press, 1927. Reprinted Freeport, N.Y.: Books for Libraries Press.

– "Marsilius of Padua." *Proceedings of the British Academy* (1935) 137–83.

Proceedings of the Third International Congress of Medieval Canon Law. Edited by Stephan Kuttner. Vatican City: Biblioteca Apostolica Vaticana, 1971.

Pronay, N., and Taylor, J. "The Use of the Modus Tenendi Parliamentum in the Middle Ages." *Bulletin of the Institute for Historical Research* 47 (1974): 11–23.

Ptolemy of Lucca (Ptolemaeus Lucensis). *Determinatio compendiosa de iurisdictione imperii auctore anonymo ut videter Tholomeo Lucense O.P.* Edited by Marius Drammer. Hanover and Leipzig: Impensis Bibliopolii Hahniana, 1909.

– "Completion of Thomas Aquinas, De regimine principum." Edited by R. M. Spiazzi. In *Divi Thomae Aquinatis opuscula philosophica*, pp. 280–358. Turin: Marietti, 1954.

Pullan, Brian, ed. *Sources for the History of Medieval Europe from the Mid-Eighth to the Mid-Twelfth Century*. Oxford: Blackwell, 1966.

Quillet, Jeannine. "L'aristotelisme de Marsile de Padoue." In *Miscellanea Mediaevalia* 2: 696–706. Edited by P. Wilpert. Berlin: 1963.

Rambaud (-Buhot), Jacqueline. "Le 'Corpus juris civilis' dans le décret de Gratien . . . "*Bibliothèque de l'Ecole des Chartes*, 1955, pp. 397–411.

– *Le défenseur de la paix*. Librairie Philosophique. Paris: Vrin, 1968.

– "L'étude des manuscrits du Décret de Gratien." Congrès de droit canonique médiéval, Louvain-Brussels, 1958. *Bibliothèque de la revue d'histoire ecclésiastique* 33 (1959): 25–48.

– "Le legs de l'ancien droit: Gratien." In *L'age classique: Histoire du droit et des institutions de l'église en occident*, edited by Georges le Bras, 7: 52–129. Paris: 1965.

– "L'organisation de la société humaine selon le *Defensor pacis* de Marsile de Padoue." In *Miscellanea Mediaevalia* 3: 185–203. Edited by P. Wilpert. Berlin: 1964.

– "Les paleae dans le Décret de Gratien." *Proceedings of the Second International Congress of Medieval Canon Law*, pp. 23–44. Citta del Vaticano: Biblioteca Apostolica Vaticana, 1964.

– "Plan et méthode de travail pour la rédaction d'un catalogue des manuscrits du Décret de Gratien." *Revue d'histoire ecclésiastique* 48 (1953): 211–23.

– *Universitas populi et représentation au XIVe siècle*. Miscellanea mediaevalia, no. 8. Berlin: Walter de Gruyter, 1971.

Rathbone, E. "Roman Law in the Anglo-Norman Realm." *Studia Gratiana* 11 (1967): 255–71.

Raymond of Pēnafort. "Summa iuris." In *Opera omnia*. Vol. 1. Edited by Jose Ruis Serra. Barcelona: Universidad de Barcelona, Facultad de Derecho, 1945.

Rees. J. C. "The Limitations of Political Theory." *Political Studies* 2 (1956): 242–52.

Regan, Richard J. "Aquinas on Political Obedience and Disobedience." *Thought* 56 (1981): 77–88.

Regesta regum Anglo-normanorum 1066–1154. Edited by H. A. Cronne et al. Oxford: Clarendon Press, 1913–69.

The Register of S. Osmund. Vetus Registrum Sarisberiense alias dictum S. Osmundi episcopi. Edited by W. H. R. Jones. 2 vols. London: Longmans, 1883–84.

Renna, Thomas J. "Kingship in the *Disputatio inter clericum et militem.*" *Speculum* 48 (1973): 675–93.

– "The Populus in John of Paris' Theory of Monarchy." *Revue d'histoire du droit* 42 (1974): 243–68.

Renouard, Yves. *The Avignon Papacy 1303–1403.* Translated by Denis Bethell. London: Faber & Faber, 1970.

Richard Fitzneale. *Dialogus de scarrario.* Edited & translated by Charles Johnson. London: T. Nelson, 1950.

Richard Fitzralph. "De pauperie salvatoris." Books 1–4 in Johannis Wycliffe, *De dominio divino libri tres,* edited by R. L. Poole, pp. 257–476. London: 1890.

Richardson, Henry Gerald. *Bracton: The Problem of His Text.* Selden Society, Supplementary Series 2. London: 1965.

– "The English Coronation Oath." *Speculum* 24 (1949): 44–75.

– "The Origins of Parliament." *Transactions of the Royal Historical Society,* 4th ser., vol. 2, 1928. Reprinted in *Essays on Medieval History,* edited by R. W. Southern. London: Macmillan, 1968.

– "Studies in Bracton—an addendum." *Traditio* 14 (1958): 399–400.

Richardson, Henry Gerald, and Sayles, G. O. *The Administration of Ireland 1172–1377.* Dublin: Stationery Office for the Irish Manuscripts Commission, 1963.

– *The Governance of Medieval England from the Conquest to Magna Carta.* Edinburgh: University Press, 1963.

– *The Irish Parliament in the Middle Ages.* Philadelphia: University of Pennsylvania Press, 1952.

– "The Origins of Parliament." *Transactions of the Royal Historical Society* 11 (1928). Reprinted in *Essays in Medieval History,* edited by R. W. Southern. London: Macmillan, 1968.

– "Parliaments and Great Councils in Medieval England." *Law Quarterly Review* 77 (1961): 213–36, 401–26.

Riesenberg, Peter N. *Inalienability of Sovereignty in Medieval Political Thought.* New York: Columbia University Press, 1956.

– "Roman Law, Renunciations and Business in the Twelfth and Thirteenth Centuries." In *Essays in Medieval Life and Thought,* edited by John H. Mundy et al., pp. 207–25. New York: Nelson, 1955.

Riess, Ludwig. *History of the English Electoral Law in the Middle Ages.* Translated by K. L. Wood-Legh. Cambridge: Cambridge University Press, 1940.

Riley, Patrick. "How Coherent is the Social Contract Tradition?" *Journal of the History of Ideas* 34 (1975): 543–62.

— *Will and Political Legitimacy. A Critical Exposition of Social Contract Theory in Hobbes, Locke, Rousseau, Kant, and Hegel.* Cambridge: Harvard University Press, 1982.

Rivière, Jean. "In partem sollicitudinis: Evolution d'une formule pontificale." *Revue des sciences religieuses* 5 (1925): 210–51.

— "Une première 'Somme' du pouvoir pontifical: Le pape chez Augustin d'Ancone." *Revue des sciences religieuses* 18 (1938): 149–83.

— *Le Problème de l'église et l'état au temps de Philippe le Bel: Etude de théologie positive.* Paris: E. Champion, 1926.

— "Sur l'expression "papa-Deus" au moyen âge." In *Miscellanea Francesto Ehrle* 2: 276–89. Rome: Biblioteca Apostolica Vaticana, 1924.

Rodding, C. M. "The Origins of Bracton's Addicio de Cartis." *Speculum* 44 (1969): 239–46.

Rodes, Robert E., Jr. *Ecclesiastical Administration in Medieval England. The Anglo-Saxons to the Reformation.* Notre Dame, Ind.: University of Notre Dame Press, 1977.

Rommen, H. A. *The Natural Law: A Study in Legal and Social History and Philosophy.* Translated by Thomas R. Hanley. St. Louis: Herder and Herder, 1959.

Roskell, J. S. "A Consideration of Certain Aspects and Problems of the English 'modus tenendi parliamentum.'" *Bulletin of the John Rylands Library* 50 (1968): 411–42.

Rothwell, H. "The Confirmation of the Charters, 1297." *English Historical Review* 60 (1945): 16–35, 177–91.

— "Edward I and the Struggle for the Charters." In *Studies in Medieval History Presented to F. M. Powicke*, pp. 319–32. Oxford: Oxford University Press, 1948.

Rouse, Richard H. and Mary A. "John of Salisbury and the Doctrine of Tyrannicide." *Speculum* 42 (1967): 693–709.

Rubinstein, Nicolai. "The Beginnings of Political Thought in Florence." *Journal of the Warburg and Courtauld Institute* 5 (1942): 198–227.

— "Marsilius of Padua and Italian Thought of His Time." In *Europe in the Late Middle Ages*, edited by John Hale, Roger Highfield, and Beryl Smalley, pp. 44–75. Evanston, Ill.: University of Illinois Press, 1965.

Rufinus. *Die Summa decretorum der magister Rufinus.* Edited by Heinrich Singer. Paderborn: Heinrich Singer, 1902.

Rup, J. *L'idée de chrétienté dans la pensée pontificale des origines à Innocent III.* Paris: Les Presses Modernes, 1939.

Russell, Jeffrey Burton. *Dissent and Reform in the Early Middle Ages.* Berkeley and Los Angeles: University of California Press, 1965.

— "Early Parliamentary Organization." *American Historical Review* 43 (1937): 1–21.

Russell, J. C. "Ranulf of Glanville." *Speculum* 45 (1970): 69–79.

Saenger, Paul. "John of Paris, Principal Author of the *Quaestio de potestate papae (Rex pacificus)*." *Speculum* 56 (1981): 41–55.

Sägmuller, Johannes V. *Die Bischofswahl bei Gratian*. Cologne: 1908.

Sait, Edward McChesney. *Political Institutions: A Preface*. New York: Appleton-Century, 1938.

Salembier, L. *Le grande schisme d'occident*. Paris: 1900. 5th ed. 1921.

Salmon, J. H. M. *The French Religious Wars in English Political Thought*. Oxford: Clarendon Press, 1959.

Salmon, Pierre. *The Abbot in Monastic Tradition. A Contribution to the History of the Office of Religious Superiors in the West*. Translated by Claire Lavoie. Cistercian Studies Series, no. 14. Washington, D.C.: Cistercian Publications, 1972.

Saltmann, Avron. *Theobald, Archbishop of Canterbury*. University of London Historical Studies, no. 2. New York: Greenwood Press, 1956.

Salvemini, Gaetano. *Johannis Viterbiensis liber de regimine civitatum*. Edited by G. Salvemini. Biblioteca juridici medii aevi, no. 3. Bologna: 1901.

Sanders, I. J., ed. *Documents of the Baronial Movement of Reform and Rebellion, 1258–1267*. Oxford: Clarendon Press, 1973.

Sawicki, J. *Bibliographia Synodorum particularium*. Vatican City: S. Congregatio de Seminariis et Studiorum Universitatibus, 1967.

Sawyer, Peter Haus. *Anglo-Saxon Charters: An Annotated List and Bibliography*. London: Royal Historical Society, 1968.

– and Wood, Ian N., eds. *Early Medieval Kingship*. Leeds, England: University of Leeds, School of History, 1977.

Sayers, J. *Papal Judges Delegate in the Province of Canterbury 1198–1254: A Study in Ecclesiastical Jurisdiction and Administration*. London: Oxford University Press, 1971.

Sayles, George O. *The Medieval Foundations of England*. Cambridge: Cambridge University Press, 1950.

Sbriccoli, M. "Politique et interprétation juridique dans les villes italiennes du Moyen Age." *Archives de philosophie du droit* (1972): 99–113.

Scharduia, Simon. *De jurisdictione, auctoritate, et praeeminentia imperiali, ac potestate ecclesiastica, deque iuribus regni et imperii, variorum authorum qui ante haec tempera vixerint, scripta; collecta et redacta in unum*. Basel: 1566.

Schelkle, K. H. "Staat und Kirche in der Patristischen Auslegung von RM. 13/1–7." *Zeitschrift für die Neutestamentliche Wissenschaft* (1952–53): 223–36.

Schilling, Otto. *Die Staats- und Soziallehre des heiligen Augustinus*. Freiburg: Herder, 1910.

– *Die Staats- und Soziallehre des heiligen Thomas von Aquin*. 2nd ed. Munich: Hueber, 1930.

Schlick, Moritz. *Problems of Ethics*. Translated by David Rynin. New York: Prentice-Hall, 1939.

Schmid, Paul. *Der Begriff der Kanonischen Wahl in den Anfungen des Investiturstreits*. Stuttgart: W. Kohlhammer, 1926.

Schnachenburg, Rudoff. "Community Co-operation in the New Testament." *Concilium* 7 (1972): 9–19.

A Scholastic Miscellany: Anselm to Ockham. Library of Christian Classics, vol. 10. London: SCM Press, 1956.

Scholz, Richard. "Marsilius von Padova und die Genesis des modernen Staatsbewusstseins." *Historische Zeitschrift* 156 (1937): 88–103.

– "Marsilius von Padova und die Idee der Demokratie." *Zeitschrift für Politik* 1 (1951): 3–36.

– *Die Publizistick zur Zeit Phillips des Schönen und Bonifaz VIII. Ein Beitrag zur Geschichte der politisches Anschauungen des Mittelalters.* Stuttgart: Vertag von Ferdinand Enke, 1903. Reissued Amsterdam: Editions Rodopi, 1969.

– *Unbekannte kirkenpolitische Streitschriften aus der Zeit Ludwigs des Baiern (1327–1354).* 2 vols. Rome: Loescher, 1911–14.

– *William von Ockham als Politischer Denker und sein Breviloquium principatu tyrannico.* Leipzig: Verlag Karl W. Hiersemann, 1944.

Schrors, Johann Heinrich. *Hincmar, erbishofver von Reims. Sein leben und seine Schriften.* Fribourg: Herder, 1884. Reprinted 1969.

Schuchman, P. "Aristotle's Conception of Control." *Journal of the History of Ideas* 23 (1962): 257–64.

Schulz, Fritz. "Bracton on Kingship." *English Historical Review* 60 (1945): 136–76.

– *History of Roman Legal Science.* Oxford: Clarendon Press, 1946.

Schuyler, R. L. "The Historical Spirit Incarnate, F. W. Maitland." *American Historical Review* 57, no. 2 (1952): 303–22.

– and Ausubel, H. *The Making of English History.* New York: Holt, Rinehart & Winston, 1952.

Schwalm, Jakob, ed. *Die Appellation Konig Ludwigs des Baiern von 1324.* Weimar: 1906.

Schwarz, E., ed. *Publizistische Sammlungen zum Acadianischen Schisma.* Abhandlungen der Bayerischer Akademie der Wissenchaften Philosophisch-Historische Abteilung. New ser., 10. Munich: 1934.

Seaver, P. W. "John of Paris, St. Thomas and the Modern State." *Dominicana* 4 (1960): 2, 119–29; 4, 305–27.

Seegrun, W. "Kirche, Papst und Kaiser nach den Anschauungen Kaiser Friedriche II." *Historische Zeitschrift* 207 (1968): 4–41.

Seliger, M. *The Liberal Politics of John Locke.* London: Allen and Unwin, 1968.

Seneca. *Ad Lucilium epistolae morales.* Translated by Richard M. Eummere. Loeb Classical Library. 3 vols. New York: Putnam, 1917–30.

Shephard, Max A. "William of Ockham and the Higher Law." *The American Political Science Review* 26 (1932): 1005–23 and 27 (1933): 24–38.

Sigmund, Paul E. *Nicholas of Cusa and Medieval Political Thought.* Cambridge: Harvard University Press, 1963.

Sikes, J. G. "John de Pouilly and Peter de la Palu." *English Historical Review* 49 (1934): 219–40.

Simon, Yves. "The Doctrinal Issue between the Church and Democracy." In *The Catholic Church in World Affairs*, edited by W. Gurian. Notre Dame: University of Notre Dame Press, 1954.

Skinner, Quentin. *The Foundations of Modern Political Thought.* 2 vols. Cambridge: Cambridge University Press, 1974.

Smalley, Bernard. *The Study of the Bible in the Middle Ages.* 2nd ed. New York: 1952. Reprinted Notre Dame, Ind.: University of Notre Dame Press, 1964.

Smalley, Beryl. *The Becket Controversy and the Schools: A Study of Intellectuals in Politics in the Twelfth Century.* Totowa, N.J.: Rowman & Littlefield, 1973.

— *The Study of the Bible in the Middle Ages.* Oxford: Oxford University Press, 1952.

Soule, C. *Les Etats-généraux de France (1302–1789): Etude historique, comparative et doctrinale.* Heule: P. C. Timbal, 1968.

Southern, R. W. *Western Society and the Church in the Middle Ages.* Harmondsworth: Penguin Books, 1970.

Spinka, M. *Advocates of Reform.* London: SCM Press, 1953.

— *John Hus: A Biography.* Princeton, N.J.: Princeton University Press, 1968.

Spufford, P. *Assemblies of Estates, Taxation and Control of Coinage in Medieval Europe.* Studies Presented to the International Commission for the History of Representative and Parliamentary Institutions, no. 31 (1965).

Stein, Peter. *Bibliographical Introduction to Legal History and Ethnology.* Edited by J. Gilissen. Brussels: Les Editions de l'Institut de Sociologie, Université libre de Bruxelles, 1965.

— "Vacarius and the Civil Law." In *Church and Government in the Middle Ages: Essays Presented to C. R. Cheney on His 70th Birthday*, edited by C. N. L. Brooke, D. E. Luscombe, G. H. Martin, and Dorothy Owen, pp. 119–37. Cambridge: Cambridge University Press, 1976.

Stelling-Michaud, S. "De Marsile de Padoue à Jean-Jacques Rousseau." *Bulletin de l'Institut National Genevois* 54 (1951): 1–35.

Stenton, Sir Frank. *Anglo-Saxon England.* 2nd ed., rev. Oxford: Clarendon Press, 1967.

Stephen of Tournai. *Die Summa des Stephanus Tornacensis über das Decretum Gratiani.* Edited by Johann Frederich van Schulte. Geissen: 1891.

Stephenson, Carl. "Taxation and Representation in the Middle Ages." In *Anniversary Essays in Medieval History by the Students of Ch. H. Haskins*, pp. 291–312. Boston and New York: 1929. Reprinted in C. Stephenson, *Medieval Institutions. Selected Essays.* Edited by B. L. Lyon. Ithaca, N.Y.: Cornell University Press, 1954.

Stickler, Alfons M. "Concerning the Political Theories of Medieval Canonists." *Traditio* 7 (1949–51) 450–63.

— "De ecclesiae potestate coactiva materiali apud magistrum Gratianum." *Salesianum* 4 (1942): 2–23, 97–119.

— "De potestate gladii materialis ecclesiae secundum 'Quaestiones Bambergenses' ineditas." *Salesianum* 6 (1944): 113–40.

— *Historia iuris canonici latini*. Turin: Libraria Pontificae Athenaei Salesiani, 1950.

— "Il 'gladius' negli atti du concilii e dei R. R. Pontifice sino a Graziano e Bernardo di Clairvaux." *Salesianum* 13 (1951): 414–45.

— "Il gladius nel Registro de Gregoria VII." *Studi Gregoriani* 3 (1948): 89–103.

— "Imperator vicarius papae." *Mitteilungen des Instituts für osterreichische Geschichtsforschung* 62 (1954): 165–212.

— "Magistri Gratiani sententia de potestate ecclesiae in statum." *Apollinaris* 21 (1948): 36–111.

— "Il potero coattivo materiale della chiesa nella Reforma Gregoriana secondo Anselmo di Lucca." *Studi Gregoriani* 2 (1947): 235–85.

— "Sacerdotium et Regnum nei decretisti e primi decretalisti." *Salesianum* 15 (1953) 575–612.

— "Sacerdozia e regno nouve ricerche attorno decretali di Gregoria." In *Miscellanea Historiae Pontificiae*, no. 18. Rome: Aedes univeritatis gregoriani, 1954.

— "Der Schwerterbegriff bei Huguccio." *Epheremides iuris canonici* 3 (1947) 202–42.

Stones, E. L. J. "The Text of the Writ *quod omnes tangit* in Stubbs's Select Charters." *English Historical Review* 83 (1968): 759–60.

Strayer, Joseph R. "Defense of the Realm and Royal Power in France." In *Studi in onore di Gino Luzzato*, 1: 289–96. Milan: Guiffrè, 1949.

— *Les gens de justice de Languedoc sous Philippe le Bel*. Toulouse: Association Marc Bloch, 1970.

— "The Laicization of French and English Society in the Thirteenth Century." *Speculum* 15 (1940): 76–86.

— *Medieval Statecraft and the Perspectives of History: Essays by Joseph R. Strayer*. Edited by John F. Benton and Thomas N. Bisson. Princeton: Princeton University Press, 1971.

— *On the Medieval Origins of the Modern State*. Princeton: Princeton University Press, 1970.

— "Philip the Fair: A 'Constitutional King?'" *American Historical Review* 62 (1956): 18–32.

Stubbs, William. *The Constitutional History of England in its Origin and Development*. 3 vols. 6th ed. Oxford: Clarendon Press, 1903.

— *Select Charters and Other Illustrations of English Constitutional History from Earliest Times to the Reign of Edward the First*. 9th ed. Rev. by H. W. C. Davis. Oxford: Clarendon Press, 1951.

Summa "Elegantius in iure divino": seu Coloniensis. Edited by G. Fransen and S. Kuttner. New York: Fordham University Press, 1969.

Sweeney, James Ross. "The Problem of Inalienability in Innocent III's Correspondence with Hungary: A Contribution to the Study of the Historical Genesis of *Intellecto*." *Medieval Studies* 37 (1975): 235–51.

Sydow, J. "Elemente von Einheit und Vielfalt in der Mittelalterlichen Stadt im

Lichte kirchen rechtlicher Quellen." *Miscellanea Medievalia* 5 (1968): 186–97.

Sykes, J. G. "John de Pouilli and Peter de la Palu." *English Historical Review* 49 (April 1934): 219–40.

Tabacco, G. *Le relazioni fra i concetti di potere temporale e di potere spirituale nella tradizione cristiana fino al secolo XIV.* Publicatione della Facola di lettere e filosofia, no. 2, facs. 5. Turin: Universita de Torino, 1950.

Tacitus. "Germania." In Tacitus, *Dialogus, Agricola, Germania.* Loeb Classical Library. New York: Putnam's, 1920.

Talmon, J. L. *The Origins of Totalitarian Democracy.* London: Secher & Warburg, 1952.

Taylor, Charles H. "Assemblies of French Towns in 1316." *Speculum* 14 (1939): 285–89.

– "An Assembly of French Towns in March 1318." *Speculum* 13 (1938): 295–303.

– "The Composition of Baronial Assemblies in France, 1315–1320." *Speculum* 29 (1954): 433–59.

– "French Assemblies and Subsidy in 1321." *Speculum* 43 (1968): 217–44.

– "Some New Texts on the Assembly of 1302." *Speculum* 11 (1936): 38–42.

Taylor, J. "The Manuscripts of the 'modus tenendi parliamentum.'" *English Historical Review* 83 (1968): 673–88.

Tallenbach, Gerd. *Church, State and Christian Society to the Time of the Investiture Contest.* Translated by R. F. Bennet. Oxford: Blackwell, 1940.

Templeman, Geoffrey. "The History of Parliament to 1400 in the Light of Modern Research." *University of Birmingham Historical Journal* 1 (1948): 202–31.

Tertullian. "To Scapula." In Tertullian, *Apologetical Works and Minucius Felix Octavius,* translated by Rudolph Arbesmann, Sr. Emily Joseph Daly, and Edwin A. Quain, pp. 151–61. Fathers of the Church 44. Washington, D.C.: Catholic University of America Press, 1950.

Testard, Maurice. *Saint Augustin et Cicéron.* 2 vols. Paris: Etudes augustiniennes, 1958.

Theiner, A., ed. *Codex Diplomaticus Dominii Temporalis Sanctae Sedis.* Rome: Imprimerie du Vatican, 1861–62.

Tholemy of Lucca. *Determinatio compendiosa de iurisdictione imperii.* Edited by M. Krammer. *MGH. Fontes* 1.

Thomas Aquinas. "De regimine principum ad regem Cypri et de regimine Judaeorum." In *Politica opuscula,* edited by Joseph Mathis. Turin: Marietti, 1948.

– *On Kingship.* Translated & edited by G. B. Phelan and I. T. Eschmann. Toronto: Pontifical Institute of Mediaeval Studies, 1949.

– *Summa theologiae.* Edited by Thomas Gilby. 61 vols. London: Eyre & Spottiswoode, 1964–81.

Tierney, Brian. "Bracton on Government." *Speculum* 38 (1963): 294–317.

- "The Canonists and the Medieval State." *Review of Politics* 15 (1953): 378–88.
- *Church Law and Constitutional Thought in the Middle Ages.* London: Variorum, 1979.
- "Collegiality in the Middle Ages." *Concilium* 7 (1965): 5–14.
- "A Conciliar Theory of the Thirteenth Century." *Catholic Historical Review* 36 (1951): 415–40.
- "The Continuity of Papal Political Theory in the Thirteenth Century. Some Methodological Considerations." *Mediaeval Studies* 27 (1965): 227–44. Reprinted in Tierney, *Church Law.*
- *The Crisis of Church and State, 1050–1300.* Englewood Cliffs, N.J.: Prentice-Hall, 1964.
- "'Divided Sovereignty' at Constance: A Problem of Medieval and Early Modern Political Theory." *Annuarium Historiae Conciliorum* 7 (1975): 238–56. Reprinted in Tierney, *Church Law.*
- *Foundations of the Conciliar Theory: The Contribution of the Medieval Canonists from Gratian to the Great Schism.* Cambridge: Cambridge University Press, 1956.
- "Hermeneutics and History: The Problem of *Haec Sancta.*" In *Essays in Medieval History for Presentation to Bertie Wilkinson*, edited by T. A. Sandquist and Michael P. Powicke, pp. 354–70. Toronto: University of Toronto Press, 1969.
- "Natura id est Deus." *Journal of the History of Ideas* 24 (1963): 307–22.
- "Ockham, the Conciliar Theory, and the Canonists." *Journal of the History of Ideas* 15 (1954): 40–70.
- *Origins of Papal Infallibility 1150–1350: A Study on the Concepts of Infallibility, Sovereignty and Tradition in the Middle Ages.* Leiden: Brill, 1972.
- "Pope and Council: Some New Decretist Texts." *Mediaeval Studies* 19 (1957): 197–218.
- "The Prince is not bound by the Laws. Accursius and the Origins of the Modern State." *Comparative Studies in Society and History* 5 (1962–63): 378–400. Also in *Atti accursiani* 3: 1245–74. Reprinted in Tierney, *Church Law.*
- "Public Expediency and Natural Law." In *Authority and Power*, pp. 298–330 (below).
- *Religion, Law and the Growth of Constitutional Thought 1150–1650.* Cambridge: Cambridge University Press, 1982.
- "Sola scriptura and the Canonists." *Studia Gratiana* 11 (1967): 345–66. Reprinted in Tierney, *Church Law.*
- "Some Recent Works on the Political Theories of the Medieval Canonists." *Traditio* 10 (1954): 594–625. Reprinted in Tierney, *Church Law.*
- and Linehan, P., eds. *Authority and Power: Studies on Medieval Law and Government Presented to Walter Ullmann on His Seventieth Birthday.* Cambridge: Cambridge University Press, 1980.

Tillman, Helene. *Pope Innocent III*. Amsterdam: North-Holland, 1980.

Todd, John M., ed. *Problems of Authority: An Anglo-French Symposium*. Baltimore: Helicon Press, 1962.

Tout, Thomas Frederick. *Chapters in Administrative History of Medieval England*. 6 vols. Manchester: Manchester University Press, 1920–33.

Treharne, Reginald Francis. "The Constitutional Problem in Thirteenth Century England." In *Essays Presented to Bertie Wilkinson*, edited by T. A. Sandquist and M. R. Powicke, pp. 46–78. Toronto: University of Toronto Press, 1969.

– *Essays on Thirteenth Century England*. London: Historical Association, 1971.

– "The Nature of Parliament in the Reign of Henry III." *English Historical Review* 74 (1959): 590–610.

Tuck, Richard. *Natural Rights Theories. Their Origin and Development*. Cambridge: Cambridge University Press, 1979.

Tunmore, Harvey P. "The Dominican Order and Parliament." *Catholic Historical Review* 26 (1941): 479–89.

Turner, Ralph V. *The King and His Courts: The Role of John and Henry III in the Administration of Justice, 1199–1240*. Ithaca: Cornell University Press, 1968.

Ullmann, Walter. "The Bible and Principles of Government in the Middle Ages." In *Settimane di studio del Centre italiano di studi sull' alto medioevo* 10: 181–227. Spoleto: 1963. Reprinted in Ullmann, *Church and Law*.

– "Canonistics in England." *Studia Gratiana* 2 (1954): 521–28.

– "Cardinal Humbert and the Ecclesia Romana." *Studi Gregoriani* 4 (1952): 111–27.

– "Cardinal Roland and Besançon." *Miscellanea Historiae Pontificiae* 18 (1954): 107–25.

– *The Carolingian Renaissance and the Idea of Kingship*. London: Methuen, 1969.

– *The Church and the Law in the Earlier Middle Ages*. London: Variorum, 1975.

– "The Cosmic Theme of the Prima Clementis and Its Significance for the Concept of Roman Rulership." *Studia Patristica* 11 (*Texte und Untersuchungen zur Geschiche der altchristlichen Literatur* 108) (1972): 85–91.

– "De Bartolo sententia concilium repraesentat mentem populi." In *Bartolo da Sassoferrato: Studi e Documenti per il VI Centenario* 2. Milan: Guiffrè, 1962. Reprinted in Ullmann, *Papacy and Political Ideas* (below).

– "Delictal Responsibility of Medieval Corporations." *Law Quarterly Review* 64 (1948): 79–96.

– "The Development of the Medieval Idea of Sovereignty." *English Historical Review* 64 (1949): 1–33.

– "The Election of Bishops and the Kings of France in the 9th and 10th Centuries." *Concilium* 7 (1972): 79–91.

– "Frederick's Opponent, Innocent IV, as Melchisedek." In *Atti del covegno internazionale di Studi Federiciani*. Palermo: 1952.

– *The Growth of Papal Government in the Middle Ages: A Study in the Ideological Relation of Clerical to Lay Power*. London: Methuen, 1955.
– "Honorius III and the Prohibition of Legal Studies." *The Juridical Review* 60 (1948): 177–86.
– *The Individual and Society in the Middle Ages*. London: Methuen, 1967.
– "The Influence of John of Salisbury on Mediaeval Italian Jurists." *English Historical Review* 60 (1944): 384–93.
– "Juristic Obstacles to the Emergence of the Concept of the State in the Middle Ages." *Annali di storia del diritto* 13 (1969): 43–58.
– "Law and the Medieval Historians." In *Rapports XIe Congrès internationale des sciences historiques* 3 (1960): 34–74.
– *Law and Politics in the Middle Ages: An Introduction to the Sources of Medieval Political Ideas*. Ithaca, N.Y.: Cornell University Press, 1975.
– "Leo I and the Theme of Papal Supremacy." *Journal of Theological Studies*, n.s., 11 (1969): 25–51.
– *The Medieval Idea of Law as Represented by Lucas de Penna*. London: Methuen, 1946.
– "The Medieval Interpretation of Frederick I's Authentic 'habita.'" In *Studi in memoria di Paolo Koschaker: L'Europa e il diritto romano*, 1: 101–36. Milan: 1953.
– *The Medieval Papacy: St. Thomas and Beyond*. London: Aquin Press, 1960.
– "The Medieval Papal Court as an International Tribunal." In *Essays Judge Dillard, Virginia Journal for International Law*, 1971, pp. 356–77.
– *Medieval Papalism. The Political Theories of the Medieval Canonists*. London: Methuen, 1949.
– "The Medieval Theory of Legal and Illegal Organizations." *Law Quarterly Review* 60 (1944): 285–91.
– "'Nos si aliquid incompetenter ... '" *Epheremides iuris canonici* 9 (1953): 275–87.
– "A Note on Inalienability with Gregory VII." *Studi Gregoriani* 9 (1971): 115–22.
– *The Origins of the Great Schism: A Study in Fourteenth Century Ecclesiastical History*. Hamden, Conn.: Shoe String Press, 1972.
– "The Origins of the Ottonianum." *Cambridge Historical Journal* 11 (1953): 110–28.
– *The Papacy and Political Ideas in the Middle Ages*. London: Variorum, 1976.
– "The Papacy as an Institution of Government." *Studies in Church History* 2 (1965): 78–101.
– *Principles of Government and Politics in the Middle Ages*. London: Methuen, 1961. 2nd ed. 1966.
– "Public Welfare and Social Legislation in the Early Medieval Councils." *Studies in Church History* 7 (1971): 1–39.

- "The Significance of Innocent III's Decretal *Virgentis*." In *Etudes d'histoire du droit canoniques dédiées à Gabriel le Bras*, 1: 729–42. Paris: Sirey, 1965.

Valls-Taberner, F. "Les doctrines politiques de la Catalunya médiéval." *Obras Selectas* 2 (1954).

Valois, Noel. *La France et le grande schisme d'Occident*. 4 vols. Paris: 1896–1902.

- *La crise religieuse du XVᵉ siècle. Le pape et le concile*. 2 vols. Paris: Picard, 1909.

Van Hove, Alfons. "Droit justinien et droit canonique depuis le Décret de Gratien jusqu'aux Décrétales de Grégoire IX." In *Miscellanea Historica in Honorem I. Van der Essen*. Brussels, Paris: Editions universitaires, 1947.

- *Prolegomena ad codicem iuris canonici*. 2nd ed. Rome: Malines, 1945.

Van Steenberghen, Fernand. *Aristotle in the West: The Origins of Latin Aristotelianism*. Translated by Leonard Johnston. Louvain: E. Nauwelaerts, 1955.

Vasoli, Caesare. *Guglielmo d'Occam*. Florence: Nuovo Italia, 1953.

Vate, John. "Quaestiones in politicam Aristotelis." Paris, Bibliothèque Nationale, Latinus, 16089, fol. 75 r-v.

Vaughan, Richard. *Matthew Paris*. Cambridge: Cambridge University Press, 1958.

Vergottini, G. de. *Studi sulla legislazione imperiale di Federico II in Italia—Le leggi del 1220*. Milan: Guiffrè, 1952.

Vermeesch, Albert. *Essai sur les origines et la signification de la Commune dans le nord de la France (XIᵉ et XIIᵉ siècles)*. Heule: VGA, 1966.

Vetulani, A. "Le décret de Gratian et les premiers décrétistes à la lumière d'une source nouvelle." *Studia Gratiana* 7 (1959): 273–353.

- "Encore un mot sur le droit romain dans le décret de Gratien." *Apollinaria* 21 (1948): 129–34.

- "Etudes sur la division en distinctions et sur les paleae dans le décret de Gratien." *Bulletin international de l'Académie polonaise des sciences et des lettres, CL. philologie, histoire, philosophie* (1933): 110–14.

- "Gratien et le droit romain." *Revue historique de droit français et étranger* 24 (1946–47): 11–48.

- "Nouvelles vues sur le Décret de Gratien." *Le Pologne au Xᵉ Congrès international des sciences historiques à Rome, 1955*. Warsaw: Académie Polonaise des Sciences, Institut d'Histoire, 1955.

- "Une suite d'études pour servir a l'histoire de Décret de Gratien conservée dans les bibliothèques polonaises." *Revue historique de droit français et étranger* 15 (1936): 343–58.

- "Une suite d'études pour servir à l'histoire du Décret de Gratien II. Les nouvelles de Justinien dans le Décret de Gratien." *Revue historique de droit français et étranger* 16 (1927): 461–79, 674–92.

Villey, Michel. "Du sens de l'expression *jus in re* en droit romain classique." *Mélanges Fernand de Visscher II. Revue internationale des droits de l'antiquité* 2 (1949): 417–36.

- La formation de la pensée juridique moderne. Paris: 1968.
- "La génèse du droit subjectif chez Guillaume d'Occam." *Archives de philosophie du droit* 9 (1964): 97–127.
- "L'idée du droit subjectif et les systèmes juridiques romains." *Revue historiques du droit*, 4th ser., 24–25 (1946): 201–28.
- "Le 'jus in re' du droit romain classique au droit moderne." *Publications de l'Institut de droit romain de l'université de Paris* 6 (1950): 187–225.
- "Les origines de la notion du droit subjectif." In *Leçons d'histoire de la philosophie du droit*, edited by Michel Villey, pp. 221–50. Paris: 1963.
- "Suum jus cuique tribuens." In *Studi in onere di Pietro de Francisci*, 2: 361–71. Milan: 1956.
Vindiciae contra tyrannos. Edited by Harold J. Laski. *Natural Law, a Defence of Liberty against Tyrants. A Translation of the Vindiciae contra Tyrannos by Junius Brutus*. London: G. Bell and Sons, 1924.
Vinogradof, P. "Les maximes dans l'ancien droit commune anglais." *Revue historique de droit français et étranger*, 4th ser., 2 (1923): 333–43.
- *Outlines of Historical Jurisprudence*. London: Oxford University Press, 1920–22.
- *Roman Law in Medieval Europe*. New York: Harper, 1909.
Vooght, Paul de. "Esquises d'une enquête sur le mot 'infallibilité' durant le période scolastique." In *L'infallibilité de l'église; journées oecuméniques de Chevetogne* (25–29 Septembre 1961), edited by O. Rousseau, pp. 99–146. Chevetogne: Editions de Chevetogne, 1963.
- *Les pouvoirs du concile et l'autorité du pape au Concile de Constance*. Paris: 1965.
- "The Results of Recent Historical Research on Conciliarism." In *Papal Ministry in the Church*, edited by H. Kung, pp. 148–57. New York: Herder and Herder, 1971.
Wahl, J. A. "Immortality and Inalienability: Baldus de Ubaldus." *Mediaeval Studies* 32 (1970): 308–28.
Waley, Daniel Philip. *The Italian City-Republics*. London: World University Library, 1969.
- *Medieval Orvieto: The Political History of an Italian City-State, 1157–1334*. Cambridge: Cambridge University Press, 1952.
- *The Papal State in the Thirteenth Century*. New York: St. Martin's Press, 1961.
Wallace-Hadrill, John Michael. *Early Germanic Kingship in England and on the Continent*. Oxford: Clarendon Press, 1971. Rev. ed. 1980.
- *Early Medieval History*. London: Blackwell, 1975.
- *The Long-haired Kings, and Other Studies in Frankish History*. London: Methuen, 1962.
- "The *via regis* of the Carolingian Age." In *Trends in Medieval Political Thought*, edited by Beryl Smalley. Oxford: Blackwell, 1965.

Walzer, Michael. *The Revolution of the Saints: A Study in the Origins of Radical Politics.* Cambridge: Harvard University Press, 1965.

Watanabe, Morimichi. "Authority and Consent in Church Government: Panormitanus, Aeneas Sylvius, Cusanus." *Journal of the History of Ideas* 33 (1972): 217–36.

– *The Political Ideas of Nicolas of Cusa, with Specific Reference to His De Concordantia Catholica.* Geneva: Droz, 1963.

Watt, John Anthony. *The Church and the Two Nations in Medieval Ireland.* Cambridge: Cambridge University Press, 1970.

– "The Constitutional Law of the College of Cardinals, Hostiensis to Joannes Andreae." *Mediaeval Studies* 33 (1971): 127–57.

– "The Development of the Theory of the Temporal Authority of the Papacy by the Thirteenth Century Canonists." In *Historical Studies*, edited by M. Roberts, pp. 17–28. Proceedings of the Irish Conference on Historians, n.d.

– "The Early Medieval Canonists and the Formation of Conciliar Theory." *Irish Theological Quarterly* 24 (1957): 13–31.

– "Medieval Deposition Theory: A Neglected Canonist from the First Council of Lyons." *Studies in Church History* 2 (1965): 197–214.

– "The Papal Monarchy in the Thought of St. Raymond of Peñafort." *Irish Theological Quarterly* 25 (1958): 33–42, 154–70.

– "The 'Quaestio in utramque partem' Reconsidered." *Studia Gratiana* 13 (*Collectio Stephan Kuttner* 3): 411–23.

– *The Theory of Papal Monarchy in the Thirteenth Century: The Contribution of the Canonists.* New York: Fordham University Press, 1965. Published originally in *Traditio* 20 (1964): 179–317.

– "The Use of the Term *plenitudo potestatis* by Hostiensis." In *Proceedings of the International Congress of Medieval Canon Law*, edited by S. Kuttner and J. J. Ryan, pp. 161–87. Monumenta iuris canonici. Ser. C, sub. 1. Vatican City: 1965.

Weber, O. *Groundplan of the Bible.* Translated by Harold Knight. London: Butterworth Press, 1959.

Webster, Wentworth. *Les loisirs d'un étranger au pays basques.* Chalons-sur-Saone: 1901.

Weigand, R. *Die Naturrechtslehre der Legisten und Dekretisten von Irnerius bis Accursius und von Gratian bis Johannes Teutonicus.* Munchener theologische Studien, Kanonistiche Abteilung 26. Munich: Hueber, 1967.

Weill, Georges. *Les théories sur le pouvoir royal en France pendant les guerres de religion.* Paris: 1891.

Weske, Dorothy Bruce. *Convocation of the Clergy. A Study of Its Antecedents and Its Rise with Special Emphasis upon Its Growth and Activities in the Thirteenth and Fourteenth Centuries.* London: Society for Promoting Christian Knowledge, 1937.

Weston, Corinne Cornstock. "The Theory of Mixed Monarchy under Charles II and after." *English Historical Review* 75 (1960): 426–33.

White, A. B. *The Making of the English Constitution.* 2nd ed. New York: G. B. Putnams, 1925.

Wieruszowski, Helen. "Roger II of Sicily, rex-tyrannus, in Twelfth Century Political Thought." *Speculum* 38 (1963): 46–78.

Wilkinson, Bertie. "The Coronation Oath of Edward II." In *Essays in Honour of James Tait,* edited by J. G. Edwards, V. H. Galbraith, and E. F. Jacob, pp. 405–16. Manchester: Manchester University Press, 1933.

– "The Coronation Oath of Edward II and the Statute of York." *Speculum* 19 (1944): 445–69.

– "English Politics and Politicians of the Thirteenth and Fourteenth Centuries." *Speculum* 30 (1955): 37–48.

– "The 'Political Revolution' of the Thirteenth and Fourteenth Centuries in England." *Speculum* 24 (1949): 502–7.

– ed. *The Creation of Medieval Parliaments.* New York: Wiley, 1972.

Wilks, Michael J. "Corporation and Representation in the Defensor Pacis." *Studia Gratiana* 15 (1972): 251–94.

– "The Idea of the Church as 'unus homo perfectus' and Its Bearing on the Medieval Theory of Sovereignty." *Miscellanea historiae ecclesiasticae Stockholm* (Louvain, 1961): 23–49.

– "Papa est nomen jurisdictionis: Augustinus Triumphus and the Papal Vicariate of Christ." *Journal of Theological Studies,* n.s., 8 (1957): 71–91, 256–71.

– *The Problem of Sovereignty in the Later Middle Ages: The Papal Monarchy with Augustinus Triumphus and the Publicists.* Cambridge: Cambridge University Press, 1963.

– "Roman Empire and Christian State in the *De civitate Dei.*" *Augustinus* 12 (1967): 489–510.

– "St. Augustine and the General Will." In *Studia patristica (Texte und Untersuchungen zur Geschichte der altchristlichen Literatur)* 94 (1966): 487–522.

William of Mandagout. *De iure electionis novorum praelatorum.* Cologne: 1602.

William of Ockham. *Breviloquium.* Edited by R. Scholz. In *Wilhelm von Ockham als politischer Denker und sein Breviloquium de principatu tyrannico.* Leipzig: 1944. Reprinted Stuttgart: 1952.

– *Opera plurima.* Lyon: 1495. Reprinted London: Gregg, 1962.

– *Opera politica.* Edited by H. S. Offler. 3 vols. Manchester: Manchester University Press, 1940–74. Vol. 1, 2nd ed.

Williams, George Huntston. *The Norman Anonymous of 1100 A.D.: Toward the Identification and the Evaluation of the So-called Anonymous of York.* Harvard Theological Studies 18 Cambridge: Harvard University Press, 1951.

Williams, Shafer. *Codices Pseudo-Isidoriani.* New York: Fordham University Press, 1951.

Williams, Watkin Wynn. *Saint Bernard of Clairvaux*. Manchester: Manchester University Press, 1953.

Wirszubski, C. *Libertas as a Political Idea at Rome during the Republic and Early Principate*. Cambridge: Cambridge University Press, 1950.

Wolfram, H. "Athanaric the Visigoth: Monarchy or Judgeship." *Journal of Medieval History* 1 (1975): 259–78.

– "The Shaping of the Early Medieval Kingdom." *Viator* 1 (1970): 1–20.

Wood, Charles T. "Personality, Politics and Constitutional Progress: The Lessons of Edward II." *Studia Gratiana* 15 (1972): 519–36.

Wood, Ian. "Kings, Kingdoms and Consent." In *Early Medieval Kingship*, edited by Peter Hayes Sawyer and Ian N. Wood, pp. 6–29. Leeds: School of History, University of Leeds, 1977.

Wood, Paul David. *Law and Society in the Visigothic Kingdom*. London: Cambridge University Press, 1972.

Woolf, Cecil N. S. *Bartolus of Sassoferrato: His Position in the History of Medieval Political Thought*. Cambridge: Cambridge University Press, 1913.

Wormuth, Francis D. *The Royal Prerogative 1603–1649: A Study in English Political and Constitutional Ideas*. Ithaca, N.Y.: Cornell University Press, 1939.

Index